THE BEAN BIBLE

THE BEAN BIBLE

A Legumaniac's Guide
to Lentils, Peas, and
Every Edible Bean
on the Planet!

by Aliza Green

Foreword by William Woys Weaver

Running Press
PHILADELPHIA · LONDON

9   8   7   6   5   4   3   2   1
Digit on the right indicates the number of this printing.

Library of Congress Cataloging-in-Publication Number 99-75092

ISBN 0-7624-0689-5

Cover and interior illustrations by Sara Love
Cover and interior design by Corinda Cook and Rosemary Tottoroto
Edited by Mary McGuire Ruggiero
Copy editing by Elizabeth Matlin of FoodWorks®, Wilmette, Illinois
Typography: Adobe Caslon and Greco Deco

This book may be ordered by mail from the publisher.
Please include $2.50 for postage and handling.
But try your bookstore first!

Running Press Book Publishers
125 South Twenty-second Street
Philadelphia, Pennsylvania 19103-4399

Visit us on the web!
www.runningpress.com

To my husband, Don Reiff, who gave me
the benefit of his highly evolved design sense
and critical palate throughout this project.
He never objected to endless nights
of bean meals and was an unfailingly willing
(and appreciative) subject for my culinary experiments.

And thanks go to my mom, Vivian Green,
who taught me to never give up
and kept encouraging me to write.
I've learned so much from her as a writer—
she is an accomplished playwright—
and as a person.

ACKNOWLEDGMENTS

My deepest appreciation and thanks go to Mary McGuire Ruggiero, my editor. Her constant encouragement and good humor made the occasionally rocky going a little smoother. After spending a week in her stimulating and entertaining company at the 1997 International Association of Culinary Professionals conference in Chicago, it became clear to me that I was ready to write a cookbook about legumes. I've also counted on Mary to make me look good and not to let the mistakes I've made slip through the cracks.

I would like to thank wholeheartedly my good friend, fellow foodie, and stalwart recipe tester, Linda Gellman, who was always cheerfully willing to try another recipe. I couldn't have written this book without her help and insightful recipe comments. I only hope she'll agree to work with me again.

I want to thank my chef and cookbook-writer friends who have generously shared their recipes for my book, including French-Asian Chef Philippe Chin; restaurateur and master of the dining room Toto Schiavone; Chef Guillermo Pernot; Certified Master Chef and 2000 U.S. Olympic Team Captain Alfonso Contrisciani; restaurateurs Amin and Jude Bitar; cookbook authors Fred and Linda Griffiths; low-fat cooking guru Don Mauer; and Lyonnais Chef Pierre Orsi.

I thank my two children, Zachary and Ginevra, who have been totally supportive of me and my crazy food work, even when it has meant that they had to FFY—fend for yourself—for dinner (unless they wanted yet another dish of beans).

CONTENTS

My first encounter with Aliza Green left a remarkable impression. It occurred almost twenty years ago when we met at The Garden restaurant with owner Kathleen Mulhern to discuss the establishment of a Delaware Valley chapter of the American Institute of Wine and Food. Even then Aliza's personal commitment to good food came through with all the enthusiasm she has since devoted to so many other worthwhile projects. We became instant friends, I guess because we believe in the same things, even though our professional lives move along slightly different paths. I have written about food from the perspective of history, from the perspective of the dining room. Aliza now writes from the heart of the kitchen. This is her bailiwick, and her huge store of creative energy seems to thrive on it. During her stint as chef at the White Dog Cafe, Aliza experimented with a long list of exciting farm-fresh products; indeed I shall never forget the memorable meal that she once cooked for me and for several of my guests from Colonial Williamsburg. For those Virginians, it was their first exposure to the culinary renaissance then under way in Philadelphia, but it was also a firsthand taste of the kind of high-quality produce that our restaurants were seeking out in the Pennsylvania countryside. The marriage of farm garden and restaurant kitchen has been one of the lasting themes in Aliza's quest for good food that not only benefits the palate and healthful eating, but also gives something back to the land. That is Aliza's special touch.

I should have realized then that lurking among all her dishes of chickpeas and lentils, all her bowls of velvety bean soup, all her smoking casseroles of flavorful favas, were the makings of this book. She calls it a bible, but I would also call it *The Essential Aliza*, for in every respect it is a guidebook to her philosophy of cuisine, plus some. For a person like myself, who is a gardener who cooks, and a cook who also writes, this is definitely the sort of exacting cookbook that needed writing long ago. I can well appreciate the love and care and no small amount of labor that went into it, for this is a huge subject and there are not many books that have tackled the bean and a host of other legumes in such a head-on, hands-on manner. *Bravo Aliza!*

I should know. I grow many of these vegetables in my own kitchen garden—at last count, over 200 sorts of beans, over 50 sorts of peas, perhaps 40 sorts of favas and cowpeas, and quite a few of the more unusual legumes that are now only coming back into vogue among aficionados—such as chickling vetch, lupine seeds, and those delightful popping beans from Peru. By bean collectors' standards, my collection is small, but I have tried to make it extremely high quality in terms of culinary merits. So oftentimes, when I have come in from the garden with a bowl full of picture-perfect flageolet chevrier verts, or African bambaras, or our own native Blue Shackamaxon beans, I have asked myself where it is I might turn to get some ideas on how to cook them. Aliza's book offers just such a refreshing perspective. Many readers will thoroughly enjoy the tidbits on bean history, and the other legumes as well. I think the legume primer, which forms the bulk of chapter two, is especially helpful because it introduces us to some of the truly good varieties that are now available, with far more detailed and useful information than what is normally provided on a typical supermarket label. That took homework, but cooks need to know their materials in order to use them to best advantage, so I think this is one part of the cookbook that will fill up quickly with the little notes and flags one finds in the cookbooks people use most. I could go on. I could crow about the delicious recipes, but words cannot replace the wonderful way they taste. They must be tried. I know there are several dishes I am going to make quite often. But what I like most about this book is that Aliza's recipes work two ways. You can follow them verbatim for easy-to-follow, great-tasting results, or you can tinker with them and use them as the basis for your own delightful creations. That, by the way, is how I like to cook, so I am especially grateful that she has jam-packed this book with nifty tips and useful advice about flavor combinations, cooking techniques, and a host of other details so important to readers who are feeling their way through certain types of dishes for the very first time. In this respect, this book is indeed a bible and an indispensable companion to anyone who wants to put good food on his or her table— and help the farmers who grew it as well.

—William Woys Weaver
December 27, 1999

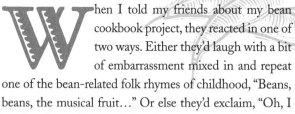

When I told my friends about my bean cookbook project, they reacted in one of two ways. Either they'd laugh with a bit of embarrassment mixed in and repeat one of the bean-related folk rhymes of childhood, "Beans, beans, the musical fruit…" Or else they'd exclaim, "Oh, I just love beans; I'm so glad you're writing this book!"

It seems that beans are a subject that inspires a lot of controversy. Unfortunately, many people have a bad association with beans—memories of eating pork and beans from a can for dinner or endless nights of baked beans, simply because these were cheap and easy dishes. I'm ashamed to admit that even I have bad memories of a classic bean dish, the Sabbath cholent (large lima beans cooked slowly with the meat and potatoes) that my mother (and probably her mother) made for cold-weather Shabbat afternoon dinners. As a child I absolutely loathed this dish. If I discovered that we were having it after Saturday morning synagogue services, I would make sure to get myself invited to a friend's house for lunch that day. Later, as a young woman and a budding chef, I was introduced to the great southwest French country-style masterpiece, cassoulet. I tasted the crusty, steaming hot, garlicky cassoulet and loved it. Only later, while doing research for this book, did I realize that the two dishes actually shared the same origin. Both cholent and cassoulet are one-pot meals (or casseroles) that can be placed in the residual heat of the baker's oven, cooked slowly overnight and served hot the next day. Their difference can be traced directly to religious beliefs. The Jewish dish cholent contains only beef (and sometimes goose), while the strongly French Catholic cassoulet normally contains a variety of pork products.

In 1991, I conducted a legume workshop sponsored by our local chapter of the American Institute of Wine and Food. During the class I demonstrated and sampled three of the recipes included in this book. I truly enjoyed the class and the participants loved the recipes. Because of this positive experience, I was inspired to take a more comprehensive look at bean cookery.

Nearly ten years later, when I was trying to focus my cookbook theme, I realized beans had been a leitmotif in my culinary career and that I had developed a broad and imaginative base of legume recipes. I didn't write this book because beans are good for you, though it doesn't hurt that they are. I wrote it because I haven't seen a book that treats beans as a culinary delight. The recipes in this book come from many sources and represent the cuisines of more than twenty-five countries that have strong repertoires of legume dishes. Some I developed during my long career as a chef and food consultant, others I tasted in my travels and had to re-create.

Beans and legumes can be as fancy as Georges Perrier's Velouté of Giant White Coco Beans with its requisite garnish of black truffles. Lentilles du Puy, the tiny French green lentils, and flageolets, the pale green ovals, both strictly controlled as to their origin and beloved by legendary French chef Auguste Escoffier, fetch a high price. Legumes can be as down-to-earth as Ful-Medames, the Egyptian porridge of fava beans with egg or the Spanish and Mexican Earthenware-Cooked Beans (*Frijoles de Olla*). They can be as complex as the Brazilian national dish, Feijoada Completa, or my own Spiced Duck in Port Wine Sauce with Green Lentils. They can be simple as a yellow mung bean dal from India, or a dish of the chickpea and sesame dip, hummus. They can be as exotic as the fermented lentil and rice pancakes from Bombay called dosa or the Indonesian bean salad, *Gado-Gado*. But don't be scared off by all the international-sounding dishes; beans can be as homey and familiar as Diner-Style Split Pea Soup or Boston Baked Beans with Steamed Brown Bread.

I've come to adore bean cookery, though I've found that a surprisingly large number of American chefs have trouble cooking beans and other legumes. If I see an interesting-looking bean dish on a menu, I'll always order it. But many times the beans turn out to be mushy and bland (obviously from a can). Other times they are hard and indigestible, probably because the chef got creative and cooked the beans with hardening substances, such as sugar, salt, and acid prior to the necessary precooking step. It's rare that I find legumes prepared as perfectly as I would like. Being so particular about this topic, I decided to "spill the beans" about how wonderful bean dishes really can be. I hope you'll agree. — *"Bean" Appétit!*

CHAPTER ONE

THE HISTORY AND GASTRONOMIC IMPORTANCE OF LEGUMES

Legumes, which include beans, peas, and lentils, are one of the most ancient human foodstuffs. They have been a staple of the diet in many parts of the world since the days of our hunter-gatherer ancestors, about 12,000 years ago. And for good reason: they are versatile, easy to grow, easy to store, inexpensive, and contain essential nutrients. No part of the bean is wasted, from its sprouts, tender young pods, and green seeds to its dry seeds, that are stored for cold winter days.

Though we may think of beans as lowly, they have enjoyed high status and been credited with possessing great powers in other eras and cultures. In his tome of kitchen science and lore, *On Food and Cooking*, Harold McGee says, "A remarkable and as yet unexplained sign of their status in the ancient world is the fact that each of the four major legumes known to Rome lent its name to a prominent Roman family: *Fabius* comes from the faba bean, *Lentulus* from the lentil, *Piso* from the pea, and *Cicero* from the chickpea."

According to history, the followers of the Greek philosopher Pythagoras were prohibited from eating beans due to the belief that to consume beans was to consume the souls of one's ancestors thus preventing them from being reincarnated. In Rome, the natural historian Pliny wrote of the belief that the souls of the dead resided in beans. Greeks and Romans reportedly banished ghosts by spitting beans at them, and at Roman funeral banquets (probably for the same reason) beans were an important part of the offering made to dead relatives.

In ancient Rome, an annual ritual was conducted during the period of Lemuria, to placate the ever-restless ghosts of the dead. The head of the household walked through the rooms of the house at midnight throwing small dark fava beans behind him, while reciting a special chant. In Japan, a parallel rite was practiced at the beginning of each new year. At midnight, the head of the house scattered roasted beans in all the rooms to drive out the demons and bring in good luck.

In the southern Italian province of Puglia, women believe that cooking dried fava beans "in their coats" (with their skins on) gives the beans special powers to increase one's physical potency. According to their folklore, fava beans cooked in their coats make the men stronger both in the fields and in the marriage bed.

Indeed, legumes have a stronghold in the traditions and, of course, the cusines of most cultures. Native Americans, such as the Algonquins, depended on corn and beans for making their traditional succotash (cooked in bear fat)—a dish that's been adapted across America. Chickpeas, sesame, and lemon combine to make the Lebanese hummus bi tahina, which has become an American vegetarian staple. Where would Israelis be without their national street food of falafel, Egyptian in origin but now often served with a Yemenite sauce containing ground fenugreek seeds (also a legume). No East Indian meal would be complete without a bowl of dal, split lentils or mung beans that can be served as a soup or side dish. And where would Mexican cooks be without the refried pinto beans that accompany just about every dish?

Beans have been around so long that many cooking traditions have evolved techniques for improving their flavor and digestibility. In Germany and Switzerland, fresh savory is known as *bohnenkraut* (the bean herb), and is always included when cooking a pot of beans. Mexican cooks invariably add sprigs of epazote, a wild wormseed plant used when cooking black beans because its special resinous oil helps reduce some of the beans' gaseous effects. Cooks in rural Italy faithfully add alkaline-rich greens like wild chicory, dandelion, spinach, or chard to balance the acidity of the beans. And according to cookbook author Madhur Jaffrey, spices used in Indian cuisine, such as fresh ginger, fennel seed, and carom (or lovage) seed,

LENTILS ARE AMONG THE OLDEST FOOD KNOWN TO HUMANITY. THEIR CULTIVATION DATES BACK AT LEAST 4,000 YEARS. THE BIBLICAL ESAU PROBABLY ATE LENTIL SOUP AS HIS POTTAGE. THEIR HIGH PROTEIN CONTENT AND EASE OF GROWING AND STORING MAKES THEM A STAPLE THROUGHOUT THE WORLD, ESPECIALLY WHERE ANIMAL PROTEIN IS SCARCE.

function as nutrition and flavor enhancers as well as carminatives (antiflatulents).

Small but Mighty: Legumes and Nutrition

The worldwide importance of legumes has much to do with their nutritional richness. The legume family is second only to the cereal grasses in its importance in the human diet. Legumes contain high percentages of protein, iron, and fiber. They contain little to no fat of their own (except for soybeans and peanuts) and no cholesterol. The only negative is that the protein contained in beans is not complete as it lacks several essential amino acids. However, all you have to do is com-

SATURNALIA AND THE BEAN KING

THE PAGAN HOLIDAY OF SATURNALIA WAS CELEBRATED BY ANCIENT ROMANS DURING THE WINTER SOLSTICE, AROUND THE SAME TIME OF YEAR AS CHRISTMAS. DURING SATURNALIA, ALL RULES WERE BROKEN, ALL RESTRICTIONS LIFTED. THE ONE WHO PICKED THE WHITE BEAN OUT OF A CONTAINER OF DARK BEANS WHILE BLINDFOLDED REIGNED OVER ALL AS THE MASTER OF REVELS. IN CHRISTIAN TIMES, SATURNALIA EVOLVED INTO THE HOLIDAY OF TWELFTH NIGHT, DURING WHICH A KING CAKE CONTAINING A LUCKY BEAN WAS SERVED. THE PERSON WHO RECEIVED THE PIECE OF CAKE WITH THE BEAN WAS SELECTED AS THE BEAN KING, ANOTHER NAME FOR THE MASTER OF REVELS.

LEGUMES AND CHILDREN'S STORIES

Two of the most famous children's stories involving riches also involve legumes. In *The Princess and the Pea*, the princess's rank was determined by testing her sensitivity. If she was a true princess, she would be able to feel a single pea while sleeping on a stack of pea-stalk hay mattresses. In *Jack and the Beanstalk*, Jack exchanges his poor, widowed mother's cow for some magic beans. Learning of her son's foolishness, she throws the beans out the window. The next day, they discover that the beans have grown into an enormous beanstalk reaching far up into the clouds—and into a giant's lair that contains riches, including a goose that lays golden eggs. Jack manages to steal the goose from the giant, who meets his fate chasing Jack back down the beanstalk.

bine the legumes with grains or a small amount of animal protein, such as eggs and cheese, and the problem is solved. It's not even necessary to eat the protein or grain in the same meal as the beans. Also, most of us eat more than enough complete protein to overcome this deficiency.

While dried legumes are a good source of iron, they should be combined with foods rich in vitamin C, such as tomatoes, dark green vegetables, or peppers (including chiles), in order to increase the body's ability to absorb this iron. For those who need more fiber (both soluble and insoluble) in their diet, there are few sources better than legumes. They also provide almost as much calcium as milk and significant amounts of other minerals, such as potassium, zinc, and magnesium.

While we know beans are good for us, some of us don't realize just how good they taste when prepared with care in a wide range of traditional and contemporary dishes. This book is full of excellent legume recipes for

both the fresh and dried varieties. My hope is that the wide-ranging selection of dishes in this book will inspire you to incorporate more power-packed legumes into your diet—and love doing so!

Legumes and Gas: Why It Occurs and How to Prevent It

Let wind and water go free, then healthy thou wilt be.
—An old Wiltshire saying

The profound effects of beans on the digestive system have generated great concern and controversy throughout the ages, and much has been written about it. According to Saint Augustine, flatulence was an unmistakable sign of man's fall from grace. Saint Jerome forbade beans to the nuns in his charge on the grounds that "they tickle the genitals."

These notions of the erotic persisted for some time. Many centuries later an English writer, Henry Buttes

⤞ ⤞ ⤞ GASTRONAUTS? ⤞ ⤞ ⤞
NASA RESEARCHES FLATULENCE

Gas or flatulence has been the subject of various research efforts in recent decades. Interestingly, research in this area became necessary with the advent of the space program. After World War II, it appeared that intestinal gas might prove to be a serious problem for test pilots for a number of reasons. Apparently it was discovered that gravitational stress, vibration, and fatigue all affect the working of the gastrointestinal tract, including gas production. The volume of a given amount of gas increases as the pressure surrounding it decreases. This means that a pilot's intestinal gas will expand as he flies higher into the atmosphere, which could ultimately cause a lot of pain. In addition, the atmosphere in extended space flights is confined and limited, and several components of human gas (including hydrogen, methane, and hydrogen sulfide) are potentially toxic to inhale.

Work in the late sixties showed that normal people averaged a daily output of about a pint of gas that contained fifty percent nitrogen, the result of swallowing air along with food and drink. Another forty percent was carbon dioxide produced by bacteria in the intestine. The remaining ten percent or so was a mixture of gases including the highly odoriferous (but not toxic) indoles and skatoles.

The precise amount and composition of gas produced by a particular person on a particular occasion (such as the middle of a fancy dinner party) depends on many different factors, such as how the food is swallowed, the bacteria present in the intestine, the general activity of the gastrointestinal tract, and the food being eaten. With so many variables, one scientist advised searching for astronauts who do not normally produce very large quantities of flatus, especially under stress.

[sic], wrote of beans' "*flatulencie*, whereby they provoke to lecher." It seems that beans were considered an aphrodisiac precisely because of the powerful aftereffects of eating them.

Pleasure of another sort is probably at the root of the perennial children's rhyme that begins "Beans, beans, the musical fruit . . ." and ends with the perverse wish ". . . so let's have beans for every meal!" The Victorian Italian culinary authority Pellegrino Artusi wrote an influential cookbook called *La Scienza en Cucina*

or *Science in the Kitchen*. In it he observed: "It seems to me that the taste of lentils is more delicate than that of beans in general and that, as for the threat of bombardment, they are less dangerous than ordinary beans and equal to the black-eyed pea." But Victorian French writer, Clement-Marius Morard, claimed that a frequent diet of lentils "produced a revolution in the organs, disturbed the head, deranged the mind, and ruined the sight."

Most of us know from experience

(or legend) that beans cause gas. But few of us really know why. It turns out that a chemical constituent in legumes, oligosaccharides, are responsible for the embarrassing consequence of their consumption. Oligosaccharides are sugar molecules linked together in such a way that human enzymes cannot digest them easily. As a result, the oligosaccharides leave the upper intestines unchanged and enter the lower intestines in a form that the body cannot absorb. Here the large resident bacterial population does the job the upper intestines are unable to do, and in the process gives off various gases as waste products.

It is this sudden increase in bacterial action, caused by the arrival of a food supply available only to the bacteria, that results in flatulence after eating legumes. The oligosaccharides are especially common in seeds because they are a form in which sugars can be stored for future use. Oligosaccharides accumulate in the final stages of bean development, so it seems that green (or immature) beans are much less troublesome than dry beans.

There must be other factors that cause flatulence because white or navy beans have a lower oligosaccharide content than soybeans, but a higher gas activity. Apparently some seeds contain an antiflatulence factor that inhibits bacterial growth. Current knowledge can be boiled down to two statements: Navy and lima beans are generally the most troublesome legumes. Peanuts generate little activity.

There have been numerous opinions on the subject of flatulence and how to solve it without giving up beans altogether. Author Patience Gray has several suggestions to offset what she calls "the explosive effects of the bean." First she recommends using the most recent crop of beans. Second, she believes cooking beans in earthenware (as is done in many places such as southern Italy, Spain, Greece, Mexico, North Africa, and Cuba) helps because the clay absorbs distressing elements. Third, she recommends cooking the beans with alkaline ingredients like wild chicory, dandelion, spinach, or chard that have been blanched, squeezed dry, then finely chopped and added during the last fifteen minutes of cooking. This would be the equivalent of adding a small amount of baking soda (an alkaline) to the water.

Julie Sahni, author of *Classic Indian Cooking*, believes that our troubles with beans arise because beans contain vegetable proteins that are harder to digest than animal proteins. Those present in certain types of unhulled beans and peas, such as black gram beans, kidney beans, and chickpeas, require more time and effort to digest. They are ideal for people who work outdoors and do heavy physical labor. For those of us who lead a modern, sedentary urban life but still want to eat beans, Sahni recommends making certain adjustments when cooking beans, such as serving them in moderate portions of no more than four to eight ounces per person. She also suggests including (or increasing the quantity of) digestive spices, such as *asafetida* (a powerfully aromatic combination of tree resins), fresh ginger, and ajwain (the seeds of a lovage plant, also called carom seeds). Smaller shelled peas and beans present less of a digestion problem. In fact, according to Sahni, lentils "are among the easiest to digest legumes."

If you're unaccustomed to eating legumes, eat them in smaller portions along with other ingredients to counteract their effects, (see Anti-Flatulence Cooking Tips, page 39). Your body will eventually be able to digest legumes more easily if you increase them gradually in your diet. Start with lentils and split peas and work your way up to soybeans, which are considered the most difficult to digest. While there is a definite connection between eating

legumes and increased flatulence, if you eat a diet high in fiber you can reduce the severity.

WHAT IS A LEGUME, ANYWAY? DEFINING TERMS

Interestingly, despite their long history and culinary significance, many of us are confused about what are and are not beans. The Greeks called them *phásela*, which became the Latin *Phaseolus* and the name for the New World bean family. The Romans called them *faba* (now *fava* in Italian, *fève* in French, and *fabas* in Spanish) and the Anglo-Saxons called them simply "beans."

According to *Webster's New World Dictionary of Culinary Arts*, a bean is "any of various legumes (mostly from the genus *Phaseolus*) with a double-seamed pod containing a single row of seeds (sometimes also called beans); some are used for their edible pods, other for shelling fresh

BEAN LANGUAGE

Because of how long they've been around and how important they are to the cuisines of many cultures, beans and legumes appear in many colorful ways in our language. For example:

- Someone who is "full of beans" is not credible.

- Something that is "not worth a hill of beans" is pretty worthless.

- Someone who is said to be "a bean counter" is a corporate penny-pincher.

- Someone who has been "beaned" has most certainly been hit on the head.

and some for their dried seeds." This includes Old World legumes, such as lentils, chickpeas, peanuts, peas, soybeans, and the black-eyed pea family, and New World varieties, such as limas, kidney beans, black turtle beans, cranberry, and cannellini.

The secondary meaning is "the ovoid or kidney-shaped dried seeds." "Pulse" is a general term for edible seeds obtained from leguminous plants, such as peas, beans, and lentils. So, it seems as though bean plants are "legumes" and the seeds are "pulses." However, the word pulse is often used to refer to lentils and peas, rather than beans.

To add to the confusion, the French and Italians use the terms *legumes* and *legumini* also to refer to all manner of vegetable dishes. In a kitchen run according to the strict French brigade system, the chef in charge of all vegetables and starches is the *legumier*. In American English, it's a bit more complicated. We differentiate between peas, beans, and lentils, and consider them very different, though they are all close relatives and meet the criterion of a plant that forms two half-seeds within an outer skin.

Without getting lost in semantics, in this book "legume" refers to all the members of the larger family, which includes peas, common beans, lentils, and chickpeas. I use "beans" when referring mainly to New World members of the common bean family, such as limas and kidney beans, and Old World beans, such as favas.

CHAPTER TWO

A LEGUME PRIMER

This chapter identifies more than 100 of the most popular or important legumes, their charateristics and culinary uses, along with some interesting heirloom varieties. Purchasing, preparation, and storage information is also included.

LEGUMES INCLUDED:

Adzuki Bean (Red Mung Bean)

Anasazi® Bean

Appaloosa Bean (Red Appaloosa Bean)

Baby White Lima Bean

Beluga Lentil

Black Appaloosa Bean

Black Chickpea

Black-Eyed Pea

Black Gram Bean (Black Mung Bean)

Black Soybean (fermented)

Black Turtle Bean

Blue Pod Capucijner

Blue Shackamaxon Bean

Bolita Bean

Borlotti Bean

Brown Lazy Wife Bean

Brown Lentil

Calypso Bean (Steuben Yellow Eye Bean, Butterscotch Calypso Bean)

Cannellini Bean

Chickpea

Christmas Lima Bean (Chestnut Lima)

Cowpea

Cranberry Bean (Roman Bean)

Cream Pea

Crowder Pea

Dark Green Chickpea

Dried Fava Bean

European Soldier Bean

Flageolet de Chevrier

French Green Lentil (Lentille du Puy)

French Horticultural Bean (October Bean)

French Navy Bean

Giant White Coco Bean

Gigante Bean (Gigandes, Hija)

Golden Split Chickpea (Channa Dal)

Goober Pea (Congo Goober, Groundnut, Bambara)

Great Northern Bean

Green Bean

Green Fava Bean (Broad Bean, Horse Bean)

Green Lima Bean (Butter Bean)

Green Mung Bean

Green Pea (English Pea, Garden Pea, Sweet Pea)

Green Romano Bean

Green Soybean

Green Split Pea

Haricot Blanc de Soisson

Haricot Lingot

Haricot Vert

Hopi Orange Lima Bean

Jackson Wonder Bean (Calico Bean)

Lady Pea

Large Brown Fava

Lupini Bean

Madeira Bean (Madera Bean)

Marrowfat Pea

Monstoller Wild Goose Bean

Mortgage Lifter Bean

Munsi Wolf Bean (Speckled Minisink)

Navy Bean (Pea Bean)

Painted Pony Bean

Peanuts, Spanish (Valencia)

Peanuts, Virginia

Pea Shoot

Pea Sprout

Petite Crimson Lentil (Crimson Lentil)

Pigeon Pea (Congo Pea, Gandules, Yellow Lentil, Toor Dal)

Pink Bean

Pinto Bean (Cabbage Bean, Crabeye Bean)

Purple Hyacinth Bean (Lablab)

Rattlesnake Bean

Red Chile Bean

Red Kidney Bean (Dark Red or Badi Rajma)

Red Lima Bean (Worcester Indian Red Pole Lima)

Red Valentine Bean (One-Thousand-For-One, Purple-Speckled Valentine Bean, Refugee Bean, Turkish Date Bean)

Rice Bean

Scarlet Runner Bean (Stick Bean)

Small Brown Fava

Small Red Bean (Peqeños)

Small White Fava

Snow Pea

Southern Checker Pea

Spanish Pardina Lentil (Spanish Brown Lentil)

Spanish Tolosana Bean (Prince Bean)

Split Fava

Split Golden Fava

Split Red Lentil (Red Chief Lentil, Egyptian Lentil, Pink Lentil)

Split White Lentil

Split Yellow Lentil

Sugar Snap Pea

Swedish Brown Bean

Tarbais Bean

Tall Telephone Pea (Dwarf Telephone Pea, Alderman Pea, Carter's Daisy Pea)

Tepary Bean

Tongues of Fire Bean

Trout Bean (Coach Bean, Dalmatian Bean, Jacob's Cattle, Torellen Bean)

Wax Bean (Crystal Bean, White Wax Bean)

White Emergo Bean (Sweet White Runner Bean)

Winged Bean (Asparagus Bean)

Yard-Long Bean (Long Beans)

Yam Bean

Yellow Indian Woman Bean

Yellow Split Mung Bean

Yellow Split Pea

Zebra Bean (Amethyst Bean)

One could devote an entire book to the botanical relationships of all legumes, of which there are literally thousands. This chart represents the major branches of the legume family and the most commonly used beans, peas, and lentils. Methods of classification vary greatly, ranging from seed type to culinary characteristics and change according to new research findings. In this book legumes have been categorized by their botanical relationships in the primer section and by their culinary uses in the cooking charts.

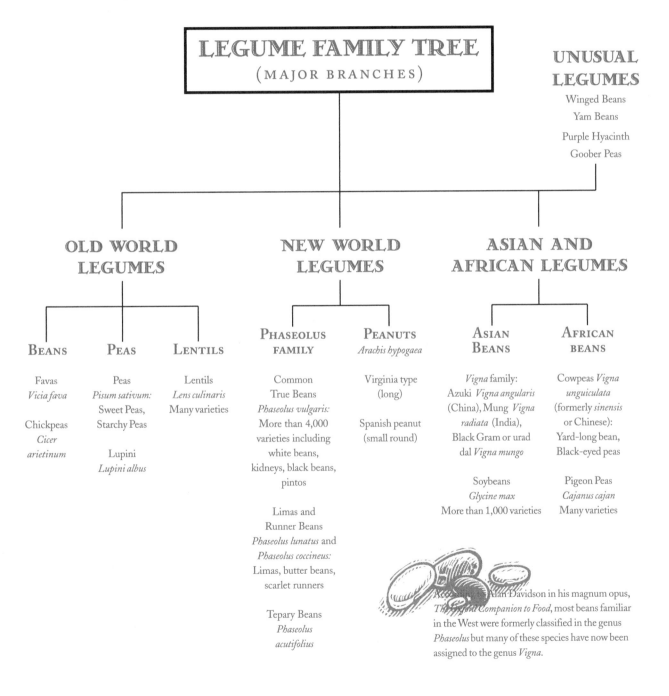

LEGUME FAMILY TREE
(MAJOR BRANCHES)

UNUSUAL LEGUMES

Winged Beans

Yam Beans

Purple Hyacinth

Goober Peas

OLD WORLD LEGUMES

BEANS

Favas
Vicia fava

Chickpeas
Cicer arietinum

PEAS

Peas
Pisum sativum:
Sweet Peas,
Starchy Peas

Lupini
Lupini albus

LENTILS

Lentils
Lens culinaris
Many varieties

NEW WORLD LEGUMES

PHASEOLUS FAMILY

Common
True Beans
Phaseolus vulgaris:
More than 4,000
varieties including
white beans,
kidneys, black beans,
pintos

Limas and
Runner Beans
Phaseolus lunatus and
Phaseolus coccineus:
Limas, butter beans,
scarlet runners

Tepary Beans
Phaseolus acutifolius

PEANUTS
Arachis hypogaea

Virginia type
(long)

Spanish peanut
(small round)

ASIAN AND AFRICAN LEGUMES

ASIAN BEANS

Vigna family:
Azuki *Vigna angularis*
(China), Mung *Vigna radiata* (India),
Black Gram or urad
dal *Vigna mungo*

Soybeans
Glycine max
More than 1,000 varieties

AFRICAN BEANS

Cowpeas *Vigna unguiculata*
(formerly *sinensis* or *Chinese*):
Yard-long bean,
Black-eyed peas

Pigeon Peas
Cajanus cajan
Many varieties

According to Alan Davidson in his magnum opus, *The Oxford Companion to Food*, most beans familiar in the West were formerly classified in the genus *Phaseolus* but many of these species have now been assigned to the genus *Vigna*.

SPECIFIC LEGUME DESCRIPTIONS AND CHARACTERISTICS

UNUSUAL LEGUMES

ASIDE FROM THE MEMBERS OF THE MAIN FAMILIES OF LEGUMES—BEANS, PEAS, AND LENTILS—THERE ARE A NUMBER OF MEMBERS OF THE LEGUME FAMILY THAT HAVE SPECIAL PROPERTIES. ALL OF THE UNUSUAL LEGUMES IN THIS SECTION ARE TROPICAL IN ORIGIN. THEY INCLUDE THE WINGED BEAN (OR GOA BEAN OR ASPARAGUS PEA), THE YAM BEAN (OR JICAMA OR MEXICAN WATER CHESTNUT), THE PURPLE HYACINTH (OR LABLAB) BEAN, AND THE GOOBER PEA (OR BAMBARRA PEA).

Winged Bean

Also known as Goa beans, Asparagus beans, Four-Angled beans, Manila beans, and Princess peas, winged beans are four-sided tropical legumes with flared ridges. A legume originally grown in limited areas of New Guinea and Southeast Asia, it is now being raised all over Southeast Asia and India. The plant produces edible shoots, leaves, flowers, tubers, pods, seeds, and a cooking oil extracted from the seeds and is comparatively high in protein. The pods are usually deep green, but may be red, pink, or purple. Each bean has four slightly ruffled wings or fins that run its length. The pods are larger than green beans but very lightweight. When cooked, they are meatier, blander, and starchier than a green bean but crunchier than a shell bean. Choose small pods with undeveloped seeds and plan to cook them within one or two days, as they don't store well. To prepare, cut off and discard the tips and then slice crosswise or on the diagonal. Wing beans are good sliced and added to stir-fries, braised and tossed in a strong-tasting sauce, or pickled.

Yam Bean

The yam bean (or jicama) is a name applied to the large, edible tubers of a leguminous plant native to Central and South America. This large, papery brown skinned root has a crisp, crunchy texture and can be eaten raw or cooked; however, the skin must be peeled before eating. Chinese cooks add yam bean to stir-fried vegetables as an easy-to-prepare alternative to fresh water chestnuts. The young pods of this plant may be eaten, but mature pods and their seeds are toxic. The enlarged root is the part of the plant sold in most supermarkets and ethnic markets. Interestingly, the tubers of leguminous plants are generally more nutritious than other tubers (such as potatoes). In the last few hundred years, yam bean (or jicama) has been introduced to most tropical and subtropical regions of the world. In Hawaii, it is supposedly called the "chop sui potato."

Purple Hyacinth Bean

The Purple Hyacinth Bean originated in tropical Asia or Africa and it thrives on heat. It has been cultivated in India since early times. Like runner beans, the hyacinth bean is cultivated both for its ornamental purple flowers and seedpods. It has a high protein content, a high yield, and the ability to stay green during droughts. It is also easy to harvest. The beans are usually black, or close to black, but some varieties are white. Note that the dry bean seeds contain toxic amounts of cyanogenic glucosides and must be boiled to become edible. Children are especially vulnerable to this toxin. They also need a long time to cook because of their thick skin. This same bean goes under many names including its Latin name *dolichos labla, moneghine* (a Venetian name meaning little nuns), lablab (its North African common name), Egyptian bean, bonavist bean, and *frijoles caballeros* (or cowboy bean).

Goober Peas

Goober peas are a legume related to fava beans that originated in West Africa. The dry beans can be ground for flour. They are similar to but not the same as peanuts. At one time they were extensively cultivated by slaves along the South Carolina coast. Other names include Congo goober, groundnut, and Bambarra. They must be cooked before being eaten and have a flavor similar to lima beans. In West Africa, they are often boiled, crushed to form them into cakes, and then fried to make a long-keeping food. A closely related species is the Hausa groundnut, which is grown in many parts of West Africa. It has seeds that are somewhat flattened, kidney-shaped, and dark brown or black. Goobers are less common now because peanuts have mostly supplanted them.

···

OLD WORLD LEGUMES

~ ❧ ~ ❧ ~ ❧ ~ ❧ ~ ❧ ~

BEANS

Favas
Vicia faba

Green Fava Beans: The venerable broad bean (fava or faba) was the only bean known to Europe until the discovery of the New World, though other legumes like chickpeas, lentils, and peas were well known. Favas are quite hardy and sturdy and have been cultivated since ancient times everywhere from Britain to Sicily and Egypt. There are also purple, deep tan, and pale beige varieties. Other names for the fava are faba, fève, broad bean, horse bean, and Windsor bean.

Fava beans grow inside large green pods about eight inches long and one inch wide with a string running down the inner side. Pull off the string, open up the pod and you'll find green fava beans nestled inside a white spongy material that helps protect the beans from any harm. Each fava bean is enclosed in a second thick, inner skin, which is normally removed before eating. Fresh favas range in color and size from the young fava beans that are a springtime delicacy, to large, yellow-white starch-laden mature beans. When picked young, these small beans are tender enough to enjoy raw with salt as a snack. The more common favas are brilliant green thumbnail-size beans or larger, more mature flattened creamy yellow beans.

For fresh favas, you must first remove the inner beans from their protective spongy pod. Break back the tips of the pods, and then pull down along the side to remove the string. The pods will then open easily. Remove the beans and discard the pods. Now you must remove the second inner skin before the final cooking stage. Bring a pot of salted water to the boil at high heat. Blanch the shelled favas, cooking them just until the water comes back to the boil. Drain and then refresh them in a bowl of ice water or under cold running water to set their color. Peel off and discard the outer skins of the fava beans, revealing the bright green inner beans. If the fresh favas are overly mature and yellow inside rather than bright green, you will need to cook them again in boiling water until they're tender. Otherwise set aside the green favas and eat as is or continue with your recipe. Because fresh favas take a fair amount of time to prepare, enjoy a few favas as a garnish to all sorts of dishes.

GREEN FAVA BEAN RECIPES
Provençal Braised Fava Beans
  and Artichokes
Minted Tender Fava Beans
Broad Bean and Nasturtium
  Soup
Trio of Savory Beans
Whole Favas with Salt
Roast Young Pigeon with Tiny
  Favas

SUGGESTED USES
• Sprinkle green favas at the last minute into any sautè of fish, seafood, or poultry to add a colorful and tasty accent.
• When cooking starches such as rice, couscous, or wheat berries, stir in favas just before serving. Add favas to pasta sauces such as fresh tomato sauce, brown butter and Parmesan sauce, or even cream-based sauces.

Dried Fava Beans: Dried favas come in many sizes, shapes, and colors. The two basic kinds are those in their skins and split favas with their inner skins removed. Large brown favas in their skins are the most common dried form, but you will also see smaller white favas and small dark brown favas. The larger dried favas have a noticeably granular texture and a strong flavor with a slightly bitter quality. Favas in their skins take longer to cook than the split, skinned varieties, which are also easier to digest. My favorite kind of dried fava is the large, split golden type that I buy at a Lebanese grocery. They cook quickly and evenly and the golden color is a real plus when making bean dips.

Chickpeas
Cicer arietinum

The Latin name for the chickpea is *Cicer arietinum*. It is said that an ancestor in the family of the Roman orator Cicero had a wart on his face that resembled a chickpea, hence the root of the first word. The second Latin word means ramlike (as in Aries, the zodiac sign of the ram) and refers to the chickpea's resemblance to a ram's head, complete with curling horns. There are many names for chickpeas including the Spanish garbanzo, the Old English calavance, the Italian ceci, and the Portuguese grao-de-bico, and the Indian gram, a term used for legumes that are whole, rather than split.

The common chickpea is tan to light brown when raw and golden brown when cooked. The bright golden yellow split chickpeas popular in India are called channa dal. Black-skinned in their unhulled form, these same chickpeas are found whole in Indian markets. Small dark green, skinned whole chickpeas are also available. In India chickpeas have been part of the diet since the second millennium BC. Chickpeas have a nutlike chewy texture that makes them satisfying in one-dish meals or hearty soups.

Chickpeas come in many forms including chickpea or gram flour, which is used in India for making fritters and pancakes, in Nice and around the Riviera for fried crunchy sticks called *panisses*, and for the snack "bread" called *socca*. Be sure to refrigerate chickpea flour to prevent insect infestation.

Dry chickpeas are notoriously hard and the most challenging of beans to cook. Check that your chickpeas come from a source that sells its stock quickly. Shriveled, dried out chickpeas will never get soft, no matter how long you cook them. I buy mine from a Mexican or Latino, Indian, or Middle Eastern grocery because those cuisines have many dishes made from chickpeas. It is necessary to soak chickpeas for at least 10 hours and as long as 24 hours before cooking them.

Many cooks recommend skinning cooked chickpeas before proceeding further with recipes. While skinning will improve the digesibility of chickpeas, for aesthetic reasons I prefer to use unskinned cooked chickpeas. To skin, place the cooked chickpeas in a large bowl of cold water. Rub vigorously between your fingers to loosen the skins, which will rise to the surface of the water. Using a wire skimmer (or your cupped hands) remove and discard the skins.

THE PEA FAMILY
Pisum sativum,
pisum culinaris

Starchy Peas

Green Split Peas: Peas are one of the oldest vegetables but early varieties were quite starchy even when young. Both the Greeks and Romans cultivated shelling peas for drying. Pease Porridge was the English wintertime staple for centuries because it "sticks

> **GREEN SPLIT PEA RECIPES**
> Diner-Style Split Pea Soup
> Hearty Dutch Green Split Pea
> Soup
> Quebec Yellow Split Pea Soup
> Moroccan Golden Split Pea and
> Pumpkin Soup

to the ribs." Yellow split pea soup still serves the same purpose for the inhabitants of Quebec. Two types of peas are now grown: the wrinkly-skinned sweet peas for eating green and the smooth-skinned starchy peas for drying as whole and split peas. Green split peas, an old-fashioned starchy pea variety without any skins, are split in half for ease of cooking.

They are sometimes found in whole form, which take longer to cook. There is also a third type of wild Mediterranean pea called the oasis or maquis pea.

Yellow Split Peas: A starchy pea variety in an attractive golden color, yellow split peas are commonly used for soups and are especially popular in Sweden, Canada, and India. In Sweden, thick yellow split pea soup is the traditional Thursday night supper, which commemorates King Eric XIV, who was poisoned with arsenic in his yellow split pea soup. Canada is now the largest source of split peas in the world. Called Channa dal in India, yellow split peas are sometimes roasted, then ground and used to bind ground meat kebabs. They can also be fried or used to thicken sauces.

Blue Pod Capucijners: This gray sugar pea is one of the more unusual pea varieties. It becomes quite leathery when mature, but is decorative with beautiful rose-pink and wine-red flowers. The deep maroon pods change to inky blue as the peas mature. Originally a Dutch variety, these peas probably were developed by Capuchin monks. They are known as *pois à cross violette* or purple cross peas in France.

Marrowfat Pea: This sought-after old English variety was thought to

taste as good and rich as the marrow fat enjoyed in dishes like osso buco.

Tall Telephone Pea: This wrinkled type of marrow pea grows on seven- to eight-foot vines with pods that hang straight down, and is also known as the Dwarf Telephone Pea, Alderman Pea, and Carter's Daisy Pea.

Sweet Peas

English Peas: Italian Renaissance gardeners originally cultivated the sweet green pea, leading to a craze for this new delicacy in the French royal court. In fact, in Louis XIV's court, the ladies would eat peas just before going to bed, in spite of the danger of indigestion. In the north and west of France, the towns of Saint-Germain and Clamart were so famous for the quality of their tiny peas that their names came to be used as culinary terms for any dishes made with *petit pois*. The people of France and Italy still celebrate spring by eating sweet young peas. Eating *risi e bisi*, a dish of creamy rice mixed with tiny peas (*piselli*), is the traditional rite of spring in Venice. The French cook the same petits pois for a matter of minutes with spring onions and butter lettuce for a dish of exquisite delicacy. Common names include garden pea and sweet pea.

Sweet peas are the familiar "peas-in-a-pod." Their parchmentlike pods are normally too stringy to eat, though they can be used to make a soup. Choose rounded pearl-shaped peas that perfectly fill their pods, the way you'd like your trousers to fit: close to the body, but not bulging. Stay away from overgrown, starchy peas that are flattened against each other and resemble a set of teeth. For the ultimate in sweet succulence, eat peas just after they're picked. But don't despair if this isn't possible. Peas will maintain almost all of their sweetness for three to four days if placed in a closed plastic bag and refrigerated.

FRESH ENGLISH PEA RECIPES
Queen Victoria's Favorite Green
   Pea Soup
Bouillabaisse of Little Peas
   Escudier
Garden Peas à la Française
Portuguese Green Peas with
   Chorizo and Poached Eggs
Venetian Rice and Peas
Spring Green Pea and Snow Pea
   Soup

Snow Peas and Sugar Snap Peas: Snow peas were probably first cultivated in Holland and originally known as Dutch peas. Sugar or snap peas are to garden peas as green string beans are to shelling beans. Sugar snaps and snow peas are both types of sugar peas, with tender, edible pods. The difference is that snow peas are completely flat with under-developed inner seeds, while sugar snaps are full rounded, closely resembling a garden pea in its pod. Other names for snow peas include *mangetout* (eat-them-alls) in France, Chinese pea, Chinese snow pea, Chinese pea

pod, and sugar pea. These flat-podded peas are hand picked and are available fresh or frozen and used in Asian dishes.

Look for barely discernible miniature peas inside snow peas. Snow peas should be light green in color and smooth and firm. Be sure to inspect the pods carefully for small circles of rot on their surface, a dead giveaway that they've been sitting too long on the shelf. Since people buy snow peas in small quantities, these peas tend to sell slowly at many supermarkets. Instead, try to buy them from Asian markets, which tend to sell them quickly and maintain a fresh inventory.

Sugar snaps and snow peas couldn't be easier to prepare. Hold the pod just below the stem between thumb and forefinger and break back the stem end. To remove the stem and strings on either side of the pod, grasp the tip of the stem and pull it down parallel to the pod. Steam or pan-fry snow peas, but always cook them quickly at high heat (for brightest color) and serve them right away.

A relatively new type of edible pod pea known as the sugar snap pea was developed in the United States by Dr. C. Lamborn of Gallatin Valley Seed Co. (now Rogers NK Seed Co.) and was introduced to gardeners in 1979. Sugar snaps are

round-podded and similar to standard pea pods in appearance. However, they are fleshier and free from pod-wall fiber when mature, and some are stringless.

Most sugar snaps are purchased fresh, though they are also available frozen and can be used as an alternative to sweet garden peas or snow peas. Snap peas should be brilliant green in color with the same smooth, firm skin as snow peas. Stay away from sugar snaps with shriveled tops or spotted sides. To maintain their brilliant color and crisp, juicy texture, cook at high heat for a very short time. They don't take well to blanching (precooking and then reheating), which is not even a timesaver because they cook so quickly. Once sugar snaps are cooked, serve them as quickly as possible because they will start to shrivel and darken within minutes.

RECIPES FOR SNOW PEAS
Green Pea and Snow Pea Soup
   for Spring
Beef Stir-Fry with Snow Peas
   and Bean Sprouts
Stir-Fried Snow Peas and Bok
   Choy with Ginger
Noodle Salad with Snow Peas,
   Bean Sprouts, and Shanxi
   Vinegar Dressing

RECIPES FOR SUGAR SNAP PEAS
Pasta Primavera with Sugar Snaps
Sesame Sugar Snaps

Pea Shoots and Pea Sprouts: Pea shoots—the very top tiny leaves and curly tendrils of snow pea vines—are a great delicacy in Chinese cooking and often the most expensive vegetables on the market. Add them to a soup just before serving or at the last-minute to a stir-fry of vegetables. They add a fresh, sweet flavor and make an outstanding garnish for any light dish. Companies that specialize in sprouts are now selling pea sprouts—the stem and first green leaves sprouted from peas. These pea sprouts are less expensive than pea shoots, and though not as sweet and spring green—only the leaf portion is green—they make a good substitute.

Lupini
Lupini albus

Lupini Beans: These flat, coin-shaped, yellow-brown beans have a small round hole at one end and are most commonly purchased cooked and pickled in glass jars. They are enjoyed as a snack with beverages in Lebanon, Italy, Spain, and Portugal, where they are called *tremoços*. To serve the lupini, drain the liquid from the jar and place the beans in a bowl. Invite guests to suck the inner beans from their skins, discarding the skins in bowls.

A member of the pea family, lupini or lupins are grown mainly for their flowers. The seeds or beans of certain species, though toxic and bitter when fresh, are treated to make them edible, and then roasted or boiled. In spite of the lengthy preparation needed to make the beans into a snack food, they have been part of the Old World diet for more than 2,000 years. Some varieties now grown can be used without preliminary preparation. The variety called *tarwi* have a high protein content.

THE LENTIL FAMILY
Lens esculenta, Lens culinaris

Brown Lentils: An important plant in the ancient world, lentils have been cultivated for close to 10,000 years in the Near East. Whole lentils are made up of two lens-shaped sides, hence the origin of its name. India accounts for about half the world's consumption of lentils and therefore has develped its own lexicon and classification for this legume. Gram is an Indian term used for legumes that are whole, rather than split, such as black gram, green chickpea, and green mung bean. Split legumes, such as red lentils, are called dal in India.

While common lentils are small, round, and earth-brown in color, lentils come in a variety of colors and sizes. There are two main types of lentils: those that are relatively large and light or yellow-colored, and those

that are small and brown, pink, or gray. In the north of India and Pakistan, the Muslim population mainly eats pink lentils. Next to soybeans, lentils have the highest protein content of all vegetables, about twenty-five percent. This may account for their being a favorite food during Lent in Roman Catholic countries.

All lentils are thin-skinned so they cook quickly without soaking. Vegetable proteins, particularly those present in certain types of unhulled beans and peas, can be very difficult to digest, but the smaller shelled peas and beans present less of a problem. Lentils are among the easiest of all legumes to digest.

Beluga Lentils: These fancy black lentils are very small and fetch a high price. Their name is a play on their resemblance to Beluga caviar, the smallest, the blackest, and the most expensive variety.

Split White Lentils: These creamy-colored skinless, lentil-like legumes commonly used in Indian cuisine are actually the inner seeds of black gram beans, also called urad dal. (See Black Gram Beans, page 28.)

French Green Lentils: Called lentilles du Puy, these special lentils are raised in Puy, a region of southwest France. They are small, speckled deep green, and firm when cooked, which only takes a short time. Because of their attractive appearance and ease of cooking, they are the darlings of French and American chefs, especially in the classic Nouvelle Cuisine dish of salmon on a bed of lentils.

Spanish Pardina Lentils: Known as Spanish brown lentils or continental lentils, they are small and richly colored (ranging from earthy brown to moss green with streaks of black), and hold their shape very well when cooked.

Split Yellow Lentils: The split yellow lentil is the seed of the plant *Cajanus cajan*, the Latin name for the pigeon pea, so yellow lentils are actually hulled split pigeon peas. In India, the classification of legumes is much looser and legumes of different families that are closely related in culinary uses are considered the same. For example, the seeds of red lentil *Lens culinaris* and the yellow lentil are both considered lentils. (See Pigeon Peas, page 33.)

Split Red Lentils: These salmon-colored small split lentils are also called red chief lentils, pink lentils, Egyptian lentils, and *masoor dal* in India. They turn golden and very soft when cooked and are ideal for soups and purées.

Petite Crimson Lentils: These tiny red lentils, which are about one-third the size of regular lentils, are originally from Turkey, Egypt, and India. They are now domestically grown and cook in only five minutes. They can be mixed with rice or made into soups such as the South Indian Vegetarian Red Lentil Soup.

New World Legumes

THE *PHASEOLUS* FAMILY:
COMMON TRUE BEANS AND LIMAS

Common True Beans Popular in America

Green Beans: We might take green beans for granted but they are a consistently satisfying, good-looking green vegetable choice. The best are bright grass-green in color (rather than faded or yellowish) and have a soft, velvety skin. Check the end where the bean has been broken off the stem; if the scar is hard and dark, it was picked too long ago. Fresh-picked beans should be crisp enough to make a "snap" sound when broken in half.

Ideally, choose slender pods with small, uniform-size seeds inside so they will cook evenly.

Green beans are still known as string beans because old-fashioned varieties had strings to remove. Because fresh picked green beans make a crisp snapping sound when the ends are broken off, they are also called snap beans. It's your choice whether to break off both ends (the stem and the pointy tip) or to just trim off the stem ends. I prefer to leave the pointy tips on for aesthetic reasons, though they are slightly tougher than the rest of the bean.

Because the pointy end deteriorates first, becoming shriveled and unsightly, green beans with their sprightly tips intact can display their freshness. For a fancier look, line up the green beans in parallel and use a sharp knife to cut off both the tops and bottoms so that the beans are all the same length. You can also French-cut the beans by slicing them on a sharp diagonal into two-inch lengths, exposing the inner flesh and tiny seeds.

Green beans react quickly to acidity, losing their attractive color and becoming more olive-colored than emerald. To cook green beans, you have several good choices. The first is to steam them using a basket steamer. The second method is to bring a large pot of salted water to a boil and blanch (partially cook) the beans, bringing the water back to a boil as quickly as possible. Also be sure to stir the beans in the pot so they will cook and color evenly. Cook two to three minutes or until bright green and crisp-tender and then drain.

The third method is to bring one to two inches of salted water to a boil in a large skillet and then add the beans, stirring them occasionally and bringing the water back to a boil as quickly as possible, and cook two to three minutes. If you're seasoning the beans with anything acidic like lemon, vinegar, white wine, or even tomatoes, toss with the beans at the last minute to preserve their color.

Note that in many countries, such as Greece, India, and Spain, green beans are cooked slowly until they are meltingly tender in a sauce that is often tomato based. Though olive in color, these beans have an appetizing quality of their own.

Wax Beans or Crystal White Wax Bean: Hybridized by Dutch plant breeders, wax beans were grown in England as a forcing bean for hothouses. Also called ice bean, this is a light green to white variety of green or snap bean that tends to be a little tougher, more like an old-fashioned green bean variety. Heirloom varieties of wax beans have a string running the length of their pods, which must be removed before cooking.

Follow the cooking directions for green beans (see page 45) if the wax beans are young with a lemony-yellow to greenish color rather than a creamy white. Colorful purple wax beans are available in markets between May and October. If your

wax beans are more mature with prominent inner seeds, follow the cooking directions for romano beans (see page 45).

Black Turtle Beans: Also called black beans or *frijoles negros*, turtle beans, and Mexican or Spanish black beans, these popular legumes are medium to small in size and maintain a dramatic shiny black color when cooked (though they are actually a very deep purple). The best black beans are considered to be the heirloom black Valentines, actually a deep purple-black. All black beans, which are closely related to kidney beans, turn purplish when cooked. They have a meaty texture and a rich, earthy flavor.

They are beloved in Cuba, Trinidad, Brazil, Mexico, and all over the southern United States, and are said to have a slightly mushroomlike flavor. Note that the black bean used in Chinese cooking (often fermented for a funky though addictive flavor) is not the same bean at all. The Chinese bean is a soybean, possibly, though not necessarily black until fermented, whereas the black turtle bean is a variety of common bean.

Dried black turtle beans are very likely to contain foreign matter, because dirt clumps or little stones are easily disguised. Always be sure to pick over black beans carefully. There are innumerable versions of black bean soup, including two in this book. Black beans make an exceptionally smooth purée.

Note that black beans seem to be particularly treacherous when it comes to creating noxious gas. To cook black beans, soak them overnight in cold water, then drain and rinse under cold water. Place in a large pot and cover generously with cold water. Bring the water to a boil, then drain, discarding the water. Add the flavoring ingredient of your choice (see Basic Cooking Chart, page 43). Cover with fresh cold water (or stock, diluted with water if concentrated). Bring to a boil again, skimming off any white foam impurities. Reduce the heat and simmer for about two hours, then stir in the salt. Continue to cook for one hour longer or until tender to the bite.

Red Kidney Beans: These large, kidney-shaped beans with a robust, full-bodied flavor and soft texture range in color from a light red to a dark, almost purple-red, that cook up to a beautiful crimson. A thick skin means these beans require long cooking and can be harder to digest, but they also hold their shape well in long-simmered dishes like chili con carne. In India, where they are called *badi rajma*, dark red kidney beans are very popular because their heartiness makes them a satisfying meat substitute. The smaller red chile bean and the pink bean, popular in Puerto Rico and sold by Goya and other companies, are close substitutes.

I've always used the gorgeous, dark red kidney beans sold in the can by the S & W Company. I find that in bean salads and other dishes where color is important, it's hard to match the brilliant color of the special variety of kidney bean used in this product. However, since I've discovered the dark red dried kidney beans sold by Vann's Spices in Baltimore and in Indian groceries, such as Kalustyan in New York, I can now achieve this same desirable color.

KIDNEY BEAN RECIPES
Pennsylvania Dutch Chow-Chow Relish
Rigatoni with Oven-Cooked Red Beans, Pepperoni, and Garlic
"Liz Taylor" Beef Chili Topped with Cornbread
Portuguese Salt Cod and Kidney Bean Salad
Tricolor Succotash
Piedmontese Red Beans in Red Wine
Baked Beans with Beef and Barley (Jewish Sabbath Cholent)
Haitian Red Beans and Rice

Great Northern Beans: One of the most popular and versatile varieties in the United States and Canada, these all-purpose, medium size oblong beans with white skins have a slightly nutty flavor and a powdery texture. Although they are slightly larger than the pea-sized navy bean, great Northern beans can be substituted for them in soups and baked bean dishes.

Navy Beans: This white bean was served so often to sailors that it became forever associated with the navy. Being small, it took less time to cook on board ship than larger beans. Navy beans have many names,

BLACK BEAN RECIPES
Black Bean Nachos
Brazilian Feijoada Completa
Corn Tortillas in Black Bean Sauce
Black Bean Quesadillas with Pepita-Tomatillo Sauce
Creamy Black Bean Pâté
Southwest Black Bean Salad with Baked Spiced Goat Cheese Rounds
Cuban Black Bean Soup with Sofrito and Smoked Turkey
Sea Isles Black Bean Purée with Dry Madeira, Lemon, and Egg Mimosa
Black Bean and Hazelnut Cakes with Steamed Clams

including haricot, Boston bean, white coco, pea bean, white pea beans, and *alubias chicas* in Spanish. This original Aztec name *ayacotl* is the root of their name haricot. Navy beans are perfect for baked beans, salads, soups, stews, and purées.

NAVY BEAN RECIPES
Boston Baked Beans with
   Steamed Brown Bread
French Navy Bean and
   Shrimp Salad
Diner-Style Baked Beans with
   Smoky Bacon
Irish Bean and Smoky Bacon Soup
Senate Bean Soup

Pink Beans: This oval pink-skinned bean with a very creamy texture is beloved in Puerto Rican cookery where it is called *habichuelas rojas* or pink bean. Pink beans can be used in all pinto and cranberry bean recipes.

PINK BEAN RECIPES
Puerto Rican-Style Pink Beans

Small Red Beans: These rounded, burgundy-red beans, called Mexican red beans and *rojos pequeños* in Spanish, are good lookers and good cookers. Because they are small, they cook quickly and evenly. These beans are popular among Hispanic people in the United States, where they are sold in large quantities by the Goya Company. Use in any creole dishes or recipes that call for kidney beans, such as chili and baked beans.

Pinto Beans: This medium-sized, oval, mottled beige and brown bean common throughout the American southwest has an earthy flavor and powdery texture. It is related to the kidney bean and turns reddish brown when cooked. The best pintos are raised at high altitude; they are quicker cooking and easier to digest. These beans are used in chili and all types of southwestern dishes, including refried beans. Pinto means "painted" in Spanish. Other colorful names for it include crabeye bean and gunga pea.

PINTO BEAN RECIPES
Earthenware-Cooked Pinto Beans
Refried Beans

Heirloom Common True Bean Varieties
Phaseolus vulgaris

Bean seeds are probably the easiest seeds of all to save from the vegetable garden and will remain viable for years if stored in a dry, cool place. Many of the heirloom varieties listed here have striking markings or special characteristics that farmers wanted to save and share. Saving heirloom bean seeds promotes genetic diversity in our crops, thus helping our food supply stay healthy. Because beans are self-pollinating, insect cross-pollination is not common. Therefore, gardeners can save seeds of common beans and peas and expect them to remain true to type.

The greater the diversity of seeds we have, the greater the possibility of overcoming problems with any one plant. Generations of gardeners and small regional growers have saved seeds for hundreds of years to preserve some of these heirloom varieties of common beans. These plants performed best for them, developed resistances to local insect and disease problems, and became adapted to specific soils and climates.

Anasazi® Beans: These burgundy and white mottled beans have a sweet flavor and meaty texture and are a close relative of appaloosa beans. Anasazi is a Navajo word meaning "the ancient ones," and refers to the Anasazi cliff dwelling Indians who lived in the four corners area (now Colorado, Utah, Arizona and New Mexico) around AD 130. This bean variety was originally found in the ruins of cliff dwellings by settlers in the early 1900s and is now registered to and grown exclusively by Adobe Milling of Dove Creek, Colorado.

Grown at high altitude (about 7,000 feet), Anasazi® beans supposedly contain seventy-five percent less of the gas-causing carbohydrates than pinto beans. They make good baking beans.

Appaloosa Beans: Though sometimes referred to as Anasazi® beans, growers insist the two beans are different. Also called red appaloosa, these beans have markings that are reminiscent of the appaloosa pony. Slender and oval with mottled burgundy to purple markings, this bean is recommended for dishes like Southwest Baked Beans because it

holds its shape well and has a rich flavor. Appaloosas make a good substitute for black-eyed peas in Smoked Turkey Chili, and may also be substituted for pintos, a close relation.

Black Appaloosa Beans: Also called cave beans, these striking black and white beans with a distinctively flat and angular shape were supposedly found in the desert soil near ancient cave dwellings in the southwest. Because of their visual appeal, they are best suited for salads and baked bean dishes, where the bean will remain whole.

Blue Shackamaxon Beans: This old variety of pole beans, preserved among Quaker farmers of southeastern Pennsylvania and south Jersey, is said to be of Lenape Indian origin. Named after a place called Shackamaxon along the Delaware River (now in the city of Philadelphia), the bean was never grown commercially. The seeds were preserved by a seedsman in Bucks County, Pennsylvania. When freshly shelled, the beans are bright navy blue; as they dry, they turn purplish-blue.

Bolita Beans: This western heirloom bean was grown by Native Americans throughout the southwest. The Spanish who settled in northern New Mexico developed them. This is a rich-tasting bean with more depth of flavor than its close relative the pinto bean, and can be used in southwest-style dishes.

Brown Lazy Wife Beans: Known as "lentil beans" among the Pennsylvania Dutch, these small and brown beans are named for how quickly they cook, and are commonly grown in the hills of western Pennsylvania, Maryland, West Virginia, and Ohio, where they may have originated. They are also popular as a soup bean in Germany, Switzerland, and northern Italy. These beans are believed to have been taken from Pennsylvania to Switzerland almost 300 years ago, and are often combined with lentils in cooking.

Calypso Bean (Steuben Yellow Eye): This thin-skinned, medium white bean with mustard colored splotches or "eyes" is a 400-year-old variety with many names, including steuben yellow eye, Maine yellow eye, and butterscotch calypso. It has a velvety texture, a mellow flavor, and plumps up well and becomes ivory to brown after cooking, making it excellent for salads and baked dishes. Supposedly this is the original bean used in colonial Boston for baked beans. Another variety of Calypso bean popular in Europe has streaked black and white markings.

European Soldier Beans: For perhaps obvious reasons, these oval, medium size white beans with red markings in the "eye" reminicent of a European toy soldier, were well known in early New England where the term "red coats" referred to the uniforms of the British soldiers. The distinctive markings are also said to resemble a soldier in Napoleon's army. They have a slightly mealy texture and should be cooked whole to maintain their markings, such as for slow-cooked dishes and soups.

French Horticultural Bean: An heirloom variety in the cranberry family, this tasty bean is also known as the October bean. It is delicious in soups, stews, and salads. Its firm texture and sweet, nutty flavor make this a favorite among bean aficionados.

Jackson Wonder Beans: This bean comes in mottled shades of beige and purplish-brown. It was popularized in Atlanta, Georgia, in the 1880s, where it became known as a good soup bean because of its creamy texture.

Madeira (Madera) Beans: This mottled brown, flat, oval-shaped bean is the largest member in the large cranberry family. These beans, originally from South America, were brought to Portugal where they became important in that nation's cuisine. They were then brought back to the United States by Portuguese and Italian immigrants. Madeiras have a floury texture and chestnutlike flavor. Though smaller, cranberry or scarlet runner beans are acceptable substitutes.

Monstoller Wild Goose Beans: The story of Civil War veteran John Monstoller, who was said to have shot down a wild goose with these beans in its craw, is very well known among heirloom seed savers. The beans were planted in 1866 and preserved ever since then by the same family. Excellent baked and in soups, this bean is very large, white on the bottom, heavily speckled with brown and maroon, and has an orange patch around the "eye."

Mortgage Lifter Beans: This extremely large white heirloom bean tastes similar to butter beans (large limas). The name comes from a farmer who was about to lose his land to the bank. Instead, his good crop of beans lifted his mortgage.

Munsi Wolf Beans: This heirloom variety was grown by the Lenape Indians in Delaware Water Gap. They are also called speckled minisink beans.

Painted Pony Beans: Similar to the appaloosa bean in that they also resemble the markings of a pony, these beans are closely related to the pinto as well. Of Mexican origin, they are slender and oval in shape, and shade from cream and beige all the way to brown and black. Rich and nutty in flavor, they are excellent in chili or other slow-cooked bean dishes.

Rattlesnake Beans: These slender, oval beans are speckled brown over a tan background. The pods twist around like rattlesnakes as they grow, hence their name. A relatively new variety, rattlesnake beans are closely related to pintos but with a richer, more intense flavor that makes them excellent in casseroles and chili.

Red Valentine Beans: These six-inch-long narrow pods are ideal substitutes for green beans. They are heavily speckled in deep-wine red over a pink background. In Germany they are called Turkish date beans. In its dried form, the bean is called one-thousand-for-one, purple-speckled valentine, and refugee bean.

Rice Beans: The seeds of this small bean of tropical Asian origin are a bit larger than rice grains, and are eaten, when dried, with or instead of rice. Ranging in color from yellow to red to brown and black, rice beans have a delicate flavor, soft texture, and are highly nutritious. These beans have been grown in the northeast of India and adjoining regions to the east, although they are difficult to harvest because they grow like vines and the seed pods open on their own, scattering the seeds. Rice beans are quick cooking, tender and slightly sweet. Their thin skins make them easy to digest.

Swedish Brown Beans: Swedish immigrants who settled in Montana introduced this toasty brown bean, a staple of Swedish cooking, to the northern United States about 100 years ago. They continue to be popular there because they mature early in the season, before the frost. When cooked, they turn honey brown and have a rich, slightly sweet flavor. They are most often used in soups, especially Swedish brown bean soup.

Trout Beans : Also known as Jacob's cattle bean, coach bean, and Dalmatian bean, these white and maroon-spotted heirloom tepary beans do indeed resemble spotted Dalmatian dogs or cattle. Originally brought to the United States from Germany, where it is called Torellen, the trout bean has been grown in New England since colonial times. These beans are suitable for growing in desert climates, and like other tepary beans, they have a relatively short growing season. When cooked, they have a velvety texture and are good in salads, relishes, and soups.

Zebra Beans: This heirloom variety, also known as the amethyst bean, is white with dark streaks that resemble a zebra's markings. It is highly prized for its superior creamy texture and full-bodied flavor, especially in Spain.

Common True Bean Varieties Popular in Europe

Green Romano Beans: This fresh Italian green bean (once only found frozen and cut into diagonals) is now a seasonal treat, especially in neighborhoods with a large Italian population. It is a flat and wide green bean that has a pronounced beany flavor. If young, these beans are quite tender, but they are often larger (as long as six inches) with visible inner bean seeds.

GREEN ROMANO BEAN RECIPES

Green Romano Bean and Navel
Orange Salad

Frittata with Romano Beans,
Prosciutto, and Italian Fontina

SUGGESTED USES

- Add to minestrone soup
- Partially cook (blanch) and toss in a pan with bacon or pancetta bits
- Served cooked and chilled with a bowl of mayonnaise-based dipping sauce
- Add to pasta salad

Larger beans should be treated more like dried beans and cooked for a longer period of time until tender. Romano beans hold up well and don't disintegrate when cooked. They take well to strong flavorings, such as tomato sauce with lots of garlic or lemon, capers, and chopped anchovy.

Choose the smallest romano beans you can find. Ideally they should be flattened in shape and only slightly wider than common green beans. The brighter the green color and the less apparent the inner bean seed, the more tender the bean. Pale or yellow beans are likely to be overgrown and tough. Using a sharp knife, trim off the stem end on a slight angle. It's your choice whether to cut off the pointy end. It will be slightly tough but adds visual interest and demonstrates the fresh-picked quality of the beans. I like to cut romano beans on the diagonal into even lengths before cooking.

If the beans vary a lot in size, separate them into two piles: one of larger beans and one with smaller beans. Cook each size separately and then mix them back together. Follow the basic cooking instructions for green beans (page 45), allowing more time for larger-seeded beans.

Haricots Verts: These pencil-thin green beans are a great delicacy in France. Most haricots verts sold in America come from Central America because of lower labor costs. Haricots verts, which simply means "green

HARICOTS VERTS RECIPES

Haricots Verts and Quail Eggs
in Truffle Vinaigrette

Haricots Verts à la Provençale

Haricot Vert and Roasted Beet
Salad with Fresh Goat Cheese

SUGGESTED USES

- Steam and refresh under cold running water and dress with a vinaigrette to serve cold.
- Steam, drain, and immediately toss in a small pan of butter or olive oil.
- Steam, drain, and serve as is or seasoned with a little sea salt and freshly ground black pepper.

beans" in French, are fashionably thin and hand-picked at just the right size. The commercial ones from Central America come all lined up like a box of green pencils, but the sweetest and plumpest haricots verts I've found come from a local organic farm. Other descriptive names include *haricots filets* (string beans) and *haricots aiguilles* (needle beans).

Prepare the haricots verts by trimming off the stem end only. (If the beans are not at their peak and their pointy tips are shriveled, trim them off also.) To cook haricots verts, set up a vegetable steamer basket with boiling water underneath and steam them for three to five minutes or until they turn a brilliant emerald green. Turn off the heat, lift out the steamer basket and refresh the beans under cold running water to set the color. (You can also cheat and add a tiny pinch of baking soda to the water when boiling. This will make them slightly less nutritious, but will insure their eye appeal.)

Borlotti Beans: Borlotti or Tuscan beans are the most popular beans of Tuscany, the land of the "bean eaters." Normally found in their dried form in this country, borlotti are plump and rounded in shape. Their background color is pinkish-tan with crimson speckles and streaks. Look for them in Italian groceries. They are similar to cranberry beans and interchangeable in use. In Italy many members of this family of small kidney-shaped speckled beans are sought after in the specific regions where they are grown, including *lamon, stregoni, scritti,* and *saluggia.*

BORLOTTI RECIPES

Florentine Borlotti Bean and
Tuna Salad

Tuscan Beans Cooked in the
Style of Wild Birds

Bolognese-Style Bean Soup

All of them share a meaty flavor and mild earthiness.

Cannellini Beans: These large white kidney-shaped beans are used extensively in Italy, and often found canned. They have a creamy smooth,

firm texture and a mild, nutty flavor that makes them extremely versatile. They are also called white kidney beans and haricots blancs in French. They are excellent in salads because their thin skins allow them to absorb flavors well. Cook cannellini gently and slowly, preferably in the oven so they keep their shape.

Cranberry Beans: Also called Roman beans, these medium-size, oval, creamy white beans have crimson speckles and streaks and are most frequently used in Italian dishes and soups. They are often found fresh in season in late summer, sold in beautiful speckled pods at Asian markets and well-stocked supermarkets.

These New World beans were enthusiastically adopted in Europe and north Africa. Old World farmers took the American beans and bred them, producing many new varieties. The cranberry bean was brought back to the United States by Italian immigrants and is now grown mostly on the California coast.

To prepare fresh shell cranberry beans, split open the pods on their slightly curved inner sides and remove the beans. These creamy, smooth, mild-tasting beans are such a treat when fresh that it's best to prepare them as simply as possible. Fresh-shelled beans do not need soaking, will keep about one week if refrigerated, and can also be frozen for later use. Simply cook them in simmering stock or water until tender and plump, generally for about half an hour. Cranberry beans are closely related to tongues of fire beans.

Tarbais Beans: This famous large white bean is cultivated in southwestern France and named for the city of Tarbes. Though rather expensive, they are available in the United States from Dean & DeLuca (see Sources, page 323). Traditionally used to make the regional masterpiece, cassoulet, this bean holds its shape extremely well, has a mild flavor and a creamy, smooth texture. Because of their large size, tarbais beans must be thoroughly soaked and cooked for a long time. Subtitute white emergo beans or large lima beans.

Tongues of Fire Beans: A close relative of the cranberry bean, this variety was originally collected from Tierra del Fuego on the far southern tip of South America. The pods are ivory white and gain red "flames" as they mature. They are a good candidate for baking and they marry very well with sausages.

Flageolets de Chevrier: These highly prized small, elongated immature bean seeds, usually light green or sometimes red, resembling the inner seeds of a common green bean are unusual in that they are picked and dried before being fully ripened. They may be cooked fresh or dried. (In the United States flageolets are generally available dried.)

A variety of haricot beans, flageolets were first developed by Gabriel

FLAGEOLET RECIPES
Roast Gigot of Lamb with
   Flageolet Gratin
Ragout of Flageolets, Chicken-
   Basil Sausage, and Spinach
Flageolets with Fennel, Tomato,
   and Green Olives
Basic Cooked Flageolets

Chevrier in Brittany in 1872 and were a particular favorite of the great French chef, Auguste Escoffier. In France they are also called chevriers or flageolets de chevrier.

Flageolets do not need soaking. They have very delicate, thin skins so cook them gently and slowly until tender but not mushy. Place the flageolets in a medium heavy-bottomed saucepan. Cover with cold water and bring to the boil. Skim off and discard the white foam that rises to the top. Reduce the heat to a bare simmer and cook slowly for about 1 hour or until the beans are close to tender without stirring, which breaks open the skins. Remove from the heat and pour off any remaining water.

Giant White Coco Beans: These large, flat French white beans are highly prized by French chefs as a side dish. They are similar in size and texture to the Emergo bean sold by specialty bean suppliers in this country.

Spanish Tolosana Beans: These beans, also known as prince beans, are well loved in Spain, where they really know their beans. With distinctive cinnamon and burgundy markings, they have a creamy texture and are especially suited to cooking with seafood, such as clams and shrimp.

French Navy Beans: The elegant and rounded French navy bean is smaller than the American navy bean. It is ivory white with a tinge of green and is especially creamy and tender. French navy beans cook quickly and are excellent for salads where their small shape is noticeably attractive.

Haricots Lingots: These large, flattened, oval white beans are grown in northern France in their place of origin, Lingot. They are higher in cost because of the care with which they are grown. These beans cook up to a creamy plumpness that makes them perfect to use in cassoulet.

Haricots Blanc de Soissons: These large white beans, grown in the region of Soissons in France, are shaped like oversized limas and taste especially meaty. In Italy they are known as *Bianchi di Spagna* (Spanish whites), *corona* or *bianco grande* (crown or large white). They are similar in size and shape, though with a different texture and flavor, to the gigante, a type of white runner bean.

Limas
Phaseolus lunatus

Lima Beans: The lima bean is a large white oblong flattish bean with a creamy texture and sweet flavor that originated in Peru. When young, limas are pale green but as they ripen they develop the pale yellow color that gives them their common name in Britain (and in older American cookbooks), the butter bean. Very large dried butter beans are also called potato beans. The name lima refers to its origin in Lima, Peru. The fact that it is now pronouced LYE-MA rather than LEE-MA comes from earlier carelessness in adopting foreign words. Another name is the Madagascar bean, because it's extensively cultivated on this island off the East Coast of Africa. The Italian name *fagioli di spagna*, meaning "Spanish bean," refers to the fact that they were originally brought to Italy by Spanish colonists. Burpee's Fordhook lima is a famous American variety developed by Atlee Burpee and named after his experimental farm, Fordhook. Once a more common alternate name for lima, sieva beans now refers to a type of smaller lima.

Young green limas in their large, flat, tough green pods are in season in late summer. Sometimes markets will sell fresh-shelled limas, saving the cook the effort of shelling. To shell, break back the tips of the pods and pull down along the sides to remove the strings and expose the insides. Remove the limas and store in a plastic bag in the refrigerator until ready to cook. The shelled limas will keep well for three to four days. If young and pale green, they will cook quickly, almost like green beans. When older and creamy yellow in color, they are starchier and will need to simmer for about thirty minutes. Frozen baby limas are an excellent product and can be added at the last minute to chowders and other vegetable-laden soups or used to make succotash. They make a good substitute for the more elusive fresh fava. *Note:* No lima beans should be eaten raw as they can contain poisonous cyanogenic glucosides. These substances have mostly been reduced to safe levels by seed selection. Proper preparation, including changing the soaking and cooking water, eliminates any poisons contained in the limas.

Dried limas come in many forms. The larger (and older) the bean, the longer it will need to soak. Thus, I soak large limas for at least twenty-four hours, changing the water at least once to discourage fermentation if the weather is warm. Their tough skins can make them difficult to digest, so be sure to blanch the beans, bringing them to a boil, discarding the water, and then starting with fresh water for the final cooking.

Christmas Lima Beans: Also called chestnut lima, this beautifully marked, large heirloom lima is dark

---

LIMA BEAN RECIPES
Crab Chowder with Limas, Green Beans, and Corn
Gratin of Summer Succotash with Crabmeat
Baked Beans with Beef and Barley (Jewish Sabbath Cholent)
Tricolor Succotash
Pennsylvania Dutch Chow-Chow Relish
Seven Vegetable and Chicken Couscous with Limas, Chickpeas, and Harissa

---

red with deep brown streaks. Very popular seventy-five years ago, it has a chestnut flavor and nutty texture. The striking markings are retained when cooked. These beans are now available from several specialty companies, including Dean & DeLuca and Kalustyan.

Hopi Orange Lima Beans: This heirloom lima has been preserved as a dry bean by the Hopi Indians, who also grind it for flour. It is very close in appearance to an ancient orange bean with dark markings found in pre-Columbian graves in Peru.

Baby White Lima Beans: These small, flat, off-white limas are probably of Guatemalan or Mexican origin. More delicate then large limas, they are in a different botanical category. They are more tender, fruity, and sweet than large limas and less mealy. Add cooked baby white limas to vegetable soups or combine them with sweet corn to make a delicate succotash.

Red Lima Beans: Also known as the Worcester Indian red pole lima, red limas were originally ground for flour by Native Americans, or served with red corn. In the South, slaves first cooked this bean with brown goober peas (close relatives of the peanut) and red sweet potatoes to make fufu (African mashed dumplings, also made of mashed plantains and other roots).

Runner Beans
Phaseolus coccineus

Runner beans originated in Mexico where possibly 6,000-year-old pods of this bean have been found in caves. These beautiful beans have both ceremonial and decorative uses in the native cultures of the American Southwest and Mexico. The Latin name, *Phaseolus coccineus*, which most likely refers to the scarlet runner variety, comes from the Greek word for the brilliant red dye called cochineal, which is extracted from the shells of a variety of ladybug.

Because runner beans can be successfully grown in cooler climates, they are a popular garden vegetable in England where many varieties have been developed. The beans grow on long runners that can produce huge pods of one foot or longer. They have large showy blossoms and are commonly grown as ornamental plants, especially in England. Consequently, runner beans are often listed in the ornamental section of garden catalogs, especially in England. White Dutch runner beans are pure white, painted lady runners have scarlet and white bicolored flowers, and scarlet runners have brilliant red blooms and lavender seeds veined with black. If you grow your own runner beans, note that the blossoms are also edible and can be added to salads and stir-fries.

Gigante Beans: Also called Gigandes and Hija, these huge, sweet-tasting, creamy-colored white beans are from the white runner bean family. They are excellent marinated in salads like Turkish White Bean Salad because they hold their shape so well. This bean was brought to the United States from Spain and Greece.

Scarlet Runner Beans: Also called stick beans, these dramatic red beans come from a plant that is often grown for its gorgeous scarlet blossoms. Scarlet runners were introduced to England by Tradescant, the gardener of King Charles I, and are still a favorite for decorative gardens.

Black Runner Beans: Black runners have long been prized both in the United States and in Great Britain for their beautiful blossoms. The beans are large with a shiny, deep black skin and a slightly sweet flavor. They hold their shape well when cooked. Serve as a side dish or marinate for a salad.

White Emergo Beans: Larger than a standard lima, Emergos are white and plump with a shape close to a half moon. These are also known as sweet white runners. They make a good substitute for the hard-to-find

gigande beans grown in Europe. They have a very fine texture and hold their shape well in marinated bean salads.

Yellow Indian Woman Beans: The Native Americans in Montana grew this very delicate type of golden runner bean. The seeds for this heirloom variety were saved and passed down through many generations of families.

RUNNER BEAN RECIPES
Scarlet Runner Beans in Brown
  Butter and Shallots
White Beans with Moroccan
  Charmoula Dressing

SUGGESTED USES:
• Cook and serve as a snack
  with a flavorful mayonnaise-
  based dipping sauce such as
  Preserved Lemon Aioli.

Tepary
Phaseolus acutifolius

Tepary Beans: The tepary bean is a New World variety (*Phaseolus acutifolius*) used dried that is especially adapted to desert conditions. It is quick growing with long roots that can reach any moisture in the ground. Tepary beans have long been grown in the Arizona desert by Native American Indians. Because of its ability to produce a quick high-protein crop in the desert, there has been recent interest in growing this bean. However, they are difficult to harvest because the pods tend to split open scattering the beans,

which are quite small. The Indians of the southwest associated a plentiful harvest of white Tepary beans with the abundant white stars of the Milky Way.

THE PEANUT FAMILY
Arachis hypogaea

Peanuts originated several thousand years ago in South America. Spanish and Portuguese traders disseminated peanuts around the world, especially to Asia and Africa. African slaves brought peanuts with them to North America, which explains why some of the first names used for it were of African (Congo) origin, including pindar and goober.

Unlike any other legume, after its flower is fertilized, the peanut buries itself in the soil where the fruit or pod develops underground, hence its other common name, groundnut.

Many types of peanuts are raised in the United States where about one-tenth of the world's crop is grown. Nearly half the United States crop is grown in Georgia. The number of kernels in a pod ranges from two to three in some varieties to as much as five to seven in others. The Virginia peanut, also called the Virginia bunch peanut, provides most of the peanuts eaten whole in the United States, both shelled and in the shell as "ballpark peanuts."

Peanuts are nutritious and high in energy, containing forty to fifty percent oil and twenty to thirty percent protein. Larger peanuts like Virginias are used for candies and roasted for snacks. Salted, roasted peanuts have become a universally popular snack, second only to potato chips in this country. Smaller peanuts like red-skinned and rich tasting Spanish or Valencias, better known in Europe, are used to make peanut butter and to press for oil. About half the peanuts grown in the United States are made into peanut butter and one-quarter more sold roasted. Many chefs, including myself, insist on peanut oil for deep-frying because of its high smoke point and nutty flavor.

Peanut butter was first concocted in the early 1900s, and quickly became an American staple. Other

PEANUT RESEARCH

GEORGE WASHINGTON CARVER (1864-1943) WAS AN OUTSTANDING INNOVA-TOR IN THE AGRICULTURAL SCIENCES WHOSE NAME IS FOREVER ASSOCIATED WITH PEANUTS. BORN TO SLAVE PARENTS IN MISSOURI, HE LEFT THE FARM AND SETTLED IN KANSAS WHERE HE WORKED HIS WAY THROUGH HIGH SCHOOL. FOLLOWING HIS GRADUATION IN 1894 FROM THE IOWA STATE COLLEGE OF AGRICULTURE AND MECHANIC ARTS (NOW IOWA STATE UNIVERSITY), HE BECAME DIRECTOR OF THE DEPARTMENT OF AGRICULTURAL RESEARCH AT TUSKEGEE NORMAL AND INDUSTRIAL INSTITUTE (NOW TUSKEGEE UNIVERSITY). THERE HE EXPERIMENTED WITH PEANUTS, DEVELOPING MORE THAN 300 INDUSTRIAL USES FOR THEM AND CONTINUALLY URGED SOUTHERN AMERICAN COTTON FARMERS TO SWITCH TO GROWING PEANUTS FOR A CASH CROP.

cultures, particularly Indonesian and Thai, have long used ground peanuts as a key ingredient to enrich and thicken their sauces.

Buy raw, shelled peanuts in bags at a natural foods store. Use these peanuts when you're going to further toast or fry the nuts. If you live in a part of the country that grows peanuts, you might be able to buy green peanuts in their shell. These are boiled for a long time in salted water and eaten as a snack in the low country regions of South Carolina and Georgia, as the Japanese do with salted green soybeans.

ASIAN AND AFRICAN LEGUMES

ASIAN BEANS

Asian Beans
Vigna unguiculata
(formerly *Sinensis*, meaning Chinese)

The small fruit of an annual plant, the Asian beans include a group of very small, slightly oblong beans with a prominent small eye. China is probably the original home of the red adzuki bean though it was introduced into Japan about 1,500 years ago. They are eaten whole in their skins, though quite often, especially in India, they are sold already shelled in the form of dal. The major varieties of these mung type beans are the green mung, black mung (or black gram), and red bean or adzuki.

Adzuki beans may be popped like corn. Green mung beans are familiar to us as bean sprouts. In China, these sprouts are called "pea" sprouts as apposed to "bean" sprouts made from soybeans. Red adzuki beans are served in many forms for holidays in both China and Japan, such as Chinese New Year dumplings and mooncakes and steamed rice and red

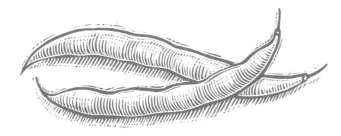

beans served in Japan for family celebrations.

Green mung beans probably originated in India though they are grown throughout Asia, the Caribbean, and in Africa. Because mung beans grow quickly, several crops a year are possible. Mung bean starch is used to make the Chinese cellophane noodles.

The black gram is the most important member of this family in India, where it has ceremonial significance in Hindu birth and death rites. However, there is much confusion over different varieties in the mung family because some black gram beans may be green. The green ones are smaller and ripen later than the black ones. The best way to tell the difference is to split them open; the urd (or black gram) is white inside, while the mung (or green gram) is yellow inside. Black gram beans need a long time to cook and they are difficult for some people to digest.

Adzuki Beans (Azuki and Aduki): Called red beans in China and Japan, these small, burgundy-red oval beans probably originated in Japan. They are especially popular in China and Japan for desserts because of their sweet, nutty flavor. Inside their rather tough skins, adzuki are velvety in texture without any discernable grain. Though not essential, I prefer to soak these beans overnight to

soften them before cooking for a more even texture.

ADZUKI BEAN RECIPE
Fried Dessert Won Tons with Red Bean Paste Filling

Green Mung Bean: This small, rounded, olive-green mung bean, from the plant *Phaseolus vigna radiata*, probably originated in India. It has a slightly sweet flavor and soft texture. When skinned and split they are yellow inside, very tender and quickly cooked. In India, this is the most widely used form of the mung bean and is known as moong dal. Yellow Split Mung Bean Dal makes an excellent vegetarian soup that is quickly prepared and easily digested. The whole green mung beans are most popular in the north and west of India. Mung beans are easily sprouted and produce the familiar small, crunchy, transparent white bean sprouts.

GREEN MUNG BEAN RECIPES
Noodle Salad with Snow Peas Bean Sprouts and Shanxi Vinegar
Asian Wrap Sandwich with Shiitakes, Bean Sprouts, and Hoisin Sauce

Black Gram Beans: Also called urad or urd beans, these small, black-skinned, oval beans are pale yellow inside. Their texture is glutinous. When split and cooked, they have a slightly viscous texture. They are also used as a seasoning in South India, where beans are thrown into hot oil to give it a red color and nutty flavor.

A member of the mung bean family, black gram beans are especially popular in northern India where they are cooked with ginger, onions, and butter to make a rich creamy purée called kali dal. When split with their skins removed, they are white inside. This white variety, called split white lentil, is easy to digest and delicious in stuffing mixes or served with curries and sautéed vegetables. Toasted and ground, they are used as an Indian spice called urad dal.

Soybeans
Glycine max

The soybean has been called "the meat of the soil," "the cow of China," and "the miracle bean." It probably originated in China and is of huge economic importance worldwide. There are more than 1,000 varieties of the extraordinarily nutritious and protein-rich soybean, ranging in color from yellow, green, and red to black, white, and mottled. Soybeans generally taste quite bland, although fresh green soybeans have a pleasingly delicate flavor and creamy texture. Unlike other legumes, soybeans are low in carbohydrates and high in protein and oil. Mild-tasting soybean oil, low in saturated fats, has long been the favored cooking fat in Chinese cuisine. Look at the label on a container labeled "vegetable oil": normally the only ingredient is soybean oil.

The soybean has been used for thousands of years in its native eastern Asia in a wide variety of forms. Its young, fresh sprouts with yellowish bean ends are eaten as a crunchy vegetable; soybeans are soaked in water to produce soy milk, from which bean curd is prepared (known as tofu). Soybeans are fermented to produce soy sauce and other condiments like miso and tamari, are ground to make flour, and are even made into a sweet dessert paste. Transformed into textured vegetable protein (seitan or tempeh), soybean products are commonly used as a fillers for ground meat products (see *Soybean Related Products, see below*).

Fresh young soybeans in their fuzzy green pods appear in the market in the summer months and are a seasonal treat, much like fresh favas. Delicious and fun to eat, fresh soybeans are a well-loved snack in China and Japan, cooked in heavily salted water and then sucked out of their pods. Green soybeans are often sold shelled and frozen (much like baby limas) in Asian markets.

(continued on page 32)

❧ ❧ ❧ SOYBEAN-RELATED PRODUCTS ❧ ❧ ❧

Since I would need to write a whole book to even begin to cover the incredibly diverse family of soybean-based products, I will give only a very simple, basic introduction to these ingredients here.

SOY SAUCE

Soy sauce has been known in the West since the seventeenth century when Dutch traders in Nagasaki exported it to Europe. It was the secret seasoning served at the court banquets of Louis XIV in France. The word soy or soya comes to us via the Dutch *soja* originally from the Japanese word *shoyu* or soy sauce. Shoyu was borrowed from the Chinese *shiyau—shi*, meaning salted beans, *yau* meaning oil.

Soy sauce was used to prevent foods from spoiling in the summer heat and to preserve foods for the winter months. In the fifteenth century Japan started to produce its own type of soy sauce. In the sixteenth century, soy sauce was commercially manufactured instead of being made by farm families for their own or local use.

This culinary bedrock of Asian cooking is a dark, salty sauce made by fermenting boiled soybeans and roasted wheat or barley with salt. A mixture of carefully selected and roasted soybeans is inoculated with a mold and then mixed with brine to make a liquidy mash (much like a wort for beer). The mash is placed in fermentation tanks to brew for one year. After brewing, the raw soy sauce is separated from any solids.

China and Japan produce all different kinds of soy sauces including light, medium, dark, thin to very thick, black soy, and mushroom soy. Chinese soy sauce is generally quite salty with a dense flavor. Japanese soy sauces have a relatively bright taste and aroma. Far more wheat is used in Japanese soy sauces, so they are sweeter and less salty than the Chinese. Japanese sauces are generally lighter and thinner than the dark, thick Chinese type.

Be sure to check that the soy sauce you buy is naturally brewed. Inexpensive but artificially brewed soy sauces with Chinese-sounding names are sold at lower prices in many supermarkets. They are brewed by chemical rather than natural fermentation in as little as three or four days rather than the one-year period necessary for natural fermentation. It's certainly worthwhile to seek out a good brand, as even the best is relatively inexpensive and it lasts indefinitely.

(continued on next page)

Artificially fermented brands list water, then salt, hydrolyzed soy protein, corn syrup, caramel color, and potassium sorbate (with no quantity given) as a preservative. A naturally brewed brand lists water, then wheat and soybeans before salt, and less than one-tenth of a percent of sodium benzoate as a preservative.

There's a huge variety among soy sauce brands. For Chinese soy sauce, a recommended brand is Pearl River Bridge from China with a label that reads "Superior Soy," for its large, round well-balanced flavor. For Japanese-style dark soy sauce, I like to buy the dark Kikkoman that is widely available and of excellent quality. Now made in Walworth, Wisconsin using American soy, wheat, and salt, Kikkoman originally began producing soy sauce in Japan in 1630.

Black soy sauce is a concentrated soy sauce made with molasses. It's perfect when you want a lot of color and flavor with less liquid, as in a cold noodle dish where the sauce should cling to the noodles. It is aged for an extra-long time and lasts indefinitely. Mushroom soy is a seasoned black sauce flavored with dried Chinese black mushrooms. It has a rounded, almost meaty flavor. I love the Pearl River Bridge brand for its smooth, deep flavor and the extra dimension of the strong mushroom taste.

Japanese light soy sauce is amber in color, thinner and saltier than the dark. It does not darken the color of the food and is salty enough to season it without heavy application. Kikkoman's light soy sauce is still produced in Japan and has a different label. Dark soy sauce has deeper color and more body, is less salty, and may be used in relatively greater quantities as a basting sauce, a marinade, or in simmered dishes.

TAMARI

This is a Japanese cousin of soy sauce, often sold in health food stores. It is a thick, very dark liquid with a stronger flavor than soy sauce and a clear soy aroma. It is made mainly of soybeans and is cultured and fermented like miso. Even in Japan, it is hard to find good-quality tamari. It is generally used in Japanese cooking as a dipping sauce or a foundation for a basting sauce. I recommend the San-J brand. I have used it extensively from the five-gallon containers in food-service dishes and it was consistently excellent.

MISO

Miso is a Japanese fermented soybean paste that has been important in the Japanese diet for centuries. It is used in a wide variety of dishes, such as a dressing for vegetables and a pickling medium. It is also spread on grilled foods as a seasoning. It is most commonly eaten in the form of *miso-shiru* or soup, the ubiquitous Japanese breakfast that is often served for lunch and dinner as well.

All of the many types of miso, each with its own aroma and flavor, color and texture, are made essentially by the same method. First boiled soybeans are crushed, then wheat, barley, or rice is added. The mixture is injected with a yeastlike mold and allowed to mature for several months or up to three years. Light, yellow miso, injected with rice mold, is relatively sweet and very good for dressings. Red miso, made with barley, is quite savory and good for winter soups. A third, fudge brown and thick type of miso, made mainly from soybeans, is very rich and salty and can be cut with a knife. Miso will keep refrigerated for up to one year.

CHINESE YELLOW AND BROWN BEAN PASTE

Bean pastes are a family of condiments made from fermented soybeans and are available in many different names and types throughout China. Hot bean paste is a frankly hot, lumpy mixture that is stirred into sauces. Sweet bean paste is a smoother, sweeter variation used in both marinades and sauces.

FERMENTED BLACK BEANS

These beans are a Chinese specialty made of small soybeans (not black turtle beans) that have been preserved in salt before packing. Because they have a pungent, salty flavor, some people rinse them before using. I normally give them a quick rinse that removes the surface salt without diluting the intense flavor that I crave. Look for Pearl River Bridge brand packed in a yellow, round cardboard box. I also like Koon Chun brand in plastic bags from Hong Kong, which is spiced with orange rind, ginger, and garlic. If I can only find plain salted beans, I add finely chopped garlic, ginger, and orange rind to them.

Bean Curd (Tofu)

Bean curd originated in China between AD 200 and 900. During this long period of time its use spread completely throughout the Far East so that today, from Indonesia to Korea to Mongolia, it is essential to the national cuisine. Bean curd's Japanese name is *tofu*, and it was probably introduced to Japan around 1,200 years ago. Japanese tofu is softer and more delicately flavored than the firmer Chinese-type of bean curd.

Like cheese, bean curd is made from curdled or coagulated liquid. It is extremely high in protein and low in cost, though quite perishable. Like fresh white cheese, it will only keep a few days. Intrinsically quite bland, bean curd absorbs flavors well. There are now modified atmosphere packages of bean curd available that have a longer shelf life as long as they are not opened. A six-ounce portion of fresh bean curd contains a mere 100 calories. More concentrated types of drained bean curd may contain over fifty percent protein.

Bean curd is made from dry soybeans that are soaked in water until softened, then crushed and boiled. The crushed mash is separated into pulp and milk. Just as in cheese-making, a coagulant is added to make the milk separate into curds and whey. The curds are poured into molds and left to settle and take shape. The molded curds are then soaked in water to firm and to keep cool and fresh. In Japan, small cakes of tofu are cut from large blocks (just like butter used to be cut from large blocks at the grocery). In this country we usually buy it already cut and packaged, except in Asian supermarkets where the fresh blocks are often available.

Chinese bean curd cakes tend to be smaller, like little pillows. Excess moisture is often pressed out beforehand, so you will see Chinese-style bean curd cakes sold dry in plastic bags in the refrigerator case. Japanese-style, water packed tofu is the most common form found in American supermarkets. It cannot be frozen successfully without becoming somewhat chewy.

There are three main types of Japanese tofu. "Regular" tofu is known in Japan as *momen* or cotton tofu. It is drained in cloth and has a slightly coarser texture than silken tofu. Silken, or *kinu*, tofu is a soft tofu that has not been drained. It is quite delicate and can't be pressed. Its fine texture is enjoyed in elegant, clear soups, especially in Japan. *Yakidotu* is tofu that has been lightly broiled. It has a light-brown mottling on its skin and a firm texture. Though it has been grilled, this tofu is packed in water. It is most often used in one-pot dishes such as sukiyaki.

For deep-frying or use in salads, tofu is pressed to remove water. Wrap the drained bean curd cakes in clean towels. Weight with two plates for about thirty minutes. You can also purchase already deep-fried bean curd called *agé*. It is golden brown in color and sold dry, like a pastry, in the refrigerator case. This type of bean curd is also cut into thin sheets and commercially deep-fried, forming pockets. These pockets can be split open along one end and stuffed with vegetables or rice.

"American households have finally emerged from their anti-bean prejudice, and today we join the world in prizing dried legumes… the interest in dried legumes among American consumers has created a massive increase of imports and availability, resulting in a dizzying variety of dried bean, pea and lentil types on American grocery shelves today. We are proud to have pioneered in this country many of the currently available types (though it's not true that we are considering a name change to Bean and Beluga)."

—David Rosengarten, Author, *Dean & DeLuca Cookbook*

❧ ❧ ❧ ❧ ❧ ❧ ❧

(continued from page 29)

AFRICAN BEANS

This is a large group of eyed peas mostly grown in the American South. The Southern peas came to the United States and to the Caribbean from Africa with the slave trade. They are thought to have first been cultivated in Ethiopia about 5,000 years ago. They are still an important crop in Africa where the seeds, leaves, and sprouts are eaten. The Southern peas, also called cowpeas, include black-eyed peas, field peas, crowder peas, and cream peas. There are many colorful names for specific varieties of Southern peas, including Mississippi silver, whippoorwill, knucklehull purple, and zipper cream.

Cowpeas
Vigna unguiculata

Cowpeas and field peas are generic terms for the varieties of Southern peas grown for cow fodder or soil enrichment rather than for human consumption. They are in the same family of African beans as black-eyed peas. They are one of the main food crops of Haiti.

Cowpeas need a hot climate to grow and in the United States, they will only grow in the South, where they were first cultivated. Cowpeas can be divided into those grown for their seeds, which are usually dried, and those grown for their immature pods. These seed plants are most often grown in Africa, India, and the United States. The pod peas are tall climbers with exceptionally long pods called yard-long beans. In Nigeria, the dried peas are a staple legume. Some tribes in West Africa eat the young shoots and leaves as a vegetable.

Black-Eyed Peas: These medium size, light cream-colored oblong beans with a small but very noticeable black circular "eye" on the curved inner side have a distinct, savory flavor and light crunchy texture. Black-eyed peas were brought into this country by slaves from Africa and are, therefore, still most popular in the southern part of the country. Black-eyed peas hold up well to strong-tasting ingredients such as chiles, garlic, and smoked pork products.

Black-eyed peas are sold in many forms, including fresh in the pod, frozen, and dried. To prepare fresh black-eyed peas, break back the tips of the pods, then pull down to remove the strings, exposing the beans inside. Remove the beans and store, refrigerated, in a plastic bag for three to four days. They can also be frozen for later use. Fresh-shelled peas do not need soaking. Simply cook in simmering stock or water until tender and plump, generally for about thirty minutes. Cook frozen black-eyed peas the same as fresh shelled. Dried black-eyed peas should be soaked overnight before rinsing, par-cooking, and proceeding with the recipe.

BLACK-EYED PEA RECIPES
African Black-Eyed Pea and
  Okra Salad with Corn
Skillet-Roasted Chicken with
  Black-Eyed Peas, Country
  Ham, and Savory
Smoked Turkey Chili with
  Black-Eyed Peas
Hoppin' John
Hoppin' Don
Texas Stuffed Tomatoes with
  Black-Eyed Pea Salad
Individual Chicken Pot Pie
  with Assorted Legumes

Yard-Long Bean: Yard-long beans (*Vigna unguiculata, sesquipedalis*) are hearty-tasting fresh beans that grow between one and three feet long. They are closely related to the black-eyed pea and are also known as long beans, dau gok, and, with winged beans, they share the nickname asparagus beans. All long beans are on the starchy side rather than being juicy like a fresh green bean. Choose thin, blemish-free beans with small seeds and plan to cook them within one or two days. Prepare for cooking by cutting off both ends. The most common variety is thin, dark green, and pliable, although there are also purple and pale green varieties.

YARD-LONG BEAN RECIPES
Chinese Yard-Long Beans with
Black Bean and Garlic Sauce
Indonesian Salad

Yard-long beans are mild tasting, but firm enough to keep their texture during braising or in stir-fries. Their chewy and slightly slippery texture lends itself well to stir-fries with strong tasting sauces, such as black bean and garlic or chili sauce. Their alternate name, asparagus bean, is misleading because they resemble asparagus only in their length and shape. The two vegetables require very different cooking methods. Yard-long beans should be blanched before adding to a stir-fry where they will finish cooking in a strongly flavored sauce.

Lady Peas: This smaller, more delicate black-eyed pea is from South Carolina. It has a very thin skin and cooks quickly to a creamy, smooth texture. Lady peas are often served with rice and green tomato relish in the style of Charleston.

LADY PEA RECIPE
Lady Peas with Carolina Rice and
Green Tomato Relish

Cream Peas: Closely related to black-eyed peas, cream peas are creamy white in color. They are most commonly found in the South. Black-eyed peas may be substituted.

Crowder Peas: Crowder peas get their name from being very crowded in their pods. All of these legumes can be cooked like black-eyed peas and substituted for them in these recipes.

Southern Checker Peas: A distant relative of black-eyed peas, Southern checker peas are small, flat, and angular. These half white and half black beans have a subtle flavor and good texture. The advantage of this bean is that it cooks without soaking in about 35 minutes.

Pigeon Peas
Cajanus cajan

Thought to be native to tropical Africa, pigeon peas are popular in the Caribbean and India because they grow well in hot climates. They are called yellow lentils, *toor dal* or *toovar dal* in India, *gandules* in Puerto Rico, congo pea or *pois Angola* (most likely because of their African origin), and googoo beans in Jamaica. Pale brown with a small "eye" on the inner ridge, they have an earthy flavor and a soft, somewhat mealy texture. These peas are best in Caribbean dishes and soups. The immature green seeds are sometimes eaten like peas or the whole young pods cooked like green beans. They are an important food staple in India, where ninety-five percent of the world's crop is grown. Some Indian groceries carry split pigeon peas that have been coated with oil as a preservative. These must be rinsed in hot water before cooking. Pigeon peas are reputed to have slightly narcotic effects when eaten.

WHERE DO OUR BEANS COME FROM?

Today, America is by far the world leader in dry bean production, due largely to climate: long, mild summers and average rainfall of about eleven to twelve inches during the growing season represent nearly perfect bean-growing conditions. Each year, U.S. farmers plant from 1.5 to 1.7 million acres of edible dry beans.

And while Americans are the chief consumers of these beans, forty percent are shipped to international markets in more than 100 different countries around the globe. The sale of these bean products to international venues generates about $275 million for the American economy annually.

Dry bean production is centered in fourteen states and includes fifteen different classes of beans. A number of states specialize in the growing of a particular bean. For instance, Michigan is one of the largest producers of navy beans. California grows the greatest portion of large and baby lima beans and black-eyed beans in the

United States, in addition to light and dark kidneys, pink beans, small whites, and chickpeas. In Idaho, pinto, pink, great Northern, and small red beans are referred to by farmers and economists as the "Big 4;" Nebraska is well-known as a producer of great Northern beans. The volume produced by each state varies, primarily due to weather conditions, but Michigan, North Dakota, Nebraska, and California usually produce the largest volume of beans year in and year out.

AMERICAN-GROWN GOURMET LEGUMES

As European growers have long known, raising high-quality beans, peas, lentils, and chickpeas requires a unique combination of soil, moisture, and climate. Many people believe that the world's best overall area for growing dry legumes is in the Pacific Northwest corner of the United States (on the borders of Idaho, Oregon, and Washington) in a region called the "Palouse." In the rain shadow of the Cascade Mountains, the Palouse region's warm, dry summer days, cool nights, and nutrient-rich volcanic soils form the ideal combination to produce high yields of top-quality dry peas, lentils, and chickpeas. The high altitude means there is less chance of fungus growth in the soil and the rich volcanic ash is excellent for growing quality beans.

Many of the heirloom varieties listed here are grown in the Palouse region in Idaho's high altitude Snake River Plain by the Zursun company. If you buy high-quality beans from a specialty food store, they may well

> ### GROWING SPECIALTY BEANS IN CALIFORNIA
>
> CHIP AND BOBBIE MORRIS, LIKE GENERATIONS OF MORRISES BEFORE THEM, GROW GOURMET SPECIALTY BEANS IN SACRAMENTO, CALIFORNIA. THIS FAMILY AGRICULTURAL TRADITION, WHICH DATES BACK TO THE 1800s, IS CARRIED ON WITH PRIDE. THE MORRISES ARE COMMITTED TO PRESERVING THE ANCIENT BEANS THAT HAVE BEEN GROWN FROM SEED AND HANDED DOWN FROM GENERATION TO GENERATION. THEY HAVE TEAMED UP WITH THE INDIAN HARVEST COMPANY TO DISTRIBUTE THEIR BEANS NATIONALLY. (SEE SOURCES, PAGE 323.)

come from the Palouse. Zursun takes pride in the high quality of its beans, which are dried in the field, rather than in ovens. This makes them less dry and easier to cook. Once harvested, the beans are sorted electronically, hand inspected, and placed in controlled low-humidity storage until shipped. It's especially important to recognize the work that specialty bean growers are doing in this country because they will help raise the status of legumes to the high position they deserve. (For information on buying specialty and heirloom beans, see Sources, page 323.)

PURCHASING LEGUMES

Dried Legumes

If you're accustomed to using canned (already cooked) legumes, you may not know how much of the dried type you'll need when a recipe calls for a certain amount of cooked legumes. Here's an easy general rule: When soaked and cooked, most varieties of small dried legumes, such as lentils, will at least double in size; medium to large size dried beans will triple in size.

When shopping for dried legumes, it pays to buy them from reputable

sources. Dried legumes from the current year's crop take less time to cook and cook more evenly. They are also easier to digest. It's certainly worthwhile spending the extra money on "gourmet" beans. Even a pound bag of fancy beans works out to an inexpensive meal. If you buy dried beans from a place that doesn't turn over stock quickly, you may get beans that are up to ten years old. If you buy beans from a specialty store that really moves its stock, you'll be more likely to get fresher beans. The older the bean, the more problems you're likely to experience, both in cooking and in digesting. I recommend Goya brand dried beans available in many supermarkets; Dean & DeLuca brand from their stores or their catalog; boxed imported European beans, such as French flageolets, lentilles du Puy, and haricots lingots; Vann's Beans available by mailorder; and beans from Indian Harvest, including many heirlooms, available by mail order or through their internet site; and Bascom's, sold boxed in specialty markets. (See Sources, page 323.)

Look for harvest dates that may be included on bean bags and boxes. I've seen this done with a very special kind of large white bean from Spain, *faves de Huelga*, which are packed in their own numbered cloth bag, with controlled origin (like Cognac or Champagne) and date of harvest tagged. In Spain there are many highly respected regional dry beans, as opposed to the United States where beans are treated as a commodity and the lowest price tends to prevail. Fortunately, stores such as Dean & DeLuca, the gourmet mecca in New York's Soho district, have been an influential proponent of heirloom and specialty beans for more than twenty years. Simple but effective packaging in clear cellophane bags and a large variety of new harvest beans has won them many customers who are committed to the cause of great bean cookery.

At one time The Spanish Table, a Spanish and Portuguese importing company in San Francisco, was selling from Sierra de Gredos a special dry white bean by the same name, but building a following for these high-priced (twelve to twenty dollars a kilo) beans proved a difficult task. Also, unlike commodity beans, these beans are harvest-dated so they have a definite and limited shelf life. However, with the growing interest in specialty legumes, The Spanish Table and other companies may once again start importing some of these Spanish dry legumes. The Spanish Table does import bottled cooked specialty legumes, including Alubias Pocha and Alubias de la Granja.

Using Frozen Legumes

The next best thing to freezing your own beans is buying them already frozen. Most supermarkets carry black-eyed peas, baby Fordhook limas, and petits pois. I can find frozen pigeon peas, favas, and cannellini beans at Latino markets and bags of frozen green soy beans, which make a great addition to stir-frys and a good substitute for green favas, at my local Asian market.

I often cook a large batch of beans and freeze them in one-quart freezer bags. Opening a bag of my homemade precooked beans is as easy as opening, rinsing, and draining canned beans. To freeze your own beans, cool them to room temperature and divide among labeled quart-size "zipper-style" freezer bags. Squeeze out the excess air and seal well. I often double-bag my beans to protect them from extraneous smells and freezer burn. Beans may be frozen for two to three months. Note: It's important to label frozen legumes (and other foods) with the name and the date. Use an indelible marker that won't rub off. Believe me, you'll never remember what was in those bags a month later.

Using Canned Legumes

What about using dried beans that have been canned, such as pinto, kidney, and black beans? By all means use them for their convenience, but be sure to try cooking your own and see if you don't prefer their texture and flavor. In a dish where beans are going to be cooked further, such as baked beans or beans and rice, canned will work fine. In soups it's hard to get a rich multi-leveled flavor of beans if they have not been cooked all the way from dried.

I would recommend both the Puerto Rican company Goya, and the Italian-American company Progresso for their large variety of canned beans. Natural and organic food companies are also a good choice for canned beans. Avoid low-priced store brands, which might not be of the best quality. I think it's worth buying the best, especially since beans are a good value, no matter how you buy them.

CHAPTER THREE

LEGUME COOKING BASICS

"There is a broad dividing line in cooking between those things which are delicious in themselves—their taste has only to be revealed—and those things which, however nourishing they may be, are more properly vehicles for absorbing flavor. So one needs to cultivate a knowledge of what flavours to communicate, and an awareness of the manner in which they are absorbed, when cooking beans."

—PATIENCE GRAY, AUTHOR, *Honey from a Weed*

To me this is a good reason for taking the trouble to cook your own dried legumes, rather than settling for canned. While cooking, you impart flavor and texture by the ingredients that go into the pot. A prosciutto bone, a country ham bone, smoked turkey legs, a head of garlic, an onion stuck with cloves, the rind of a lemon, fragrant bay leaves, a chunk of pastrami, fennel, coriander, cumin, and caraway seeds each gives its own taste. By following my directions for soaking and cooking, you can also diminish, if not eliminate, any digestive problems.

GENERAL LEGUME COOKING TIPS

USE SOFT WATER

When cooking beans, the most important ingredient may be water! Always use cold water; hot water can pick up lead and other undesirable minerals from the pipes. If you live in an area that has very hard, mineral-laden water, you may not ever have been able to cook the beans until soft. The solution is to add a pinch of baking soda to the water to neutralize the acid. Don't overdo it as this will cause the skins to separate and fly off the beans. In hard water areas, use $1/8$ teaspoon of baking soda per pound of beans. The beans will actually absorb more liquid if cooked in a smaller, rather than larger, amount of water. Give the beans enough water to soak up and swell, but don't drown them.

GET THE DIRT OUT

Many bean recipes start with the admonition to pick through and rinse the beans. In most cases this isn't necessary. I have noticed, however, that black turtle beans and certain imported beans often contain small lumps of dirt, small stones, or debris. So picking over your beans and rinsing them is probably still a good idea, just to be on the safe side.

PREVENT FERMENTATION

When cooking beans, keep in mind that they are prone to ferment. I would basically skip cooking beans on very hot humid days because they are more likely to spoil. If you do make a large pot of beans, place the pot of beans in a sink half-filled with ice water to chill them quickly. Once cold, beans can either be refrigerated in an airtight container for up to four days or frozen. Do not leave the cooked beans at room temperature because they ferment easily. I have found this out the hard way; be especially attentive in hot humid weather or during low-pressure weather patterns, such as before a thunderstorm, when spoilage seems to happen more quickly.

BLANCH BEANS FOR INCREASED DIGESTIBILITY

In the most isolated and tradition-bound areas of the Mediterranean, beans, known as "the poor man's meat," are cooked by a time-honored method: they are blanched or parcooked (placed in an earthenware pot or heavy pan with plenty of cold water and a pinch of baking soda, brought to a boil and cooked for five minutes, then drained and rinsed under cold water). In her book, *Honey from a Weed*, Patience Gray says "This preliminary blanching is a definite ritual with regard to any bean of the species *Phaseolus vulgaris* (all the kidney bean varieties) fresh or dried, in Italy, Spain, and Greece."

In Tunisia, a country whose cuisine is rich in legumes like chickpeas, favas, and lentils, this preliminary blanching is done as a matter of course. My Portuguese friend, Maria Mata, never fails to blanch beans for dishes like Salad of Salt Cod and Red Beans. While testing bean recipes, I have found that blanching is an effective way to make dried beans more easily digested. If I skip this step, I often have trouble, especially with black beans and chickpeas.

ADD HARDENING INGREDIENTS LAST

Beware of cooking legumes with salt, sugar, or acid (such as vinegar, tomato, or molasses), all of which harden the skin of the beans and prevent them from softening. This is why, to make good Boston baked beans, you must first cook the beans at least halfway *before* adding the sweet and salt ingredients. I've included three baked bean recipes that contain sweeteners. It is especially important in these dishes that the beans be softened, though not mushy, before the final baking step. If the beans are too hard to begin with, they'll never absorb enough liquid to get tender, no matter how long you cook them.

SHAKE—DON'T STIR—BEANS

If you carefully shake the pot rather than stir it, especially near the end of cooking, you'll avoid breaking up the soft beans. The fewer the broken beans, the better the texture.

KNOW *When* TO SALT

I like to salt beans halfway through their cooking, after the skins have softened but when there is enough liquid left in the pot to dissolve the salt. You can, of course, salt after cooking, but there's no substitute for the mellow flavor you get when the salt is evenly distributed throughout the beans rather than sprinkled over the top. If you pressure-cook your beans, salt them *before* cooking to prevent them from becoming mushy under high pressure. Also, if you soak beans for a full twelve hours, you can add salt to the soaking liquid to help keep them whole. It is especially helpful to add salt both to the soaking liquid and cooking water of beans with fragile skins such as flageolets, soybeans, and limas to help keep their skins intact.

ANTI-FLATULENCE COOKING TIPS

Some of us have trouble digesting beans. To minimize the gas-producing effects of certain legumes, try the following tips:

• Purchase the most recent crop of dried beans. The older the bean, the more gastrointestinal problems you're likely to experience. Buy dried beans from a specialty store that turns over its stock quickly.

• Always soak and drain your beans first. Soak the beans for at least four hours in a bowl of cold water, changing to fresh water once or twice, especially in hot and humid weather (to prevent fermentation). The longer you soak, the more of the offending oligosaccharides are leached out into the soaking water. Drain and rinse the beans thoroughly before cooking, discarding the soaking water.

• Always blanch or precook beans of the common bean family, such as kidney, black beans, cannellini, and pinto.

To precook beans, bring a large pot of unsalted fresh water to a boil. Add the beans and cook five minutes, skimming off and discarding any white foam impurities that rise to the surface. Drain and rinse, discarding the cooking water. Continue cooking the beans as the recipe directs; otherwise freeze the beans for later use.

• Remove the skin from beans or eat skinless legumes, such as split peas, split mung beans, and split chickpeas.

When making a puréed soup, especially from beans with tougher skins, such as black beans, white beans, limas, and red kidney beans, strain the soup through a food mill or a sieve to remove the skins. When preparing chickpeas, rub off the skins before using them.

• Cook southwestern-style beans, such as pintos, red kidney beans, and especially black beans, with epazote leaf (a strong tasting leaf called wormseed in English that has anti-carminative properties).

• Cook Indian-style legumes with seasonings such as ginger, turmeric, tiny quantities of asafetida (dried plant resin), fennel seed, and ajwain seeds (lovage or carom seeds), all of which taste great and aid in digestion.

• Cook Mediterranean-style bean

dishes with alkaline-rich greens such as wild chicory, dandelion, spinach, or chard to balance the acidity of the beans.

To do this, simply add the blanched, drained, and chopped greens during the last fifteen minutes of cooking. Alternatively, you can add a small amount of baking soda (also an alkaline) to the water when cooking legumes. Although this method does leach some of the nutrients into the water, it solves the problem.

• When using a pressure cooker to cook beans, add a strip of dried kombu (a type of seaweed sold at natural food stores), which makes the beans more digestible.

• If all else fails, try a commercial natural enzyme product, such as Beano®, which breaks down the oligosaccharides before they are acted upon by gas-producing bacteria. In its powdered form, this product is sprinkled on food. Note that the enzyme is destroyed by heat, so it must be added directly to the finished dish. In its pill form, it is taken by mouth just before eating.

TO SOAK OR NOT TO SOAK?

The purpose of soaking is to rehydrate dried legumes, ensure even cooking, and shorten the cooking time. Another benefit of soaking beans is to remove indigestible oligosaccharides that can cause gas. These oligosaccharides are soluble in water. For even better results in removing them, change the water up to three times over the soaking period. Be sure to drain and thoroughly rinse the beans before covering with cold water and cooking. Remember to never cook the beans in the same soaking liquid.

Because legumes vary so much in size, texture, and shape, the soaking and cooking methods aren't uniform. Many kinds of small legumes, such as lentils, peas, and mung beans, don't require soaking because they are small enough to cook through without this preliminary step. Whole beans and peas must be soaked in water because their skins are impermeable. Water can only enter beans through the "hilum" (the eye or point at which each bean was attached to its pod). Therefore, rehydrating the flesh inside the skin is a slow process. However, if you know the beans are freshly picked from the current year's crop, it is *not* necessary to presoak them.

Generally, beans are soaked in cold water for at least eight hours. Small, thin-skinned beans can take as few as four hours. I prefer to soak all large beans up to twelve hours in a bowl of cold water to cover. The larger (and older) the bean, the longer it will need to soak. Thus, I soak large, thick-skinned dried favas and limas for at least twenty-four hours, changing the water frequently to discourage fermentation if the weather is warm. To save time, you can also quick-soak beans (see Soaking Chart opposite). To check if the beans have been soaked long enough, cut a bean crosswise in half. If the bean has no opaque center the bean is ready to cook.

If you plan to soak beans for the full overnight period (eight to ten hours), add salt to the beans while soaking. The salt helps keep the skins firm and intact and promotes more even cooking, resulting in a better shaped bean. Add 1 teaspoon of table salt (2 teaspoons of kosher salt) to the soaking water per pound of beans.

ON THE OTHER HAND...
Interestingly, not every authority recommends soaking beans. I remember working with Chef Bradley Ogden for a special event. He asked me not to soak the black beans because their color would lighten from jet black to a deep purple. While I have to agree that unsoaked black beans are definitely darker and more dramatic in color, I am willing to forego a bit of color to ease the digestion of my meal.

Diana Kennedy, a culinary authority I've admired greatly ever since her seminal book, *The Cuisines of Mexico*, also has strong opinions about preparing beans. She recommends not soaking beans to avoid the unpleasant odor the skins can produce. However, if the beans are soaked, she recommends not throwing out the soaking water because it contains all the minerals and flavor.

My advice is to experiment and find out what works best for you.

QUICK SOAKING DRIED LEGUMES

QUICK-SOAKING CAN BE DONE IN ABOUT ONE AND A HALF HOURS FROM START TO FINISH. THE ADVANTAGE OF THIS METHOD IS THAT YOU DO NOT NEED TO BLANCH OR PAR-COOK AND DRAIN THE BEANS BEFORE THEIR FINAL COOKING IN ORDER FOR THEM TO BE DIGESTIBLE. HOWEVER, THE BEANS TEND TO BREAK UP MORE AS THEY COOK WHEN QUICK-SOAKED, SO IT'S BETTER TO USE THIS METHOD FOR DISHES WHERE THE BEANS DON'T NEED TO KEEP THEIR SHAPE, SUCH AS IN SOUPS WHERE BROKEN-UP BEANS ACT AS A THICKENER.

BASIC QUICK-SOAK METHOD

FOR EVERY POUND (2 CUPS) OF DRIED LEGUMES, ADD 10 CUPS COLD WATER. BECAUSE MOST BEANS WILL REHYDRATE TO DOUBLE THEIR DRY SIZE, BE SURE TO START WITH A LARGE ENOUGH POT. HEAT TO BOILING, LET BOIL 2 TO 5 MINUTES, DEPENDING ON THE SIZE OF THE BEAN (THE LARGER THE BEAN, THE LONGER THE COOKING TIME). REMOVE FROM HEAT, COVER, AND SET ASIDE FOR AT LEAST ONE BUT NO MORE THAN FOUR HOURS. DRAIN AND DISCARD THE WATER AND RINSE THE BEANS. PROCEED WITH ANY RECIPE THAT CALLS FOR SOAKED BEANS. *Note:* THE LONGER THE SOAKING TIME, THE GREATER THE AMOUNT OF GAS-CAUSING PROPERTIES THAT WILL DISSOLVE IN THE WATER, THUS HELPING TO IMPROVE DIGESTION OF BEANS. WHETHER YOU SOAK THE BEANS FOR AN HOUR OR SEVERAL HOURS, REMEMBER TO DISCARD THE SOAK WATER.

SOAKING CHART FOR DRIED LEGUMES

When soaking beans for recipes, figure that most dried beans will double in size when soaked and triple in size when cooked. For example, 1 cup dried beans will yield at least 2 cups soaked and 3 cups cooked.

SOAKING IS HIGHLY RECOMMENDED FOR THE FOLLOWING LEGUMES:

Type of Dried Beans	Slow-Soak Times in Cold Water	Quick-Soak Times
Large, thick-skinned beans: *brown favas, large lima beans, white emergo beans, gigandes, giant white cocos, Christmas limas, scarlet runners*	12 hours at room temperature; change the water once to prevent fermentation in hot humid weather	Bring to a boil and cook 5 minutes; remove from heat and let soak 1 hour.
Whole chickpeas, whole starchy peas	10 hours at room temperature; change the water once to prevent fermentation in hot humid weather	Bring to a boil, cook 3 minutes (add a pinch of baking soda to cooking water for chickpeas); remove from heat and let soak 1 hour.
Medium-sized thick-skinned beans: *black beans, cannellini, red kidney, pinto, navy*	6 hours at room temperature (Note: Soak in lightly salted water if you plan to cook these beans in a pressure cooker so that their skins will stay intact under pressure.)	Bring to a boil and cook 2 minutes; remove from heat and let soak 1 hour.
Small thin-skinned beans: *French navy beans, pea beans, rice beans, red chile beans*	4 hours at room temperature	Bring to a boil and cook 1 minute; remove from heat and let soak 1 hour.
Small thick-skinned beans: *azuki, mung*	8 hours at room temperature	Bring to a boil and cook 1 minute; remove from heat and let soak 1 hour.

SOAKING IS NOT NECESSARY FOR THE FOLLOWING LEGUMES:

Skinned split beans: *split favas, split yellow and green peas, split chickpeas*

Flageolets (dried seeds are immature and not starchy)

Shell beans or fresh-shelled pod beans: *limas, cranberry, roman, black-eyed peas*

Lentils (with and without skins)

Field-dried beans from current year's crop (rather than oven-dried)

Frozen shelled beans: *black-eyed peas and limas*

All fresh green beans and peas: *garden peas, green favas, green limas, green beans, yard-long beans, green romanos*

COOKING METHODS FOR LEGUMES

Here is some general information on cooking all types of beans by all types of methods. Although some methods allow for deeper, richer flavors because they involve longer, slower cooking times, you can use any method you choose to cook legumes and still get terrific results—especially if you season your beans while they cook. So, if you're lucky enough to own a pressure cooker, why not use it to cook all your legumes? On the other hand, if you're a fan of ovenware, like those pieces made in wonderful colors by the French company Le Creuset, by all means use them. And never fear—if all you have is a big pot, you can still boil up a great dish of beans.

USING A POT

Cooking dried legumes in a pot on the stovetop (see chart opposite) is one of the fastest methods and the easiest alternative to using canned beans. In general, dried legumes take 30 minutes to 2 hours to cook. Avoid using a pot made from a reactive metal, such as aluminum, as the beans can pick up an unpleasant metallic taste. Choose a heavy-bottomed pot for best results.

For simple boiled beans, place the soaked, rinsed, and drained beans in a large pot with fresh cold water. If you use this method, be sure to add plenty of liquid; you can always pour off the excess later, although some people say that beans will plump more if cooked in less water. This way, you'll never have to worry about the beans sticking and burning—a disaster in the

making. The water level should come to about one inch above the beans. For each pound (2 cups) of dried legumes, you can add one tablespoon cooking oil to reduce foaming, which should be skimmed off and discarded.

Boil beans for 10 minutes, then cover the pot, reduce the heat to low and simmer until tender (approximately 1 to 2 hours, depending on the variety), checking the beans occasionally. Add seasonings (see chart opposite) during the cooking time, if desired. Never add anything acidic, such as tomatoes, vinegar, wine, or citrus juices, while the beans are cooking. Add acidic ingredients only after the beans are almost tender. Stir occasionally to prevent heavy beans from sinking to the bottom. The beans will keep their shape much better if you stir them gently with a rubber spatula or wooden spoon. Salt the beans halfway through cooking. Their skins should be soft enough to absorb the salt. Allow the beans to cool at least partially in their cooking liquid before draining them, long enough to begin firming up without drying out.

USING A DUTCH OVEN

A fail-safe way of cooking legumes is to combine the flavorings, legumes,

and liquid in a heatproof casserole with a lid. Bring it to a boil on the stove top, then place in a preheated moderate (300°F) oven and cook until the liquid has been absorbed and the beans are soft but not mushy.

USING AN EARTHENWARE BEAN POT OR SLOW-COOKER

Like many rustic-style cooks in the Mediterranean, Diana Kennedy prefers to cook dried beans in the Mexican style—in an earthenware pot that retains all the bean flavors. Since care must be taken that the beans do not scorch, Mexican cooks place a small *cazuela* (a shallow-sided earthenware casserole) filled with water over the top of the bean pot. This cuts down on the evaporation and keeps steaming hot water handy for adding to the beans, if necessary.

Kennedy also recommends using an electric slow-cooker with a ceramic liner. (These once ubiquitous cookers can often be found at yard sales for a couple of dollars.) She leaves her beans cooking on medium heat overnight. Look for a slow-cooker with a glass, rather than plastic, top. Kennedy prefers the slow-cooker over the pressure cooker because she believes beans taste better if they're not cooked in metal.

LEGUME VOLUMES: DRIED VS. COOKED

MOST DRIED LEGUMES TRIPLE IN VOLUME WHEN SOAKED AND COOKED.
HERE IS AN EASY REFERENCE FOR MEASURING:

1 LB. DRIED BEANS = 2 CUPS DRY = 6 CUPS COOKED

1 CUP DRIED BEANS = 3 CUPS COOKED

BASIC COOKING CHART FOR DRIED LEGUMES

Here is an easy guide to the simplest method of cooking dried legumes—in a pot of water on a stove top.

Type of Dried Beans	Water Amounts and General Cooking Times	Flavoring Suggestions (for all legumes)
Large thick-skinned beans: *brown favas, butter beans, emergo beans, gigandes, giant white cocos, Christmas limas, scarlet runners, red kidney beans*	Use 3 parts water to 1 part beans. Boil 10 minutes (remove skins of favas); simmer covered on low heat 2½ hours.	• ham or smoked turkey bones • goose or duck legs and wings • bacon rind or *la cotenna* (the skin of prosciutto) • whole unpeeled onion stuck with 3 or 4 whole cloves (peel onion for white beans) • head of garlic with the top half inch sliced off • bay leaves and/or small bunch of fresh thyme, marjoram, sage, rosemary, or savory tied up with string; several whole carrots. • dried and fresh hot chile pepper pods: green jalapeños, smoky dried chipotles, dark and rich chile anchos, or salty-strong Korean red pepper. • strips of lemon and orange peel or a wedge of orange • toasted, ground seeds: coriander, fennel, cumin, caraway, dill, and anise
Whole chickpeas Whole, starchy green peas	Use 3 parts water to 1 part beans. Boil 10 minutes (add a pinch of baking soda to cooking water for chickpeas); simmer covered on low heat 2½ hours.	
Soaked medium-sized thick-skinned beans: *black turtle beans, cannellini, black-eyed peas, pinto, navy*	Use 2 parts water to 1 part beans. Boil 10 minutes; simmer covered on low heat 1½ hours.	
Small thick-skinned beans: *adzuki, mung*	Use 3 parts water to 1 part beans. Bring to a boil, then simmer covered on low heat 1 hour.	
Small thin-skinned beans: *French navy beans, pea beans, rice beans, red chile beans*	Use 3 parts water to 1 part beans. Bring to a boil, then simmer covered on low heat 45 minutes to 1 hour.	

I would agree with that and I avoid any reactive metals, especially aluminum. However, to my mind, a stainless steel pressure cooker or pot doesn't adversely affect the beans.

Using a Pressure Cooker

While testing the recipes for this book, I convinced Linda Gellman, my dear friend and intrepid recipe tester, to try out my pressure cooker. When she returned it, Linda told me, "I fell in love with a pot today,"

and immediately went out to buy her own. Though not inexpensive, a good stainless steel pressure cooker is a lifetime investment in good results. Once you're tried a modern pressure cooker (newly popularized because of improved features) you'll be convinced. Nothing is faster and more reliable. There are many excellent brands for sale now, most imported from Europe where they've been standard kitchen equipment for years. Mine is a

large, 7½-quart model called a Duromatic, made by the Kuhn-Rikon Company of Switzerland.

The exception to the rule of not adding salt until the beans are soft is when you're using a pressure cooker. The directions on my box of imported French haricots lingots instructed me to add the salt from the beginning of cooking. Because of the great buildup of pressure in the pot, the salt doesn't prevent the beans from softening as it would in standard cooking methods.

Pressure cookers produce dramatic time savings when cooking beans. Most beans can be cooked in one-third to one-half the time of conventional cooking methods. Exact times are impossible to give because of variables such as the age and dryness of the beans.

Once the pressure builds up in your pressure cooker, reduce the heat to medium pressure—about 15 p.s.i. (pounds per square inch). Lentils, split peas, and lima beans should be cooked at low pressure—about 8 p.s.i. Don't fill the pressure cooker more than halfway with beans, as they will need enough room to expand. Adding about 1 teaspoon of vegetable oil to the pressure cooker will reduce the foaming, especially for chickpeas. Because the foam can cause the steam vent to clog, you may need to press the vent occasionally to let off steam, which unclogs it.

Instead, it helps them keep their shape by making them a bit more firm. They will also retain their shape because you won't break them up when stirring in salt near the end of cooking.

A good way to prevent foaming and tenderize beans is to add a strip of kombu (a type of seaweed sold in dehydrated strips at health food stores). Rinse the kombu quickly before placing a strip on top of the beans. Discard the kombu after cooking.

KNOWING WHEN DRIED BEANS ARE DONE

According to food maven Paula Wolfert in her book *Mediterranean Grains and Greens*, "You can tell when the beans are almost done by removing one or two beans with a spoon and blowing gently on them—the skins will burst." New England cooks have long used the same method when making baked beans to tell if the beans are sufficiently soft to absorb hardening ingredients like sweet molasses and salt pork. The American Dried Bean Board recommends tasting a few beans to see if they are done: they should be tender, but not mushy. When cooling cooked legumes, keep them in their cooking liquid to prevent them from drying out. When reheating them, add a tablespoon or two of water.

STORING COOKED LEGUMES

When cooking dried legumes, why not make more than you need for immediate use? Extras are very easy to store—especially if packaged in moisture-proof containers. Cooked legumes may be kept in the freezer for up to six months. Bean dishes may be kept four or five days in the refrigerator.

BASIC COOKING CHART FOR FRESH LEGUMES

Beans that are fresh-shelled and not dried for storage are sometimes sold in-season, especially in farm markets and at roadside stands. These beans should be treated like fresh vegetables and cooked in salted, boiling water until tender. They do not need any soaking. Keep in mind that green beans will lose their bright, attractive color if cooked with anything acidic in the water, such as lemon or vinegar. They keep the best color and flavor if cooked as quickly as possible over the highest heat with salt added to the water, or by using steam, which is hotter than boiling water. If precooking the beans, drain and rinse them under cold running water to set their color. Otherwise, drain and serve immediately. There is no better way than tasting to judge their doneness, because beans vary so much in maturity and tenderness.

TYPES OF LEGUMES	THREE METHODS OF COOKING
Green Beans Fresh Limas Green Romano Beans Fresh Favas All "shell" beans, such as fresh cranberry beans or black-eyed peas sold fresh in their pods	**I. Steaming** Steam the beans in a basket steamer over a pot of boiling water until tender and brightly colored. **II. Boiling** Bring a large pot of salted water to a boil and add the beans. Bring the water back to a boil as quickly as possible, making sure to stir the beans so they will cook evenly. Cook until tender and brightly colored. Be sure to rinse under cold water to stop the cooking and set the color, unless serving immediately. **III. Pan Cooking** In a large skillet, bring 1 to 2 inches of salted water to a boil. Add the beans, stirring them occasionally and bringing the water back to the boil as quickly as possible. Cook until tender and brightly colored. (If seasoning the beans with acidic ingredients, such as lemon, vinegar, wine, or tomatoes, toss with the beans at the last minute to preserve their bright green color.)

CHAPTER FOUR

SNACKS AND DIPS

CHILE-SPICED CHICKPEAS

As a young teen, I was lucky enough to spend two summers living and traveling in Mexico. I lived first in Mexico City and then in the colonial university city of Puebla. Our apartment, complete with maid's quarters, was up in a luxury high-rise building with only four apartments on each floor. Downstairs was a wonderful supermarket where I became addicted to the combination of these chili-spiced chickpeas with an exotic mango or watermelon frozen fruit bar. You could also vary this recipe by tossing the fried chickpeas with a good curry powder, such as Madras style from India or S & B brand from Japan.

Advance preparation required. Serves 8 (6 cups) •

1 pound (2 cups) dried chickpeas, soaked 24 hours

3 cups soybean oil

2 tablespoons chile ancho powder

2 tablespoons ground oregano

1 tablespoon garlic powder

1 tablespoon popcorn salt, or fine sea salt

2 teaspoons ground allspice

1. Drain the soaked chickpeas. Bring a large pot of unsalted water to a boil. Cook the chickpeas for 10 minutes, then drain. Spread out on paper or cloth towels to dry completely.

2. In a large heavy skillet or a wok, heat the oil until shimmering hot but not smoking, about 340°F on a deep-frying thermometer. Fry the chickpeas, in about 1 cup batches, for 3 to 4 minutes, or until the chickpeas are golden brown and crunchy. Using a slotted spoon or wire skimmer, scoop out the chickpeas and drain on paper towels. Repeat until all the chickpeas have been fried, then toss the beans with the chile ancho powder, oregano, garlic powder, salt, and allspice. Serve as a snack with a pitcher of frosty margaritas. Store in an airtight container for up to 2 weeks.

The Romans regarded chickpeas as food for peasants and the poor. Interestingly, when sickened by city life, the Roman poet Horace purportedly longed for a simple dish of chickpeas.

SPICY HOMEMADE BEER NUTS

In 1970, just out of high school, I spent three months hiking and camping out in Jasper National Park in the middle of the Canadian Rockies. My funds were extremely limited but the local lager at the village tavern was cheap. I learned to enjoy it like the Canadians, with a tomato juice chaser and several packages of beer nuts to round out my "meal." Needless to say, I spent many an evening in convivial company. This is my crunchy spicy version of the packaged beer nuts I used to eat. The raw peanuts are available at most natural food stores.

Serves 6 (3 cups) •

1 pound raw Virginia peanuts
  (about 2½ cups)
1 cup sugar
1 cup water
1 tablespoon ground coriander
2 teaspoons Korean red pepper flakes
  (see below), or cayenne
1 teaspoon freshly ground black pepper
1 tablespoon paprika
Popcorn salt, or fine sea salt for seasoning

ABOUT KOREAN RED PEPPER FLAKES

I'VE BECOME A RABID FAN OF THE KOREAN STAPLE OF GROUND, SALTED, HOT RED PEPPER FLAKES. THERE IS ONE AISLE IN MY LOCAL KOREAN MARKET THAT SHELVES NOTHING BUT DIFFERENT BRANDS, GRADES, AND PACKAGE SIZES OF THIS SPICE. THE BRILLIANT RED-COLORED, SEEDLESS FLAKES ARE SPICY HOT BUT ALSO HAVE A FULL VEGETABLE TASTE OF THE PEPPER. KEEP IT REFRIGERATED TO MAINTAIN ITS COLOR AND POTENCY.

1. Preheat the oven to 350°F. Spread the peanuts onto a baking sheet and toast for 10 minutes or until just starting to brown. Remove from the oven and reserve, keeping the oven on.

2. In a large saucepan, make a syrup by bringing the sugar and water to a boil. When the syrup is clear, remove from the heat and stir in the coriander, red pepper flakes, black pepper, and paprika. Stir in the peanuts and return to the heat. Cook on medium heat for about 10 minutes or until the syrup has thickened, shaking often.

3. Spray a baking sheet with nonstick vegetable spray or line with parchment paper. Spread the nuts along with their syrup out on the prepared baking sheet. Bake at 350°F for about 15 minutes, stirring once or twice, or until the peanuts are evenly browned and the syrup has crystallized on the nuts. Remove the peanuts from the oven and cool slightly. Season to taste with salt and cool completely before serving. Store in an airtight container, such as a cookie tin, for up to 2 weeks.

FRIED FAVAS
WITH SMOKED SPANISH PAPRIKA

You will need to start this dish two days before serving it in order for the favas to have sufficient time to soak. Similar preparations of fried favas eaten as a snack are found everywhere from Portugal, Spain, and the South of France, to Morocco, Egypt, and Lebanon, and as far away as Mexico, South America, and even Korea. After frying, sprinkle the favas with the smoky Spanish paprika *(pimentón)*, or substitute cayenne, Korean red pepper flakes, Italian-style red pepper flakes, or ground red Aleppo pepper.

Advance preparation required. Serves 8 to 12 (about 4 cups) •

1 pound (2 cups) large split golden fava
   beans (without skins)
1 cup extra-virgin olive oil, for frying
3 cups soy bean or canola oil, for frying
Fine sea salt, or popcorn salt,
   for seasoning
1 teaspoon pimentón, or ½ teaspoon
   cayenne, or hot red pepper flakes
½ teaspoon garlic powder

1. Soak the favas overnight in about 16 cups (4 quarts) of water. The next day, drain, rinse and cover again with cold water. Repeat 2 more times, changing the water every 12 hours or so, for a total of 36 hours. The beans should expand greatly and soften somewhat. Remove and discard any remaining skin pieces. Bring a large pot of unsalted water to a boil. Add the beans and cook for 5 minutes, then drain. Spread out on paper or cloth towels to dry completely.

2. In a large heavy skillet, heat both kinds of oil until shimmering hot but not smoking, about 340°F on a deep-frying thermometer. Fry the dry precooked favas, in about 1 cup batches, for 3 to 4 minutes. Scoop out with a slotted spoon or skimmer and drain on paper towels. Repeat until all the favas have been fried, then toss the beans with salt to taste, the pimentón, and the garlic powder. Serve as a snack with a pitcher of drinks, such as margaritas or sangria. Store in an airtight container for up to 2 weeks.

STEAMED GREEN SOYBEANS
IN THE POD *(Eda mame)*

Young soybeans in their fuzzy green pods appear in the market in the spring and summer months. Delicious with drinks and fun to eat, they are a well-loved seasonal snack in China and Japan. The Japanese call green soybeans *eda mame* or "branch beans." Their name in Chinese translates to "hairy beans." They are sold as bunches of stalks with the pods attached in Asian markets. When the soybeans pods are shelled, the soybeans inside are green, smooth, sweet, and crunchy. In the springtime, fresh green soybeans beans, salted and cooked in their pods, are a traditional Chinese and Japanese snack served with drinks.

Serves 4

1 bundle young green soybeans on the
  stalks (about 1 pound)
2 tablespoons salt

SNACKING ON LEGUMES

IN ANOTHER PART OF THE WORLD, LUPINI BEANS ARE A FAVORITE SNACK. THESE OLD WORLD BEANS, RELATED TO FLOWERING LUPINES, ARE MUSTARD-YELLOW WITH A DISTINCTIVE SMALL ROUND HOLE AT ONE END. COOKED AND LIGHTLY PICKLED, THE SOUTHERN ITALIANS CALL THEM *lupini* WHILE THE PORTUGUESE REFER TO THEM AS *tremoços*. IN LEBANON, LUPINI ARE WRAPPED UP IN A NEWSPAPER CONE AND EATEN AS STREET FOOD.

IN SOUTH CAROLINA'S LOW COUNTRY, SUMMERTIME ROADSIDE STANDS SELL A REGIONAL FAVORITE LEGUME AS A SNACK: BOILED GREEN PEANUTS. THESE ARE FRESHLY DUG PEANUTS BOILED IN SALTED WATER FOR UP TO TWELVE HOURS UNTIL SOFT AND TASTY. YOU CAN ALSO PURCHASE BOILED PEANUTS IN A CAN (SEE SOURCES, PAGE 323).

1. Separate the pods from the stalks. Using a scissors, snip off a bit of the stem end of each pod to allow the beans to be easily squeezed out of their pods after cooking. Place the beans pods in a bowl and sprinkle with the salt. Rub the beans with the salt until evenly coated. Let them rest for 15 minutes to absorb the salt (this enhances the color of the beans and accents their sweet flavor).

2. Bring 16 cups (4 quarts) of water to a boil. Add the beans and boil over high heat for 7 to 10 minutes. Taste test for doneness after 7 minutes (the bean should be crisp-tender) and continue cooking for the remaining time if you prefer a softer bean.

3. Serve the soybeans in baskets or bowls with drinks, along with a bowl for the discarded pods. To eat the soybeans, squeeze the pods between your lips, pressing the beans into your mouth. For best flavor, eat the beans the same day they are cooked.

CRISPY LENTIL WAFERS *(Pappadums)* WITH COCONUT-CILANTRO CHUTNEY

In the early nineties, I got the chance to plan the initial menu for a landmark project. It was to be named the Dock Street Brewing Company and Restaurant. Former owner and founder, Jeff Ware, started his company by contract, producing an extremely well-received microbrew called Dock Street Amber. After petitioning for a change in legislation in Harrisburg, Ware got the permits to open his own microbrewery and restaurant. These thin lentil wafers, called *pappadums*, flavored with fenugreek, garlic, nigella seeds, cumin, and chile, were a popular snack food served at the bar.

Serves 10 to 12 •

2 cups Coconut-Cilantro Chutney
  (see page 292), for dipping
4 cups peanut or vegetable oil
1 (12-ounce) package plain or flavored
  lentil pappadums

1. Prepare the Coconut-Cilantro Chutney. Reserve.

2. Using an electric skillet or deep, heavy-bottomed pot, heat the oil to 365°F on a deep-frying thermometer. One at a time, carefully place the pappadums in the oil, cooking 4 to 5 in a batch. Fry for about 1 minute, or until small bubbles form over the surface of the pappadum. Using tongs, turn the pappadum over and continue to fry until bubbles form again. The pappadums should not brown, but should be crispy and light. Remove the pappadums from the oil and drain on paper towels. Keep them warm in a 200°F oven while frying the remaining pappadums. Serve with the Coconut-Cilantro Chutney.

Cook's Note ❧ ❧ ❧

Pappadums or poppdoms, poppadums, papdoms—whatever way you spell them (the Oxford English Dictionary *lists eleven spellings)—are crispy, thin savory lentil pancakes are served in Indian restaurants in the West as a nibble before the first course. Don't be tempted to overcook them while frying. Once they begin to brown, they develop an unpleasant bitter aftertaste. Purchase dried pappadam wafers at Indian groceries or specialty food markets.*

CROSTINI WITH CANNELLINI BEAN SPREAD AND OVEN-ROASTED PLUM TOMATOES

*C*rostini or *bruschetta* is a frugal peasant's way of using up day-old bread by brushing it with olive oil, then toasting it. Endlessly versatile, crostini can be topped with anything from Tuscan-style chicken liver spread to a seasonal Piedmontese specialty of anchovy-garlic butter topped with thin slices of fresh white truffle. In this recipe, crostini are brushed with a rosemary-infused oil before being toasted and spread with white beans. Plump, herb-marinated roasted tomatoes contrast beautifully with the creamy bean topping. You can prepare the bean spread up to two days ahead and the tomatoes up to 2 weeks ahead.

Serves 10 to 12 (about 36 pieces) •

36 (about) Oven-Roasted Plum
  Tomatoes (see page 289), drained

CANNELLINI BEAN SPREAD

1 cup dried cannellini beans, cooked and
  drained (see Basic Cooking Chart,
  page 43), or 3 cups canned cannellini
  beans, rinsed and drained
2 tablespoons extra-virgin olive oil
2 cloves garlic, peeled
1/2 cup chopped fresh sage
  (about 1 bunch)
1/4 cup chopped fresh marjoram
  (about 1/2 bunch)
1/2 teaspoon hot red pepper flakes
Salt and freshly ground black pepper

CROSTINI

1/2 cup fresh rosemary, leaves picked-off
  and finely chopped (about 1 bunch)
6 tablespoons extra-virgin olive oil
1 round or oblong loaf fresh Italian
  country bread, cut into 1/2-inch-
  thick slices

1. Prepare the Oven-Roasted Plum Tomatoes and cannellini beans. Reserve.

2. Prepare the Cannellini Bean Spread: In a medium sauté pan, cook together the olive oil, garlic, sage, marjoram, and hot red pepper flakes until the aromas are released. Add the beans and cook until the mixture thickens and starts to come away from the side of the pan.

3. In a food processor or blender, purée the bean mixture to a paste. Season to taste with salt and black pepper. Reserve.

4. Prepare the Crostini: Preheat the oven to 350°F. Combine the rosemary and the remaining 6 tablespoons olive oil in a small bowl. Cut the bread slices into 2 x 3-inch pieces. Arrange the pieces in a single layer on a baking sheet. Brush the rosemary oil lightly on each side. Toast for 5 minutes, then turn the pieces and toast for 5 minutes longer or until the crostini are golden.

5. Reduce the oven temperature to 325°F. Spread the crostini with a 1/4- to 1/2-inch layer of the bean mixture. Top each crostino with 1 drained Oven-Roasted Plum Tomato half. Arrange on a baking sheet and bake for 10 minutes, or until heated through. Serve immediately.

CLASSIC HUMMUS DIP

Here is my favorite version of the Lebanese chickpea spread hummus, enriched with a splash of good-quality fruity green olive oil. I make it piquant by sprinkling in Philly Chili brand chipotle hot sauce (see Sources, page 323). I'm also a big believer in the value of toasting spice seeds like coriander and particularly cumin—and I can't resist the flavor of cilantro, even though it's hardly traditional.

Serves 12 to 16 (8 cups)

1 pound (2 cups) dried chickpeas, soaked (see Soaking Chart, page 41)

¼ cup fresh lemon juice (about 2 lemons)

3 cloves garlic, peeled

2 cups sesame tahini, preferably Lebanese

1 tablespoon chipotle hot sauce, or chopped chipotles in adobo sauce, or pimentón (smoked Spanish paprika)

2 tablespoons salt

1 tablespoon plus 1 teaspoon ground toasted cumin seeds (see Toasting Seeds, page 217)

1 teaspoon paprika, for garnish

1 tablespoon extra-virgin olive oil, for garnish

2 tablespoons chopped fresh cilantro, for garnish

Pita bread, for serving

1. Rinse the soaked chickpeas and place in a large saucepan. Add 8 cups cold water. Bring to a boil, then cook for 5 minutes. Discard the water, cover again with 8 cups fresh water and bring to a boil. Reduce the heat and simmer until the chickpeas are tender, about 2 to 3 hours. Skim off and discard any white foam that appears on the surface. Drain the chickpeas and rinse under cold running water.

2. In the bowl of a food processor, purée the chickpeas, reserving a few whole beans for garnish, along with the lemon juice and garlic. Add a little water, only as much as necessary, to blend. Scrape the purée into a bowl and whisk in the tahini, chipotle hot sauce, salt, and 1 tablespoon of the cumin. The mixture should be smooth, creamy, and thick enough to hold its shape.

3. To serve, mound the hummus in the center of a large flat serving dish. Using the back of a spoon, smooth the hummus from the center out so there is a slight hollow in the center. Decorate the hummus in a star pattern with sprinkles of paprika and the remaining 1 teaspoon cumin. Drizzle the olive oil into the center. Garnish with chopped cilantro and the reserved whole chickpeas. Heat the pita bread and cut into wedges. Serve with hummus for dipping.

RED BEAN DIP WITH
CRUNCHY PITA CHIPS AND VEGETABLES

During the years that I worked as a food stylist for cookbook authors at QVC, I prepared hundreds of dishes, many of them low fat because these kind of books always sold well. This spread, which I adapted from my original inspiration of a lower fat chickpea spread in *Lighter, Quicker, Better* by Marie Simmons and the late Richard Sax, is a real winner. Bring it to your next potluck buffet and watch it disappear.

Serves 12 to 16 (3 cups) •

1 cup dried small red beans (see Basic
   Cooking Chart, page 43)
1/2 cup fresh lemon juice (about 4 lemons)
2 tablespoons extra-virgin olive oil
2 tablespoons roasted Japanese sesame oil
1 head roasted garlic, cloves peeled
   and puréed
1 whole chipotle chile in adobo sauce,
   chopped
Salt and black pepper
Salt and freshly ground pepper
1/2 cup chopped fresh cilantro (about 1 bunch)
1/2 cup chopped fresh Italian parsley
   (about 1 bunch)
Paprika, for garnish

CRUNCHY PITA CHIPS
2 tablespoons extra-virgin olive oil
1 tablespoon chopped garlic
1 tablespoon ground cumin
1/2 teaspoon hot red pepper flakes (optional)
1 package pita breads, each cut into
   6 wedges
Paprika, for garnish
1 English (seedless) cucumber, half-peeled
   in stripes and cut diagonally into rounds,
   for serving
1/2 pound carrots, peeled and cut
   diagonally into long slices, for serving
2 heads Belgian endive, separated into
   leaves, for serving

1. Prepare the small red beans. Reserve.

2. In a blender or food processor, purée the reserved beans with the lemon juice, olive oil, sesame oil, garlic, chile, and season to taste with salt and black pepper. Strain through a food mill or sieve to remove skin pieces if desired (this step will make the beans more digestible). Combine the cilantro and parsley. Fold three-fourths of the herbs into the bean mixture. Spoon the bean mixture into the serving dish, then sprinkle the remaining herbs over the top.

3. Prepare the Crunchy Pita Chips: Preheat the oven to 350°F. In a small bowl, combine the olive oil, garlic, cumin, and hot red pepper flakes. Brush each pita wedge with the oil mixture. Arrange in a single layer on a baking sheet. Bake 6 to 8 minutes, then turn over and bake for 2 to 4 minutes longer, or until lightly and evenly toasted. Reserve.

4. Serve the dip sprinkled with the paprika and accompanied by the carrots, cucumber, endive leaves, and pita chips.

BLACK BEAN NACHOS

These colorful nachos are always a satisfying snack while watching "the game"—especially when served with Mexican beer. For a more crunchy, crusty texture, make these nachos in a paella pan, a shallow, slope-sided stainless steel pan with a flat bottom.

Serves 4 to 6 •

2 cups Black Turtle Beans with Epazote
   (see page 222)
1 cup Pico de Gallo Salsa (see page 300)
1 recipe Spicy Guacamole (see page 295)
1 (21-ounce) bag restaurant-style
   (thick) tortilla chips
¹/₂ cup sour cream
¹/₄ pound thinly sliced pepperoni
¹/₄ pound oil-cured Sicilian olives, or
   Kalamata olives, pitted and halved
¹/₄ pound shredded sharp Cheddar cheese

1. Prepare the Black Turtle Beans with Epazote, Pico de Gallo Salsa, and Spicy Guacamole. Reserve.

2. Preheat the oven to 450°F. Spray a 15 x 10-inch metal jelly-roll pan with nonstick vegetable spray.

3. Spread the chips out in a reasonably even layer on the pan. Spoon dollops of the beans onto the chips. Spoon dollops of guacamole Pico de Gallo Salsa, and sour cream in between. Sprinkle with the pepperoni slices and olives. Cover the whole pan with the shredded cheese. Bake on the top oven shelf for about 15 minutes, or until the cheese is browned and bubbling. Allow to cool slightly before serving directly from the pan.

A "beanery" is a small, inexpensive restaurant such as a diner. There is a life-sized sculpture named The Beanery permanently installed in Amsterdam's Stedlijk Museum. Inside the 3-D sculpture, artist Jim Dine has created every authentic detail of a beanery restaurant, a surrealistic combination of the ultrarealistic and the nonsensical.

CORN TORTILLAS IN BLACK BEAN SAUCE
(Enfrijoladas)

This typical Oaxacan dish is ideal served at a light brunch. It is unusual because the tortillas are fried and then dipped in a bean sauce, which results in a texture that is crunchy on the inside and soft on the outside.

Serves 6 to 8

1 recipe Earthenware-Cooked Beans
    (see page 235) prepared with black
    turtle beans
1/2 head garlic
1/4 cup lard, or vegetable oil
1 small onion, sliced
1 or 2 small whole dried red chile peppers
1 tablespoon crumbled dried epazote,
    or avocado leaves (see Cook's Note)
Kosher salt
1/4 cup vegetable oil
1 package 6-inch corn tortillas (about 12)
1 white onion, sliced into thin rings,
    for serving
1/2 cup crumbled Mexican queso fresco,
    or mild French feta, or ricotta salata,
    or fresh farmer cheese, for serving
1/4 cup sliced pickled jalapeños, for serving

Cook's Note

In Oaxaca, charred avocado leaves are used for flavoring. To prepare, hold a sprig of the tender avocado leaves or half a dozen larger leaves over a flame to singe them slightly and just bring out their aroma. Cool and crumble the leaves, discarding the stems. Use in place of the epazote in this recipe.

1. Prepare the Earthenware-Cooked Beans. Reserve.

2. Char the head of garlic on a hot grill, over a gas flame, or on an electric coil till the skin is blackened. Cool, peel, and reserve.

3. In a large skillet, heat 2 tablespoons of the lard. Fry the sliced onion and dried chiles until lightly browned. Transfer the mixture to a blender (with or without the chiles depending on how hot you'd like the dish), or use a hand-held blender. Add the epazote, garlic cloves, and about 1/2 cup water. Purée until smooth. Working in batches, if necessary, add the beans and their liquid and blend until smooth. If necessary, add about 1/2 cup more water to blend.

4. Heat the remaining 2 tablespoons lard in a skillet; stir in the bean purée. Cook about 10 minutes over medium heat, stirring up from the bottom to prevent sticking. Season to taste with salt. Partially cover, so the bean sauce doesn't form a crust but has enough air circulation to prevent fermentation, and reserve.

5. Just before serving the dish, reheat the bean sauce, adding a little water if it has thickened. It should be thin enough to lightly coat the tortillas.

6. In a skillet, heat the oil and fry the tortillas just until they begin to get crispy and are thoroughly heated. Drain on paper towels. Immerse the tortillas, 1 at a time, in the warm bean sauce and then fold into quarters. Sprinkle each serving of 1 to 2 tortillas with onion rings, crumbled cheese, and several slices of pickled jalapeños.

CHILE ANCHO EMPANADAS
WITH FRIJOLES FILLING

Recently I tasted empanadas made with a chile-ancho-flavored dough. I really liked the taste of the pastry, though the lobster they were filled with wasn't appropriate for this book. I decided to adapt a recipe I had seen for black-bean-filled empanadas. This would be a good make-ahead dish for a stand-up cocktail party. Serve with Pico de Gallo Salsa (see page 300) or sour cream mixed with lime juice and cilantro, if desired.

Serves 12 (24 empanadas) •

4 cups Refried Beans (see page 236), chilled

CHILI ANCHO DOUGH

3½ cups unbleached all-purpose flour

½ cup whole-grain cornmeal

2 tablespoons chile ancho powder, or commercial chili powder

1 teaspoon salt

1 cup vegetable shortening or lard

¼ cup butter, chilled and cut into bits

1 egg, lightly beaten

¾ cup ice water

2 eggs, lightly beaten, for sealing

¼ cup milk or light cream, for sealing

Cook's Note ❧ ❧ ❧

Prepare the empanadas complete with their filling and egg wash, then arrange them on a single layer on a baking sheet and freeze. Once the empanadas are frozen solid, transfer them to a plastic bag, sealing well. Proceed with the directions for baking, but you'll need to add about 15 minutes if they're frozen.

1. Prepare the Refried Beans. Reserve in the refrigerator to chill.

2. Prepare the Chili Ancho Dough: Into the bowl of a food processor, measure the flour, cornmeal, chile ancho powder and salt. Pulse until combined. Add the shortening and butter; pulse until the mixture resembles oatmeal. Combine the 1 egg and ice water. With the machine running, pour into the dry ingredients. Processing just until the dough comes together in a dryish, but not crumbly, ball. Do not overprocess. Remove the dough from the processor, place in a plastic bag, seal, and chill for 1 hour.

3. To prepare the empanadas, roll out the dough on a floured surface to a ⅛- to ¼-inch thickness. Cut out 4- to 5-inch circles using a large jar top (such as from a mayonnaise jar) as a pattern or a cookie cutter. Gather all the dough scraps together and reroll them once. Discard any remaining dough scraps as a third rolling might result in tough pastry.

4. In a small bowl, mix together the eggs and milk; reserve. Place a tablespoonful of the filling in the center of each dough circle. Using a pastry brush, apply the egg-wash mixture around the edges of the circles and fold over to form half-moons. Press or crimp the edges with a fork to seal tightly. When all the empanadas have been filled, brush them with the remaining egg wash. Poke each pastry with a fork to form steam holes. (Empanadas may be frozen at this point as directed in the Cook's Note.)

5. Preheat the oven to 350°F. Arrange the empanadas on parchment paper-lined baking sheet, leaving about 1 inch between them. Bake for 25 to 30 minutes or until the filling starts to bubble up through the fork holes. Cool slightly before serving.

CHICKPEA FRIES
(Paniccia Rivierasca)

In the early eighties, I immersed myself in studying Italian and even proposed translating the great classic (and still not translated) *Le Ricette Regionale d'Italia (Italian Regional Recipes)*, now in its ninth edition. According to author Anna Gosetti della Salda, if you go to the seaside city of Savona from April to September and try the frying places *(friggitorie)*, you can taste this rustic but superb specialty. Many dishes cross the border with some modifications from France to Italy. After all, Nice was part of the Italian Principality of Savoy for many years, which is why you will find *raioules* in Nice (ravioli) and *paniccia* in Italy. Alice Water's Berkeley restaurant, Chez Panisse, commemorates this dish in its name. The French version, *panisse*, is characteristic of Nice and immortalized by the great Provençal writer Marcel Pagnol.

Serves 6

2 tablespoons olive oil

1½ cups chickpea flour

4 cups cold water

4 cups peanut oil, for frying

Salt and freshly ground black pepper

½ cup freshly shredded Parmigiano-Reggiano (or other strong-flavored hard grating cheese)

1. Generously brush an 8 x 8-inch square cake pan with the olive oil. Place the chickpea flour into a bowl and vigorously whisk in the cold water. Keep whisking until you have a smooth paste. Pour the batter into a heavy-bottomed pot and bring to a boil over medium heat, stirring constantly with a wooden spoon. Cook for 5 to 10 minutes or until the mixture thickens and comes away from the side of the pan (as with polenta). Remove from the heat and beat until very smooth. Using a rubber spatula, scrape the batter into the oiled pan and cool, then chill in the refrigerator.

2. When ready to finish the dish, cut the cold batter into 2½-inch sticks (like French fries). Heat the peanut oil to 365°F on a deep-frying thermometer. Fry about one-fourth of the sticks at a time. When they are crispy, golden, and covered with blisters, remove them carefully using a wire skimmer or slotted spoon, and drain on paper towels. Sprinkle with salt and pepper to taste.

3. To finish, preheat the broiler. Arrange the chickpea fries in a single layer on a shallow baking pan and sprinkle generously with salt, pepper, and the cheese. Broil for 5 to 10 minutes or until the cheese is lightly browned and crusty. Serve immediately.

YELLOW SPLIT PEA (Dosa) PANCAKES WITH CUCUMBER-YOGURT RAITA

This large, lacy, ground split pea and rice pancake is flavored with onions, cilantro, and fresh ginger. You'll need to start the naturally fermented batter of split pea and rice purée a day ahead of time. An unusual but delicious pancake, dosa is related to other Indian flatbreads made with lentils or dals, such as *pappadum* and *dohkla*. Serve the dosa with the Green and Yellow Bean Curry with Cauliflower (see page 193) for an Indian vegetarian meal. The Indian-style toasted clarified butter, *ghee*, is used as a cooking fat here and gives further dimension to these simple pancakes. The *raita* is a simple, refreshing, and nutritious salad/relish made from thick yogurt, cucumber, and mint.

Advance preparation required (makes six 9-inch pancakes) • • • • • • • • • • • • • • • • • • •

½ cup dried yellow split peas

1½ cups raw long-grain rice, preferably basmati

1¼ cups cold water

2 cups Cucumber-Yogurt Raita (see page 288)

½ cup finely chopped onion

¼ cup finely chopped cilantro leaves (about ½ bunch)

2 tablespoons grated fresh ginger

1 jalapeño pepper, halved, seeded and thinly sliced

2 teaspoons salt

3 tablespoons ghee (see Making Ghee, page 61) or vegetable oil

1. Rinse both the yellow split peas and rice separately in cold water. Place in separate bowls and cover each with cold water. Soak at room temperature for 12 hours or overnight. Drain the split peas and purée in a blender along with ½ cup of the cold water. (The mixture should be smooth like a pancake batter.) Transfer the pea purée into a large bowl. Drain the rice and purée with ½ cup of the cold water, then combine with the split pea purée. Stir well, cover with a damp towel and set aside at room temperature to ferment for at least 24 hours and up to 2 days, or until the mixture is bubbly and slightly sour tasting.

2. The next day, prepare the Cucumber-Yogurt-Raita. Reserve. Stir the onion, cilantro, ginger, jalapeño, salt, and the remaining ¼ cup cold water into the fermented batter to make a soupy mix.

3. In an 8- or 9-inch nonstick skillet, melt 1 teaspoon of the ghee. Pour in ¾ cup of the batter, tilting the pan so the batter spreads out evenly, as if you were making a crepe. Cook for 2 to 3 minutes, or until bubbles form across the surface. Drizzle ½ teaspoon more ghee over the top. Cover the pan with a large heatproof plate, then flip over. Slide the uncooked side of the pancake back into the pan and cook for 2 minutes longer or until lightly browned. Keep the dosa warm in a 200°F oven. Serve with the Cucumber-Yogurt Raita on the side for dipping.

❧ ❧ ❧ MAKING GHEE ❧ ❧ ❧

To make ghee place at least 1 pound of cut-up butter into a small heavy pot and melt over very low heat. Cook slowly until the white butter solids, which first foam up, turn to a nutty brown color. Be careful not to burn the ghee, especially when it's almost ready. Skim off and discard the remaining butter solids floating on the surface. Strain the hot ghee through a paper towel or cheesecloth-lined sieve to remove any remaining particles. It should be completely clear without any solids, which could cause it to spoil or to burn. The ghee will keep indefinitely in the refrigerator.

MEXICAN SEVEN-LAYER SALAD WITH HOMEMADE TORTILLA CHIPS

It seems like seven is the magic number for this super-popular party dish. Of course you could leave out a layer, but it might be missing a bit of magic. To get the full effect of this salad, you will need a large, footed, glass trifle dish or a glass salad bowl with straight sides. Layer the ingredients in the order given for the best color contrast. You can make the salad early in the day it is served, but not any sooner or the colors will start to fade. Serve with the Homemade Tortilla Chips.

Serves 10 to 12 •

2 cups Basic Black Turtle Beans
    (see page 231)
1 recipe Pico de Gallo Salsa
    (see page 300)
1 recipe Avocado Mousse
    (see page 296)
Homemade Tortilla Chips
    (see recipe at right)
1 head romaine lettuce, washed
    and shredded
½ pound sharp Cheddar cheese
    (preferably orange colored), shredded
1 pint (2 cups) sour cream
½ cup pimiento-stuffed green olives,
    cut into halves or slices (depending on
    the size)
½ cup pitted Kalamata olives, cut into
    halves or slices (depending on the size)

1. Prepare the Basic Black Turtle Beans, Pico de Gallo Salsa, Avocado Mousse, and Homemade Tortilla Chips. Reserve.

2. Arrange the following layers in a clear glass, straight-sided, large salad bowl or trifle dish, making sure to spread out each layer evenly to the edges so it can be seen from the side: romaine lettuce, Pico de Gallo Salsa, Basic Black Turtle Beans, Avocado Mousse, cheese, and sour cream. Decorate the top with the green and Kalamata olives. Serve with the homemade tortilla chips.

HOMEMADE TORTILLA CHIPS

1 (12 OUNCE) PACKAGE FRESH (6-INCH) CORN TORTILLAS
CORN OR SOYBEAN OIL, FOR FRYING
1 CONTAINER POPCORN SALT (USUALLY SOLD WITH THE POPCORN)
OR FINE SEA SALT

Cut each tortilla into 6 to 8 wedges. In a deep, heavy-bottomed pan or fryer, heat the oil to 365°F on a deep-frying thermometer. Place tortilla wedges into the oil one at a time so they won't stick together, adding as many as will fit in a single layer. Stir with a pair of metal tongs or a spoon so they brown evenly. When they start to brown and turn stiff, remove from the oil using a wire skimmer or a pair of metal tongs. Drain on paper towels, sprinkle lightly with salt, and keep warm in a low oven, if desired.
To crisp tortilla chips, place in a 200°F oven for 10 minutes. Store in a cookie tin if possible.

PENNSYLVANIA-DUTCH CHOW-CHOW

The name of this brightly colored and prominently spiced version of the traditional sweet-and-sour bean relish, is derived from Chinese word for miscellaneous, *cha*. It refers to either a ginger-spiced fruit preserve or a mustard-flavored mixed vegetable and pickle relish.

Serves 32 (1 gallon) •

³/₄ cups dried dark red kidney beans, cooked and drained (see Basic Cooking Chart, page 43), or 2 cups canned dark red kidney beans, rinsed and drained

³/₄ cups dried black turtle beans, cooked and drained (see Basic Cooking Chart, page 43), or 2 cups canned black turtle beans, rinsed and drained

1 pound green beans, cut into 1-inch lengths

1 head cauliflower, cut into small florets

1 (10-ounce) package frozen baby lima beans

3 (10-ounce) packages frozen white corn kernels

¹/₂ stalk celery, cut into ¹/₂-inch lengths

2 red bell peppers, cut into 1-inch strips

2 yellow bell peppers, cut into 1-inch strips

SPICED SYRUP

2 cups sugar

4 cups cider vinegar

2 cups water

¹/₄ cup Kosher salt

2 tablespoons ground turmeric

2 tablespoons black peppercorns

1 (2 to 3-inch) stick cinnamon

1 tablespoon whole allspice

6 whole bay leaves

2 whole chile red pepper pods

¹/₄ cup yellow mustard seeds

1 tablespoon celery seeds

1. Prepare the kidney and black beans. Reserve.

2. Steam the green beans and then the cauliflower for 5 minutes each. Drain and rinse with cold water to stop the cooking. Place the limas and corn in a colander and rinse under lukewarm water to separate the pieces. Rinse the kidney and black beans, then drain and combine with the green beans, cauliflower, limas, corn, celery, and bell peppers in a large bowl. Reserve.

3. To prepare the Spiced Syrup: In a large saucepan, bring the sugar, cider vinegar, water, salt, turmeric, peppercorns, cinnamon, and allspice to a boil. Simmer together 30 minutes. Strain out the spices and pour the syrup back into the pot. Add the bay leaves, red pepper pods, mustard seeds, and celery seeds. Simmer for 10 minutes longer. Pour the syrup over the vegetables and mix well. Cool. Spoon the chow-chow and syrup into clean glass jars and store in the refrigerator for 1 week before serving. The chow-chow keeps at least 1 month in the refrigerator.

CHICKPEA FLOUR TART *(Socca)* NIÇOISE WITH ROASTED PEPPERS AND GOAT CHEESE

This crispy-thin delicious chickpea flour tart, called "socca" in Provençal dialect, is served hot as a snack is common in Nice, France and on both the French and Italian Rivieras. Chickpea flour is available at most Indian groceries and health food stores. Be sure to keep the flour in the freezer to prevent spoilage.

Serves 6 •

CHICKPEA FLOUR TART *(Socca)*

½ cup olive oil

2 cups chickpea flour

3 cups water

Salt and freshly ground black pepper

ROASTED BELL PEPPER TOPPING

1 tablespoon chopped fresh herbs, such as marjoram, thyme, or savory

4 cloves garlic, peeled

2 teaspoons salt

¼ cup extra-virgin olive oil

½ teaspoon freshly ground black pepper

4 red or orange bell peppers, cut into quarters and seeded

¼ pound fresh mild goat cheese, crumbled, for serving

1. Prepare the Chickpea Flour Tart: Generously brush a 12-inch round pizza pan with 1 tablespoon of the olive oil. Mix the chickpea flour, 6 tablespoons oil, water, and salt and pepper to taste in a bowl. Stir well to create a batter and let stand at room temperature for 1 hour.

2. Prepare the Roasted Pepper Topping: Preheat the oven to 400°F. Chop together the herbs, garlic, and salt until mixture is chunky. Mix with the olive oil and black pepper in a large bowl. Add the quartered pepper and toss. Spread the peppers in a single layer on a baking sheet. Roast for 15 to 20 minutes, or the until peppers are well-browned at the edges. Cool.

3. Preheat the broiler. Pour a thin layer (about ⅛ inch) of the reserved tart batter into the prepared pizza pan. Place the pan under the broiler, as close to the heat source as possible. Broil for 5 minutes. Remove from the oven, and sprinkle with the remaining tablespoon olive oil. Broil for 5 to 10 minutes longer, or until the tart is crispy and golden. Sprinkle with salt and pepper to taste. Slide onto a serving platter and cut into 2-inch squares. Top each square with a few of the roasted peppers and sprinkle with the crumbled goat cheese. Serve immediately.

ITALIAN CHICKPEA TORTE
(Torta di Ceci)

According to the great Italian culinary authority, Anna Gosetti della Salda, the oven should ideally be a wood-burning bread oven because of the smoky flavor it imparts. This dish is not served at the table, but is tasted and savored throughout the day as a snack. Cut the torte into diamond shapes and accompany it with apéritifs like Martini & Rossi, half sweet and half dry; Lillet with orange; Dubonnet, or a glass of Italian spumante (sparkling wine).

Serves 6 •

1 pound (2 cups) chickpea flour

3 quarts (12 cups) cold water

2 teaspoons salt

$1/2$ cup extra-virgin olive oil

1 large onion, sliced paper thin

2 tablespoons finely chopped fresh
    rosemary (about $1/4$ bunch)

Freshly ground black pepper

1. Place the chickpea flour in a bowl. While whisking constantly, beat in the water. Add the salt and let the batter rest in the refrigerator for 1 hour or overnight. Using a skimmer, remove and discard any white scum that forms on the surface.

2. Preheat the oven to 425°F. Generously brush a 12-inch round pizza pan with 1 tablespoon of the olive oil. Beat 6 tablespoons of the remaining oil into the chickpea batter. Pour the batter into the pan, cover with the onion slices and rosemary, and place in the oven. Bake, on the top rack, for 10 to 15 minutes, or until the torte is golden and crispy. Drizzle the top with the remaining 1 tablespoon of oil and sprinkle with black pepper. Cut immediately into diamond shapes and serve.

CRUNCHY FALAFEL WITH YEMENITE FENUGREEK (*Hilbeh*) SAUCE

I never get tired of eating falafel. Don't ask me why. Perhaps it's the seasoning or the combination of fried crunchy bean cakes with the juicy vegetables and creamy, sour yogurt-cucumber dressing. I haven't been in Israel for over 20 years, but I still remember the streets of falafel stands in the beautiful hillside seaport of Haifa. On one steep street, falafel stands abounded, each with an elaborate assortment of condiments, relishes, sauces, and toppings with which to embellish the basic falafel in pita. The traditional Yemenite *Hilbeh* Sauce, made with lots of fenugreek and served with the falafel, is very popular in Israel.

Serves 6 •

1 cup Yemenite Fenugreek Sauce (see page 293)

1 pound (2 cups) dried chickpeas, soaked (see Soaking Chart, page 41)

1 egg, lightly beaten

3 tablespoons salt

1 teaspoon freshly ground black pepper

1 teaspoon turmeric

¹/₂ cup chopped fresh cilantro leaves, (about 1 bunch)

1 teaspoon ground coriander seeds

¹/₂ teaspoon ground cardamom

¹/₂ teaspoon cayenne

3 cloves garlic, peeled

2 tablespoons sesame tahini

¹/₂ cup fresh white bread crumbs

¹/₂ cup sesame seeds (preferably natural, or unhulled)

4 cups canola, soybean, or peanut oil, for frying

1 (8-ounce) package pita bread

1. Prepare the Fenugreek Sauce. Reserve.

2. Drain the soaked chickpeas. Using a meat grinder or food processor, grind the chickpeas to a paste. Add the egg, salt, pepper, turmeric, cilantro, coriander, cayenne, garlic, tahini, and bread crumbs and process again until well combined. (The mixture should be soft, but firm enough to hold its shape.) Using a small ice cream scoop or tablespoon, form the falafel mixture into 1-inch balls with the tops slightly flattened. Dip the tops of the falafel into the sesame seeds, pressing them in lightly. Cover and chill in the refrigerator until ready to cook.

3. In a large heavy-bottomed pot, heat the oil to 365°F on a deep-frying thermometer. Gently place the falafel into the oil 1 at a time until about one-fourth are added. Fry until crisp and evenly browned. Using a slotted spoon, remove the falafel and drain on paper towels. Continue frying the remaining falafel in batches. Serve with Fenugreek Sauce and pita bread.

TRADITIONAL CONDIMENTS FOR FALAFEL

FOR A TRADITIONAL SPREAD, SERVE THE FALAFEL WITH SMALL BOWLS OF YOGURT TAHINI SAUCE; *torshi* OR THE MAGENTA-COLORED BEET-PICKLED TURNIPS (AVAILABLE FROM MIDDLE EASTERN GROCERIES); YEMENITE FENUGREEK SAUCE (SEE PAGE 293); AND A LARGER BOWL OF ISRAELI SALAD (DICED CUCUMBER, RED ONION, AND TOMATO IN LEMON JUICE AND OLIVE OIL). OTHER GARNISHES COULD INCLUDE MARINATED HOT PEPPERS, MARINATED OLIVES, SMALL PICKLED GHERKINS FROM ISRAEL OR KOSHER-STYLE PICKLES, AND HOT GRILLED PITA BREAD ALONG WITH *za'atar* PITA BREAD IF YOU HAVE A LEBANESE BAKERY IN YOUR AREA.

BLACK BEAN QUESADILLAS WITH PEPITA-TOMATILLO SAUCE

At the lovely high-style Mexican Camino Real Hotel in Cancun, salty-strong aged *Cotija* cheese was sprinkled on the black beans I ate every morning at the fabulous buffet. The best substitute is a Romano cheese from Italy, or perhaps the slightly sour-tasting white cheese from England called Wensleydale. In this dish, charred poblano peppers and onions are layered with tasty black beans on tortillas. The creamy but acidic Pepita-Tomatillo Sauce lightens the dish while giving it another dimension of flavor. If you'd like a crunchy garnish, toast green pumpkin seeds *(pepitas)* in a 300°F oven for about 10 minutes and then sprinkle on top just before serving.

Serves 6 •

2 cups Basic Black Turtle Beans
   (see page 231), or Black Turtle Beans
   with Epazote (see page 222)
2 cups Pepita-Tomatillo Sauce
   (see page 285)
4 poblano peppers
2 large onions, unpeeled and quartered
1 tablespoon vegetable oil
1 (12-ounce) package corn tortillas
1/4 pound crumbled Cotija cheese, or
   French feta, or ricotta salata

1. Prepare the Basic Black Turtle Beans and Pepita-Tomatillo Sauce. Reserve.

2. Preheat a grill until hot. Rub the poblano peppers and onions with the oil and grill until the skins are blackened but the flesh is still firm, about 10 minutes. When cool enough to handle, peel both the poblanos and the onions. Seed the poblanos and remove the stems. Cut into strips. Cut the onion into strips and combine both vegetables in a bowl.

3. Spread about a 1/4-inch-thick layer of the reserved black beans over half of the tortillas. Top with a portion of the poblano mixture and cover with a second tortilla. Preheat the broiler. Grill the quesadillas on both sides until browned and scattered with bubbles. Arrange the grilled quesadillas in a shallow, broiler proof baking dish. (I would use a steel paella pan here.) Ladle the reserved sauce over top and sprinkle with the Cotija cheese. Place under the broiler long enough for the sauce to get bubbling hot and serve.

PAN-GRILLED FALAFEL WITH SALAD IN GARLIC DRESSING

Amin and Jude Bitar run one of Philadelphia's culinary treasures: Bitar's Grocery and Pita Hut. The two brothers have carried on the business started by their father when he brought his family here from Beirut in 1974. Lebanese Christians, the Bitar brothers reach out to whole food community in the city: Christians, Muslims, Jews, and others. As the city's Arabic-speaking population has grown, so has the demand for sometimes hard-to-find foods like pomegranate molasses, fava beans, labni yogurt, Aleppo pepper, sumac, apricot leather, and zaatar spice. Amin developed this popular recipe for his customers who were looking for a lighter version of falafel.

Serves 6 •

FALAFEL

¼ pound (½ cup) dried split fava beans, presoaked (see Soaking Chart, page 41)

¼ pound (½ cup) dried chickpeas, pre-soaked (see Soaking Chart, page 41)

½ cup seeded diced green bell pepper

½ cup chopped Italian parsley leaves (about 1 bunch)

1½ teaspoons garlic powder

1½ teaspoons onion powder

1 teaspoon salt

¼ teaspoon freshly ground black pepper

½ teaspoon ground cumin

¼ teaspoon baking soda

½ teaspoon olive oil, for cooking

1. Prepare the Falafel: Drain the presoaked favas and chickpeas. Place in a food processor and blend to a pasty texture. Add the bell pepper, parsley, garlic powder, onion powder, salt, black pepper, cumin, and baking soda. Process until well mixed. Transfer the mixture to a bowl. Form into balls about 1-inch in diameter and arrange on a waxed-paper-lined tray. Cover and chill thoroughly in the refrigerator, for at least 1 hour.

2. Preheat a nonstick skillet over medium heat, then lightly grease with the ½ teaspoon olive oil. Pat the falafel balls into thin patties and add to the pan. Cook falafel patties on both sides, (as you would pancakes). When browned on both sides, remove from the pan.

3. Prepare the Garlic Dressing: Using a hand-held blender, or in a blender, blend the lemon juice, 2 tablespoons olive oil, and garlic to a creamy liquid. Toss with the lettuce, tomatoes, parsley, and pickles, and divide among plates. Serve the falafel on top of the salad accompanied by heated or grilled pita breads.

GARLIC DRESSING

$^1/_2$ cup fresh lemon juice (about 4 lemons)

2 tablespoons extra-virgin olive oil

1 teaspoon minced fresh garlic

1 head lettuce (romaine, iceberg, green leaf), shredded

2 large ripe tomatoes, seeded and diced

1 cup chopped Italian parsley leaves (about 2 bunches)

2 sour dill pickles, diced

6 zaatar-spiced, or white or whole wheat pita breads

❧ ❧ ❧ FALAFEL'S ORIGIN ❧ ❧ ❧

These small vegetarian fried cakes supposedly originated in Egypt where they are known as falafel in Alexandria and *ta'amia* in Cairo. Because Alexandria was a port city, it must have exported this name to Syria, Lebanon, and Israel where the same dish is made with either all chickpeas, or chickpeas mixed with favas as in this Lebanese recipe for Pan-Grilled Falafel.

CREAMY BLACK BEAN PÂTÉ

The strong flavors in this modern pâté, inspired by a recipe in Joyce LaFray's *Cocina Cubana*, make it a natural to serve with drinks such as margaritas. You will need to start the pâté the day before, but you can also make it up to three days ahead of time. I've added the classic Mexican liquor, tequila, made from the fermented and distilled sap of the agave, called *maguey* in Spanish. In Mexico, there are many specially distilled and aged tequilas that are searched out and sampled with the same dedication as lovers of single-malt Scotches. Tequila's strong, unmistakable punch reinforces the flavor of the black beans. You will need a 6-cup mold or deep bowl, preferably metal, to mold the pâté.

Advanced preparation required. Serves 12 •

1 recipe Black Turtle Beans with Epazote
  (see page 222)
Homemade Tortilla Chips (see page 62)
3 packages unflavored gelatin
1/2 cup cold water
1/2 cup tequila
1 tablespoon chopped garlic
2 tablespoons chile ancho powder, or
  chili powder
2 tablespoons Pickapeppa Sauce,
  or Worcestershire, or A-1 Sauce
2 tablespoons salt
1 tablespoon ground cumin (preferably
  toasted, see Toasting Seeds, page 217)
2 teaspoons ground allspice
1 cup sour cream
1 medium red onion, diced fine
1/2 cup chopped pimiento-stuffed green
  olives
1/2 cup sliced dry-pack sun-dried
  tomatoes (see page 79)
2 bunches fresh cilantro,
  1 bunch chopped (about 1/2 cup)
4 limes, sliced and halved

1. Prepare the Black Turtle Beans with Epazote and the Homemade Tortilla Chips. Reserve. In a small bowl, soften the gelatin in the cold water for 5 minutes, until it "blooms" or absorbs the liquid. Place the bowl over a pan of hot water until the mixture become thin and clear. Stir in the tequila with the gelatin and remove from the heat.

2. Place 4 cups of the black beans, the garlic, chile ancho powder, Pickapeppa Sauce, salt, cumin, and allspice into the bowl of a food processor. Purée until smooth. Add the sour cream and reserved gelatin mixture and process again to combine. (If a smoother pâté is desired, strain the mixture through a food mill or sieve.) Transfer to a bowl and fold in the red onion, green olives, sun-dried tomatoes, and chopped cilantro. Using a rubber spatula, fill a 6-cup mold with the mixture. Bang the mold on the counter to remove any air pockets. Cover and chill until firm, 4 hours or overnight.

3. To serve, dip the mold briefly into a bowl of very hot water, then unmold onto a large platter. Fill the center of the mold with the whole cilantro and surround with half-moon-shaped lime slices. Chill again until ready to serve, accompanied by Homemade Tortilla Chips.

CHAPTER FIVE

HEARTY SALADS

INDONESIAN SALAD *(Gado Gado)*

An impressive and decorative party dish, *gado gado* really can't be made in small quantities because of the number of ingredients used. The legume family contributes five members to this dish: tofu, Chinese long beans, bean sprouts, peanuts, and soybean oil for frying. It has a rich spicy sauce based on peanuts and coconut milk. The pungent undertone of the dressing comes from trassi or blanchan, a paste made from salted, dried and fermented shrimp. The special ingredients called for here are all dried, and will keep well in your pantry.

Serves 12 to 15 •

Tofu

¼ cup tamarind liquid
   (see Preparing Tamerind, page 291)
1 teaspoon salt
1 pound fresh, firm tofu, cut into 2-inch
   cubes
Soybean oil for frying
1 package Asian shrimp wafers (optional)

Dressing

¼ cup soybean oil
1 medium onion, chopped
1 tablespoon chopped garlic
1 tablespoon chopped fresh ginger
2 teaspoons trassi or fresh blanchan
2 cups crunchy peanut butter
2 (12-ounce) cans unsweetened
   coconut milk
¼ cup dark brown sugar
¼ cup tamarind liquid
1 stalk lemon grass, tender inner heart
   only, thinly sliced
1 tablespoon hot chile paste

1. Prepare the tofu: Combine the ¼ cup tamarind liquid and salt in a bowl. Add the drained tofu cubes and marinate for 10 to 15 minutes, turning once or twice.

2. In a large heavy pot, heat a 2-inch depth of oil to 365°F on a deep-frying thermometer, (or until a haze forms on the oil, just before it starts to smoke). Fry the tofu for 2 to 3 minutes or until golden brown and crispy. Drain on paper towels. Cut into ½-inch-wide strips. Reserve. If using the optional shrimp wafers, fry them in the same oil until they puff up and get crispy, about 2 minutes, then drain on paper towels.

3. Prepare the Dressing: Combine the ¼ cup oil, onion, garlic, and ginger in a medium heavy pot, about 2 minutes. Cook until softened but not browned. Add the trassi and mash until well blended with the other ingredients. Stir in the peanut butter, coconut milk, brown sugar, tamarind liquid, lemongrass, and chile paste. Simmer for 15 minutes or until just thick enough to hold its shape in a spoon. Add water, if necessary, to thin the sauce. Cool and reserve.

4. Prepare the Salad: Bring a pot of salted water to a boil. Add the long beans and cook until bright green and crisp-tender, about 10 minutes. Scoop from the water and refresh under cold running water to set the color. If desired, cook the carrots for 1 minute and rinse under cold water (or serve them raw). Add the potatoes to the boiling water and cook until still firm but tender in the center (about 10 minutes). Drain and reserve.

SALAD

1 pound fresh Chinese long beans, or
green beans, trimmed and cut into
4-inch lengths

1 pound carrots, thinly sliced

1 pound golden potatoes,
sliced ½ inch thick

1 small head green cabbage, cored
and shredded

1 pint mung bean sprouts

4 to 6 hard-cooked eggs, sliced,
(see Hard-Cooking Eggs, page 159)
for garnish

1 English (seedless) cucumber, halved
lengthwise and sliced

5. To serve the gado gado, cover a large serving platter with the shredded cabbage, then arrange the potatoes, long beans, bean sprouts, tofu, carrots, and egg slices over it in strips. Surround the salad with the cucumber slices. Serve the dressing on the side with a bowl of the fried shrimp wafers to garnish each portion.

TURKISH WHITE BEAN SALAD

In 1974, I spent two weeks exploring Istanbul and some of the surrounding areas, including its fascinating old Jewish neighborhood. Passing an impressive building, which turned out to be the largest synagogue in Istanbul, I went in and talked to the caretaker who invited me back that evening for the start of Passover. After the lovely services, conducted in both Ladino (the ancient Spanish dialect still spoken there more than 500 years after the ancestors of these Jews were expelled from Spain) and in Hebrew, I was invited to a marvelous seder at the home of a prominent Turkish Jewish family. I remember eating tiny crispy deep-fried whitebait fish and a version of this salad. I only wish I had known enough then to write down everything I ate.

Serves 8 •

1 pound (2 cups) dried large white beans, such as white emergo beans, cannellini, or haricots lingots, soaked (see Soaking Chart, page 41)

1/2 cup lemon juice (about 4 lemons)

1/2 cup extra-virgin olive oil

1/2 teaspoon hot red pepper flakes

Salt and freshly ground black pepper

1/2 cup chopped Italian parsley leaves (about 1 bunch)

1 bunch scallions, thinly sliced

Seeds of 1 pomegranate

1. Drain and rinse the soaked beans. Place in a large pot with 6 cups cold water and bring to a boil. Simmer, partially covered for 1½ to 2 hours, or until the beans are tender. Drain the beans, reserving about 1/4 cup of the cooking liquid.

2. Whisk together the lemon juice, olive oil, red pepper flakes, and salt and black pepper to taste. Place the hot cooked beans, reserved cooking liquid, parsley, and scallions in a bowl. Toss gently with the dressing mixture. Taste for seasoning and serve immediately or refrigerate until needed. The salad may be made up to 2 days in advance but will need a little extra lemon juice and salt before serving. Garnish with the pomegranate seeds just before serving.

AFRICAN BLACK-EYED PEA AND OKRA SALAD WITH CORN

In this colorful dish, I combine three native African foods: black-eyed peas, okra, and peanuts. African slaves brought these foods to America where they became incorporated into our cuisine through the skillful cooks who worked in the "big houses." Black-eyed peas have a crunchy texture and lively look. Fresh okra can be delicious and won't get slimy if you cook it quickly. Choose smaller okra pods for less gumminess. If you grow your own okra, their large, beautiful, edible blossoms (related to the hibiscus) will reward you. Make this salad in summer when fresh okra and corn are in both in season.

Serves 8

1½ cups Barley Malt Vinaigrette
  (see page 285)
½ pound (1 cup) dried black-eyed peas,
  or 4 cups frozen black-eyed peas
1 head garlic
1 whole dried red chile pepper
2 cups fresh corn kernels (about 4 ears),
  or 2 (10-ounce) packages frozen corn
  kernels
1 pound fresh young okra pods, sliced
  into ½-inch pieces, or 1 (10-ounce)
  package frozen sliced okra
2 tablespoons peanut oil
3 to 4 ribs celery, thinly sliced
1 medium red onion, diced
2 bell peppers (red, yellow, and/or
  orange), seeded and diced
Salt and freshly ground black pepper
¼ pound roasted Virginia peanuts,
  coarsely chopped (about ½ cup),
  for garnish
2 tablespoons chopped fresh parsley,
  for garnish

1. Prepare the Barley Malt Vinaigrette. Reserve.

2. Place the dried black-eyed peas in a medium-sized heavy pot with 6 cups cold water. Bring to a boil, skimming off and discarding any white foam that rises to the surface. Drain and rinse the peas. Place in the same pot with 6 cups fresh cold water. Cut ½ inch off the top of the garlic head. Add the garlic, beans, and the pepper pod. Bring to a boil, reduce the heat and simmer until quite soft, about 2 hours. (Note: If using frozen black-eyed peas, proceed as follows: Combine 3 cups of cold water with the garlic and hot pepper pod. Bring to a boil, then reduce heat and simmer for 30 minutes. Add the frozen black-eyed peas and cook for 10 to 15 minutes, or until the beans are tender.) Remove from the heat. Discard the garlic and pepper pod and allow the beans to cool slightly. Drain off any excess liquid and rinse the beans. Reserve.

3. Quickly sauté the corn and okra in the peanut oil until crisp-tender. Remove from the heat and then stir in the celery, onion, and bell peppers. Transfer to a bowl, and stir in the black-eyed peas. Pour the vinaigrette over and toss together gently. Season generously to taste with salt and black pepper. Sprinkle with peanuts and parsley. Serve.

NOODLE SALAD WITH SNOW PEAS, BEAN SPROUTS, AND SHANXI VINEGAR DRESSING

Noodle salads are so popular. They make a great hot weather entrée or buffet dish. This version includes a few of my favorite Asian ingredients: fresh ginger, Shanxi vinegar, mushroom soy sauce, and fermented black beans. The Shanxi vinegar, also known as China's Secret, is a wonderful product fermented from barley, sorghum, and peas. Made in a remote Northern province of China, the vinegar has been brewed in the traditional way for thousands of years. With a mellow, sweet taste reminiscent of balsamic vinegar, it is drunk in small quantities as a pick-me-up and used as a versatile seasoning. If you have a food processor with a slicing blade, use it to cut the carrots and radishes.

Serves 8

1½ cups Chinese Shanxi Vinegar Dressing (see page 287)
¼ pound fresh snow peas, trimmed (see sidebar below)
1 pound imported whole wheat spaghetti
1 bunch scallions, thinly sliced on the diagonal
2 cups bean sprouts, rinsed and drained
½ pound carrots, thinly sliced
1 small bag radishes, thinly sliced
½ cup fermented black beans, lightly rinsed under cold water and drained
½ cup chopped fresh cilantro leaves (about 1 bunch)
½ cup toasted sesame seeds, for garnish

1. Prepare the Chinese Shanxi Vinegar Dressing. Reserve.

2. Bring a large pot of salted water to a boil. Add the snow peas and cook only until they turn bright green, 1 to 2 minutes. Scoop out and rinse under cold water to set the color and stop the cooking.

3. Bring the water back to a boil and add the spaghetti. Cook until almost done, about 6 minutes (you should still be able to see a small white pearly heart in the center of the noodles. Don't overcook or the noodles will become mushy when dressed.) Rinse under cold water, drain, and reserve. (Recipe may be prepared 1 day in advance up to this point.)

4. To serve, toss the scallions, bean sprouts, carrots, radishes, black beans, cilantro, snow peas, and noodles with the dressing in a large bowl. Divide the salad among large salad bowls and garnish with the toasted sesame seeds.

> ## TRIMMING SNOW PEAS
> To trim snow peas, hold the pod just below the stem between the thumb and forefinger and break back the stem end. To remove the stem and string on side of the pod, grasp the tip of the stem and pull it down parallel to the pod.

WHITE BEAN SALAD CONTADINA

Here is a hearty, country-style main course salad that tastes great made a day or so ahead. Serve as part of a buffet dinner, or arrange individual servings on a bed of salad greens. The caperberries are the fruit of a caper bush and have a similar flavor to the regular capers. However, they are larger, oval in shape, and pickled complete with stems. Nonpareil capers will work fine but they won't be as noticeable in the salad because they're so much smaller.

Serves 8 •

SALAD

6 cups (1 recipe) Oven-Cooked Italian-Style Beans (see page 228), prepared with cannellini beans

1 cup sliced Oven-Roasted Plum Tomatoes (see page 289), or 1 cup dry-pack sun-dried tomatoes (see Cook's Note below)

1/4 pound Genoa salami, cut into small dice

1/2 cup oil-cured black olives, pitted and halved (about 1/4 pound)

1/2 cup caperberries or capers, drained and rinsed

1 cup coarsely chopped Italian parsley leaves (about 2 bunches)

DRESSING

3/4 cup balsamic vinegar

3/4 cup extra-virgin olive oil

1 tablespoon Dijon mustard

1 tablespoon finely chopped fresh thyme (about 1/4 bunch)

1 teaspoon crushed red pepper flakes

Freshly ground black pepper

1. Prepare the Salad: Prepare the Oven-Cooked Italian-Style Beans and Oven-Roasted Plum Tomatoes. Reserve.

2. Place the tomatoes, salami, olives, caperberries, and parsley in a large mixing bowl, reserving a bit of each to sprinkle on top for garnish. Combine the cooled beans (which should be soft and creamy but still hold their shape) with the salad ingredients.

3. Prepare the Dressing: In a medium bowl, whisk together the vinegar, oil, mustard, thyme, red pepper flakes, and black pepper to taste. Toss the salad with enough dressing to coat well. If making ahead, taste again just before serving as bean salads absorb liquids. The flavor is best if served at room temperature. Just before serving, sprinkle the salads with the reserved garnishes.

Cook's Note ❧ ❧ ❧

If you want a quick substitute for the Oven-Roasted Plum Tomatoes, bring 1 cup water and 1 cup red wine to a boil in a small pan. Turn off the heat and add 1 cup dry-pack sun-dried tomatoes. Allow the tomatoes to cool and plump in the liquid, about 1 hour. Use or store in the refrigerator in the liquid for up to 1 week.

PROVENÇAL CHICKPEA SALAD WITH TUNA CAVIAR

This salad uses a fish roe preparation that is a specialty of the Riviera—both French and Italian. Called *poutargue* in French and *bottarga* in Italian, this strong-flavored pressed and dried mullet or tuna roe was known to the people of Crete and imported to Marseilles and the rest of Provence by Phoenician sailors. Related to the Greek *tarama* made from mullet roe, it is used as an accent flavor, like anchovies or cured olives.

Serves 6 •

1 recipe Basic Cooked Chickpeas
    (see page 234)
1 cup Lemon-Garlic Vinaigrette
    (see page 287)
2 green bell peppers, cut into
    julienne strips
2 red bell peppers, cut into
    julienne strips
2 ounces poutargue, or Greek tarama
2 ounces whole anchovy fillets packed in
    olive oil, well drained, for garnish
1/4 pound small Niçoise olives
Freshly grated nutmeg, for garnish
1/2 cup chopped fresh Italian parsley
    (about 1 bunch), for garnish

MAYONNAISE
2 cloves garlic, peeled
2 onions, diced
2 teaspoons salt
1/2 teaspoon freshly ground black pepper
2 tablespoons Dijon mustard
7 tablespoons chopped fresh fine herbs
    (mix of parsley, chives, thyme, chervil,
    and tarragon)
2 cups extra-virgin olive oil
1/4 cup fresh lemon juice (about 2 lemons)

1. Prepare the Salad: Prepare the Basic Cooked Chickpeas and Lemon-Garlic Vinaigrette. Reserve.

2. Toss the chickpeas and bell peppers in a bowl with the Lemon-Garlic Vinaigrette. Arrange in a mound in a large salad bowl. Grate the poutargue over the chickpeas (or sprinkle with the tarama); reserve.

3. Prepare the Mayonnaise: Using a garlic press, squeeze the garlic into a blender jar. Combine with the onions, salt, pepper, mustard, and herbs. Blend for 1 minute, then gradually stir in 1 cup of the olive oil. Continue to add the remaining 1 cup oil slowly waiting until it is absorbed before adding more. Stir in the lemon juice and taste for seasoning.

4. Place a large mound of the mayonnaise on top of the chickpeas, then garnish with the anchovy fillets and olives. Sprinkle with the nutmeg and parsley.

CURRY NOODLE SALAD WITH SUGAR SNAP PEAS AND PEANUTS

This colorful noodle salad is full of flavor, from the curry dressing to the red cabbage cooked with ginger and garlic. You could use either the Japanese curry recommended in the sidebar below or a Madras-type curry powder. Use a French mandoline or a Japanese Benriner cutter to make perfect julienne matchsticks of the vegetables. If you have an old-fashioned cabbage slicer, cut thin even rounds, then cut the rounds into matchsticks with a knife. The back-up plan is to shred the vegetables with a box grater or a food processor shredder blade. These will work but won't produce the same neat look.

Serves 8 •

DRESSING

2 tablespoons roasted Japanese sesame oil

1 tablespoon dry mustard

1 tablespoon curry powder
   (see sidebar below)

2 tablespoons soy sauce

$1/4$ cup Dijon mustard

$1/4$ cup peanut oil

$1/4$ cup rice wine vinegar

SALAD

1 pound linguine

1 tablespoon roasted Japanese sesame oil

2 tablespoons peanut oil

2 tablespoons chopped fresh ginger

2 teaspoons chopped garlic

1 small head red cabbage, cut into
   1-inch squares

2 tablespoons rice wine vinegar

1 rutabaga, or butternut squash, or
   carrots, peeled and cut into matchsticks

$1/2$ pound sugar snap peas, strings
   removed

2 red bell peppers, cut into matchsticks

1 bunch scallions, cut diagonally into
   1-inch slices

1 cup chopped toasted peanuts

1. Prepare the Dressing: Whisk together the 2 tablespoons sesame oil, dry mustard, curry powder, soy sauce, Dijon mustard, $1/4$ cup peanut oil, and $1/4$ cup vinegar. Reserve.

2. Prepare the Salad: Bring a large pot of salted water to a boil. Add the linguine and cook for about 8 minutes or until firm to the bite. Drain and rinse under cold water, then mix with the 1 tablespoon sesame oil. Reserve.

3. Place the 2 tablespoons peanut oil, ginger, and garlic in a sauté pan. Add the cabbage and 2 tablespoons vinegar and cook until the cabbage is wilted and the liquid has been absorbed. Remove from pan; reserve.

4. In the same pan, quickly stir-fry the rutabaga and then the sugar snaps. Combine with the linguine, cabbage mixture, most of the scallions, most of the peanuts and the dressing. Garnish with the remaining scallions and peanuts.

ABOUT S & B BRAND CURRY POWDER

I'VE BECOME ENAMORED OF S & B (SUN BIRD BRAND) CURRY POWDER FROM JAPAN. AVAILABLE IN MOST ASIAN MARKETS, IT COMES IN A SMALL ROUND RED AND YELLOW TIN. ITS FLAVORS ARE SWEETLY AROMATIC, FRESH AND WELL BALANCED, WITHOUT TOO MUCH INEXPENSIVE ACRID-TASTING TURMERIC.

FLORENTINE BORLOTTI BEAN AND TUNA SALAD

As a young and ambitious chef at Philadelphia's fine northern Italian restaurant, DiLullo's, I was determined to learn Italian so that I could travel and be able to converse and read Italian cookbooks in their original language. After studying intensely for six months, I went off on my own on a trip to Italy. During my stay in Florence, I enjoyed this classic Tuscan salad at the wine bar, Cantina Antinori, where the gracious wait staff made me feel right at home by complimenting my questionable Italian. You might not immediately think of combining beans and tuna, but trust me—they're a naturally compatible pair. The borlotti beans called for here are the Tuscan bean of choice. Available in Italian groceries, borlotti look like fat, rounded cranberry beans with a tan background.

Serves 6 •

6 cups (1 recipe) Oven-Cooked
  Vegetarian Beans (see page 230) prepared with borlotti, or cranberry beans
1/2 cup red wine vinegar
1 cup extra-virgin olive oil
2 teaspoons red pepper flakes
1/4 cup Dijon mustard
Salt and freshly ground black pepper
1 cup chopped Italian parsley leaves
  (about 2 bunches)
2 tablespoons finely chopped fresh
  rosemary (about 1/4 bunch)
1 (9-ounce) can tuna in oil
  (preferably olive oil), well drained
1/4 cup pitted cured black olives
1/2 cup red radishes, quartered or sliced
Lemon wedges, for garnish

1. Prepare the Oven-Cooked Vegetarian Beans. Reserve and keep warm.

2. Whisk together the vinegar, olive oil, red pepper flakes, and mustard. Season to taste with salt and black pepper. Reserve.

3. Gently toss the warm beans, parsley, rosemary, and reserved dressing together. (Dress the beans while still warm so the flavors will be absorbed.) Mound the beans into the centers of 6 large salad plates. Top each plate with a portion of tuna and garnish with black olives, radishes, and lemon wedges.

FRENCH NAVY BEAN AND SHRIMP SALAD

ere is a French variation on the Tuscan custom of serving white beans with tuna. In this dish I garnish a salad of tiny French navy beans tossed in a tarragon-shallot vinaigrette with vermouth-poached shrimp. A sprinkling of delicate chives completes the dish. If you happen to grow chives, make this salad when they blossom. Remove the lavender-colored flower heads, separate them into small florets and then sprinkle the salad with these delicious sweet onion-perfumed blossoms.

Serves 6 •

6 cups Oven-Cooked Vegetarian Beans
    (see page 230) prepared with French
    navy beans
1½ cups French Tarragon-Shallot
    Vinaigrette (see page 288)
4 cups water
½ cup dry white vermouth
2 bay leaves
6 sprigs fresh thyme
2 tablespoons fresh lemon juice
    (about 1 lemon)
1½ pounds large shrimp (16 to 20 per
    pound), peeled and deveined
Sea salt and freshly ground black pepper
Grated zest of 1 lemon
¼ cup snipped fresh chives
    (about 1 bunch)

1. Prepare the Oven-Cooked Vegetarian Beans and French Tarragon-Shallot Vinaigrette. Reserve.

2. Place the water, vermouth, bay leaves, thyme, and lemon juice in a medium stainless steel or enameled pot with a lid. Bring to a boil and simmer 15 to 20 minutes to flavor the cooking liquid. Bring the liquid to a rolling boil, add the shrimp, and stir to distribute evenly. Cover and turn off the heat. Allow the shrimp to set in the steaming water for 3 to 4 minutes, or until they are curled and opaque. (Cut a shrimp in half through the thickest part if you need to check). Drain and reserve, discarding the bay leaves and thyme.

3. To assemble the salad, cut the shrimp into 1-inch lengths, reserving 1 whole shrimp (for each portion) for garnish. Toss the beans (preferably while still warm) with the shrimp and the vinaigrette. Season to taste with salt and pepper. Serve immediately, garnished with the lemon zest and chives.

HARICOTS VERTS AND ROASTED BEET SALAD WITH FRESH GOAT CHEESE

A dish served at the Union Square Café in New York inspired this strikingly beautiful salad. I was so pleased when this café opened on historic Union Square, which had unfortunately become seedy and rather scary. Because my grandfather had his musical instrument business on Union Square, I spent a lot of time there while growing up. His offices happened to be in the same building that housed Andy Warhol's studio. We would ride the elevator up and on the way it would stop and open on the happenings in the famous studio. This salad appropriately uses ingredients readily available from the marvelous Union Square Greenmarket.

Serves 6

Hazelnut Vinaigrette

1 tablespoon coarse-grain mustard

2 large shallots, finely minced

¼ cup imported French red wine vinegar

½ cup hazelnut oil, or use ¼ cup hazelnut oil and ¼ cup canola or soybean oil

1 teaspoon salt

¼ teaspoon freshly ground black pepper

Salad

1 pound medium-sized fresh beets

1 pound haricots verts, stems trimmed

1 bunch young arugula leaves, washed and dried

¼ pound fresh goat cheese, crumbled

½ cup skinned, toasted hazelnuts, coarsely chopped

Cook's Note

I love goat cheese. My favorite brands include Canadian Madame Chevre, Silver Goat from Israel, or Coach Farms from New York State.

1. Prepare the Hazelnut Vinaigrette: Combine the mustard, shallots, vinegar, hazelnut oil, salt, and pepper in a glass jar with a wide lid. Close the lid tightly and shake vigorously to combine. Reserve.

2. Preheat the oven to 350°F. Wrap the beets in aluminum foil and roast 45 minutes to 1 hour, or until tender when pierced with a fork. Cool slightly, then peel by rubbing off skins. Cut the beets into wedges and toss with about one-third of the Hazelnut Vinaigrette and reserve.

3. Over boiling water, steam the haricots verts until bright emerald green, then rinse under cold water to set color. Reserve. Toss the haricots with one-third of the vinaigrette. Toss the arugula with the remaining vinaigrette.

4. To serve the salad, place a small mound of arugula on each of 6 large salad plates. Form the arugula into a nest and top with a portion of the haricots verts. Divide the beets among the plates. Sprinkle each salad with the goat cheese and the chopped hazelnuts.

FRENCH GREEN LENTIL SALAD
WITH BACON AND TOMATO

This appetizing salad of French green lentils marinated in a classic French Tarragon-Shallot Vinaigrette is colorful because of the red and gold tomatoes, and green chives. This salad not only got the most raves at my tastings, it was also a favorite with Linda Gellman, my tireless recipe tester. Turn this salad into a main dish by topping each portion with a crispy-oven roasted Confit of Duck Leg (see page 310) or a grilled rich-oily type fish, such as tuna, salmon, or mahi-mahi. Or, make a Lentil B-L-T salad by serving each portion on a nest of tender Boston lettuce.

Serves 4 to 6 •

2 cups Basic Cooked French Green
   Lentils (see page 233)
1/2 cup French Tarragon-Shallot
   Vinaigrette (see page 288)
1/2 pound thick-sliced bacon, cut into
   matchsticks
2 ripe red and/or yellow tomatoes, diced
Salt and freshly ground black pepper
1/4 cup snipped fresh chives
   (about 1 bunch)

1. Prepare the Basic Cooked French Green Lentils. Reserve in a medium bowl.

2. Prepare the French Tarragon-Shallot Vinaigrette. Pour the vinaigrette over the lentils while they're still warm, tossing to coat.

3. Cook the bacon until crispy and browned, then drain on paper towels. Add most of the bacon and tomatoes to the lentils, reserving some for garnish. Season the salad with salt and pepper to taste and serve warm, garnished with the reserved bacon, tomato, and chives.

NIÇOISE PASTA SHELL SALAD WITH GREEN BEANS, CHICKPEAS, AND TUNA

One of the great American contributions to the salad bar and deli counter in the last ten or fifteen years has been the pasta salad. These salads are popular because they are inexpensive and relatively easy to make. Often I find them bland and mushy, because pasta is starchy and continues to absorb flavors and liquid after it's cooked. To prevent this, I use an imported Italian brand of pasta. I especially enjoy this salad as a summertime meal. If you can find the imported canned tuna fish packed in olive oil, this is a great way to enjoy it.

Serves 8 •

2 cups Basic Cooked Chickpeas
(see page 234), well drained

$1^{1}/_{2}$ cups Lemon-Garlic Vinaigrette
(see page 287)

$^{1}/_{2}$ pound fresh green beans, cut
diagonally into 1-inch pieces

2 large, ripe beefsteak tomatoes,
seeded and diced

$^{1}/_{2}$ cup pimiento-stuffed green olives,
sliced

1 large red onion, cut into thin rings

1 (9-ounce) can tuna in oil
(preferably olive oil), well drained

1 pound medium pasta shells, cooked and
drained

$^{1}/_{2}$ bunch fresh basil leaves, cut into thin
strips (about 1 cup)

1 head escarole, washed and shredded

2 tablespoons caperberries or tiny capers
(optional)

1. Prepare the Basic Cooked Chickpeas and Lemon-Garlic Vinaigrette. Reserve.

2. Bring a small pot of lightly salted water to a boil. Add the green beans and cook for 3 minutes. Drain and run under cold water to stop the cooking and set the color.

3. In a large bowl, mix together the green beans, tomatoes, olives, chickpeas, red onion, tuna, pasta shells, and basil. Add the vinaigrette with salad ingredients and toss to coat evenly. Serve the salad over a bed of escarole leaves and sprinkle with caperberries.

PORTUGUESE SALT COD AND KIDNEY BEAN SALAD

(Salada de Bacalhau e Feijãos)

My close friend Maria Marta is a wonderful Portuguese cook who makes the rustic but extremely tasty dishes her country is known for. Here she combines poached and grilled salt cod or *bacalhau* with kidney beans in a red-wine vinaigrette. With its garnish of sliced eggs and black olives, this dish makes a colorful and satisfying main-dish salad. Start at least one day ahead to allow time for soaking the salt from the cod.

Advance preparation recommended. Serves 6 •

2 pounds whole salt cold (on the bone)

½ pound (1 cup) dried dark red kidney beans, cooked and drained (see Basic Cooking Chart, page 43), or 3 cups canned red kidney beans, rinsed and drained

2 red bell peppers

2 green bell peppers

½ cup chopped Italian parsley leaves (about 1 bunch)

1 cup extra-virgin olive oil

½ cup red wine vinegar

Freshly ground black pepper

6 hard-cooked eggs, sliced (see Hard-Cooking Eggs, page 159)

½ cup cured black olives, pitted

ABOUT CODFISH AND THE PORTUGUESE

NOT LONG AFTER THE DISCOVERY OF THE NEW WORLD, INTREPID PORTUGUESE FISHERMEN WERE COMBING NEWFOUNDLAND'S GRAND BANKS FOR COD. BY 1506, CODFISH, OR *bacalhau*, WAS ALREADY A SIGNIFICANT PART OF THEIR CATCH AND THE PORTUGUESE, WHO LEARNED TO SALT THE COD WHILE STILL AT SEA TO PRESERVE IT, ARE SAID TO KNOW 365 WAYS TO COOK IT. WHOLE BACALHAU CAN BE FOUND IN ITALIAN AND SPANISH MARKETS.

---

1. Place the whole salt cod in a large bowl of cold water. Soak for 24 hours, changing the water several times. In hot weather, cover and refrigerate; in cold weather, it can be soaked at room temperature.

2. Prepare the kidney beans. Reserve.

3. Drain the soaked cod, then rinse and drain again. (When it has soaked sufficiently, it should be white, pliable, and plump.) Bring a large pot of unsalted water to a boil. Add the cod and poach gently for about 5 minutes or until partially cooked. Drain and cool. Reserve.

4. Brush the grill lightly with oil and preheat. Grill the bell peppers, charring the skins on all sides. Remove and cool. Peel and discard the blackened skins and cut the peppers into thin strips. Clean the grill with a wire brush if necessary and grill the parcooked cod until completely cooked, about 5 minutes per side. Remove from the grill and cool. Remove and discard the skin and bones, then, using your fingers, flake the cod meat into large chunks.

5. In a mixing bowl, combine the kidney beans, cod, bell pepper strips and most of the parsley. Add the olive oil, vinegar, and black pepper and toss gently and thoroughly. (You probably won't need salt because the cod is salty, but adjust the seasoning here as necessary.) Arrange the salad on a large shallow platter. Decorate with the egg slices and olives and sprinkle with the reserved parsley. Serve at room temperature for best flavor.

ROMANO BEAN AND NAVEL ORANGE SALAD

Fresh romano beans are in season in late summer. They do take a little more cooking than the usual green beans unless they are extremely young. Here I combine them with orange slices trimmed until only the flesh is left, in a technique called *à vif*, or "to the quick," in French. By all means, if dramatic red-streaked blood oranges are in season, substitute them for the navel oranges.

Serves 6

ORANGE-HONEY DRESSING
¾ cup olive oil
¼ cup sherry vinegar
Grated zest of 1 orange
2 tablespoons whole-grain mustard
2 tablespoons honey
1 tablespoon finely chopped fresh rosemary leaves
1 tablespoon finely chopped garlic
1 tablespoon salt
¼ teaspoon freshly ground black pepper

SALAD
2 pounds romano beans, ends trimmed and diagonally cut into 1½ inch-pieces, or 2 (12-ounces) boxes frozen romano beans, rinsed
4 navel or blood oranges
1 red onion, cut into thin slices

1. Prepare the Orange-Honey Dressing: Whisk together the olive oil, vinegar, orange zest, mustard, honey, rosemary, garlic, salt, and pepper. Reserve.

2. Bring a large pot of salted water to a boil. Cook the fresh romano beans for 5 minutes. Drain and rinse under cold water and reserve. (Skip this step if using frozen beans.)

3. Using a sharp paring knife, cut away all the white pith of the oranges, exposing all the flesh inside. Cut the oranges into halves from end to end, and then cut half-moon-shaped slices from each half. (Only bright orange slices without any pith or membrane should be left.)

4 Combine the romano beans, orange slices, red onion, and dressing in a large bowl, tossing together gently, so as not to break up the orange sections.

SOUTHWEST BLACK BEAN SALAD WITH BAKED SPICED GOAT CHEESE ROUNDS

This hearty and spicy black bean salad is a good example of the modern salads popularized by Texas and Santa Fe chefs. These chefs have been exploring local culinary traditions while updating flavors and presentations. Purple-black, red, yellow, orange, white, and green: these are the eye-appealing colors of this salad. The tangy spiced goat cheese rounds which accent the flavors, are an addition popularized by influential chefs from the southwest, such as Mark Miller and Steven Pyles.

Serves 8 ●

SPICED GOAT CHEESE ROUNDS

1/2 pound log mild goat cheese

2 tablespoons black sesame seeds, or poppy seeds

2 tablespoons chile ancho powder, or New Mexican red chile powder

1/4 cup snipped fresh chives (about 1 bunch)

BLACK BEAN SALAD

1 recipe Black Turtle Beans with Epazote (see page 222)

1 recipe Cumin-Lime Citronette Dressing (see page 296)

2 bell peppers (red, yellow, green and/or orange), seeded and diced

1 red onion, diced

2 bunches scallions, cut into 1/2-inch slices

8 whole ripe plum tomatoes, seeded and diced

1 or 2 poblano chiles, seeded and diced

Salt and freshly ground black pepper

1. Prepare the Spiced Goat Cheese Rounds: Using a sharp knife dipped into hot water, cut 8 rounds from the goat cheese. Place the sesame seeds, chile powder, and chives in 3 small bowls. Dip 1 edge of the goat cheese rounds into the black sesame seeds, and then dip the opposite edge into the red chile. Sprinkle the centers with the chives. Place the rounds chive sides up, on a shallow metal dish such as a foil pie plate, small foil baking pan, or folded-over piece of heavy-duty foil. Reserve in the refrigerator.

2. Prepare the Black Bean Salad: Prepare the Black Turtle Beans with Epazote and the Cumin-Lime Citronette Dressing. Reserve.

3. To assemble the salad, combine the bell peppers, red onion, scallions, tomatoes, poblano chiles, and beans in a large bowl. Pour in the citronette dressing and toss to coat lightly and evenly. Season to taste with salt and pepper.

4. When ready to serve, preheat the oven to 400°F. Place the goat cheese rounds in the oven. Bake for 10 minutes, or until the cheese begins to crack through the spice coating. Remove from the oven and cool slightly. Arrange the bean salad on individual plates. Using a spatula, lift up 1 baked goat cheese round at a time and place in the center of each salad portion.

THREE-BEAN SALAD RING
WITH AVOCADO MOUSSE

I always knew that jellied salads and desserts, popular in the 1950s, were slated to have a big comeback. Recently, I've noticed prize-winning dessert jellies and a growing popularity of the Italian jellied cream dessert, *panna cotta*. It's only a matter of time before colorful, refreshing, natural-tasting jellied dishes, like this variation on the classic American picnic dish Three-Bean Salad, regain their popularity. Here the beans are suspended in a clear jelly with a vegetable juice base. For a winning combination, serve this dish with an accompanying bowl of cool Avocado Mousse on the hottest summer day.

Advanced preparation recommended. Serves 8 •

¾ cup dried red kidney beans, cooked and drained (see Basic Cooking Chart, page 43), or 2 cups canned red kidney beans, rinsed and drained

¾ cup dried black turtle beans, cooked and drained (see Basic Cooking Chart, page 43), or 2 cups canned black turtle beans, rinsed and drained

4 cups Light Chicken Stock (see page 301)

1 large (46-ounce) can vegetable juice

¼ cup egg whites (about 2 eggs)

½ pound fresh ground beef

1 tablespoon salt

½ teaspoon freshly ground black pepper

½ cup red wine vinegar

½ cup water

¼ cup (8 envelopes) unflavored gelatin

1 (12-ounce) package frozen baby lima beans, rinsed and drained

½ cup diced roasted red peppers (use a commercially prepared imported brand)

1. Prepare the kidney and black turtle beans and the Light Chicken Stock. Reserve. Have ready a 2-quart decorative mold.

2. In a large stockpot, combine the stock, juice, egg whites, ground beef, salt, and black pepper. Slowly bring to a boil, whisking until the mixture begins to get hot. Allow an egg white and beef "raft" to coagulate on top, which will take about 20 minutes. Remove and discard using a slotted spoon or skimmer. Strain the broth through a sieve lined with a double layer of cheesecloth to obtain a clear broth. Reserve the strained broth.

3. In a pot, mix the wine vinegar and water. Sprinkle in the gelatin and stir gently to mix. Allow the gelatin to "bloom" (absorb the liquid and soften), about 5 minutes. Add the reserved broth to the bloomed gelatin and place over low heat. Cook until clear, about 3 minutes.

4. Pour the gelatin/broth mixture into a bowl. Cool it by placing over a second larger bowl filled with ice water. Stir frequently to cool evenly, using a spoon (rather than a whisk, which will stir up unwanted bubbles). When the mixture is syrupy and starts to gel, remove from the ice water bath. Fold in the kidney beans, black beans, lima beans, roasted peppers, celery, red onion, cilantro, and hot sauce. Pour into the mold and chill until set, about 3 to 4 hours, or overnight.

3 ribs celery, diced

1 red onion, finely diced

½ cup chopped fresh cilantro leaves (about 1 bunch)

1 tablespoon hot sauce pepper, or cayenne

1 recipe Avocado Mousse (see page 296), for serving

5. Prepare the Avocado Mousse. Reserve chilled.

6. Unmold the salad by dipping the mold briefly (about 10 seconds) into a deep bowl of hot water and shaking to loosen. Turn the mold out onto a decorative platter and serve accompanied by the reserved Avocado Mousse.

TEXAS STUFFED TOMATOES
WITH BLACK-EYED PEA SALAD

The idea for this dish came from a recipe in *The Junior League Centennial Cookbook*, a compilation of the best of this country's many junior league cookbooks, which I had the pleasure of food styling for QVC. I make this dish in late summer when the sweetest locally grown Jersey and Pennsylvania tomatoes and corn are in season. It's a tasty and inexpensive first course with a dramatic presentation. Frozen black-eyed peas are found in some supermarkets and many ethnic markets.

Serves 6 •

1 cup dried black-eyed peas
   (see Basic Cooking Chart, page 43),
   or 2 (12-ounce) packages frozen
   black-eyed peas, rinsed
1 cup Cumin-Lime Citronette Dressing
   (see page 296)
2 cups white corn kernels (about 4 ears),
   or 1 (12-to 15-ounce) package frozen
   white corn
2 large, ripe beefsteak tomatoes,
   seeded, diced, and drained
2 red, yellow, or orange bell peppers,
   roasted (see page 314), seeded,
   and diced
1 bunch scallions, thinly sliced
1 to 2 red or green jalapeño peppers,
   seeded and minced
6 large, ripe beefsteak tomatoes,
   for serving
1 teaspoon salt
$^{1}/_{2}$ cup sour cream, for serving
2 limes, cut into wedges, for serving

1. Prepare the black-eyed peas and Cumin-Lime Citronette Dressing. Reserve.

2. In a bowl, mix together the black-eyed peas, corn, tomatoes, roasted peppers, scallions, and jalapeños. Add the citronette dressing and toss lightly. Reserve.

3. Cut off the top 1-inch of the tomatoes. Using a tablespoon, scoop out the insides, leaving the outside wall as the shell, about $^{1}/_{2}$ inch thick. Sprinkle the insides of the tomatoes with salt and turn them upside-down on a double-thick layer of paper towels to drain for about 15 minutes.

4. Fill the tomato shells with the salad. Garnish each tomato with a spoonful of sour cream and a lime wedge. Serve cold or at room temperature.

KIDNEY BEAN SALAD IN MUSTARD VINAIGRETTE

Before smooth-style Dijon mustard, the oldest types of prepared mustard had large visible grains of mustard seeds. One of the most venerable brands is Moutarde de Meaux, which has been made in the town of Meaux, France since 1632. This kind of mustard gives a crunchy texture to the beans and its milder flavor means you can use it generously without making the salad too "hot." Mustard and tarragon have a long standing marriage in France, where rabbit in mustard sauce with tarragon is a Sunday standard. As much as I'm a fiend for fresh herbs, dried tarragon is one of the few herbs that keeps a reasonably close resemblance to its fresh counterpart.

Serves 6 •

1 pound (2 cups) dried red kidney beans, cooked and drained (see Basic Cooking Chart, page 43)

½ cup extra-virgin olive oil

¼ cup sherry or balsamic vinegar

¼ cup coarse-grain mustard

2 tablespoons chopped fresh tarragon (about ½ bunch), or 2 teaspoons dried

Salt and freshly ground black pepper

3 or 4 ribs celery (preferably from the heart where the celery is white and mild), sliced

¼ cup finely chopped shallots

1. Prepare the kidney beans. Reserve and keep warm.

2. Whisk together the olive oil, vinegar, mustard, tarragon, and salt and pepper to taste. Pour the mixture over the beans and toss well to combine. Marinate the beans for at least 2 hours at room temperature, or preferably overnight in the refrigerator, then stir in the celery and shallots. Serve.

WHITE BEANS WITH MOROCCAN CHARMOULA DRESSING

I got the idea for this salad while consulting for the Moroccan-French restaurant Tangerine. This delicious and unusual salad didn't fit into the opening menu, which was built around cold-weather dishes. However, I tested it by bringing it to the annual picnic of the Philadelphia chapter Chef's Collaborative 2000, where it was a big hit, especially among the many vegetarian growers who attended.

Serves 8 •

1 pound (2 cups) dried white emergo beans, cooked and drained (see Basic Cooking Chart, page 43)

2 tablespoon nigella seeds (see About Nigella Seeds, page 126)

$1/2$ cup extra-virgin olive oil

$1/4$ cup red wine vinegar

$1/4$ cup fresh lemon juice (about 2 lemons)

1 tablespoon finely chopped garlic

2 tablespoons sweet Spanish paprika

2 teaspoons hot paprika

2 teaspoons ground toasted cumin seeds (see Toasting Seeds, page 217)

2 teaspoons salt

$1/2$ teaspoon freshly ground black pepper

1 preserved lemon

$1/4$ cup chopped fresh cilantro leaves (about $1/2$ bunch)

1. Prepare the white emergo beans. Reserve.

2. In a heated dry skillet, toast the nigella seeds, shaking constantly until their aroma is released. Remove from the heat and cool. Reserve.

3. Using a hand-held or standard blender, blend the olive oil, vinegar, lemon juice, and garlic. When smooth and creamy, blend in the sweet and hot paprikas, cumin, salt, and pepper.

4. Scrape off and discard the pulp and white pith from the preserved lemon; finely dice the lemon. Pour the dressing over the beans and toss with most of the nigella seeds, most of the cilantro and most of the lemon. Serve the salad garnished with the remaining nigella seeds, cilantro, and lemon.

PINTO BEAN SALAD
WITH SMOKED TURKEY SAUSAGE

This simple but flavorful pinto bean salad is hearty enough to serve as a main course. If possible, try using Southwest-Style Turkey Sausage from Aidell's Sausage Company (see Sources, page 323), for a wonderful flavor.

Serves 8 •

1 pound (2 cups) dried pinto beans, cooked and drained (see Basic Cooking Chart, page 43)

1 pound smoked turkey sausage

$^1/_2$ cup vegetable oil

1 chipotle in adobo sauce, chopped with about 2 tablespoons of the liquid

$^1/_2$ cup balsamic vinegar

2 teaspoons ground toasted cumin seeds (see Toasting Seeds, page 217)

Salt and freshly ground black pepper

2 teaspoons dried oregano

2 bunches scallions, thinly sliced

2 green bell peppers, seeded, and diced

$^1/_2$ cup coarsely chopped Italian parsley leaves (about 1 bunch)

1. Prepare the pinto beans. Reserve and keep warm.

2. Remove and discard the sausage skin. Cut the sausage into small cubes. Heat the oil in a large pan over medium heat. Add the sausage and cook, shaking the pan occasionally, for about 10 minutes or until the sausage is nicely browned on all sides. Remove from the heat and reserve both the oil and sausage.

3. Whisk together the reserved oil, chipotle vinegar, cumin, salt, pepper, and oregano. Pour over the beans. Stir in the reserved sausage, scallions, green pepper, and parsley.

LENTIL SALAD WITH SALT COD *(Bacala)* FRITTERS AND PRESERVED LEMON AÏOLI

Spanish Pardina lentils are a small, prized lentil that cook quickly and keep their shape well. Here I've combined them in a salad seasoned with Spanish sherry vinegar. *Bacala* (or salt cod) fritters—a favorite for the little tapas plates that accompany drinks during the long, leisurely drinking hour in Spain—accompany the salad. Note that the salt cod requires 24 hours of soaking, so be sure to plan ahead before making this dish. The preserved lemon aioli is a variation on the classic olive-oil mayonnaise served in Spain with fried fish dishes. The preserved lemon, actually cured in salt, give the salad a zesty flavor with a slight sharp-bitter aftertaste that awakens the palate.

Advanced preparation required. Serves 6 to 8 •

PRESERVED LEMON AIOLI

4 egg yolks
1 egg
½ cup lemon juice (about 4 lemons)
2 cups extra-virgin olive oil
¼ cup finely chopped shallots
Finely diced rind of 1 preserved lemon
   (see Sources, page 323), or grated zest
   of 1 lemon
Freshly ground black pepper

LENTIL SALAD

3 cups Basic Cooked French Green
   Lentils (see page 233) made with
   Spanish pardina lentils
¼ cup sherry vinegar
½ cup extra-virgin olive oil
1 red onion, diced
1 teaspoon salt
¼ teaspoon freshly ground black pepper

1. Prepare the Preserved Lemon Aioli: Place the egg yolks, whole egg, and lemon juice into the bowl of a food processor. Process for 1 minute, or until creamy. With the machine running, slowly pour the oil through the feed tube, waiting until the oil has been absorbed before adding more. Continue until each addition of it is completely absorbed and the aioli is thick.

2. Transfer the aioli from the processor to a bowl and stir in the shallots, preserved lemon, and black pepper to taste. Taste for seasoning. Because the lemons are cured in salt, you probably won't need to add any additional salt. If you substitute lemon zest, add salt to taste. Also, if you are immune sensitive and wish to avoid raw eggs, combine a good quality purchased mayonnaise with the fresh lemon juice, chopped shallots, and the preserved lemon or lemon zest.

3. Prepare the Lentil Salad: Prepare the Basic Cooked French Green Lentils. Reserve.

4. Combine the lentils, sherry vinegar, oil, red onion, salt, and black pepper in a large bowl; toss to combine and reserve.

Salt Cod Fritters

1 pound salt cod fillet

2½ cups all-purpose unbleached flour

1 teaspoon baking powder

1½ cups buttermilk

3 eggs, separated

1 teaspoons hot red pepper flakes

1 white onion, chopped finely

1 teaspoon chopped garlic

¼ cup chopped fresh cilantro leaves (about ½ bunch)

Olive or vegetable oil, for deep-frying

5. Prepare the Salt Cod Fritters: Prepare the salt cod fillet in a large bowl of cold water. Soak for 24 hours, changing the water after 12 hours. In hot weather, cover and refrigerate; in cold weather it can be soaked at room temperature.

6. Prepare the fritter batter by combining flour and baking powder in a large bowl. Whisk in the buttermilk, egg yolks, and pepper flakes. Allow the batter to rest, covered, in the refrigerator for 30 minutes to make it more tender.

7. Drain the soaked cod, then rinse under cold fresh water. Place the cod in a pot and cover with cold water. Bring to a boil. Reduce the heat to a simmer and poach for about 10 minutes, or until the fish flakes easily. Remove from the water and flake. You should have about 2 cups of flaked fish.

8. Stir the flaked salt cod, white onion, garlic, and cilantro into the batter. Beat the egg whites until they form soft peaks. Fold in the egg whites. In a deep-fryer or heavy-bottomed deep pan no more than one-third full of oil, heat the olive oil to 365°F on a frying thermometer. Carefully drop the batter by tablespoonfuls into hot oil, frying until browned on all sides. Drain on paper towels and repeat if necessary.

9. Place a mound of the lentil salad in the center of each plate and surround the salad with the hot fritters and top each one with a dollop of preserved lemon aioli. For a more stylish presentation, filling a ring mold or clean tuna can with top and bottom removed with the lentil salad (pressing down firmly to make the salad more compact) to create a molded vertical salad on each plate when you remove the ring.

TABBOULI SALAD WITH LENTILS, LEMON, AND MINT

Tabbouli is a type of cracked wheat that is cooked and then dried. It is popular in Turkey, Lebanon, Syria, and Israel. Contrary to common American practice, tabbouli salad is not really a grain salad, but rather a parsley and vegetable salad that contains tabbouli. In this recipe lentils are added, making the dish into a hearty main-course salad. I prefer to use kirby cucumbers (the small firm cucumbers used to make crispy sour dill pickles) or the European variety of cucumbers that don't need to be peeled. These "burpless" cukes (so-called because of their small seeds) are generally hothouse grown and often come from Canada.

Serves 6 to 8 •

2 cups Basic Cooked French Green
   Lentils (see page 233), well drained
1 cup bulghur wheat
1 cup extra-virgin olive oil
1/2 cup fresh lemon juice
   (about 4 lemons)
1 tablespoon chopped garlic
2 teaspoons ground cumin, preferably
   toasted
Salt, freshly ground black pepper,
   and cayenne
4 plum tomatoes, seeded and diced
1 bunch scallions, thinly sliced
1 European cucumber, diced
   (or 4 or 5 kirby cukes)
1 small bag red radishes, diced
3 cups coarsely chopped Italian parsley
   (about 2 bunches)
1/2 cup coarsely chopped fresh mint
   (about 1 bunch)

1. Prepare the Basic Cooked French Green Lentils. Reserve.

2. Soak the bulghur in boiling water to cover for 10 minutes, or until the grains become soft and plump. Drain off any excess water.

3. In a small bowl, whisk together the olive oil, lemon juice, garlic, cumin, salt, black pepper, cayenne. Combine the dressing with the bulghur and lentils. Stir in the tomatoes, scallions, cucumber, radishes, parsley, and mint. Taste for seasoning and serve.

CHAPTER SIX

SOUPS

SENATE BEAN SOUP

This white bean soup, flavored with smoked ham hocks, has been served for almost one hundred years in the United States Senate's restaurant, operated for senators and their guests. Credit for creating the soup—or at least introducing it to the Senate restaurant—has gone to Senator Fred Dubois of Idaho in the 1890s and to Senator Knute Nelson of Minnesota in the early part of the twentieth century. The soup couldn't be simpler.

Serves 6 •

1 pound (2 cups) dried navy bean beans, soaked (see Soaking Chart, page 41) and drained
8 cups (2 quarts) cold water
1 ham hock
1 cup diced onion
1 cup diced celery, including leaves
1 cup potato, diced small
2 teaspoons chopped garlic
$1/4$ teaspoon ground clove
Salt and freshly ground black pepper
$1/4$ cup chopped Italian parsley leaves (about $1/2$ bunch)

1. Drain the soaked navy beans. Combine with the water and ham hock in a stockpot and bring to a boil. Reduce the heat and simmer about $1^{1}/_{2}$ hours, or until the beans are tender.

2. Remove the ham hock from the pot. Cool the meat and reserve, discarding the bone. Add the meat to the pot, along with the onion, celery, potato, garlic, and clove. Bring the soup back to a boil. Reduce the heat and simmer until the potato is soft, about 20 minutes.

3. Remove the soup from the heat. Using a potato masher or a heavy whisk, mash the mixture until it becomes creamy, leaving some beans whole for texture. Season to taste with salt and pepper, and stir in the parsley. Serve hot.

BOLOGNESE BEAN SOUP
(Minestra di Fagioli Bolognese)

In Italian, a *minestra* is a thick soup made from a few simple ingredients, as opposed to a *minestrone*, which is more of a meal in a bowl, or a *zuppa*, which is based on a clear broth. Fresh, pink-streaked cranberry beans are commonly sold fresh in the pod during the summer months. These creamy, smooth, mild-tasting beans are such a treat in season that it's best to prepare them as simply as possible, topped with the nutty, sweet flavor of freshly grated, imported Parmigiano-Reggiano, as in this vegetarian Bolognese soup.

Serves 8 •

1½ pounds fresh cranberry beans, shelled, or ½ pound (1 cup) dried borlotti beans

4 to 6 cloves garlic, peeled

½ cup extra-virgin olive oil

¼ cup chopped Italian parsley leaves (about ½ bunch), for garnish

2 cups tomato purée

½ pound fresh egg pasta dough, cut into coarsely-shaped squares

Salt and freshly ground black pepper

Freshly grated Parmigiano-Reggiano cheese, for serving

1. In a large pot, cover the shelled cranberry beans with 8 cups cold water and bring to a boil. Cover and simmer for 30 minutes or until tender to the bite. Remove from the heat and reserve. Do not drain.

2. Cook the garlic cloves in the olive oil until golden. Add 3 tablespoons of the parsley and the tomato purée. Simmer together for 5 minutes, then add the reserved beans and their cooking liquid (which should equal about 8 cups). Bring the soup to a boil, then scoop out 2 to 3 cups of the beans and purée in a blender. Stir the puréed beans back into the soup, season to taste with the salt and pepper and bring back to a boil.

3. Add the pasta squares and simmer for 3 to 4 minutes or until the pasta is tender. Ladle the soup into serving bowls. Garnish each portion with some of the remaining 1 tablespoon parsley and serve with a separate bowl of Parmigiano-Reggiano to sprinkle on top.

YELLOW SPLIT MUNG BEAN DAL WITH TADKA

The *moong dal* or mung beans used here are actually the tiny, golden-yellow, oval split seeds that remain after the green skins of the mung bean (the same one used for sprouting) have been removed. *Tadka* is an ancient Indian topping used to give bright, fresh flavor to relatively bland foods like legumes. It is made by cooking ghee (Indian nutty-tasting browned and clarified butter) with fragrant spices and seasonings at high heat to release the aromatic oils.

Serves 6 •

DAL

1 pound (2 cups) dried yellow split mung
  beans (*moong* or *mung dal*),
  pick over and rinsed
1 teaspoon turmeric
1 tablespoon grated fresh ginger
1 tablespoon salt
2 tablespoons fresh lemon juice
  (about 1 lemon)

TADKA

¼ cup ghee or clarified butter
  (see Making Ghee, page 61)
2 teaspoons black mustard seeds
1 to 2 small green chiles
  (such as jalapeño or serrano),
  seeded and thinly sliced
¼ cup chopped cilantro
  (about ½ bunch), for serving

1. Prepare the Dal: Place the beans, turmeric, and ginger in a large heavy-bottomed saucepan with a lid. Add 8 cups cold water and bring to a boil, stirring occasionally (these beans stick easily). Reduce the heat, partially cover the pan, and simmer for about 30 minutes or until the beans are soft when pressed between your fingers. Continue to stir occasionally, especially near the end of the cooking time when the beans are starting to thicken. The beans should disintegrate to form a thick soupy purée. Reserve.

2. Prepare the Tadka: Heat the ghee in a small pan with a lid over high heat until it shimmers but is not yet smoking. Add the black mustard seeds and cover the pan immediately because the seeds will pop and jump like popcorn. When the seeds have all popped and turned gray, stir in the chiles. Cook for about 1 minute, then remove from heat.

3. Just before serving, stir the salt and lemon juice into the dal, and reheat if necessary. Pour the hot tadka over the dal and sprinkle each portion generously with the cilantro.

❧ ❧ ❧ ABOUT DAL ❧ ❧ ❧

Dal is often made from the pea-like seeds of the tropical mung bean that is widely eaten in Africa, India, and the Caribbean. The Hindu name dal is a derivative from the Sanskrit word dal, meaning split. This is because the seeds in India are commonly split and dried for storage. Dal has come to refer to all kinds of dried and split legumes, as well as porridge-like dishes made with mung beans, onions, and spices.

CANNELLINI AND CHICORY SOUP
(Minestra di Cicoria e Cannellini)

A dish of the *cucina povera* (the cuisine of frugality), this simple soup is a meal on its own. Traditionally made with wild chicory or *cicoria*, here I call for curly endive, our closest substitute. This recipe comes from my friend, restaurateur Toto Schiavone, who's originally from Calabria (the instep of Italy's "boot"). Close to Greece geographically and culturally, the region is filled with fig, olive, and hazelnut trees, bitter wild onions, and homemade sun-dried tomatoes like prunes, that hang in bunches and wreaths from the whitewashed houses that characterize this region.

Serves 4

1 cup dried cannellini beans, cooked and
   drained (see Basic Cooking Chart, page
   43)
2 large bunches curly endive,
   cut into 2- to 3-inch pieces
¼ cup finest extra-virgin olive oil
1 tablespoon chopped garlic
1 cup broken Crostini (see page 53)
1 cup Light Chicken Stock
   (see page 301)
Salt and hot red pepper flakes
½ cup grated Pecorino Romano cheese

1. Prepare the cannellini beans. Reserve.

2. Fill a large bowl with cold water and add the endive pieces. Swish the water around to release any dirt. Let the dirt settle, then scoop out the endive. Bring a pot of salted water to a boil. Cook the endive for about 5 minutes, or until completely wilted. Drain and rinse under cold water. Gently squeeze out the excess water. Reserve.

3. In a large, heavy-bottomed saucepan, place the olive oil and the garlic. Cook together over medium heat for 3 to 4 minutes or until the garlic releases its fragrance, but isn't browned. Reduce the heat and add the endive and let it cook slowly for 8 to 10 minutes.

4. Stir in the Crostini and beans. Add the Light Chicken Stock little by little and cook until the broth has been absorbed. Season to taste with the salt and red pepper flakes. Let the soup rest for a few minutes before serving. Serve with the grated cheese.

HARICOT BEAN AND OVEN-ROASTED TOMATO SOUP WITH SMOKED SPANISH PAPRIKA

This soup gets its wonderful flavor from fabulous oven-roasted tomatoes, which I first tasted when I worked at an event with Michael Romano of Union Square Café in New York. For the smoky flavor in this recipe, you can use any one of a number of items, including *pimentón*, smoked Spanish paprika from the Extremadura (my first choice), smoked chipotles, or good-quality sweet Hungarian or Spanish paprika, which will still give you a good soup with a lovely pinkish-orange color.

Serves 8

2 cups Oven-Roasted Plum Tomatoes
   (see page 289)
4 cups Smoked Turkey Stock
   (see page 302)
1 pound (2 cups) dried great Northern
   beans, soaked (see Soaking Chart,
   page 41)
2 onions, peeled and quartered
6 cloves garlic, peeled
2 tablespoons olive oil
1 teaspoon dried oregano
2 teaspoons ground cumin
2 tablespoons pimentón (see About
   Pimentón, page 224) or chipotle chile
4 cups water
1/4 cup fresh cilantro leaves (about 1/2
   bunch), chopped

1. Prepare the Oven-Roasted Plum Tomatoes and Smoked Turkey Stock. Reserve.

2. Drain the soaked beans. Place them in a large pot and cover with cold water. Bring to a boil, then drain the beans, discarding the liquid. Reserve.

3. Preheat the oven to 400°F. Combine the onions, garlic, olive oil, oregano, and cumin in a small roasting pan. Cook for 1 hour, turning vegetables once or twice, or until roasted and well browned.

4. In a large soup pot, place the roasted vegetables with pan juices, the Oven-Roasted Plum Tomatoes, blanched beans, pimentón, Smoked Turkey Stock, and water. Bring to a boil, reduce the heat to a simmer and cook for 2 hours, or until the beans are tender. Allow the soup to cool somewhat, then purée in a food processor or blender until smooth. Strain through a sieve, if desired, to remove any skin pieces. Garnish with chopped cilantro.

❧ ❧ ❧ ABOUT HARICOT BEANS ❧ ❧ ❧ ❧

Haricot bean is an antiquated term for any member of the New World bean family. Old New England cookbooks refer to what are now known as great Northern, navy, Boston, and pea beans as haricots. In France, a haricot (or haricot lingot) is a large white bean perhaps most famous in cassoulet. The Aztec name for these beans was *ayacotl*, which was eventually transformed into haricot.

QUEBEÇOIS YELLOW SPLIT PEA SOUP

As an 18 year old, I spent a month in Montreal where I first sampled this hearty, satisfying soup in a traditional Quebeçois restaurant in Montreal's Old Quarter. It was a rare treat for me to eat in an actual restaurant, so maybe that's why this soup tasted so good and was so memorable. Serve it piping hot in large bowls accompanied by thick slices of buttered multi-grain bread, preferably in front of a roaring fireplace.

Serves 6 to 8 •

3 pounds smoked ham hocks

3 bay leaves

16 cups (4 quarts) water

2 teaspoons celery seeds,
  or 1 tablespoon celery salt

1 pound (2 cups) dried yellow split peas

2 large onions, diced

4 ribs celery, sliced

Salt

1. Place the ham hocks, water, bay leaves, and celery seeds in a large soup pot. Bring to a boil. Cover with a lid, reduce the heat and simmer for 2 hours.

2. Add the yellow split peas, onions, and celery and bring back to a boil. Reduce the heat and cook, covered, for 1 hour, or until the yellow split peas are very soft. Remove the ham hocks, cool and pick the meat from the bones. Stir the meat back into the soup, remove and discard the bay leaves, and season to taste with salt. Serve immediately or cool and freeze.

Beans have even been used to describe weather. Herman Melville wrote in his Journal of a Visit to London and the Continent 1849, *"Upon sallying out this morning, [I] encountered the old-fashioned pea soup London fog."*

SUMMER MINESTRONE
WITH PESTO ALLA GENOVESE

My garnish for this summer version of minestrone is an all-too-short-lived delicacy: female zucchini blossoms—the sweetest, most succulent vegetable you can imagine. If you grow your own zucchini, the females are the blossoms from which the zucchini grows. These blossoms have a thick, fleshy inner stalk and won't last much longer than a day or two after picking. The male blossoms, which grow along the stalk of the plant don't produce fruits. These are also good, though to my taste, not nearly as desirable as the females. Serve this soup as they do in the summer in Milano, at cool room temperature.

Serves 8 •

Pesto alla Genovese

¹/₂ cup extra-virgin olive oil

10 to 12 cloves fresh young garlic, peeled

¹/₄ pound pine nuts

1 large bunch basil, leaves picked, washed, and dried

Soup

1 pound shelled fresh cranberry beans

¹/₂ pound fresh romano beans, diagonally sliced, or 1 (10-ounce) package frozen beans

1 pound fresh plum tomatoes, blanched, peeled, and seeded

2 leeks, sliced and washed

8 cups Light Chicken Stock (see page 301)

¹/₂ pound yellow squash, sliced into half moons

1. Prepare the Pesto alla Genovese: Place the olive oil, garlic, and pine nuts in a food processor or blender and process to a paste. A handful at a time, add the basil leaves and process again until a bright green paste forms. Reserve.

2. In a large soup pot combine the cranberry beans, tomatoes, leeks, and Light Chicken Stock. Bring to a boil, reduce the heat and simmer for 15 to 20 minutes or until the beans are almost tender. Skim off any white foam that rises to the surface. Add the romano beans, yellow squash, zucchini, and ditalini and bring back to a boil. Reduce the heat and simmer for 5 to 8 minutes or until the pasta is cooked through and the romano beans are tender.

3. Just before serving stir in the zucchini blossoms, then remove the pot from the heat. Season to taste with salt and pepper. Divide the soup among serving bowls. Top each with a generous spoonful of the pesto. Combine the grated Parmigiano and Pecorino cheeses in a small bowl and serve with the soup.

When making the green pesto, it is most important to first sharpen your food processor blade or bring it to a knife sharpening service. A dull blade will bruise and blacken rather than cut the basil. Then add the ingredients in the proper order: fats first (oil and cheeses), greens last. In addition to basil, other herbs make great pestos (an Italian word simply meaning "paste"). I like to make a southwest version using cilantro, pumpkin seeds, garlic, aged Monterey Jack or Asiago cheese, and a little fresh green chile. I also make a sage leaf pesto with hazelnuts to stir into hearty white bean soup (see Hazelnut-Sage Pesto, page 114).

$1/2$ pound small zucchini, sliced into half
 moons

$1/2$ pound ditalini, or short-cut penne

12 female zucchini blossoms, for garnish
 (optional)

Salt and freshly ground black pepper

$1/2$ cup grated Parmigiano-Reggiano

$1/2$ cup grated Pecorino Romano

HOT AND SOUR SOUP
WITH DUCK, PEA SHOOTS, AND TOFU

Just about every time I eat in a Chinese restaurant, I have to order hot and sour soup. Sometimes it is quite wonderful, with a hotness that makes my eyes tear and my nose run, but too often it is overly thickened with cornstarch. I just had to include a recipe for this soup, though it's not at all traditional. Here, inspired by a soup I tasted at Barbara Tropp's China Moon Restaurant in San Francisco, I've made a lighter version using her suggestion of duck breast instead of the traditional pork shreds. I also added tender fresh pea shoots, fresh shiitakes, and tofu.

Advance preparation recommended. Serves 6 to 8 •

1 recipe Rich Chicken Stock
  (see page 303)
½ pound boneless, skinless duck breast
1 tablespoon mushroom soy sauce
2 teaspoons ground Szechuan
  peppercorns (optional)
1 tablespoon saké, or dry sherry
1 teaspoon minced fresh ginger
1 teaspoon minced garlic
1 tablespoons finely chopped
  cilantro leaves
1 tablespoon cornstarch
¼ cup mushroom soy sauce
¼ cup rice wine
2 teaspoons roasted Japanese sesame oil
2 tablespoons cornstarch
½ pound shiitake mushrooms,
  stems removed and caps sliced
½ pound fresh "cotton" or firm tofu,
  drained on paper towels and
  cut into ½-inch cubes
1 bunch fresh pea shoots,
  washed and trimmed
1 bunch scallions, sliced into thin rings
¼ cup rice wine vinegar
2 teaspoons hot pepper flakes

1. Prepare the Rich Chicken Stock. Reserve.

2. Chill the duck meat in the freezer for 30 minutes, then cut into matchsticks. Reserve.

3. In a large bowl combine the 1 tablespoon mushroom soy sauce, peppercorns, 1 tablespoon saké, ginger, garlic, cilantro, and 1 tablespoon cornstarch; stir until mixed. Add the duck and toss to coat in the marinade. Cover and refrigerate for at least 2 hours or up to overnight.

4. Place the duck and marinade in a small pot and bring to a boil, stirring constantly, to lightly cook the duck. Drain the duck, discarding the liquid, and spread the meat out onto a plate to cool.

5. Combine the ¼ cup mushroom soy sauce, ¼ cup rice wine, sesame oil, and 2 tablespoons cornstarch in a small bowl and reserve.

Pea shoots, the very top tiny leaves and curly tendrils of snow pea vines, are a great delicacy in Chinese cooking and often the most expensive vegetable on the market. Add them to a soup just before serving, or as a last-minute addition to a vegetable stir-fry. They add a fresh, sweet, springtime flavor to dishes and make an outstanding garnish for any light dish. Companies that specialize in sprouts are now selling pea sprouts. These pea sprouts are less expensive than pea shoots, and though not as sweet and spring green—only the leaf portion is green—they make a good substitute. Use pea sprouts in salads and as a crunchy sandwich green instead of lettuce.

6. Place the Rich Chicken Stock in a soup pot and bring to a boil. Add the shiitake mushroom slices and the cooled duck meat, stirring to combine. Pour in the reserved cornstarch/soy mixture. Bring back to a boil, stirring occasionally so the cornstarch is evenly distributed. Just before serving, stir in the tofu, pea shoots, and scallions. Add the rice wine vinegar and red pepper flakes. Serve immediately in large soup bowls.

TUSCAN WINTER MINESTRONE

This Tuscan-style soup is a hearty but simple white bean and savoy cabbage minestrone flavored with pancetta. It is infused with the herb flavors of Italian parsley, thyme, rosemary, and basil. Savoy cabbage, called *la verza* in Italian, is a mild-flavored, tender cabbage with beautiful "savoyed" or curly dark and light green leaves. It has much less of the strong cabbagey aroma associated with common green or white cabbage, and balances well with the beans here. You can substitute a small green cabbage if you can't find the savoy, but it's really worth looking for. This soup is served without cheese in Tuscany, but because many Americans enjoy cheese in their soup and this minestrone has a hearty flavor and full body, I recommend serving it with shredded aged Provolone cheese, either domestic or imported.

Serves 6 •

1 cup dried cannellini beans, soaked (see Soaking Chart, page 41)

Salt

¹/₄ pound pancetta

2 carrots, trimmed and peeled

1 rib celery

3 cloves fresh garlic, peeled

1 large sprig fresh basil leaves

1 large sprig fresh rosemary leaves

¹/₂ cup extra-virgin olive oil (preferably Tuscan)

1 medium onion, thinly sliced

2 cups chopped plum tomatoes (fresh or canned)

1 small savoy cabbage, cored and shredded

1 tablespoon chopped fresh thyme

Salt and freshly ground black pepper

¹/₄ pound ditalini or other small tubular pasta

1 bunch fresh Italian parsley, chopped for garnish

¹/₄ pound shredded aged Provolone cheese, for serving (optional)

1. In a large pot, cover the beans with plenty of cold water and bring to a boil. Simmer until the beans are tender to the bite. In a food processor or blender, purée half the beans and strain through a food mill or sieve to remove the skin pieces. Stir the purée back into the whole beans and their cooking liquid and reserve.

2. Chop together (either by hand or in the food processor) the pancetta, carrots, celery, garlic, basil, and rosemary until it becomes a chunky paste. Place the mixture into a large, heavy Dutch oven and add the olive oil and onion. Cook over medium heat for several minutes, or until the aromas are released. Stir in the tomatoes, cabbage, thyme, and the cooked beans with their liquid. Bring to a boil, stirring occasionally, then season to taste with salt and pepper. (The soup can be covered and refrigerated for up to 2 days at this point before finishing with the pasta.)

3. When ready to serve the soup, bring it back to a boil, add the pasta and cook until the pasta is al dente, about 6 minutes. Garnish with the parsley. Serve immediately with the cheese.

SPRING GREEN PEA AND SNOW PEA SOUP

There's nothing quite like enjoying a lovely lunch at Takashimaya's stylish tea room in New York City to celebrate spring. Owned by the top Japanese department store chain, this store appeals to all the senses. As you walk in there is a fragrant flower shop filled with blossoming branches of Japanese cherry and irises, and pots of lacy white hydrangea blossoms. Downstairs is the tea emporium, filled with big boxes of fine loose teas and all the exquisite paraphernalia for tea preparation. The adjoining tea room serves light, exquisitely presented foods, including this delicate green spring soup I loved so much I had to adapt it for this book.

Serves 6 to 8

2 pounds fresh young green peas, shelled

1 pound snow peas

2 bunches scallions, sliced

4 cups Light Chicken Stock
  (see page 301)

¼ cup cornstarch

½ cup saké

1 (2-inch) length fresh ginger,
  peeled and grated

¼ cup light soy sauce

½ bunch fresh pea shoots, or pea pod
  sprouts, for garnish

½ bunch Chinese flat chives, thinly
  sliced (about ¼ cup), for garnish

1. In a stainless steel or enameled soup pot, place the peas, snow pea, scallions and Light Chicken Stock. Bring to a boil, reduce the heat and simmer for 15 to 20 minutes. Purée the mixture using a hand-held blender or by placing it in a blender in batches. Strain through a sieve or food mill.

2. Wash out the pot and place the strained soup mixture back into it. Bring to a boil. In a small bowl, combine the cornstarch, saké, ginger, and soy sauce. Slowly pour into the boiling soup while whisking constantly until well combined. Bring back to a boil, then remove from the heat. Divide the soup among serving bowls and sprinkle each bowl with pea shoots and chives.

CANNELLINI BEAN SOUP WITH HAZELNUT-SAGE PESTO

Pesto, which we usually think of as a basil sauce, is made of toasted hazelnuts and fresh sage in this creamy white bean soup recipe. Hazelnuts are so much more common in Europe than here, but I happen to adore their special taste. For the pesto, I combine the hazelnuts with a wonderful French hazelnut oil. Though more expensive even than walnut oil, it's worth trying. Store the oil in the refrigerator as nut oils quickly become rancid at room temperature.

Serves 8 •

1 pound (2 cups) dried cannellini beans,
    soaked (see Soaking Chart, page 41)
8 cups Light Chicken Stock
    (see page 301)
2 bay leaves
1 small whole dried hot red chile pepper
1/2 pound bacon, chopped in
    food processor
1 large onion, diced
2 leeks, white and light green parts only,
    sliced and washed
1/2 rib celery, sliced
Salt and freshly ground black pepper

HAZELNUT-SAGE PESTO
1/2 cup hazelnut or walnut oil
10 cloves fresh young garlic, peeled
1/4 pound hazelnuts, lightly toasted
    and skinned
1 large bunch fresh sage leaves
    (about 1 cup)
1/2 cup grated Parmigiano-Reggiano
1/2 cup grated Pecorino Romano

1. Prepare the Soup: Drain the soaked beans. Combine the beans, Light Chicken Stock, bay leaves, and hot pepper in a large pot. Bring to a boil, reduce the heat and simmer for 2 1/2 hours.

2. In another pot, cook the chopped bacon, onion, leeks, and celery until softened but not browned. Reserve. After the beans have cooked for 2 1/2 hours, add the bacon/onion mixture to them. Continue cooking for 30 minutes or until the beans are very soft.

3. Prepare the Hazelnut-Sage Pesto: Combine the hazelnut oil, garlic, and hazelnuts in a food processor and process to a paste. A handful at a time, add the sage leaves and process again until the mixture becomes a chunky green paste. Stir in the cheeses and reserve.

4. Purée the soup in a food processor or blender, then strain through a food mill to remove the bean skins. Season to taste with salt and black pepper. Divide the soup among soup bowls and top each with a dollop of pesto.

BROAD BEAN AND NASTURTIUM SOUP

This recipe is adapted from a dish served in season at the Souk Harbour House, a small but world-renowned thirteen-room inn on the west coast of Vancouver Island that has won countless awards. The menu changes daily and focuses on fresh local organic seafood, often caught right off their own shores, as well as meat and produce. Their herb and edible flower gardens have about 400 varieties of herbs, greens, vegetables, edible flowers, and trees that inspire their chefs' culinary creations. According to my friends who've visited there, the place is as dreamy as it sounds and the food is spectacular. Here nasturtium blossoms, a member of the watercress family, are used to add a special flavor and lovely color to a soup of fresh green fava beans.

Serves 6 to 8 •

6 tablespoons unsalted butter

1 medium onion, diced

4 cloves garlic, finely minced

¼ cup cider vinegar

½ cup dry white wine

2 pounds fresh fava beans, hulled,
   or ½ pound frozen green favas

4 cups Light Chicken Stock
   (see page 301)

Pinch of freshly grated nutmeg

Salt and freshly ground black pepper

1 cup heavy cream, whipped

12 to 16 nasturtium flowers and
   12 to 16 small nasturtium leaves,
   for garnish (optional)

1. Melt the butter in a large, heavy-bottomed soup pot. Cook the onions until translucent. Stir in the garlic and cook for about 30 seconds. Add the cider vinegar and white wine and bring to a boil. Cook until almost all the liquid has evaporated. Add the favas and Light Chicken Stock and bring to a boil. Season with nutmeg, and salt and pepper to taste. Reduce the heat and simmer for 3 to 5 minutes, or until the beans are tender. Stir in the whipped cream.

2. Purée the soup in a food processor or blender, and strain through a sieve to remove the bean skins. Garnish with the nasturtium flowers and leaves.

FRESH TOMATO SOUP WITH WHITE BEANS

Cookbook authors Linda and Fred Griffith tell me that their garden usually includes twenty varieties of heirloom tomatoes, so they have developed a large store of fresh tomato recipes including this soup. One usually expects a bean soup to be rather sturdy. However, this particular soup is very light and refreshing because of the special flavor it gets from fresh-from-the-garden tomatoes. Sweet onion and some garlic add other flavor nuances. Freeze this soup and you will enjoy the pleasure of garden-fresh flavors in the middle of winter.

Serves 12 •

1 pound (2 cups) dried great Northern beans, soaked (see Soaking Chart, page 41)

¼ cup olive oil

½ cup minced sweet onion

2 large cloves garlic, minced

6 pounds vine-ripened beefsteak tomatoes, coarsely chopped

1 rounded teaspoon sugar

1 tablespoon salt

¼ teaspoon freshly ground white pepper

8 cups (2 quarts) Light or Rich Light Chicken Stock (see page 301 or 303)

1 bouquet garni (2 sprigs Italian parsley, 2 sprigs thyme, 1 bay leaf, 1 whole clove, 1 tablespoon slightly crushed white peppercorns tied in a cheesecloth bag)

12 tablespoons shredded sharp Cheddar cheese

Minced fresh chives, for garnish

1. Drain the soaked beans. Reserve.

2. Heat the olive oil over low heat in a heavy-bottomed 3-quart pot. Add the onion and garlic. Cover and cook over very low heat until the onion becomes transparent, 5 to 8 minutes. Stir in the tomatoes. Cook, covered, for 20 minutes. Stir in the sugar, salt, and white pepper. Cook, uncovered, over low heat for 40 minutes.

3. While the tomatoes cook, place the drained beans and Light Chicken Stock in a 5-quart soup pot. Bring to a boil over medium heat. Reduce the heat; simmer for 40 minutes.

4. When the tomatoes have finished cooking, remove them from heat and let cool for 15 minutes. Purée the tomatoes in a food mill, discard the skins and seeds.

5. Add the tomato purée and bouquet garni to the bean mixture. Simmer, partially covered, for 2 hours, or until the beans are tender. (If the soup needs thickening, uncover completely, increase the heat, and simmer briskly for an additional 15 to 30 minutes.) Adjust seasonings to taste. Remove and discard the bouquet garni.

6. To serve, ladle into flat soup plates and garnish with the shredded cheese, chives, and additional freshly ground white pepper.

CRAB CHOWDER WITH LIMAS, GREEN BEANS, AND CORN

This lovely summer soup is fancy enough to serve for your next dinner party. For best results, place the corn, crab, and tomatoes in the bottom of each bowl and ladle the creamy broth over the top.

Serves 8 to 10 •

4 ears sweet white corn, husked

8 cups (2 quarts) milk

1 whole peeled onion,
   stuck with 3 to 4 whole cloves

2 teaspoons ground allspice

1 tablespoon whole coriander seed

3 bay leaves

1 pound Yukon or other golden
   potatoes, peeled and diced

1/4 pound bacon, cut into small strips

1 onion, diced

1/2 pound fresh green beans,
   cut into 1/4-inch slices

1 (12-ounce) package frozen baby limas,
   thawed and drained

3 tablespoons unbleached all-purpose
   flour

1 cup light cream

Salt and freshly ground black pepper

Freshly grated nutmeg

1 pound jumbo lump crabmeat,
   cartilage removed, for serving

1 pound ripe beefsteak tomatoes, peeled,
   seeded, and diced, for serving

1/4 cup chopped fresh chervil (1 bunch),
   for serving

1/4 cup chopped fresh thyme leaves
   (1 bunch), for serving

Pinch cayenne

1. Cut the corn kernels off the cobs. Reserve. Place the cobs in a large soup pot with the milk, onion, allspice, coriander seeds, and bay leaves. Bring to a boil. Reduce the heat and simmer for about 30 minutes, stirring occasionally to prevent the milk from scorching. Strain through a sieve, reserving the aromatic milk and discarding the solids.

2. Return the milk to the pot and add the potatoes. Simmer over medium heat until the potatoes are tender when pierced with a fork, about 15 minutes. Reserve.

3. In a medium pan, cook the bacon until crisp. Transfer the bacon to a paper towel, reserving the bacon drippings. Sauté the onion in the bacon drippings until transparent. Add the green beans and limas. Stir in the flour and cook together for 3 minutes, continuing to stir until thickened.

4. Transfer the beans to the potato mixture and bring to a boil. Add the cream and remove the soup from the heat. (If you want to serve the soup the next day, cool the soup quickly by placing the pot in an ice water bath, then remove and refrigerate. The next day, slowly heat the soup, just until it boils.)

5. When ready to serve, season the soup broth to taste with salt, black pepper, and nutmeg. Divide the reserved corn, crabmeat, and diced tomato among the individual soup bowls. Ladle the soup into the bowls. Sprinkle each portion with the remaining herbs, cayenne, and the reserved bacon bits. Serve immediately.

VELOUTÉ OF WHITE COCO BEANS
AND BLACK TRUFFLES

This marvelous soup is served at Le Bec-Fin, the world-class restaurant run by Philadelphia's magnificent chef, Georges Perrier. Inspired by an unforgettable meal he enjoyed at Joël Robuchon's former restaurant in Paris, he recreated the dish for his own menu using fresh truffles. In this version of the soup, I have substituted less expensive and more accessible black truffle paste from France. For best results, use small white beans such as the French coco or American navy beans.

Serves 8 •

1$\frac{1}{2}$ cups dried small white beans, preferably white coco beans, soaked (see Soaking Chart, page 41)

16 cups (4 quarts) Rich Chicken Stock (see page 303)

1 smoked ham hock

4 bay leaves

2 tablespoons chopped fresh thyme leaves (about $\frac{1}{2}$ bunch)

3 leeks, white part only, sliced

$\frac{1}{2}$ pound bacon, diced

1 white onion, diced

3 ribs celery, sliced

2 teaspoons chopped garlic

2 cups heavy cream

Sea salt and finely ground white pepper

1 (3.5-ounce) jar black truffle paste

1 bunch fresh chives, finely chopped, for garnish

1. Prepare the Rich Chicken Stock. Reserve.

2. Drain the soaked beans. Combine the beans, ham hock, stock, bay leaves, and thyme in a large soup pot. Bring to a boil. Reduce the heat, cover, and simmer for 1$\frac{1}{2}$ hours.

3. Soak the leek slices in a large bowl of cold water, swishing around several times to release any sand. Skim the leeks off the surface of the water and drain, leaving any sand at the bottom of the bowl. Cook the bacon in a medium skillet until lightly browned. Add the leeks, onion, celery, and garlic and cook for 10 minutes or until softened but not browned.

4. After cooking the beans for 1$\frac{1}{2}$ hours, scrape the leek mixture into the soup. Simmer for 30 minutes or until the beans are soft but not mushy. Remove and discard the ham hock and bay leaves.

5. Using a hand-held blender (or working in small batches in a blender), purée the soup. Strain through a fine sieve or food mill. Return to the pot. Stir in the heavy cream. Bring the soup to a simmer and season to taste with salt and white pepper. Reserve until ready to serve.

6. Reheat the soup if necessary, stirring constantly, then ladle into 8 heated soup plates. Spoon a generous teaspoonful of black truffle paste into the center of each bowl. Sprinkle with the chives and serve immediately.

HEARTY WINTER MINESTRONE WITH GREEN AND WHITE BEANS

Minestrone can be varied infinitely according to region and season. Here I use pearl barley and cannellini beans to thicken and fortify the soup. I like using the barley because it doesn't get mushy like pasta when cooked in soup. This soup is even better reheated the next day and it makes a wonderful meal in a bowl, sprinkled with shredded aged Provolone. Serve with Crostini (see page 53), if desired.

Serves 8 •

1 cup dried cannellini or cranberry beans,
   cooked and drained (see Basic Cooking
   Chart, page 43), or 3 cups canned
   cannellini beans, rinsed and drained
1 large onion, diced
3 leeks, white and light green parts only,
   sliced and washed
$^{1}/_{2}$ pound carrots, diced
1 celery root, pared and diced
2 tablespoons chopped garlic
$^{1}/_{2}$ pound prosciutto, rind cut off,
   chopped in food processor or ground
8 cups (2 quarts) Light Chicken Stock
   (see page 000)
1 (28-ounce) can chopped plum
   tomatoes, or 1 (25-ounce) box POMI
   brand Italian chopped tomatoes
1 cup medium pearl barley
$^{1}/_{2}$ pound fresh green beans,
   cut into 1-inch lengths
1 head savoy cabbage, shredded
$^{1}/_{2}$ cup chopped Italian parsley leaves
   (about $^{1}/_{2}$ bunch)
Salt and freshly ground black pepper
   to taste
$^{1}/_{4}$ pound grated aged Provolone cheese
   (about 1 cup)

1. Prepare the cannellini beans. Reserve.

2. In a large soup pot, cook the onion, leeks, carrots, celery root, garlic, and prosciutto until softened but not browned. Add the Light Chicken Stock and tomatoes and bring to a boil. Add the barley and simmer until half-tender, about 20 minutes, stirring occasionally.

3. Add the cannellini beans, green beans, and cabbage. Return to a boil and simmer about 20 minutes, or until the vegetables are tender. Stir in the parsley and season to taste with salt and black pepper. Serve with a bowl of grated aged Provolone for each person to sprinkle onto the soup.

MOROCCAN GOLDEN SPLIT PEA AND PUMPKIN SOUP

There is a rich culinary tradition among many Moroccan Jews, who at one time made up fully ten percent of the population. Each city in Morocco has its own special dishes. In Marrakesh, Jews typically served this symbolically golden soup on the first night of Rosh Hashanah, the Jewish New Year. The use of precious saffron and other spices shows that the dish was hardly for everyday. This soup is also made with chickpeas so you could substitute the split golden chickpeas, called *channa dal*, if you are fortunate enough to find these little beauties.

Serves 8 to 10 •

1 recipe Rich Chicken Stock (page 303)
4 cups (1 quart) cold water
1 pound (2 cups) dried yellow split peas
3 bay leaves
½ cup olive oil
2 large onions, chopped
1 tablespoon ground cinnamon
1 tablespoon ground ginger
2 large pinches saffron threads, crumbled
2 pounds peeled and diced red pumpkin, butternut squash, or calabaza
Salt and freshly ground black pepper

1. Prepare the Rich Chicken Stock.

2. In a large soup pot, combine the stock, water, yellow split peas, and bay leaves and bring to a boil. Skim off and discard any white foam that forms on the surface. Reduce the heat and simmer for about 1 hour or until the split peas become tender.

3. In a separate pan, heat the olive oil over a medium heat. Add the onions, cinnamon, ginger, and saffron. Cook until the onions are softened but not browned. Add this mixture to the soup along with the pumpkin cubes. Simmer for 30 minutes longer or until the pumpkin is quite soft. Remove and discard the bay leaves. Season to taste with salt and pepper and serve.

❧ ❧ ❧ ABOUT FRENCH RED PUMPKINS ❧ ❧ ❧

The firm, red-fleshed pumpkin called for in this recipe is similar to the French *potiron rouge*. Grown in the United States by a few specialty growers, it is sometimes known as a Cinderella pumpkin and has a flattened shape and strikingly beautiful brick red skin. A favorite of chefs in nineteenth-century Paris, this pumpkin is considered especially good for soup because of its mild flavor and pleasing color. The closest easily available substitute is butternut squash, some times sold already peeled and cut into chunks in the supermarket produce section. Calabaza, a squash that is greenish on the outside and orange on the inside, is also a good substitute. Our Jack-o'-Lantern pumpkins are too stringy to use here.

CREAMY LENTIL SOUP
WITH CELERY ROOT

This simple soup, which I developed for the Omni Hotel at Independence Park in Philadelphia when it first opened, is a regional Pennsylvania (Eastern Heartland or Mid-Atlantic) specialty that combines homely brown lentils with the sweet, earthy taste of celery root. Substitute smoked turkey legs if you don't want to use the ham hocks.

Serves 8 •

2 smoked ham hocks

16 cups (4 quarts) cold water

4 bay leaves

1/4 cup chopped fresh thyme leaves
   (about 1 bunch)

2 teaspoons whole peppercorns

1 pound (2 cups) dried brown lentils

1 pound celery root, peeled and finely
   diced

1/2 cup chopped fresh sage leaves
   (about 1 bunch)

2 tablespoons chopped garlic

2 teaspoons ground coriander

1/2 teaspoon cayenne

1/4 cup unsalted butter

Salt

1. In a large pot, combine the ham hocks, water, bay leaves, thyme, and peppercorns. Bring to a boil, reduce the heat, and simmer for 2 hours. Add the lentils and cook for 1 hour, or until the lentils are very soft. Remove the ham hocks and, if desired, pick the meat from the bones when cool enough to handle. Reserve the meat and discard the bone. Remove and discard the bay leaves.

2. Let the soup cool slightly, then purée in a blender (or with a hand-held blender) and strain through a sieve or food mill. Stir in the reserved meat and return to the same pot.

3. In a medium pan, cook the celery root, sage, garlic, coriander, and cayenne in the butter until softened but not browned. Add the vegetable mixture to the puréed lentils and simmer for 10 minutes or until the celery root is tender when pierced with a fork. Season to taste with salt. Serve in soup plates.

CUBAN BLACK BEAN SOUP
WITH SOFRITO AND SMOKED TURKEY

Cuban cookery often includes a flavorful *sofrito*, aromatic vegetables slowly cooked in annatto oil. Annatto or achiote is an extremely hard red seed used for its beautiful deep red color and delicate flavor. I make this soup with smoked turkey legs instead of the traditional, higher-fat smoked ham hocks. A piping hot bowl of this smoky dark soup followed by a green salad and a loaf of whole-grain bread makes a delicious, filling meal. Black turtle beans are very popular for soup because they make an exceptionally smooth purée.

Serves 8 to 10 •

1 pound (2 cups) dried black turtle beans, soaked (see Soaking Chart, page 41)

1 onion, peeled and stuck with 8 whole cloves

3 bay leaves

1 pound smoked turkey legs

4 cups (1 quart) Light Chicken Stock (see page 301)

4 cups (1 quart) cold water

1 large white onion, diced

1 tablespoon chopped garlic

1 tablespoon ground toasted cumin seeds, (see Toasting Seeds, page 217)

2 tablespoons annatto oil, or peanut oil plus 1 tablespoon paprika

1 (15-ounce) can plum tomatoes, chopped

2 tablespoons malt or sherry vinegar

Salt and freshly ground black pepper

1. Drain and rinse the soaked black turtle beans. In a large soup pot, add the beans and enough water to cover. Bring the water to a boil, reduce the heat, and simmer for 5 minutes. Drain the beans, discarding the water.

2. Place the beans back in the pot along with the whole onion, bay leaves, and turkey legs. Cover with the Light Chicken Stock and 16 cups cold water. Bring to a boil, skim off any white foam impurities that rise to the surface and reduce the heat to a simmer. Cook very slowly until the beans are quite soft, about 2 hours. (Alternatively, cook the beans in a pressure cooker for 25 minutes, starting the timer after the steam has built up pressure in the pot.) Remove the onion and bay leaves and discard. Remove the turkey legs, and when cool enough to handle, dice the meat and reserve.

3. Purée three-fourths of the beans, along with their liquid, in a blender or a food processor. Leave the remaining beans whole. To make the soup easier to digest, strain the bean purée through a sieve or food mill to remove the skins. Return to the pot with the whole beans.

4. In a skillet, sauté the diced onion, garlic, reserved diced turkey meat, and cumin in the oil until softened. Add the tomatoes and vinegar. Add the sautéed vegetable mixture to beans. Bring the soup back to a boil and season to taste with salt and pepper.

DINER-STYLE SPLIT PEA SOUP

Every old-fashioned diner should serve a rib-sticking split pea soup (where a spoon inserted in the middle of a bowl can stand upright). This version has a unique depth of flavor because of the three aromatic resinous herbs used in the soup: savory, thyme, and sage. For a mouth-pleasing contrast of texture, serve the soup topped with some garlic croutons. This soup freezes and reheats so well, why not make a big batch and have it ready for a cold drizzly day or unexpected company?

Serves 10 to 12 •

1 pound (2 cups) green split peas

1 pound smoked ham hocks

4 quarts (1 gallon) water

3 leeks, sliced and washed

2 large onions, diced

$^1/_4$ cup bacon fat or chicken fat,
    or unsalted butter

1 tablespoon chopped garlic

2 tablespoons chopped fresh summer or
    winter savory leaves (about $^1/_4$ bunch),
    or $1^1/_2$ teaspoons dried

2 tablespoons chopped fresh thyme leaves
    (about $^1/_2$ bunch), or 2 teaspoons dried

$^1/_4$ cup chopped fresh sage, (about $^1/_2$
    bunch), or 1 tablespoon dried

3 cups Light Chicken Stock
    (see page 301)

Salt, freshly ground black pepper,
    and cayenne

1. Bring the split peas, ham hocks, and water to a boil in a large pot. Cover and reduce the heat and simmer for 2 hours or until split peas are soft. Remove the ham hocks and pick the meat from the bones when cool enough to handle, and discard the bones. Place the meat back in the pot.

2. Cook the leeks and onions in bacon fat until softened. Add the garlic, savory, thyme, and sage and cook for 5 minutes longer. Add the vegetable mixture to the peas. Add the Light Chicken Stock and return to a boil. Season to taste with salt, black pepper, and cayenne.

ABOUT PEA AND PEASE
❧ ❧ ❧

"Pease" was the old English name for the pea and is actually a singular, not plural, form. In what must be the ancestor of split pea soup, the English staple back then was a rib-sticking thick pease soup. Its enduring importance is shown in the nursery rhyme: "Pease porridge hot, pease porridge cold, pease porridge in my pot, nine days old." The word "pea" itself is a very old term, and the Greek, Italian, old Irish, French, and English share variations on the same word.

EGYPTIAN FAVA BEAN SOUP
(Ful Medames)

The national dish of Egypt, *Ful Medames*, is so basic to the Egyptian diet that it is more than a dish, it's a way of life. In Egypt, small brown fava beans, called *ful*, are cooked in a special pot that tapers to a narrow neck. As the steam from the cooking beans condenses on the sloping sides, it drops back into the pot keeping all the flavorful juices in the beans. It is yet another member of the family of narrow-necked, usually earthenware, bean pots, including the Italian *fiasco*, the Spanish and Mexican *olla*, and the good old American Boston bean pot.

Serves 6 •

1½ pounds dried brown fava beans,
   soaked (see Soaking Chart, page 41)
16 cups (4 quarts) water
3 cloves garlic, finely chopped
2 tablespoons extra-virgin olive oil
¼ cup fresh lemon juice (about 2 lemons)
1 tablespoon salt
½ teaspoon freshly ground
   black pepper
4 hard-cooked eggs, sliced for garnish
   (see Hard-Cooking Eggs, page 159)
2 tablespoons finely chopped Italian
   parsley leaves, for garnish

1. Preheat the oven to 300°F. Drain the fava beans, place in a heavy ovenproof Dutch oven, and cover with the cold water. Bring to a boil on top of the stove, then cover and place in the oven. Bake for 3 to 4 hours, or until the beans are soft but still mostly whole. Remove from the oven.

2. Stir in the garlic, olive oil, lemon juice, salt, and pepper. Ladle into 6 large soup bowls, garnish with the sliced eggs and sprinkle with the parsley.

IRISH BEAN AND SMOKY BACON SOUP

On a long ago trip hitchhiking, camping, and hosteling throughout Ireland, I learned to love this emerald-green country and its warm people. I ate inexpensive, filling soups very much like this one on that trip. Years later Jack Downey, the owner of Philadelphia's best known pub at the corner of Front and South Streets, Downey's, asked me to help develop recipes for his high-end canned soups under the Downey's name. This Irish Bean and Smoky Bacon Soup sold quite well—but not quite as well as his star soup, Lobster Bisque.

Serves 8 •

1 pound (2 cups) dried navy beans

4 bay leaves

1 large white onion, peeled and left whole

4 sprigs fresh thyme

4 tablespoons chopped fresh sage leaves

8 cups (2 quarts) Light Chicken Stock
   (see page 301)

1/4 pound smoky bacon, cut into strips

1 large white onion, diced

1/2 pound good-quality ham,
   cut into small dice

2 leeks, cleaned well and diced
   into 1/2-inch pieces

2 cloves garlic, chopped

2 cups light cream

Salt and freshly ground black pepper

1. Place the beans in a large pot, cover with cold water, and bring to a boil. Simmer for 5 minutes, then drain.

2. Return the bean to the pot, add the bay leaves, whole onion, thyme, 2 tablespoons of the sage, and the Light Chicken Stock, and bring to a boil. Cover, reduce heat and simmer until tender, about 1½ hours. Remove and discard the whole onion, thyme sprigs, and bay leaves. Purée half of the beans in a blender or food processor, leaving the remaining beans whole. Strain the purée through a food mill, if desired, and return to the pot.

3. Cook the bacon in a pan until lightly browned. Add the diced onion, ham, leeks, garlic, and the remaining 2 tablespoons sage. Cook for 3 minutes, or until softened but not browned.

4. Add the cooked mixture to the beans and bring to a boil. Stir in the cream and return to a boil. Season to taste with salt and pepper. Serve immediately.

MULLIGATAWNY SOUP
WITH CHICKEN, RICE, AND LIME

My trusty *Oxford Diner's Dictionary* tells me that employees of the great East India Company originally brought this soup to England. The soup as it has evolved in England bears little resemblance to its aromatic south Indian original. The name comes from a Tamil word *milakutanni*, which means "pepper water." I admit that I've taken liberty in naming this soup "mulligatawny." I just loved the name and when I wanted to entice customers to order this delicious, hot and spicy red lentil soup with chicken, I called it mulligatawny.

Serves 8 •

1 recipe Light Chicken Stock
  (see page 301)
2 pounds skinless chicken thighs
2 medium onions, diced
1/2 cup chopped fresh ginger
1/2 cup chopped garlic
2 jalapeño peppers, seeded and chopped
6 tablespoons unsalted butter
3 tablespoons ground toasted cumin
  seeds (see Toasting Seeds, page 217)
3 tablespoons ground toasted coriander
  seeds (see Toasting Seeds, page 217)
2 tablespoons turmeric
2 tablespoons whole black mustard seeds
1 pound (2 cups) split red lentils
Salt
Juice of 3 limes
3 cups cooked basmati rice, for serving
2 tablespoons nigella seeds, for garnish

1. In a large soup pot, bring the Light Chicken Stock to a boil. Add the chicken thighs, and return to a boil. Reduce the heat, cover, and poach the chicken for 20 minutes, or until the large bone jiggles freely in its joint. Remove the thighs from the stock. When cool enough to handle, remove the meat from the bones. Shred the meat, being careful to remove and discard any fat and connective tissue. Cover the chicken meat and refrigerate until ready to use.

2. In a medium pan, cook the onions, ginger, garlic, and jalapeños in the butter until softened. Add the cumin, coriander, turmeric, and mustard seeds, and cook for 5 minutes. Add the mixture into the soup pot with the lentils. Bring to a boil. Reduce the heat and simmer for 1 hour, or until the lentils are soft.

3. Cool the soup slightly, then purée using a food processor or blender and season to taste with salt. When ready to serve, stir in the lime juice, cooked rice, and reserved chicken meat. Sprinkle each portion with nigella seeds and serve piping hot.

ABOUT NIGELLA SEEDS

THE ANGULAR BLACK SEEDS, CALLED VARIOUSLY *nigella, kalonji,* OR *charnushka,* USED AS A GARNISH IN THIS RECIPE HAVE A DISTINCTIVE AROMA AND MILD FLAVOR, ACRID AND NUTTY AT THE SAME TIME, A BIT LIKE A PUNGENT POPPY SEED. IRRESISTIBLE TO ME, THEY ARE THE SEED OF CHOICE ON THE RUSSIAN-STYLE BLACK AND RYE BREADS BAKED IN NEW YORK CITY, WHERE THEY ARE CALLED *charnushka.* THE SAME SEED IS ALSO MIXED WITH BREAD DOUGH TO MAKE AN ADDICTIVELY DELICIOUS INDIAN NAN BREAD AND IS OFTEN COMBINED WITH LEGUMES AS IN THE NIGELLA-STUDDED LENTIL PAPPADUM WAFERS. THERE ARE TWO COMMON NAMES FOR THIS SEED THAT IS USED EXTENSIVELY IN INDIA TO FLAVOR LEGUMES. IN THE NORTH IT IS KNOWN AS *kala jeera* (ALSO THE NAME FOR BLACK CUMIN, A TOTALLY DIFFERENT PLANT); ELSEWHERE IN INDIA, IT IS CALLED *kalonji.*

PASTA AND BEANS *(Pasta e Fagioli)* FROM THE VILLA CIPRIANI

When I turned 45, I promised myself a birthday present: a trip to France and Italy with my daughter, Ginevra, who was then eight years old. One of the high points was a day trip to the beautiful artist's colony of Asolo in the foothills of the Italian Dolomites. The Cipriani family runs a lovely country inn along one of the narrow steep stony streets of the town. We enjoyed a totally sybaritic lunch in the dining room with its spectacular view of the countryside on the plains below. After demolishing my bowl of *Pasta e Fagioli*, I asked our gracious waiter if I might have the recipe. Perhaps because my daughter was charming him, he introduced me to their chef, Secondo Ceccato, who gladly dictated his recipe to me as I scrawled it onto a scrap of paper. He wouldn't let me leave without a bagful of *fagioli di lamon belluno*, the special beans he uses in this unctuous soup.

Serves 8 •

1 pound (2 cups) dried cranberry beans, soaked (see Soaking Chart, page 41)

1/2 pound ditalini pasta

1 (6-ounce) piece pancetta

1 (6-ounce) piece cotenna (the skin of a prosciutto), or pork rind

2 cloves garlic, peeled

16 cups (4 quarts) cold water

2 tablespoons beef concentrate (such as Marmite or Knorr brands) or fresh beef drippings

6 ounces grated Parmigiano-Reggiano

Sea salt and freshly ground black pepper

1/2 cup extra-virgin olive oil, for garnish

1. Drain the soaked cranberry beans. Reserve.

2. Bring a pot of salted water to a boil. Add the pasta and cook for 3 minutes. Drain and rinse well under cold running water. Reserve.

3. In a large pot, combine the beans, pancetta, cotenna, garlic, and water. Bring to a boil, skim off any white foam, and reduce the heat. Cover and cook very slowly for 4 hours. Remove from the heat; discard the pancetta and cotenna.

4. Purée half of the soup in a blender or food processor, and then pass through a food mill to remove the bean skins. Combine the purée with the remaining beans. Stir in the beef concentrate and cheese. Season to taste with salt and pepper.

5. Just before serving, reheat the soup and add the reserved pasta. Serve in wide shallow bowls and, at the table, drizzle each serving with about 1 tablespoon of extra-virgin olive oil.

QUEEN VICTORIA'S FAVORITE GREEN PEA SOUP WITH BUTTERED CROUTONS

This recipe for green pea soup, flavored with mint and scallions and enriched with butter, is adapted from Lafcadio Hearn's cookbook. His name alone is enough to inspire thoughts of romance and exotic locales. Hearn was a journalist, restaurateur, cartoonist, and novelist in New Orleans in the 1880s and later traveled to Japan. His cookbook *La Cuisine Creole: A Collection of Culinary Recipes* was published in 1885. Now considered a classic, the book is filled with recipes Hearn had collected from the many New Orleans homes he visited.

Serves 8 to 10 •

BUTTERED CROUTONS

1 (1-pound) loaf of dense white
  sandwich bread, sliced
1/4 pound (1 stick) unsalted butter,
  melted

SOUP

1 recipe Rich Chicken Stock
  (see page 303)
3 (12-ounce) packages frozen green peas,
  thawed under cold running water
1/2 cup (about 1 bunch) Italian parsley
  leaves, coarsely chopped
1/2 cup (about 1 bunch) fresh mint
3 bunches scallions, sliced
2 tablespoons cornstarch
1/4 cup water
1/2 pound (2 sticks) unsalted butter,
  cut up
2 tablespoons sugar
Salt and freshly ground black pepper
Freshly grated nutmeg

1. Prepare the Buttered Croutons: Preheat the oven to 300°F. Cut the crusts from the bread slices and discard. Cut the bread slices into small cubes. Toss with the melted butter and spread out onto a shallow baking pan. Bake for 15 minutes. Stir and bake again for 10 minutes longer, or until the croutons are golden brown. Reserve.

2. Prepare the Soup: Prepare the Rick Chicken Stock.

3. In a large soup pot, bring the stock to a boil. Add the thawed peas, parsley, mint, and scallions and return to a boil. Reduce the heat to low. Combine the cornstarch and the water. Add to the soup and simmer for 5 minutes, stirring occasionally, until thickened.

4. Using a hand-held or traditional blender, purée the soup until smooth. Strain through a sieve or food mill to remove the pea skins and then transfer back to the pot. Stir in the butter one piece at a time, and sugar, heating until the butter is melted. Season to taste with salt, black pepper, and nutmeg. Serve each portion of soup topped with a small handful of the Buttered Croutons.

SEA ISLES BLACK BEAN PURÉE WITH DRY MADEIRA, LEMON, AND EGG MIMOSA

South Carolina's Sea Isles (Pat Conroy territory, author of *The Water Is Wide*) is home to a very special culture, that of Gulla-speaking African-Americans who have lived in these rather isolated islands for centuries. The cuisine is special there too for featuring shad, mullet, porgy, oysters, and shrimp, as well as all kinds of rice dishes. Here is a subtly flavored version of black bean soup, laced with Madeira, the fortified wine made in the Portuguese island of Madeira and imported into our coastal cities since precolonial times. The chopped egg mimosa, which enriches the soup, is named for its resemblance to the small rounded yellow blossoms of the mimosa tree.

Serves 6 to 8

1 pound (2 cups) dried black turtle beans, soaked (see Soaking Chart, page 41)

2 smoked ham hocks

8 cups (2 quarts) Light Chicken Stock (see page 301)

2 bay leaves

2 large yellow onions, coarsely chopped

½ pound carrots, peeled and chopped

3 to 4 ribs celery, sliced

1 tablespoon chopped garlic

¼ cup unsalted butter

2 tablespoons cider vinegar

½ cup dry Madeira

Grated zest of 1 lemon

2 tablespoons fresh lemon juice (about 1 lemon)

1 teaspoon ground mace or nutmeg

Salt and freshly ground black pepper

1 lemon, sliced into thin rings, for garnish

2 hard-cooked eggs (see Hard-Cooking Eggs, page 159), chopped, for garnish

2 tablespoons chopped Italian parsley leaves, for garnish

1. Drain and rinse the soaked black turtle beans. In a large soup pot, place the beans, ham hocks, Light Chicken Stock, and bay leaves. Bring to a boil and skim off any white foam impurities that rise to the surface. Reduce the heat and simmer for 2 hours.

2. In a separate pan, cook the onions, carrots, celery, and garlic in the butter over medium heat until softened but not browned. Transfer the mixture to the soup pot and continue simmering until the beans are soft enough to be easily mashed with a fork against the side of the pot, about 30 minutes. Remove and discard the bay leaves and ham hocks.

3. In a blender or food processor, purée the soup. Strain through a food mill or sieve to remove any bean skins. Return the purée to the soup pot and stir in the vinegar, Madeira, lemon zest, lemon juice, and mace. Season to taste with salt and pepper, then pour into individual bowls. Garnish each portion with a lemon slice, chopped egg, and parsley.

DUTCH GREEN SPLIT PEA SOUP
(Erwtensoep)

I spent a year living in Holland as a young child and even learned to speak good Dutch back then. I don't remember much about that time, though I have a clear recollection of gorging myself on rich butter cookies. I ate so many that I couldn't stand the smell of butter cookies for years afterward. Holland has a simple, hearty cuisine with dishes like apple *pannekoecken* (thick apple pancakes), herring in all forms (including their delicacy of raw, live herring eaten whole), tasty aged Gouda and Edam cheeses, and this soup. Perfect for a cold, rainy day, make a meal of it with buttered whole-grain bread, sliced aged Gouda, and a good Dutch apple cake for dessert.

Serves 8 •

2 ham hocks

1/2 pound piece salt pork, rinsed (optional)

16 cups (4 quarts) water

1 pound (2 cups) green split peas

1 pound potatoes (gold varieties, russets, or all-purpose), peeled and cut into small dice

1 bunch leeks (white and light green parts only), sliced and washed

1 celery root, pared and cut into small dice

Heart of 1 stalk celery (including the leaves), cut into thin slices

1 tablespoon chopped fresh summer savory, or 1 teaspoon dried

1/2 pound cooked smoked sausage (such as kielbasa), sliced into rounds

Salt and freshly ground black pepper

1. Place ham hocks, salt pork, and water in a large soup pot and bring to a boil. Skim off and discard any white foam impurities that rise to the surface. Reduce the heat and simmer, covered, for 1 hour. Add the green split peas and return to a boil. Reduce the heat and simmer for 2 hours. Remove the salt pork and ham hocks; reserve until cool.

2. Add the potatoes, leeks, celery root, celery heart, and savory. Simmer for 30 minutes longer. Cut the salt pork into small dice and remove the meat from the cooled ham hock. Add the salt pork, ham hock meat, and sausage to the pot and season to taste with salt and black pepper. Simmer for 5 to 10 minutes to thoroughly heat the meat. Serve the soup in large bowls.

In upper New England, a French-Canadian person is often referred to as a "pea soup."

GREEK LENTIL SOUP

This lentil soup is called *faki* in Greek. It is a popular dish during the Lenten season when meat is not eaten. To be strictly vegetarian, use a vegetable stock instead of the chicken stock. Soups similar to this have been part of the Greek diet since the Golden Age of Greece. Imported Greek oregano, sold dried on the branch, is highly resinous and full of a powerful aroma obtained by plants that have struggled to grow in rocky soil under the rays of a blazing sun. Like wine grapes, the more struggle, the more flavor.

Serves 6 to 8 •

1 pound (2 cups) dried brown lentils

8 cups (2 quarts) Light Chicken Stock (see page 301)

2 cups chopped onions

1 cup diced carrots

1 cup sliced celery

1 tablespoon chopped garlic

$^1/_2$ cup tomato sauce (purchased or homemade)

$^1/_2$ cup extra-virgin olive oil

1 tablespoon crumbled oregano (preferably Greek)

Salt and freshly ground black pepper

$^1/_4$ cup red wine vinegar or fresh lemon juice (2 lemons)

1. Place the lentils in a soup pot with the Light Chicken Stock and bring to a boil. Reduce the heat and simmer for 1 hour.

2. Add the onions, carrots, celery, garlic, tomato sauce, olive oil, oregano, and salt and pepper to taste. Continue cooking for 30 minutes, or until the lentils are tender and the soup is slightly thickened.

3. Just before serving, stir in the vinegar. Divide among soup bowls.

LENTIL SOUP WITH HOT DOGS

Growing up in a kosher home, my mother often used garlicky kosher hot dogs in dishes like this lentil soup. It's easy to make and a real kid-pleaser. This soup freezes extremely well, so serve half and freeze the other half for a quick cold-weather meal. While it's not necessary to use kosher hot dogs, I happen to believe their quality is outstanding because by law only beef muscle meat can be used. They are also more highly flavored with garlic than standard dogs.

Serves 6 •

8 cups (1 recipe) Rich Chicken Stock
   (see page 303)

$^1/_4$ cup vegetable oil

1 large onion, diced

2 carrots, diced

2 leeks, sliced and washed

2 ribs celery, sliced

2 teaspoons chopped fresh thyme leaves,
   or 1 teaspoon dried

1 teaspoon chopped fresh sage leaves,
   or $^1/_2$ teaspoon dried

1 pound (2 cups) dried brown lentils

1 pound kosher high-quality hot dogs,
   cut into $^1/_2$-inch slices

Salt and freshly ground black pepper

1. Prepare the Rich Chicken Stock. Reserve.

2. Heat the oil and add the onion and carrots. Sauté until well browned, stirring often, and then add the leeks, celery, thyme, and sage. Cook for about 5 minutes, stirring often, until softened but not browned.

3. Add the Rich Chicken Stock and lentils and bring to a boil. Reduce the heat to very low and simmer for $^1/_2$ hour. Add the hot dog slices and continue cooking until the lentils are quite soft. Season to taste with salt and pepper.

SOUTH INDIAN VEGETARIAN RED LENTIL SOUP

This is an easy-to-make vegetarian soup of quick-cooking split red lentils. You could also substitute split yellow mung beans, split yellow chickpeas, or yellow split peas. The key to many Indian dishes is the warm, nutty flavor of popped black mustard seeds. They pop just like popcorn, so you'll need to use a pot with a lid when making them.

Serves 6 •

6 cups (1½ quarts) Vegetable Stock (see page 304)

2 tablespoons vegetable oil

2 tablespoons whole black mustard seeds

1 large white onion

¼ cup chopped fresh ginger

1 tablespoon chopped garlic

2 jalapeno peppers, seeded and finely chopped

¼ cup ghee (see Making Ghee, page 61) melted butter

2 tablespoons Madras-type curry powder

1 pound (2 cups) red lentils

1 teaspoon salt

¼ teaspoon freshly ground black pepper

2 tablespoons freshly squeezed lime juice (about the juice of 1 lime)

¼ cup chopped fresh cilantro

1 cup plain yogurt

1. Prepare the Vegetable Stock. Reserve.

2. In a small pot with a lid, heat the vegetable oil with the black mustard seeds. Be sure to cover the pot, or the seeds will start popping out of it. Cook for about 4 minutes, or until the popping sound stops. Reserve.

3. In a soup pot, cook the onion, ginger, garlic, and jalapeno in the ghee or butter. Add the curry powder and cook for 2 minutes longer. Stir in the lentils, stock, salt, and black pepper. Bring to a boil, reduce the heat, and simmer until soft, about 1 hour, stirring occasionally. Using a potato masher, partially mash the lentils to thicken the soup.

4. Just before serving stir in the mustard seeds with their cooking oil, the lime juice, and cilantro. Garnish each serving with a dollop of yogurt and sprinkle with cilantro.

❧ ❧ ❧ REHEATING THICK SOUPS ❧ ❧ ❧

Most thick soup will thicken even more when refrigerated overnight. When reheating, cover the bottom of the pot with ½ inch water and bring to a boil. Then add the cold soup. Reduce the heat to low and bring back to a boil, stirring often to prevent burning and heat thoroughly.

SPANISH CHICKPEA SOUP
WITH GARLIC-MINT PESTO

This simple Spanish peasant soup is an example of how a few inexpensive ingredients can be transformed into a hearty and satisfying meal. The use of chickpeas here shows the Arabic origin of the soup.

Serves 8 •

4 cups dried chickpeas, cooked and
   drained (see Basic Cooking Chart,
   page 43)
1 recipe Rich Chicken Stock
   (see page 303)
3/4 cup extra-virgin olive oil
1/2 loaf country-style white bread
   (about 1/2 pound), crust trimmed,
   cut into small squares
2 tablespoons chopped garlic
2 teaspoons salt
1/2 cup chopped Italian parsley leaves
1/2 cup chopped fresh mint leaves,
   or 2 tablespoons dried

1. Prepare the chickpeas and Rich Chicken Stock. Reserve.

2. Preheat the oven to 350ºF. Make the croutons by tossing 1/2 cup of the olive oil with the bread cubes. Spread out on a baking pan and toast in the oven for 15 minutes, stirring after about 10 minutes for even browning. Remove from the oven and reserve.

3. In a food processor or blender, process the remaining 1/4 cup olive oil with the garlic, salt, parsley, and mint to a thick green paste. Remove and reserve.

4. Bring the stock to a boil and add the chickpeas. Reduce the heat and simmer for 15 minutes. To serve the soup, ladle the chickpeas and broth into individual bowls. Let each person add a spoonful of the mint pesto to their bowl, stirring to release the aroma. Then top with the croutons.

In Italy, a cicerone (meaning large chickpea) is the word used to describe a suitably unthreatening companion that accompanies a beautiful woman.

CHAPTER SEVEN

APPETIZERS AND LIGHT MEALS

FRENCH GREEN LENTILS WITH BLACK TRUFFLES AND CARAMELIZED SHALLOTS

We think of lentils as earthy, even plebeian, but not in this dish which I adapted from the cookbook I coauthored with the great chef, Georges Perrier. At his *"restaurant classique"* he serves the lentils with glazed freshly peeled pearl onions. Here I've substituted shallots—I prefer their taste and they're easier to peel than pearl onions.

Serves 6 •

4 cups (1 quart) Rich Chicken Stock (see page 303)

1 (12 ounces) package dried French green lentils

1 whole fresh black winter truffle (scrubbed and peeled), or 1 canned winter truffle plus 2 tablespoons truffle juice

2 tablespoons unsalted butter

1/2 cup rendered duck fat (see About Duck Fat, page 310) or unsalted butter

1/2 pound firm, fresh shallots, peeled

1 tablespoon sugar

Salt and freshly ground black pepper

1 bunch fresh chives, thinly sliced

1. Prepare the Rich Chicken Stock.

2. Place the lentils and the stock in a heavy-bottomed pot and bring to a boil. Reduce the heat to very low and simmer for about 45 minutes, or until the lentils are cooked through but still firm—the skins shouldn't split open. (You can also cook the lentils in a 300°F oven, covered, until they're tender but still firm.) Drain off and reserve any cooking juices and keep lentils warm in their cooking pot.

3. Cut the truffle into tiny dice. In a small pot, reduce the lentil cooking juices (and the juices from the canned truffle if using) to 1/4 cup and mix in the diced truffles. Whisk the butter into this reduction then reserve.

4. Preheat the oven to 300°F. In an ovenproof pan over a medium heat, heat the duck fat until sizzling, then add the shallots. When they begin to brown, add the sugar and cover with a lid or aluminum foil. Place the pan in the oven and roast the shallots until tender, about 15 minutes. Drain off and discard the duck fat.

5. Have ready 6 shallow soup plates, preferably heated. Season the lentils to taste with salt and pepper. Ladle each portion into a soup plate. Cover each portion of lentils with the reserved truffle sauce, making sure each serving has its portion of truffle. Divide the caramelized shallots among the 6 plates and sprinkle each portion with chives.

PORTUGUESE GREEN PEAS WITH CHORIZO AND EGGS

Here is a simple, filling dish from Portugal's southern Algarve coastal country that is perfect for a brunch menu. If you live near a Portuguese neighborhood, look for *linguiça*, a long, thin tongue-shaped sausage flavored with lots of garlic and paprika. Otherwise, a Spanish-style chourico, chorizo, or even Italian pepperoni will do. Poaching is one cooking technique that reveals if an egg is fresh. A fresh egg will poach into a neat, firm oval; an older egg will be runny and hard to form.

Serves 6 •

2 tablespoons olive oil

1 onion, chopped

2 red bell peppers, cut into thin strips

1/2 pound linguiça, chourico, or chorizo, or pepperoni, sliced thin

2 pounds fresh green peas, shelled, or 2 (12-ounce) packages frozen green peas, rinsed

1/2 cup water

Salt and freshly ground black pepper

2 tablespoons white vinegar

4 cups water

1 tablespoon salt, for poaching

6 very fresh jumbo eggs, preferably organic

2 tablespoons chopped fresh cilantro leaves

1. In a medium heavy pot with a lid, heat the oil and sauté the onion, bell peppers, and linguiça until the onion is softened but not browned. Reduce the heat as low as possible, cover and cook for 15 to 20 minutes or until a jamlike consistency. Add the peas and 1/2 cup water and continue cooking until the peas are tender. Season with salt and pepper to taste.

2. In a medium pan, add the vinegar to 4 cups of water. Bring to a full rolling boil. Break open each egg and carefully drop, 1 at a time, into the center of the pan. After all the eggs are in the water, reduce the heat and gently poach the eggs for about 3 minutes or until the whites have set, but the yolks are still liquid.

3. To serve, divide the pea mixture among 6 shallow bowls. Form a hollow in the center of each bowl and place a poached egg in it. Sprinkle with the chopped cilantro and serve immediately.

ASIAN WRAP SANDWICHES WITH SHIITAKES, BEAN SPROUTS, AND HOISIN SAUCE

In the last few years, every restaurant trade magazine has been filled with stories about wraps, the purported "sandwich of the future." For a while, it seemed as though they were everywhere. Although the publicity may have waned, the sandwiches are still good—especially when they're stuffed full of flavorful ingredients with plenty of textural contrast and cooked to order. This Asian vegetarian wrap combines crunchy bok choy cabbage and bean sprouts with the smoky, earthy flavor of shiitake mushrooms and a combination of assertive Chinese seasonings: hoisin sauce, roasted Japanese sesame oil, and mushroom soy sauce.

Serves 6

1 cup water

1/2 cup raw long-grain rice

1/2 cup hoisin sauce

1/4 cup mushroom soy sauce

2 tablespoons roasted Japanese sesame oil

2 tablespoons grated fresh ginger

1/4 cup peanut oil

1 head bok choy cabbage, sliced into
   1-inch shreds

1 pound shiitake mushrooms, stems
   removed, caps sliced

2 cups fresh bean sprouts, rinsed
   and drained

1/2 cup chopped fresh cilantro leaves
   (about 1 bunch)

1 bunch scallions, thinly sliced

6 (10-inch) whole wheat tortillas

1. In a small pan with a lid, bring the water to a boil. Add the rice. Cook, covered, for 15 minutes over very low heat until tender and fluffy. Remove from heat and cool. Reserve.

2. In a small bowl, combine the hoisin, soy sauce, sesame oil, and ginger. Reserve.

3. In a wok or large skillet, heat 2 tablespoons of the peanut oil. Add the bok choy and stir-fry until bright green and slightly softened, about 3 minutes. Remove the bok choy from the wok and reserve in a bowl. Wipe out the wok with paper towels.

4. Heat the remaining 2 tablespoons peanut oil in the same wok. Add the mushrooms and stir-fry until softened and lightly browned. Pour in the reserved hoisin sauce mixture and bring to a boil. Transfer the mushroom mixture into the bowl with the bok choy. Add the cooked rice, bean sprouts, cilantro, and scallions to the bowl, mixing well.

5. Lightly heat the tortillas for 15 seconds in the microwave (or wrap in foil and bake at 350°F for 5 to 10 minutes). Spread the tortillas out on a flat surface. Place one-sixth of the filling (about 1¼ cups) on the bottom half of each tortilla, forming it into a 6-inch by 2-inch rectangle. Fold in the right and left sides of the tortilla to the center over the filling. Fold the bottom edge over the filling, then fold and continue to roll up like an egg roll. Place seam side down on a baking pan. (If desired, refrigerate the wraps, covered with plastic wrap for up to 1 day.)

6. Preheat the oven to 350°F. Wrap each sandwich individually in foil and place on a baking sheet. Bake for 15 to 20 minutes or until the wrap steams when pricked through the foil with a fork.

BEAN AND HAZELNUT CAKE
WITH STEAMED CLAMS

Derek Davis, chef owner of the Main Street Restaurants Group in Philadelphia, has made a name for himself as the kingpin of the city's old Manayunk neighborhood. An old and proud working class neighborhood, in recent years it has become a magnet for boutiques and restaurants. This recipe is from Derek's California restaurant, Sonoma. I love the combination of flavors he uses. You could make the full recipe of the black bean cakes and freeze half of them. Prepare half the steamed clam recipe. Then next time, you'll only need to defrost the black bean cakes in the microwave, brown the cakes, and prepare the steamed clam portion.

Serves 12 as an appetizer; 6 to 8 as an entrée •

BLACK BEAN CAKES

1 pound (2 cups) black turtle beans, picked over and rinsed well

1 small white onion

1 poblano pepper

2 jalapeño peppers

6 cloves garlic, peeled

1/2 cup hazelnuts, toasted, skinned, and coarsely chopped

Salt

1/2 to 1 cup bread crumbs

2 tablespoons unsalted butter

CLAMS

6 dozen littleneck clams, scrubbed and soaked in cold water until completely sand-free

2 cups chopped plum tomatoes

2 cups diced tomatillos

2 tablespoons chopped garlic

1 cup dry white wine

1/4 pound (1 stick) unsalted butter

3 tablespoons chopped fresh cilantro leaves

12 fresh cilantro sprigs, to garnish

1. Prepare the Black Bean Cakes: Cover the black turtle beans with cold water and bring to a boil. Reduce the heat and simmer for 30 minutes. Add the onion, poblano and jalapeño peppers, and garlic. Cook until the beans are very soft, about 1 hour longer. Remove from the heat. Drain, reserving the cooking liquid.

2. Place the bean mixture into the bowl of a food processor and pulse until smooth, adding a little of the reserved cooking liquid, if necessary, to get the paste going. (Note: the drier the paste is, the fewer bread crumbs it will need to make a proper texture.) Fold in the hazelnuts. Season to taste with salt. When cool, add enough bread crumbs so the mixture holds its shape. Using about 1/2 cup of the mixture for each, form into small hockey-puck-sized cakes. The cakes may be prepared several days ahead and refrigerated (or even frozen). Just before serving, heat the butter in a pan over medium heat. Add the cakes and cook for 5 minutes, until browned. Flip the cakes over and repeat.

3. Prepare the Clams: Place the clams, tomatoes, tomatillos, garlic, and wine in a pot with a lid. Steam over high heat for about 8 minutes. When the clams are open, stir in the butter and chopped cilantro. (Note: discard any clams that don't open.)

4. To serve, place each black bean cake in the center of a large plate (about 12 inches in diameter). Surround each cake with 6 clams. Spoon the butter sauce over the clams. Garnish with fresh cilantro sprigs.

BOUILLABAISSE OF LITTLE PEAS ESCUDIER

When Jean-Noël Escudier (AKA Monsieur Provence) published his classic cookbook *La Véritable Cuisine Provençale* in France in 1953, it was the first anthology of authentic Provençal recipes. As an inveterate flea market treasure hunter, I picked up Peta Fuller's English version of the book, titled *The Wonderful Food of Provence*, for a mere two dollars and proceeded to fall in love. According to the book, this simple dish of tiny peas cooked in the style of a bouillabaisse is actually one of the multiple forms of bouillabaisse. It is an ancient Provençal way of dressing peas with fennel, potatoes, poached eggs, and bread. Note that in Provence, fennel grows wild and is quite pungent. Our American domesticated Florence fennel or sweet anise is much sweeter and more delicate.

Serves 4

2 medium onions, diced

¼ cup extra-virgin olive oil

1 (28-ounce) chopped plum tomatoes

½ pound potatoes, peeled and cut into thick slices (preferably Yukon or Finnish Golds)

8 cups (2 quarts) boiling water

1 bouquet garni Provençal-style (1 sprig thyme, 2 sprigs Italian parsley, 1 bay leaf, 1 strip orange peel, and 1 tablespoon fennel seeds tied together or placed in a cheesecloth bag)

3 cloves garlic

1 small fennel bulb, diced

Salt and freshly ground black pepper

6 cups shelled little peas, or 2 (12-ounce) boxes of frozen petit pois rinsed in cold water

4 cups of water

2 tablespoons white vinegar

4 eggs

1 tablespoon salt, for poaching

½ loaf country-style bread (about ½ pound), sliced about ½ inch thick and toasted

1. In a large pan, cook the onions in the oil until transparent. Add the tomatoes and potatoes and toss. Pour in the boiling water and add the bouquet garni, garlic, fennel, and salt and pepper to taste. Boil the mixture, covered, over high heat until the potatoes are almost tender, about 5 minutes. Add the peas and cook for 2 to 3 minutes longer.

2. In a shallow, wide, medium-sized pan, bring the 4 cups water to a simmer. Stir in the vinegar and salt. Break open each egg and drop carefully, 1 at a time, into the simmering water. Cook for 3 to 4 minutes, depending on how you prefer the yolks cooked. (The whites should be firm and opaque and the yolks still liquidy in the middle.) Remove the eggs using a slotted spoon and gently place on a clean towel or paper towels to drain.

3. To serve, lay a toasted bread slice in each of 4 large soup plates. Top with a poached egg, then ladle some of the bouillabaisse over the top.

FRITTATA WITH ROMANO BEANS, PROSCIUTTO, AND ITALIAN FONTINA

Why is a frittata different from other egg dishes? It's more of an egg cake than an omelet, similar to the Spanish tortilla. A frittata is an ideal lunch or light supper dish. It can easily be made an hour or two ahead, then either briefly reheated in the microwave or served at room temperature as is common in Italy. Growing up, I loved the boxes of bias-cut "Italian beans" my mother would buy from the freezer case. It took a trip to Italy to discover the real thing: fresh romano beans. They have a distinct beany flavor, chewy texture and, when they're young, lovely velvety skin that begs to be caressed. Together, these two—the prosciutto and romano bean—work wonderfully.

Serves 6 •

1 pound fresh romano beans, cut into
 $1/2$-inch lengths

$1/4$ cup extra-virgin olive oil

1 large onion, diced

$1/4$ to $1/2$ pound prosciutto cut into
 small dice

12 eggs, lightly beaten

$1/2$ pound imported Italian Fontina
 cheese, shredded

Salt and freshly ground black pepper

1. In a medium pan, precook the beans in boiling water for 4 minutes or until crisp-tender. Drain and rinse under cold running water. Reserve.

2. In a large (12-inch) ovenproof skillet, heat 2 tablespoons olive oil. Add the onion and prosciutto, and cook over medium heat until lightly browned. Add the reserved beans, then remove the skillet from the heat. Transfer the bean mixture to the eggs, along with half of the cheese, and salt and pepper to taste.

3. Preheat the broiler to high. Wipe out the same skillet with a paper towel. Add the remaining 2 tablespoons olive oil and heat over medium heat. Pour in the egg mixture and cook for about 6 minutes, shaking occasionally, until most of the egg sets (the top should be soft and liquidy). Sprinkle the frittata with the remaining $1/4$ pound cheese and place the skillet under the broiler for 2 to 3 minutes, or until the cheese is bubbling and browned and the eggs are set on top.

4. Cool slightly and then cut into wedges. Serve accompanied by roasted potatoes, if desired.

HARICOTS VERTS AND FRIED QUAIL EGGS IN TRUFFLE VINAIGRETTE

Haricots verts, which simply mean "green beans" in French, are fashionably pencil-thin green beans hand picked at just the right size. The commercial ones from Central America come all lined up like a box of green-colored pencils, but are often a bit shriveled. The sweetest and plumpest haricots verts I've ever eaten came from Buck's County's Branch Creek Farm, organic growers of the finest vegetables, herbs, and greens. Haricots verts keep their brilliant emerald green color best if steamed rather than boiled. I find the best and most reasonably priced quail eggs not in a fancy gourmet supermarket, but at my local Korean grocery store.

Serves 6 •

TRUFFLE VINAIGRETTE

1 tablespoon (or more) black truffle, minced fresh or jarred

2 large shallots, minced

1/4 cup champagne vinegar, or rice wine vinegar

1/2 cup olive oil, or walnut or hazelnut oil

Salt and freshly ground black pepper

SALAD

1 1/2 pounds haricots verts, top stems removed

2 tablespoons unsalted butter

6 to 8 quail eggs (allow a few extra in case any break)

1 ripe tomato, cut into small dice

1/4 cup snipped fresh chives (about 1 bunch)

1. Prepare the Truffle Vinaigrette: In a small bowl, whisk the truffle, shallots, vinegar, oil, and salt and pepper to taste. Reserve. (If you are using canned truffles, add a little of their liquid to the dressing.)

2. Prepare the Salad: Have ready a bowl of ice water. Place the haricots verts in a steamer basket over a pot of rapidly boiling water. Steam for 3 to 4 minutes or until bright green. Drain and refresh in the bowl of ice water. Drain and reserve.

3. In a small nonstick skillet, heat the butter over medium heat until sizzling. Using a serrated knife, gently slice through the rather tough inner membrane of the quail eggs without breaking the yolks. Add the quail eggs, 1 at a time, to the skillet as if making miniature sunny-side up-eggs. Sprinkle each fried egg with salt and pepper to taste. Cover and cook for about 1 minute, then remove the pan from the heat.

4. To serve the salad, toss the haricots verts with the vinaigrette. Divide among 6 serving plates. Top each serving with a fried quail egg, then sprinkle with the tomato and chives. Serve immediately.

RANCH-STYLE EGGS AND REFRIED BEANS

(Huevos Rancheros y Frijoles Refritos)

This dish has been a personal favorite since I lived in Mexico as a teenager. There's something about the warm spiced flavor of Mexican Tomato Sauce with Allspice (see page 290) soaked into corn tortillas, and topped with runny, rich fried eggs and dense, concentrated refried beans that I crave on a regular basis. Maybe it's just because the whole thing evokes good memories. For whatever reason this dish is a classic.

Serves 4

2 cups Refried Beans (see page 236), heated thoroughly

2 cups Mexican Tomato Sauce with Allspice (see page 290)

2 tablespoons corn or peanut oil

1 (12-ounce) package corn tortillas

8 eggs

¼ pound shredded Monterey Jack or Cheddar cheese

½ cup chopped fresh cilantro leaves (about 1 bunch), for garnish

1. Prepare the Refried Beans; keep hot. Prepare the Mexican Tomato Sauce with Allspice; keep hot.

2. Heat a thin film of corn oil in a heavy cast-iron skillet. Add tortillas, 1 at a time, and cook for 30 seconds on each side or until toasted, adding a bit more oil for each tortilla. Place 2 overlapping tortillas per portion on the bottom of a shallow ovenproof baking dish, or in individual baking dishes.

3. Preheat the broiler. Spread the tomato sauce over the tortillas, using a spoon to form 2 rounded hollows on the surface. Carefully break 2 eggs per person into the hollows in the sauce. Sprinkle with the cheese.

4. Broil for 8 to 10 minutes or until the cheese is bubbling and the egg whites are set. Serve accompanied by a generous dollop of hot refried beans. Garnish with cilantro.

LENTIL CAKES *(Khaman Dhokla)* WITH DATE-TAMARIND CHUTNEY

This unusual spongy lentil cake served with a tasty, dark-sweet chutney is a specialty of the city of Bombay. Tamarind is one of the most common ingredients in many countries, used for its sour pruny flavor and the thickening powder of its pulp. Tamarind is most often sold dried and pressed into blocks, which must be soaked in water to rehydrate and then strained to remove the large seeds. Tamarind concentrate is also available, but it tends to be salty, so you would need to adjust the seasoning.

Advance preparation recommended. Serves 8 •

1 recipe Date-Tamarind Chutney
  (see page 291)
1 pound (2 cups) dried yellow split peas,
  soaked for 12 hours
1/2 cup plain yogurt
1 teaspoon salt
1 teaspoon finely chopped fresh green
  chile (such as jalapeño)
1 teaspoon grated fresh ginger
3 tablespoons corn oil
1/2 teaspoon black mustard seeds
1/2 teaspoon sesame seeds
2 tablespoons chopped fresh cilantro
  leaves

1. Prepare the Date-Tamarind Chutney. Reserve.

2. Drain the soaked split peas, discarding the water. Combine with the yogurt and salt, place in a blender, and purée until smooth. (The mixture should be thick enough to hold its shape without running.) Place the mixture in a bowl and cover. Let stand overnight at room temperature to allow the mixture to ferment. The next day, it should be bubbling and light. Stir the batter well to remove excess bubbles. Stir in the chili and ginger.

3. Lightly oil a Chinese bamboo steamer or the perforated insert to a pasta pot. Bring a pot of water to boiling. Pour the batter into the steamer to a thickness of 1/4 inch. Cover and steam the thin cake for 15 minutes or until a knife stuck in the middle comes out clean. Cool for 10 minutes, then using a sharp knife, cut the cake into 1-inch diamond shapes.

4. In a small pan with a lid, heat the oil with the mustard seeds. Cook, covered, until the seeds pop (like popcorn). Add the sesame seeds and remove from the heat.

5. Drizzle the hot spice oil over the diamonds and leave for 5 minutes to absorb the flavors. Garnish with the cilantro and serve with the reserved chutney.

INDIAN VEGETABLE TEMPURA IN CHICKPEA BATTER

I prepared this fragrant, flavorful vegetable tempura for the first legumes class I ever taught. Everyone loved it. The nutty chickpea flour, the toasted seeds, and the tangy yogurt combine to make a frying batter with considerable intrinsic flavor. By choosing an imaginative variety of vegetables for frying, you can make a memorable dish from simple ingredients. I've listed fifteen vegetables that all cook up firm and tasty without being too watery.

Makes 4 cups batter, enough for 3 to 4 vegetables •

2 cups Cucumber-Yogurt Raita
  (see page 288)
2 cups chickpea flour
1 cup cold water
2 teaspoons salt
1 teaspoon ground toasted cumin seed
  (see Toasting Seeds, page 217)
1 teaspoon ground toasted coriander seed
1 teaspoon ground toasted fennel seed
2 teaspoons ground fenugreek
$1/2$ teaspoon cayenne
2 teaspoons turmeric
1 cup plain yogurt
Soybean or peanut oil, for deep-frying
6 cups assorted vegetables, such as:
  Butternut squash, pared and cut into
    $1/2$-inch-thick half-slices
  Carrots, cut into 2- to 3-inch sticks,
    or whole baby carrots
  Cauliflower, cut into small florets
  Daikon radish rounds, peeled and cut
    into $1/2$-inch-thick coins
  Fennel, trimmed, outer layer removed,
    cut into wedges and rubbed with a
    little lemon juice

1. Prepare the Cucumber-Yogurt Raita. Reserve.

2. In a medium bowl, whisk together the chickpea flour, water, salt, cumin, coriander, fennel, fenugreek, cayenne, turmeric, and yogurt to make a thick batter. Cover and let the batter rest in the refrigerator for 30 minutes.

3. Preheat the oven to 200°F. Fill a large, heavy-bottomed pot or wok no more than one-third full with oil. Preheat the oil to 365°F on a deep-frying thermometer. Dip bite-sized chunks of vegetables, 1 at a time, into the chickpea batter. (If the batter is too thick, add more water a little at a time. The batter should be thick enough to coat the vegetables) Gently lay each vegetable onto the surface of the hot oil, making sure not to crowd the vegetables. For crisp results, each vegetable should be surrounded by oil. Deep-fry in batches until light brown and crispy, about 6 minutes. Drain vegetables on paper towels. Spread out in a single layer on a baking sheet or ovenproof platter and keep warm in the oven while continuing to fry. Serve with the reserved Cucumber-Yogurt Raita.

Japanese eggplant, cut lengthwise
into ½-inch-thick slices

Romano beans, blanched 3 minutes
in boiling salted water if fresh
(or use frozen)

Salsify, peeled and cut into 2- to
3-inch sticks, rubbed with a little
lemon juice

Spinach leaves, stems removed

Sweet potatoes, pared and cut into
½-inch-thick half-moons

Sweet white or red onions, roots
trimmed but not removed,
each cut into 6 to 8 wedges

Taro root, pared and cut into
½-inch-thick slices

White mushrooms, wiped clean,
quartered if large

White or yellow turnip, pared and
cut into thin wedges

Yellow squash, scrubbed and cut on
the diagonal into ½-inch-thick slices

TUNISIAN FAVA BEAN STEW WITH MERGUEZ LAMB SAUSAGE *(Bisara)*

Tunisia is a land with an ancient history. It has been influenced at one time or another by just about every civilization surrounding the Mediterranean including the indigenous Berber peoples the Phoenicians—founders of the city of Carthage—and the Romans during the height of their empire. Later came the Arabic tribes, Ottoman Turks, and Italians—all of whom contributed to the cuisine. Tunisian food is based on the sun-ripened products of the Earth, including their highly fragrant olive oil called for here. Tunisians also favor the spicy merguez lamb sausage featured in this dish. Two sizes of fava beans are called for here; the smaller size will dissolve into the sauce and the large ones will remain whole.

Serves 6 •

1 pound (2 cups) dried split fava beans, preferably half small and half large, soaked (see Soaking Chart, page 41)

¼ cup extra-virgin olive oil

2 tablespoons tomato paste

4 to 5 ripe plum tomatoes, diced

3 cloves garlic, finely chopped

3 cups water

1 pound merguez, or smoked turkey sausage

2 teaspoons ground coriander

1 teaspoon ground caraway seed

2 teaspoons salt

1 teaspoon cayenne (optional)

1. Drain and rinse the soaked favas. Reserve.

2. In a heavy Dutch oven, heat the olive oil. Add the tomato paste and cook for 5 minutes, stirring to combine. Stir in the tomatoes and garlic and continue to cook for 5 minutes. Add the water and bring to a boil. Add the reserved favas and cook for 25 minutes. Add the sausage, coriander, caraway, salt, and cayenne. Continue cooking for 15 minutes, stirring occasionally, or until the favas are tender and the sausage is thoroughly cooked. Serve.

Cook's Note ❧ ❧ ❧

If only whole caraway is available, grind it in a clean coffee grinder or with a mortar and pestle.

PASTA PRIMAVERA WITH SUGAR SNAPS

When Sirio Macchioni of the world-class New York restaurant, Le Cirque, first brought pasta primavera into the consciousness of American diners back in the seventies, he had an extraordinarily long-lasting and widespread effect. For a time—and even now—it seemed like every self-respecting chef in America had a version of this dish on their menu. Every ingredient here plays a roll in providing color, texture, and juiciness. Don't leave anything out and you'll understand why it was such an instant hit.

Serves 4 •

1 pound linguine pasta

1 tablespoon chopped garlic

½ head broccoli, cut into small florets

2 tablespoons olive oil

1 pint ripe red cherry tomatoes,
  cut into halves

½ pound fresh sugar snap peas, trimmed

1 bunch scallions, cut into 1-inch lengths

½ cup heavy cream

1 bunch fresh basil leaves washed and
  coarsely torn (about 1 cup leaves)

½ cup grated Parmigiano-Reggiano

Salt and freshly ground black pepper

¼ cup toasted pine nuts

1. Bring a large pot of salted water to a boil. Add the pasta and cook until firm but tender, about 7 minutes. Drain and reserve in the pot to keep warm.

2. While the pasta is cooking, sauté the garlic and broccoli in the olive oil in a large skillet for 2 to 3 minutes or until crisp-tender. Add the cherry tomatoes and cook for 2 minutes. Stir in the sugar snaps, scallions, and cream. Bring the mixture to a boil, then turn off the heat. Add the basil and cheese. Add the vegetable mixture to the pot of pasta. Toss to coat evenly. Season to taste with salt and pepper, sprinkle with pine nuts and serve immediately.

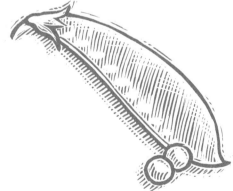

RAVIOLI WITH SPRING GREENS FILLING AND CREAMY WHITE BEAN AND SAGE SAUCE

When I was in Bologna, I had the great pleasure of watching pasta being prepared by the women in the kitchen of the restaurant, Diana. Theses expert craftswomen would take a huge wooden rolling pin, as long as a table, and use it to stretch and roll out a thin but textured sheet of pasta dough. After filling the ravioli with a simple ricotta and spinach stuffing, or a filling made from pumpkin and chopped amaretti cookie, or this spring greens stuffing, they would arrange them one by one on a wood-framed wire trays, that kept the air circulating and prevented the ravioli from sticking. I admit that it's a formidable task to make your own ravioli, but otherwise you'll never get the chance to taste these tender plump pillows hand-stuffed with fresh greens.

Serves 6 to 8 •

1 recipe Durum Pasta Dough
(see page 306)

CREAMY WHITE BEAN AND SAGE SAUCE
1 cup dried cannellini beans, cooked and
drained (see Basic Cooking Chart, page
43)
2 tablespoons olive oil
1/4 cup chopped garlic
2 cups Light Chicken Stock
(see page 301)
1 cup shredded fresh sage leaves
(about 2 bunches)
1/2 cup heavy cream
Salt and freshly ground black pepper

1. Prepare the Durum Pasta Dough and reserve.

2. Prepare the Creamy White Bean and Sage Sauce: Prepare the cannellini beans. Reserve.

3. Heat the olive oil in a medium pot, add the garlic and cook for 3 to 4 minutes. Do not brown. Add the beans, Light Chicken Stock, and sage. Bring to a boil, reduce the heat, and simmer for 20 minutes.

4. In the blender or food processor, purée half the beans, then stir the purée into the remaining beans. Add the heavy cream and cook over low heat until hot. Season to taste with salt and pepper. Keep warm, or else refrigerate if preparing ahead.

5. Prepare the Filling: Bring a large pot of water to a boil. Add the sorrel, spinach, mustard greens, and endive and cook just until wilted and soft. Drain and run under cold water to chill. Squeeze out the greens in your hands, removing as much water as possible. In a large bowl, mix the squeezed greens with the ricotta, Parmigiano, eggs, nutmeg, salt, and pepper. Cover and refrigerate until ready to fill the ravioli.

FILLING

1 bunch fresh sorrel, stems trimmed,
   leaves cut into narrow shreds

1 bunch fresh spinach, stems trimmed,
   leaves cut into shreds

1 bunch young fresh mustard greens,
   stems trimmed, leaves cut into shreds

1 head curly endive, stalks removed,
   leaves cut into shreds

$1/4$ pound whole milk ricotta cheese

$1/4$ pound grated Parmigiano-Reggiano

4 eggs

1 teaspoon freshly ground nutmeg

2 teaspoons salt

1 teaspoon freshly ground black pepper

2 tablespoons chopped Italian parsley
   leaves, for garnish

6. To assemble the ravioli, use a ravioli plaque. Lay 1 sheet of dough onto the bottom of the plaque, pressing to make indentations for the filling. (If the dough is dry, brush the edges with water; if it's moist enough to stick together well, this won't be necessary.) Fill each indentation with 1 tablespoon of the filling, being careful not to smear any on the edges. (The dough will only stick to more dough, not to filling.) Cover with a second sheet of dough, then roll over the top with a rolling pin to seal. Use your fingers to press down on all the edges to strengthen the seal. Arrange the filled ravioli on a clean flour-dusted portable wire window screen (used for this purpose), or on a perforated pan or flour-dusted waxed paper. Repeat with the remaining dough and filling. Reserve until ready to cook.

7. Bring a large pot of salted water to a boil. Drop in the filled ravioli 1 at a time. Bring the water back to a boil, stirring the ravioli gently with a wooden spoon. When all the ravioli have floated to the surface, cook for 2 to 3 minutes longer. Scoop out using a skimmer or a wire sieve. Drain by shaking off the water, then gently toss with the Creamy White Bean and Sage Sauce (reheat if necessary). Sprinkle with parsley and serve immediately.

Cook's Note ❧ ❧ ❧

If you don't have a ravioli plaque you can shape the ravioli by hand: Roll out 1 sheet of the pasta dough as wide as the machine will allow. Fold the sheet in half lengthwise, then unfold it, to make a crease. Starting from the left side, place 1 tablespoon of the filling 1 inch from the edge of the dough, just below the crease. Repeat, making sure to leave 1 inch between each spoonful of filling. When the dough has been filled, brush around all of the mounds with cold water. Fold the top half of the dough over the bottom half. Press firmly between and around all of the mounds of filling to seal the edges pressing out all the excess air pockets. Using a knife or ravioli cutter, cut between each of the ravioli to make half-moon shapes.

ARTICHOKES WITH FAVA BEANS *(Barbouiado)*

This old-time Provençal dish, called *barbouiado* in the regional dialect, combines two vegetables I can never get enough of—fresh favas and artichokes. Naturally, they both take a seemingly inordinate amount of time to prep. You have the choice of making the dish from scratch to serve to highly discriminating guests or taking the easy way out and using frozen green favas (sold in Asian and Mediterranean markets) and frozen artichoke hearts. (If you can find Birdseye brand frozen artichoke hearts, they're my absolute first choice. Cara Mia brand is more common but has too much citric acid for my taste.)

Serves 6

1 pound fresh shelled green favas, or 1
  (1-pound) bag frozen green fava beans
4 large fresh artichokes, trimmed (see
  Preparing Fresh Artichokes below), or
  1 (12-ounce) box frozen artichokes
1/4 cup extra-virgin olive oil
1 large sweet onion, sliced into strips
1/2 cup dry white vermouth
1/2 teaspoon freshly grated nutmeg
Salt and freshly ground black pepper

1. Bring a pot of salted water to a boil and add the favas. Cook for 2 minutes, then drain and rinse. Remove and discard the inner skin. Refill the pot with water and bring to a boil. Cook the skinned favas for 5 to 10 minutes or until nearly tender. Drain and reserve.

2. In a medium pan, brown the artichoke strips (or frozen wedges) in the olive oil over high heat. Add the onion, and cook for 3 minutes, or until the onion is softened. Pour in the vermouth. Bring the mixture to a boil, add the favas and nutmeg, and season to taste with salt and pepper. Toss to combine well. Serve immediately.

PREPARING FRESH ARTICHOKES

HAVE READY A BOWL OF COLD WATER WITH 2 TABLESPOONS LEMON JUICE ADDED (ABOUT 1 LEMON). USING A STAINLESS STEEL KNIFE, SLICE OFF THE STEMS OF THE ARTICHOKES SO THEY SIT UPRIGHT. SLICE OFF THE TOPS OF THE ARTICHOKES, LEAVING ABOUT 1 1/2 INCHES OF LEAVES ON THEM. TURN THE ARTICHOKES UPSIDE-DOWN. WORKING IN A SPIRAL, GRASP ONE LEAF AT A TIME, FIRST BENDING IT BACK AT THE POINT WHERE THE LEAF MEETS THE ARTICHOKE BOTTOM AND THEN BREAKING IT OFF. KEEP BREAKING OFF LEAVES, GOING IN ORDER AROUND THE ARTICHOKE UNTIL ALL THE LEAVES HAVE BEEN REMOVED BUT THE INNER LIGHT-GREEN SECTION. NOW, USING A SHARP PARING KNIFE, PARE AWAY ALL THE TOUGH DARK GREEN OUTER SKIN FROM THE ARTICHOKE BOTTOM. YOU SHOULD HAVE ONLY LIGHT GREEN FLESH LEFT. AS YOU FINISH TRIMMING EACH ARTICHOKE PLACE IT IN THE LEMON WATER. USING A MELON BALLER OR A HEAVY STAINLESS STEEL TEASPOON, SCRAPE OUT AND DISCARD THE INEDIBLE HAIRY PORTION IN THE CENTER OF EACH ARTICHOKE, CALLED THE "CHOKE." CUT THE TRIMMED ARTICHOKE BOTTOMS INTO 1/4-INCH-THICK SLICES AND RESERVE IN THE LEMON WATER UNTIL READY TO COOK. (*Note:* DO NOT ATTEMPT TO GRIND THE ARTICHOKE TRIMMINGS IN A SINK DISPOSAL. THEY ARE MUCH TOO FIBROUS AND SHOULD BE DISCARDED IN THE TRASH).

SPINACH AND BEEF FILET TIP SALAD WITH FERMENTED BLACK BEANS

This dish of roasted beef filet in a dark, Korean-style marinade features fermented black beans, and is served over fresh spinach making it a perfect main-dish salad. The beef tastes best if served hot or at room temperature rather than ice cold, which dulls the flavors.

Serves 6

MARINADE

$1/4$ cup molasses

$1/4$ cup peanut oil

2 tablespoons roasted Japanese sesame oil

$1/4$ cup grated fresh ginger

$1/4$ cup mushroom soy sauce

$1/4$ cup Shanxi vinegar

$1/4$ cup hoisin sauce

$1/4$ cup fermented black beans, rinsed, drained, and chopped

4 beef filet tips (about 1 pound total), trimmed, silverskin removed

DRESSING

2 tablespoons soy sauce

2 tablespoons rice wine vinegar

2 tablespoons Shanxi or balsamic vinegar

1 tablespoon grated fresh ginger

$1/2$ teaspoon freshly ground black pepper

1 tablespoon Dijon mustard

2 tablespoons roasted Japanese sesame oil

6 tablespoons peanut oil

1 white onion, thinly sliced, soaked in salted ice water for 10 minutes, then drained

1 (10-ounce) bag spinach, stems removed

1. Prepare the Marinade: In a large shallow dish, blend the molasses, peanut and sesame oils, ginger, soy sauce, vinegar, hoisin, and beans. Add beef tips, turning to coat, marinate overnight in the refrigerator.

2. Preheat the oven to 450°F. Drain off and discard marinade from the beef tips. Place in a small roasting pan and roast the beef tips in the hot oven until rare, about 135°F on a meat thermometer. Cool to room temperature, then thinly slice with a sharp knife, preferably an electric knife. Reserve.

3. Prepare the Dressing: Place the soy sauce, rice wine and Shanxi vinegars, ginger, black pepper, and mustard into a blender. Blend until well combined. Slowly pour in the sesame and peanut oils, continuing to blend until the mixture is creamy looking. Reserving a few onion slices, toss about half the dressing with the spinach and remaining onions.

4. Divide the spinach mixture among 6 large salad plates. Arrange the beef slices over the top with sprinkle with the reserved onion slices. Drizzle the remaining dressing over the beef.

FRENCH LENTIL AND FOIE GRAS-STUFFED WON TON RAVIOLI WITH TOMATO AND TRUFFLE OIL

I've had the pleasure of tasting this dish two or three times prepared by my friend, Philippe Chin, chef/partner of the elegant Philippe on Locust. Chin specializes in French-Asian fusion cuisine with an emphasis on the French techniques he learned in school in his native Paris. From his Chinese grandfather, he learned about Asian ingredients and techniques, and has been incorporating more and more of them into his own stylish cuisine. Here, Chin fills won ton ravioli skins with firm, almost meaty green lentils and luscious ultra-rich fresh foie gras. This extraordinarily good filling could only be properly set off by the light tomato sauce drizzled with truffle oil. The aroma that wafts over the table when the waiters uncover the cloches (the hat-shaped lids) is indescribably intoxicating.

Serves 6 •

FILLING

1 cup Cooked French Green Lentils
   (see page 233)
6 (1-ounce) slices fresh foie gras
   (see Sources, page 323)
Salt and freshly ground black pepper
1/4 cup well-cleaned chopped leek
1 tablespoon chopped carrot
1 teaspoon olive oil
12 round thin won ton wrappers
1 egg yolk mixed with 1 tablespoon water

SAUCE

1 tomato, peeled, seeded, and diced
1 tablespoon extra-virgin olive oil
1/2 cup tomato juice
1 1/2 cups Light Chicken Stock
   (see page 301)
Salt and freshly ground black pepper
2 tablespoons (or more) truffle oil,
   for serving
6 fresh basil leaves, for garnish

1. Prepare the Filling: Prepare the Basic Cooked French Green Lentils. Reserve.

2. Preheat a large nonstick skillet over high heat. Season the foie gras with salt and pepper. Add in 2 batches to the hot pan, and sear on each side, cooking just long enough to brown the outside. Transfer the foie gras slices to a platter, cover, and refrigerate, reserving the fat from the pan separately.

3. In a pan, cook the leek and carrot in the olive oil for about 3 minutes or until the leek is translucent. Add the lentils and foie gras fat. Season generously to taste with salt and pepper (some of the seasoning will be absorbed by the won ton skins). Cover and refrigerate the filling. (Step 1 through 3 can be done up to 1 day ahead.)

4. Place 6 won ton wrappers on a clean surface. Brush around the edges with the egg yolk mixture. Place about 1 tablespoon of the chilled filling in the center of each wrapper. Top each with a slice of the foie gras. Cover the filled won tons with the remaining 6 wrappers. Seal the ravioli by pressing lightly all around the edges. Let dry for a few minutes before cooking.

5. Prepare the Sauce: Cook the diced tomatoes in 1 teaspoon of the olive oil in a small saucepan. Add the tomato juice and Light Chicken Stock. Bring to a boil, reduce the heat, and simmer for 10 minutes. Purée the tomato mixture in a blender, or with a hand-held blender, slowly adding the remaining 2 teaspoons olive oil. Season to taste with salt and pepper. Reserve.

6. When ready to serve, bring a large wide pot of salted water to a boil. Add the ravioli, dropping each in, 1 at a time, so they don't stick together. Cook for about 4 minutes, then scoop out using a slotted spoon or wire skimmer. Shake off the excess water and immediately place in 6 heated large, shallow soup bowls. Top with the tomato sauce and a drizzle of truffle oil. Garnish each won ton with a basil leaf.

GOLDEN GARLIC AIOLI WITH HARICOTS VERTS AND SUGAR SNAPS

This variation on a traditional Niçoise specialty makes a lovely dish to serve on a hot summer night. Everything can be made ahead of time, though the vegetables and eggs will taste best if they're cool but not icy-cold. Serve with a chilled carafe of rosé wine preferably from Provence, such as Bandol. I happen to love the flavor of the caramelized garlic in the aioli. It also makes this dish a little more user-friendly because the cooked garlic doesn't leave a strong aftertaste.

Serves 6 (makes 3 cups sauce) •

Roasted Garlic Aioli

1 cup peeled garlic cloves

1/2 cup olive oil

2 tablespoons finely chopped fresh thyme
   leaves (about 1/2 bunch)

2 tablespoons Spanish, or sweet
   Hungarian paprika

1/4 cup red wine vinegar

2 cups high-quality prepared mayonnaise

2 teaspoons salt

1 teaspoon hot pepper sauce

Salad

1/2 pound haricots verts, or green beans,
   stems trimmed

1/2 pound sugar snap peas, tops trimmed
   and strings removed

1 pound young beets

1/2 pound fresh artichoke wedges (see
   Preparing Fresh Artichokes, page 154),
   or frozen artichoke hearts, thawed and
   drained on paper towels

1 fennel bulb, trimmed, cut into thin
   wedges (and soaked in lemon juice and
   ice water)

12 hard-cooked eggs, quartered (see
   Hard-Cooking Eggs, page 159)

1. Prepare the Roasted Garlic Aioli: Place the garlic cloves, oil, and thyme in a small pot and cook over medium heat shaking often, until the garlic begins to turn golden. Remove from the heat and cool to room temperature. Transfer the mixture to a food processor and purée to a fine paste. Add the paprika, vinegar, mayonnaise, salt, and hot sauce. Purée again until smooth. Taste for seasoning. (The sauce will keep well for 2 weeks if tightly covered and refrigerated.)

2. Prepare the Salad: In a vegetable steamer basket over boiling water, steam the haricots verts for 3 to 5 minutes, or until they turn a brilliant emerald green. Lift out the steamer basket and rinse the beans under cold running water to stop the cooking and set the color. If you like, briefly steam the sugar snap peas for about 1 minute or until they turn a light, bright green. Rinse under cold running water. (The sugar snaps are delicious raw or cooked. They are fresher and crunchier when raw and more tender and bright when cooked.)

3. Set the steamer up again, adding enough water to the pot to reach a depth of at least 1 inch. Trim off the beet greens, if any, leaving about 1 inch of stems attached to the tops. (Be careful not to cut into the root end of the beets or they will bleed and lose much of their bright magenta color.) Steam the whole beets

for 20 to 30 minutes, or until tender when pierced with a fork. When cool enough to handle, rub the skins off the warm beets and trim off the root ends. (To prevent staining, wear gloves and cut the beets on a nonporous surface.) Cut into wedges.

4. In a medium pot, bring the fresh artichoke wedges and their soaking liquid to a boil over high heat. Reduce the heat and cook for about 8 minutes, or until the artichokes are tender when pierced with a fork. Drain, cool, and reserve.

5. Transfer the aioli to a small bowl. On a large platter, arrange the haricots verts, sugar snaps, artichokes, beets, raw fennel, and eggs in a decorative pattern with the bowl of aioli in the center for dipping.

❧ ❧ ❧ HARD-COOKING EGGS ❧ ❧ ❧

To avoid rubbery, overcooked eggs with a green halo around the yolk, don't boil your eggs. Instead, place the eggs in a medium pot and add 1 tablespoon salt and enough cold water to cover them by about 2 inches. Cover, bring to a boil, and allow the water to a boil for 1 minute. Turn off the heat and let the eggs continue to cook in the hot water for 6 minutes for European-style eggs (soft in the center), or 8 minutes for firm eggs. Place the eggs in a large bowl of cold water to chill, changing the water once or twice, until the eggs are cold. Peel immediately and cut into quarters, as desired. (Adding salt to the cold water helps to cleanly separate the shells from the eggs.)

SHRIMP AND BEAN THREAD SPRING ROLLS WITH PEANUT DIPPING SAUCE

Is it *really* worth making your own spring rolls? I find most spring roll fillings to be overcooked and heavy. Here the filling is light because of the slippery bean thread noodles and crunchy because of the napa cabbage shreds. You can certainly serve the rolls as is without the sauce, but if you have time, give it a try. The sauce can be made several days ahead of time. The spring rolls can be filled and rolled up to one day ahead of time. Be sure to use fresh soybean oil for frying. The lightest results come from the first frying in clear, fresh bubbly oil.

Makes 12 spring rolls •

2 cups (1 recipe) Spicy Peanut Dipping Sauce (see page 298)

2 ounces bean thread, or cellophane noodles

2 teaspoons chopped garlic

1 tablespoon chopped fresh ginger

1 tablespoon peanut oil

1 tablespoon roasted Japanese sesame oil

$^1/_2$ pound small shrimp, peeled

$^1/_4$ head napa cabbage, shredded

2 carrots, shredded

1 tablespoon mushroom soy sauce

$^1/_2$ teaspoon hot red pepper flakes

1 tablespoon cornstarch

$^1/_4$ cup rice wine, saké, or dry sherry

$^1/_4$ bunch scallions, sliced

$^1/_4$ cup chopped fresh cilantro leaves (about $^1/_2$ bunch)

12 egg-roll wrappers

1 egg white mixed with 1 tablespoon cold water

Soybean oil, for frying

1. Prepare the Spicy Peanut Dipping Sauce. Reserve.

2. Soak the bean thread noodles in cold water to cover until softened, about 15 minutes.

3. Drain and reserve. In a medium pan over medium heat, cook the garlic and ginger in the peanut and sesame oils. Add the shrimp and sauté until just cooked through. Remove from heat and reserve.

4. In another pan over medium heat, cook the cabbage until wilted. Remove from the heat and stir in the carrots. Add the shrimp and noodles to the cabbage mixture and toss to combine. Transfer to a colander set over a bowl; drain and reserve the excess liquid, then transfer to a bowl.

5. In a small pot, over medium heat, cook the reserved liquid, reducing until syrupy. Stir in the soy sauce and pepper flakes. In a small bowl, combine the cornstarch and wine. Whisk into the reduced liquid and bring to a boil, stirring constantly. Remove from the heat and stir into the reserved shrimp-vegetable mixture. Add the scallions and cilantro. Cover and refrigerate mixture for about 1 hour, until well chilled.

6. Arrange the egg-roll wrappers on a large, clean surface. Divide the filling into 12 equal portions. Place 1 portion on each wrapper, forming it into an oblong shape, leaving a 1-inch border all around the edges. Brush the egg white mixture all around the edges of the wrappers. Roll up, envelope style, pressing to seal the packets well. Refrigerate until ready to cook.

7. When ready to serve, preheat the oven to 200°F. Fill a large, heavy-bottomed pot, deep-fryer, or wok no more than one-third with oil. Heat to 365°F on a deep-frying thermometer. Fry a few spring rolls at a time, leaving plenty of room in the pot, until brown, about 4 minutes. Drain well on paper towels and then transfer to a paper-towel-lined baking sheet. Place in the oven to keep warm while cooking the remaining spring rolls. Serve with the spicy peanut sauce.

GRATIN OF SUMMER SUCCOTASH WITH CRABMEAT

Here is a lovely seasonal variation on the classic succotash. The basic combination of limas and sweet corn is preserved, but I've enhanced it with crabmeat in a creamy sauce. I love sweet blue crabmeat but it's so expensive to buy the top-quality jumbo lump. In this dish, it's mixed with enough other ingredients so one pound will easily feed six people. In the summer at Philadelphia's 100-year-old culinary treasure, the Reading Terminal Market, you can buy little bags of fresh shelled baby limas from the Amish farmers who sell their wares. What a treat! I love anything made with crab, corn, Jersey tomatoes, and field-grown basil, and this dish has it all.

Serves 6 (makes one 6-cup gratin) •

1 pound shelled fresh baby lima beans

1 bunch scallions, sliced into 1-inch lengths

1/4 cup unsalted butter, melted

1 pound jumbo lump crabmeat, carefully picked over

4 cups sweet white corn kernels (about 8 ears)

4 large red, ripe beefsteak tomatoes, seeded and diced

1 cup shredded basil (about 1 bunch)

1/2 cup heavy cream

Salt and freshly ground black pepper

1 cup fresh white bread crumbs

1. Place the lima beans in a medium pot with enough cold water to cover. Bring to a boil. Reduce the heat and simmer for about 10 minutes, or until bright green and almost tender. Drain and reserve.

2. Preheat the oven to 400°F. Cook the scallions in 2 tablespoons of the melted butter, just until bright green. Remove from the heat. Fold in the limas, crabmeat, corn, tomatoes, basil, and cream. Season to taste with salt and pepper. Spoon the mixture into an ungreased 6-cup shallow gratin dish.

3. Combine the bread crumbs and the remaining 2 tablespoons butter in a small bowl. Sprinkle evenly over the top of the gratin. Bake for 20 to 30 minutes or until bubbling and browned on top.

CRUNCHY SPROUTING BEAN SALAD

If you can find the packages of mixed sprouting beans (not bean sprouts) sold in many supermarkets, especially those with a large natural food selection, this salad is a cinch to make. Follow the directions for Home-Grown Bean Sprouts (see page 308) if you'd like to make your own bean sprouts. Children greatly enjoy the process of making bean sprouts, though they might not necessarily be willing to eat them.

Serves 6 •

3 cups mixed fresh sprouting beans
   (about 2 pints)

3 carrots, cut into small dice

2 red, yellow, or orange bell peppers,
   seeded and cut into small dice

1 bunch scallions, thinly sliced

¼ cup chopped Italian parsley leaves
   (about ½ bunch)

1 teaspoon finely chopped garlic

1 small red onion, diced

3 tablespoons balsamic vinegar

6 tablespoons olive oil

Salt and freshly ground black pepper

1 pint ripe red cherry tomatoes

1. Heat a pot of salted water to a boil. Add the sprouted beans and cook for 30 minutes or until crunchy-tender and still brightly colored. Drain and run under cold water to set the color and stop the cooking.

2. In a large bowl, combine the sprouted beans, carrots, bell peppers, scallions, and parsley.

3. In a small bowl, combine the garlic, onion, and vinegar. Pour in the oil slowly while whisking. Season to taste with salt and pepper. Pour the oil mixture over the vegetables and toss to combine. Cover and refrigerate overnight to give the flavors a chance to meld.

4. When ready to serve, garnish the salad with cherry tomatoes.

RED LENTIL AND
RED BELL PEPPER TERRINE

This red lentil terrine is not only light and colorful but also relatively low in fat. The pimiento-colored vinaigrette that accompanies the terrine enhances its orangy-red color. This terrine is great for serving at a party because it's easy, inexpensive, and can be made one or two days ahead of time. To make perfect terrine slices, try using an electric knife. Vary the flavor of the terrine by adding about one tablespoon curry powder or chili powder to the lentils while they are cooking.

Serves 6 •

1/2 cup Roasted Red Pepper Vinaigrette
  (see page 286)
1 cup split red lentils
2 cups Light Chicken Stock
  (see page 301)
1 tablespoon unflavored gelatin
1/2 cup dry white vermouth
Salt, freshly ground black pepper, and
  cayenne
1 bunch fresh swiss chard, stems trimmed
2 bunches scallions; 1 cut into 2 1/2-inch
  pieces, 1 diced
1 tablespoon olive oil
1 fennel bulb, finely chopped
1 large yellow or orange bell pepper,
  seeded and finely chopped

1. Prepare the Roasted Red Pepper Vinaigrette. Reserve.

2. Spray a 6-cup terrine mold or a 9 x 5 x 3-inch rectangular bread pan with nonstick vegetable spray.

3. Combine the lentils and Light Chicken Stock in a large pot. Bring to a boil. Skim off any foam impurities that rise to the surface, reduce the heat and simmer gently until the lentils are soft, about 30 minutes. Drain, return the lentils to the pot, and reserve.

4. In a small bowl, add the gelatin to the vermouth until it "blooms" or absorbs the liquid and softens slightly. Add the gelatin mixture to the pot with the reserved warm lentils, stirring well to make sure that the gelatin melts completely. Season with salt, pepper, and cayenne. Cool the lentils to room temperature. (To do this quickly, place the pot in a larger pot containing ice water.)

5. In a wide, shallow pan, bring about 1/2 inch water to a boil. Add the swiss chard and cook until just wilted. Drain and immediately run under cold water to refresh and set the color. Lightly squeeze out the excess water and reserve.

The Latin word for lentil, lens, gives us our word for a lentil-shaped piece of glass, a term used ever since the seventh century.

6. Bring a small pot of salted water to a boil and drop in the 2½-inch long scallions, stirring to cook evenly. As soon as their color brightens, about 30 seconds, drain and run under cold water to set the color. In the same pan over medium heat combine the olive oil, diced scallions, fennel, and bell pepper. Cook for 2 minutes or until slightly softened. Remove from the heat and combine with the lentils.

7. In the prepared terrine mold, arrange half of the reserved swiss chard, rib sides facing up, so that they overlap each other and the edges of the mold by about 1 inch. Spread half the lentil mixture into the mold. Arrange the 2½-inch scallion pieces lengthwise in rows down the center of the mold. Cover with the remaining lentil mixture. Top with the remaining spinach leaves as before. Fold the overlapping edges over the top to enclose the lentils completely. Bang the filled terrine sharply on a hard surface to force out any air bubbles. Cover and refrigerate at least 2 hours, preferably overnight, or until the mixture is firm enough to cut.

8. Unmold the terrine by dipping it briefly into hot water and then inverting. Cut into ¼-inch-thick slices preferably using an electric knife. Ladle the reserved vinaigrette onto large chilled plates and arrange 1 slice of terrine on each plate and serve immediately.

CHAPTER EIGHT

MAIN DISHES

RIGATONI WITH OVEN-COOKED ITALIAN-STYLE BEANS, PEPPERONI, AND GARLIC

This is a great party recipe to serve with red Zinfandel wine. Hearty, full-flavored, and inexpensive, I've had nothing but raves every time I've served this dish. The sauce makes enough for two pounds of pasta, but it keeps and reheats quite well: about four days in the refrigerator, or two months in the freezer. Note that when cooking pasta it will be done just past the point where you can see a small center of hard pearly-looking dough. The color should still be creamy yellow; overcooked pasta is whitish in color.

Serves 8 to 10 •

4 cups (1 recipe) Oven-Cooked Italian-Style Beans (see page 228) prepared with red kidney or chili beans

¼ cup extra-virgin olive oil

1 cup peeled garlic cloves

½ pound pepperoni, diced

1 whole hot red chile pepper

3 cups tomato sauce (homemade or purchased)

Salt and freshly ground black pepper

1 pound imported rigatoni (or other ridged, tube-shaped pasta)

1 cup chopped Italian parsley leaves (about 2 bunches)

¼ pound grated aged Provolone (or other grating cheese such as Kefalotiri or dry Jack), for serving

1. Prepare the Oven-Cooked Italian-Style Beans. Reserve, including the cooking liquid.

2. Combine the olive oil and garlic in a small pot. Cook over medium heat until the cloves turn a light golden brown. Remove from the heat and strain the oil, reserving both the oil and garlic.

3. In the reserved garlic oil, sauté the pepperoni and chile pepper until lightly browned. Add the garlic cloves, tomato sauce, and the reserved Oven-Cooked Italian-Style Beans with their cooking juices. Simmer liquid for 10 to 15 minutes, stirring occasionally. Season to taste with salt and pepper.

4. Cook the pasta in plenty of boiling salted water until al dente, or barely cooked through. Drain well and toss with about one-third of the sauce and the chopped parsley. Serve on large heated pasta plates, adding another spoonful of the sauce on top. Pass the cheese in a small bowl and the remaining sauce in a gravy boat, if desired.

CHOOSING GARLIC

I'M A GARLIC LOVER SO I'M VERY PARTICULAR ABOUT THE QUALITY OF GARLIC I BUY. I REALLY DESPISE THE BITTER TASTE OF COMMERCIAL CHOPPED GARLIC IN OIL. ON THE OTHER HAND, EVEN I DON'T ALWAYS HAVE THE PATIENCE TO PEEL MY OWN—THOUGH IF I COME ACROSS HEADS OF HARD-NECKED, PINK-SKINNED GARLIC FULL OF JUICY CLOVES, I DON'T PASS UP THE OPPORTUNITY TO ENJOY GARLIC AT ITS BEST. CHEFS HAVE BEEN ABLE TO BUY HIGH-QUALITY PEELED GARLIC CLOVES FOR A LONG TIME BUT IT'S ONLY RECENTLY THAT I'VE SEEN WHOLE PEELED GARLIC CLOVES IN THE PRODUCE SECTION OF MY MARKET. IF YOU SPOT CREAMY-LOOKING, SMOOTH, PEARLY CLOVES, BUY THEM FOR THIS HEARTY, SOUL-SATISFYING DISH.

TOTO'S PASTA "FAZOOL" *(Pasta e Fagioli)*

Toto Schiavone, owner of the super-stylish restaurant Toto, is a person who has had a major influence on my life. As *direttore* (managing director) of the original Ristorante DiLullo, Toto was the king of maître d's. A born restaurateur, his generous and outgoing nature endeared him to customers, who continued coming back for both the food and his legendary hospitality. As a boy growing up in Taranto (the instep of the Italian boot), Toto ate the traditional rustic foods of the region, including lots of fish and seafood like calamari and mussels, and this cold weather dish of pasta with beans (made in different ways throughout Italy). I always loved it when he cooked this dish for me and so I asked him to share his mother's recipe for this book. He makes it using pork broth but I've substituted chicken broth.

Serves 6 •

3 cups (1/2 recipe) Oven-Cooked Italian-
Style Beans (see page 228) prepared
with cranberry beans

1 pound Durum Pasta Dough
(see page 306), cut into maltagliati
shapes, or 1 (1-pound) package small
dried pasta shells

1/4 cup extra-virgin olive oil

1/2 red onion, chopped (about 1/4 cup)

1/2 fennel bulb, finely chopped

6 individually-cut pork ribs

1 cup fresh crushed tomatoes

3 cups Light Chicken Stock
(see page 301)

1/2 cup finely diced carrots

1/2 cup finely shredded arugula leaves
(about 1 bunch)

2 teaspoons salt

1/4 teaspoons freshly ground black pepper

1/2 cup grated Parmigiano-Reggiano

2 tablespoons extra-virgin olive oil,
for serving

1. Prepare the Oven-Cooked Italian-Style Beans. Reserve.

2. Prepare and cut the Durum Pasta Dough. Reserve.

3. Heat the 1/4 cup oil in a large, heavy-bottomed pan. Add the pork ribs and cook over medium heat until brown. Remove from the pan. Add the fennel and onions. Cook until the vegetables are soft. Add the tomatoes and simmer for about 7 to 10 minutes.

4. Add the reserved beans, mix well and stir in the Light Chicken Stock. Bring to a boil, reduce heat and simmer for 30 minutes adding the carrots the last 5 minutes. Remove the pork ribs from the pot. Cool then remove the meat from the bones. Remove about 1 cup of the bean mixture to a bowl and mash with a fork. Place the pork meat and the mashed beans back into the pot.

5. Bring a large pot of salted water to a boil. Cook the pasta until firm to the bite (2 to 3 minutes for fresh pasta; 8 minutes for dried). Drain, reserving 1/2 cup of the pasta cooking water.

6. Add the reserved pasta water to the bean mixture along with the arugula, salt and pepper, and grated cheese. Let the mixture rest for 5 minutes and then serve, dividing the meat among the plates. As Toto says, "Drizzle each plate with one hair of oil."

ROASTED GIGOT OF LAMB WITH FLAGEOLET GRATIN

Flageolets and lamb are a classic combination in France where the "gigot," or leg of lamb, is much appreciated for its robust flavor. We Americans eat relatively little lamb but are starting to get to know it better as a result of the huge wave of new Mediterranean restaurants. Assertively flavored lamb rubbed with resinous herbs, like rosemary, thyme, and oregano, marries very well with creamy-textured but flavor-absorbing legumes. Start this dish the day before you plan to serve it so the meat has a chance to absorb the flavors of the rub. The flageolets can be prepared up to the point of baking them as much as three days ahead.

Advanced preparation recommended. Serves 8 •

LAMB

¼ cup chopped fresh rosemary leaves
   (about ½ bunch)
¼ cup chopped fresh thyme leaves
   (about 1 bunch)
2 tablespoons chopped garlic
Grated zest of 2 lemons
1 tablespoon kosher salt
1 teaspoon freshly ground black pepper
¼ cup olive oil
1 (8- to 10-) pound leg of lamb, outer fat
   trimmed off (see Cook's Note, page 171)
1 cup dry white vermouth
1 cup water

1. Prepare the Lamb: Combine the rosemary, thyme, garlic, lemon zest, salt, and pepper in a small bowl. Stir in the oil and rub the seasoning paste all over the surface of the lamb. Place the lamb in a roasting pan just large enough to hold it, cover lightly and marinate in the refrigerator for at least 4 hours or overnight. (You could use a disposable foil roasting pan for this.) About 3 hours before you plan to serve the lamb, start the flageolets.

2. Prepare the Flageolet Gratin: Place the flageolets, clove-studded onion, lemon zest, and bay leaves into a medium, heavy-bottomed pot. Add the 6 cups water to cover and bring to a boil. Skim off and discard the white foam impurities that rise to the top. Reduce the heat to a bare simmer and cook slowly for about 1 hour, or until the beans are almost tender. Remove from the heat and pour off and reserve the liquid. Discard the onion, lemon zest, and bay leaves. Reserve the beans and their cooking liquid.

3. Heat ¼ cup of the olive oil in a sauté pan. Add the shallots, garlic, and thyme and cook for 2 to 3 minutes, while stirring constantly. Add the Light Chicken Stock and bring the mixture to a boil. Add the reserved flageolets along with their cooking liquid and remove from the heat.

FLAGEOLET GRATIN

1 (12-ounce) package imported flageolets

1 whole peeled onion stuck with
  4 whole cloves

1 (3- to 4-inch) strip lemon zest (yellow
  part only)

2 bay leaves

6 cups water

$\frac{1}{2}$ cup extra-virgin olive oil

$\frac{1}{2}$ cup sliced shallots

2 tablespoons chopped garlic

2 tablespoons chopped fresh thyme
  leaves (about $\frac{1}{2}$ bunch)

3 cups Light Chicken Stock
  (see page 301)

$1\frac{1}{2}$ cups fresh bread crumbs, prepared
  from country-style white bread

Cook's Note 🐦 🐦 🐦

*Ask your butcher to completely trim
the leg of lamb and remove the aitch
bone (the partial hip bone at the large
end of the leg) to make it easier to
carve. You should see little to no outer
connective tissue, with the muscle
meat exposed. (The fat of the lamb is
strong tasting and the herb rub won't
penetrate if this step is not done.)*

4. Lightly rub the insides of a shallow 2-quart oval gratin dish or large shallow baking dish with a little oil. In a separate bowl, combine the remaining $\frac{1}{4}$ cup oil with the bread crumbs and reserve. Fill the gratin dish with the bean mixture, spreading it evenly with a spoon. Sprinkle generously with the bread crumbs. Reserve in the refrigerator for up to 3 days.

5. About 2 hours before serving, preheat the oven to 375°F. Place the marinated lamb on the bottom shelf of the oven and roast for about 1 hour, or until it reaches 100° to 110°F on a meat thermometer. Place the gratin on the top shelf in the oven and cook with the lamb for about 1 hour longer, or until the top of the gratin is browned and bubbly and the lamb reaches 135°F on a meat thermometer inserted into its thickest part (for medium-rare).

6. Remove the lamb from the oven, place on a cutting board and allow it to rest for about 15 minutes before carving it into thin tongue-shaped slices and arrange on a platter. Pour off and discard the excess fat from the roasting pan. If the pan is metal, place it directly over a burner. If not, add the vermouth and place the pan back in the oven to soften the browned bits. Add the vermouth and 1 cup water. Bring the liquid in the pan to a boil, scraping up the browned bits with a wooden spoon. Strain through a sieve into a small pot. Cook for 5 to 10 minutes to reduce the liquid by one-fourth. Transfer it to a gravy boat.

7. To serve, place a scoop of the gratin, including some crust, onto each plate and top with a couple lamb slices. Pour the juices over the top.

BEER-BRAISED LAMB SHANKS ON A BED OF DRUNKEN BEANS

If you like lamb and meat that's falling-off-the-bone tender, then lamb shanks are for you. Here, I braise the lamb shanks in an old-fashioned way of slow-cooking tough but tasty meats in small amounts of liquid. There's nothing like the meltingly rich consistency of braised meats, especially in winter. Many times meat markets will only have two to four lamb shanks on hand. You can either order them ahead, or buy them as you see them and freeze them well-wrapped until you decide to make this dish. The beer evolves into a dark, subtly sweet sauce for the lamb. The drunken beans follow the same theme by simmering in a potful of beer.

Serves 6 •

DRUNKEN BEANS

1 pound (2 cups) dried white haricot
    beans, such as great Northern beans,
    soaked (see Soaking Chart, page 41)
2 (12-ounce) bottles dark beer
2 bay leaves
4 cups cold water
1/4 cup olive oil
2 large onions, diced
1 teaspoon ground allspice
1 teaspoon ground coriander
Salt and freshly ground black pepper
1/4 cup chopped Italian parsley leaves
    (about 1/2 bunch)

1. Prepare the Drunken Beans: Drain and rinse the soaked white beans, then place in a large heavy pot with a lid. Add the beer, bay leaves, and water and bring to a boil. Cover, reduce the heat and simmer for about 2 hours, or until the beans are cooked through but still firm. Drain off and discard any excess liquid.

2. Heat the olive oil in a pan and cook the onions over medium heat until well browned, stirring often. Stir in the allspice and coriander. Stir the onion mixture into the beans. Season to taste with salt and pepper and continue to cook for another 5 to 10 minutes, stirring occasionally. Remove from the heat and stir in the parsley. Reserve.

3. Prepare the Lamb Shanks: Preheat the oven to 325°F. In a bowl, combine the flour, salt, and pepper. Dredge the shanks in the flour mixture.

4. In a large Dutch oven with a lid, heat the oil. Brown the shanks on all sides in the oil, turning several times. Remove the shanks and keep them warm. Drain off and discard most of the fat from the pan. In the same pan, add half the carrots, half the garlic, and half the celery root. Brown the vegetables over medium heat, then pour in the beer to deglaze the pan, scraping up

Lamb Shanks

1 cup unbleached all-purpose flour,
  for dusting

1 tablespoon kosher salt

1 teaspoon freshly ground black pepper

6 large lamb shanks, excess fat trimmed
  (about 5 to 6 pounds total)

2 tablespoons olive oil

1 pound carrots, diagonally sliced

1 cup peeled garlic cloves

1 large celery root, pared and diced

3 (12-ounce) bottles dark beer

½ cup chopped fresh winter or summer
  savory leaves (about 1 bunch)

any browned bits. Add the savory and bring the liquid to a boil. Place the shanks back into the Dutch oven and bring to a boil on top of the stove. Cover and braise in the oven for about 2 hours, turning once, until the shanks are tender but still whole.

5. Remove the shanks from the oven, cool slightly so the shanks don't fall apart, then remove and reserve them. Strain the Dutch oven liquid through a sieve, pressing the solids to extract the juices. Discard the solids. Add the remaining half of vegetables to the Dutch oven along with the reserved shanks and liquid and cook together until the vegetables are tender, about 20 minutes.

6. To serve, place a mound of the beans on each plate and top with a lamb shank, a portion of the vegetables, and the sauce.

BRAZILIAN FEIJOADA COMPLETA

Feijõada, from the Portuguese word, *feijõas*, meaning beans, is the national dish of Brazil. It is based on a central dish of black beans that is surrounded by a large variety of smoked and cured meats. I once held a tasting party for a take-out food project I was working on. Seventy-five or so guests came, tasted a menu of about twenty items, and then had to fill out a survey. This dish was the all-around favorite.

If you have access to a home smoker and you want to include the amazing spiced and smoked short ribs and the home-smoked chorizo, you'll need to start this dish three days ahead of time. Otherwise, simply substitute with corned beef or smoked pork butt and smoked kielbasa. Here I serve the black beans surrounded with spiced short ribs, smoked chorizo, Brazilian rice, and braised greens, and accompanied by the spicy lemon-pepper mojo or salsa.

Advance preparation required. Serves 12 to 16 •

MEAT

3½ pounds Spiced and Smoked Short Ribs (see page 175), or 3 pounds cooked corned beef or smoked pork butt (see Cook's Note, opposite)

2½ pounds Home-Smoked Chorizo (see page 175), or 3 pounds smoked kielbasa, cut into ¾-inch diagonal slices (see Cook's Note, opposite)

BLACK BEANS

6 cups (1 recipe) Basic Black Turtle Beans (see page 231)

2 large white onions, diced

2 tablespoons chopped garlic

1 tablespoon ground toasted cumin (see Toasting Seeds, page 217)

¼ cup bacon fat or olive oil

1 (28-ounce) can plum tomatoes, seeded and diced, juice strained and added

½ cup malt vinegar, or cider or sherry vinegar

1 tablespoon Mexican oregano

2 tablespoons hot pepper sauce

2 tablespoons salt

1. Prepare the Spiced and Smoked Short Ribs. Reserve.

2. Prepare the Home-Smoked Chorizo. Reserve.

3. Prepare the Black Beans: Prepare the Basic Black Turtle Beans. Reserve. Preheat the oven to 300°F. In a large, heavy Dutch oven with a lid, cook the onions, garlic, and cumin in the bacon fat until softened but not browned. Stir in the tomatoes, vinegar, oregano, hot sauce, salt, and bring to a boil. Stir in the reserved cooked beans, cover and transfer to the oven. Bake for 2 hours or until the beans are soft and plump. Reserve.

5. Prepare the Brazilian Rice: Bring the Light Chicken Stock, the saffron, water, salt and pepper to a boil in a medium pan. Remove from the heat and cover. In a large, heavy Dutch oven, cook the onions in the olive oil until softened but not browned. Add the rice and sauté until transparent but not browned. Add the hot stock mixture and tomatoes to the rice and bring to a boil. Reduce the heat and simmer, covered, for 15 to 20 minutes or until all the liquid has been absorbed.

6. Prepare the Lemon-Pepper Mojo and the Mixed Greens with Garlic and Olive Oil. Reserve.

7. To serve, arrange the beans in the center of a large platter. Place

BRAZILIAN RICE

2 cups Light Chicken Stock
  (see page 301)
1/2 teaspoon saffron threads
2 cups water
Salt and freshly ground black pepper
1 onion, thinly sliced
2 tablespoons olive oil
2 cups raw long-grain rice
1 (28-ounce) can chopped plum tomatoes

1 1/2 cups Lemon-Pepper Mojo
  (see page 284)
6 cups Mixed Greens with Garlic and
  Olive Oil (see page 299)
Orange slices and ruby red grapefruit
  slices, for garnish

SPICED AND SMOKED SHORT RIBS

Makes 3 1/2 pounds smoked ribs

2 tablespoons kosher salt
2 tablespoons molasses
2 tablespoons sugar
2 tablespoons grated fresh ginger
1 tablespoon cracked black peppercorns
1/2 cup chopped garlic
2 tablespoons cracked coriander seed
2 tablespoons ground fennel seed
5 pounds cross-cut short ribs of beef

1. To prepare the Spiced and Smoked Short Ribs, place the salt, molasses, sugar, ginger, peppercorns, garlic, coriander, and fennel in a blender or food processor and process to a paste. Rub all over the surface of the short ribs and cure, covered, in the refrigerator for 3 days.

2. Wipe off the excess paste and hot-smoke according to smoker manufacturer's directions for 4 hours, or until tender and well browned. Cover and reserve in a 200°F oven.

the reserved short ribs on one side of the beans and the chorizo on the other. Garnish the platter with the orange and grapefruit slices. On a second large platter, arrange the rice on one side and greens on the other. Place the mojo in a bowl alongside.

Cook's Note ❧ ❧ ❧

If using corned beef instead of beef ribs, purchase a 5- to 6-pound corned beef brisket. Remove it from the package, drain well, and place in a large soup or braising pot. Cover with chicken, beef, vegetable stock, or water and bring the liquid to a boil. Reduce the heat and simmer very gently for 3 hours, or until the meat is tender when pierced with a fork. Cool in its cooking liquid for juiciest results and reserve the liquid. To serve, slice thinly across the grain of the meat and reheat in the reserved cooking liquid. Cover and reserve in a 200°F oven.

If using smoked pork instead of beef ribs, purchase a 4-pound boneless smoked pork loin. To cook, preheat the oven to 325°F. Place the meat in a roasting pan with about 3 cups of liquid (white wine, beef or chicken stock, or water). Cover with foil and bake for 1 hour, or until steaming hot. Remove from the oven and cool for about 10 minutes before slicing. Cover and reserve in a 200°F oven.

If using kielbasa instead of chorizo, brown the slices in a skillet over medium heat. Drain and reserve in a 200°F oven.

HOME-SMOKED CHORIZO

Makes 2 1/2 pounds smoked chorizo

3 pounds raw chorizo links

To prepare the Home-Smoked Chorizo, hot-smoke the chorizo according to the smoker manufacturer's directions for 1 hour, or until it bubbles inside when pricked with a fork and is evenly browned. Cover and reserve in a 200°F oven.

INDONESIAN LAMB SATÉ
WITH SPICY PEANUT SAUCE

This classic saté of lamb might be sold by an Indonesian street vendor with a small charcoal brazier. An easy make-ahead dish, serve this saté at your next cookout. If you cook on a natural charcoal grill, the flavor will be even better.

Here, strips of lean lamb are marinated in tamarind (a tart tropical fruit), ginger, and soy sauce and then threaded on bamboo skewers. The lamb is grilled and accompanied by a spicy peanut sauce. This is an inexpensive and tasty dish that your guests will snap up and you won't even need any silverware. You can vary this dish by making it with beef strips.

Serves 8 •

2 tablespoons tamarind pulp
  (see Preparing Tamarind, page 291),
  seeded and chopped
2 pounds fresh boneless leg, or shoulder of
  lamb, or beef chuck
1 small onion, coarsely chopped
2 cloves garlic, chopped
2 tablespoons mushroom soy sauce
1/4 teaspoon cayenne
1 1/2 teaspoons ground coriander
1 (2-inch) length fresh ginger
1 tablespoon peanut oil
1 cup Spicy Peanut Dipping Sauce
  (see page 298)

1. Prepare the tamarind pulp. Reserve.

2. Place the lamb in the freezer for about 30 minutes to chill and firm. Remove and trim off any surface fat. Cut the meat into thin finger-shaped strips, 2 to 3 inches long and reserve. In a shallow glass dish, combine the meat, onion, garlic, soy sauce, cayenne, coriander, ginger, tamarind pulp, and oil. Cover and marinate in the refrigerator for 24 hours.

3. Prepare the Spicy Peanut Sauce. Reserve.

4. Drain and discard the marinade. Thread the meat onto bamboo skewers lengthwise, threading them accordion-style so they resemble snakes. Reserve the skewered meat, covered, in the refrigerator until ready to cook.

5. When ready to serve, heat a grill, preferably hardwood charcoal, to white hot. Grill the skewers on both sides, until browned and crusty, about 5 minutes on each side. Serve the skewers with the Spicy Peanut Sauce.

BEEF STIR-FRY WITH SNOW PEAS AND BEAN SPROUTS

This quick stir-fry is a popular choice for lunch at a longtime favorite Philadelphia restaurant, Friday-Saturday-Sunday. (Originally it was open only those days. More than twenty years later, it's open seven days.) Crunchy bean sprouts and sweet snow peas represent the legume family here. The large white mild daikon radish called for is sold in many supermarkets. It's a versatile vegetable, delicious shredded raw in salads or cooked in stir-fries. Substitute white turnip if daikon isn't available.

Serves 4 to 6 •

1 tablespoon roasted Japanese
   sesame oil

¼ cup soy sauce

¼ cup molasses

½ teaspoon hot red pepper flakes,
   such as Korean red pepper flakes
   (see About Korean Red Pepper Flakes,
   page 49)

2 tablespoons cornstarch

2 tablespoons peanut or soybean oil

1 pound London broil, cut into
   2- to 3-inch-long thin strips

2 tablespoons chopped fresh ginger

2 tablespoons chopped garlic

1 large white onion, peeled and cut
   into strips

1 red bell pepper, cut into ½-inch
   wide strips

½ pound daikon radish, peeled and cut
   into half-moon slices

¼ pound snow peas, trimmed

1 pint fresh bean sprouts, trimmed

3 cups steamed rice, for serving (optional)

1. In a small bowl, whisk together the sesame oil, soy sauce, molasses, red pepper flakes, and cornstarch. Reserve.

2. Heat the peanut oil in a wok or a large skillet until it just begins to smoke. Add the beef and stir-fry for about 5 minutes or until browned. Remove from the pan and reserve in a warm place.

3. In the same pan, cook the ginger and garlic for 1 minute. Add the onion, bell pepper, and daikon. Stir-fry for 2 minutes, then add the reserved beef, snow peas, cornstarch mixture, and bean sprouts. Cook until the sauce thickens and the snow peas turn bright green. Serve with steamed rice, if desired.

A WORD ABOUT SNOW PEAS

THE FRENCH TERM *mangetout* (LITERALLY EAT-IT-ALL) USUALLY REFERS TO YOUNG BEANS THAT ARE EATEN PODS AND ALL, AND ARE KNOWN IN THIS COUNTRY AS SNOW PEAS. IN ENGLAND THE SAME TERM IS APPLIED TO THE RELATIVE NEWCOMER "THE SUGAR SNAP PEA." SNOW PEAS, WHICH HAVE BEEN CULTIVATED FOR AT LEAST THREE HUNDRED YEARS, HAVE PODS WITH NO HARD INNER SKIN. THEY ARE PICKED BEFORE THE PEAS INSIDE GROW LARGE ENOUGH TO BE VISIBLE FROM THE OUTSIDE. THE PEA PODS USED TO BE CALLED "PEA CODS" AS IN CODPIECE.

GRILLED LAMB PATTIES *(Kofte)*
WITH TURKISH WHITE BEAN SALAD
AND MARINATED CARROTS

In the early seventies, I stayed in the old section of Istanbul, near the Souk and across from the famous Blue Mosque. Every night we played *shesh-besh* (backgammon) in the hotel's courtyard. In spite of my limited funds, I ate well, enjoying Istanbul's varied offerings: a melange of eastern Mediterranean and north African dishes. Most days I would go to the same restaurant to enjoy this dish, their "working man's lunch special."

Serves 4 •

2 cups Turkish White Bean Salad
   (see page 76)

MARINATED CARROTS

1 pound carrots, peeled and shredded

1/2 cup fresh lemon juice (about 4
   lemons)

1/2 cup extra-virgin olive oil

1 sweet onion (such as Vidalia, or Texas
   100), or white onion, thinly sliced

Salt and freshly ground black pepper

2 teaspoons sumac (optional)

LAMB PATTIES

1 pound ground lamb

1 egg

1 teaspoon finely chopped garlic

1 small onion, grated

2 teaspoons chopped fresh mint leaves,
   or 1/2 teaspoon dried

1/4 teaspoon hot red pepper flakes

1/4 teaspoon ground cinnamon

1/4 teaspoon ground allspice

2 teaspoons salt

1/4 teaspoons freshly ground black pepper

Olive oil, for brushing

Kosher salt, for grilling

1. Prepare the Turkish White Bean Salad. Refrigerate and reserve.

2. Prepare the Marinated Carrots: In a bowl, combine the carrots, lemon juice, olive oil, onion, and salt and pepper to taste, mixing well. Refrigerate until needed, for up to 3 to 4 days. If dried out, sprinkle with the sumac before serving.

3. Prepare the Lamb Patties: In a large bowl, combine the lamb, egg, garlic, onion, mint, pepper flakes, cinnamon, allspice, salt, and black pepper. Knead together by hand until well combined. Form into 8 oblong patties. Cover and refrigerate for 30 minutes or for up to 1 day.

4. When ready to cook, preheat a grill. Lightly brush the lamb patties with olive oil and sprinkle with kosher salt to help keep them from sticking. Place the patties on an angle on the grill and cook 5 to 7 minutes or until they release freely from the grill when you try to turn them. Rotate the patties a half-turn and continue to grill for 5 minutes, then turn them over and repeat, cooking for another 5 to 7 minutes. The patties should be medium to medium-rare when cooked.

5. To serve, place a mound of the bean salad on each plate. Top with 2 grilled lamb patties and surrounded with 3 to 4 small mounds of the marinated carrots.

ISRAELI COUSCOUS WITH EGGPLANT ROLLS AND CHICKPEAS

In the early sixties, many of Morocco's large Jewish population left the country and settled in Paris, bringing with them their highly developed cuisine. On a trip to Paris in 1964, I tasted my first couscous and loved the way the fluffy grain soaked up the subtly spiced cooking juices. Later, my mother's Moroccan Jewish friend in Washington, D.C. taught her how to make her version of couscous, which I've adapted for this book, using the large-grain Israeli-style couscous.

Serves 8 •

1 cup dried chickpeas, cooked and drained (see Basic Cooking Chart, page 43)

EGGPLANT ROLLS

1 large eggplant, sliced into 16 $^1/_4$-inch thick pieces

1 pound ground beef, formed into 16 walnut-sized meatballs

2 eggs, well beaten

Salt and freshly ground black pepper

1 cup unbleached, all-purpose flour, for coating

Olive oil, for frying

2 cloves garlic, crushed

2 pounds beefsteak tomatoes, seeded and diced, juices strained and reserved

2 cups Light Chicken Stock
 (see page 301)

ISRAELI COUSCOUS

2 tablespoons olive oil

2 cups Israeli large-grained couscous

4 cups Light Chicken Stock (see page 301), simmering

2 teaspoons salt

1. Prepare the chickpeas. Reserve.

2. Prepare the Eggplant Rolls: Lay the eggplant slices on a clean flat surface and salt lightly. After 30 minutes, pat the eggplant slices dry. Place a meatball in the center of each slice. Roll the eggplant around the meat to form a tube, secure with a toothpick or skewer. When all the eggplant slices have been stuffed, dip them first in the egg and then roll them in salt- and pepper-seasoned flour to coat, shaking off the excess. Reserve on a platter.

3. Heat $^1/_2$-inch depth of olive oil in a large skillet over medium heat. Add the eggplant rolls and brown on both sides, then remove from the pan and reserve. Pour off and discard almost all the oil.

4. Reduce the heat and add the garlic to the pan, stirring to cook evenly. Add the tomatoes and juice, reserved chickpeas, and 2 cups Light Chicken Stock. Increase the heat and bring to a boil. Place the eggplant rolls in the stock mixture, reduce the heat and simmer for 30 minutes, until tender.

5. Prepare the Israeli Couscous: Heat the olive oil over medium heat in a medium pot. Add the couscous and lightly brown, stirring constantly. Add the 4 cups simmering Light Chicken Stock and salt. Bring to a boil and cover. Reduce the heat and cook about 15 minutes or until the stock has been absorbed. Reserve.

6. To serve, have a large platter ready, heated if possible. Place the couscous in a mound in the center. Surround it with the eggplant rolls. Serve topped with the remaining sauce from the pan.

ROASTED PIGEONS WITH FRESH FAVA BEANS

(Pigeonneau Rôti aux Fèvettes)

I had the great pleasure of spending a day and evening in the kitchen of Chef Pierre Orsi's wonderful and charming restaurant in Lyons. Chef Orsi was a generous and hospitable host and patiently answered my many questions about his kitchen and cuisine. He shared two of his recipes with me, which I've adapted.

Serves 4

4 whole young pigeons
  (about 3 pounds total)
Salt and freshly ground black pepper
10 tablespoons unsalted butter
½ cup vegetable oil
¼ cup dry white wine
½ cup Light Chicken Stock
  (see page 301)
2 tablespoons Cognac
4 slices country-style white bread, crusts
  trimmed and cut into neat oval shapes
½ cup raw wild rice, cooked according to
  package directions (1½ cups cooked)
½ cup blanched and skinned fresh,
  young fava beans (see About Young
  Fava Beans, page 181)
2 tablespoons fresh basil leaves,
  snipped into fine shreds

1. Preheat the oven to 400°F. Rinse and dry the pigeons. Remove the giblets, reserving the livers. Sprinkle them inside and out with salt and pepper, then tie them with butcher's string to make a neat compact shape.

2. In a large ovenproof Dutch oven, heat about 6 tablespoons of the butter with the oil until foamy. Add the pigeons and brown on all sides, keeping the butter foamy. Place the pigeons, still in the pan, into the oven and roast for 10 minutes, basting several times.

3. Remove the pan from the oven and transfer the pigeons to a cutting board, draining and reserving any juices from the birds. Reduce the oven to 300°F. Using a heavy knife or kitchen shears, cut down along both sides of each pigeon's backbone. Remove and reserve the bone. Turn the pigeon halves over and use your fingers to pull out the rib cage and reserve. Reserve the semi-boned pigeon halves on ovenproof platter and cover with foil.

4. Pour off most of the fat from the Dutch oven into a small sauté pan and reserve. Add the wine to the Dutch oven, place over medium heat and bring to a boil, scraping up any browned bits with a wooden spoon. Add the Light Chicken Stock and the reserved pigeon bones and juices and bring to a boil. Reduce the heat and simmer for 30 minutes, then strain the liquid, discarding the bones. Pour the liquid into a small pan and boil until reduced by about half. The liquid should be slightly syrupy. Season to taste with salt and pepper.

5. Heat the sauté pan of reserved roasting fat. Add the pigeon livers and cook over high heat until well browned. Season with salt and pepper. Remove the livers to a small bowl with a slotted spoon. Add 2 tablespoons of the butter and mash. Add the Cognac to the mixture and mash again until fairly smooth. Stir this mixture into the reduced pigeon liquid to make the sauce.

6. In a small pan over low heat, heat the remaining 2 tablespoons butter until foamy. Add the bread ovals and lightly brown on both sides. Remove the bread ovals from the pan and reserve.

7. Reheat the wild rice, if necessary (you can do this in the microwave oven). When ready to serve, have ready 4 large heated dinner plates. Place the platter with the pigeon halves into the 300°F oven to reheat for about 10 minutes. At the last minute, bring the pigeon sauce to a boil, add half the fava beans and simmer for 2 minutes.

8. Place one bread oval in the center of each dinner plate. Place two pigeon halves onto the bread and baste with the liquid from the pigeon sauce. Surround the pigeon with a ring of wild rice and sprinkle with some of the remaining fava beans, the basil shreds, and the remainder of the pigeon sauce. Serve immediately.

ABOUT YOUNG ❧ ❧ ❧ FAVA BEANS ❧ ❧ ❧

Tender young fava beans are a springtime legume. Before you cook them, it is necessary to blanch them in salted water and refresh them in ice water in order to remove the outer skin, which is not edible. Then, separate each one into two halves.

SEVEN VEGETABLE AND CHICKEN COUSCOUS

Couscous grains are actually small balls of semolina flour rolled around a core of coarse semolina, although sometimes it is made from whole wheat flour or from toasted barley grits. All types of couscous—from vegetarian to lamb, poultry, seafood, and even sweet versions—are popular in the cuisines of Tunisia, Morocco, and Algeria. I definitely have an affinity for north African cuisines. As the former chef of a Mediterranean bistro owned by two Tunisian-born brothers, I learned how to prepare couscous, harissa sauce, *chakchouka* (a dish of roasted vegetables mixed with egg), brik, and preserved lemons. It's only in the past few years that I've started seeing these dishes and ingredients served commonly.

Serves 6 to 8 •

3 cups Basic Cooked Chickpeas
   (see page 234)
½ cup Tunisian Harissa Sauce
   (see page 297)
5 cups Rich Chicken Stock
   (see page 303)
3 pounds chicken thighs
Salt and freshly ground black pepper
2 cups couscous
6 tablespoons extra-virgin olive oil
Salt
1 small onion, diced
1 large butternut squash, pared, seeded
   and cut into 1-inch dice
1 rutabaga or white turnip, pared and cut
   into 1-inch dice
1 (12-ounce) package frozen artichoke
   hearts, thawed and drained
1 (12-ounce) package frozen baby limas,
   thawed and drained
1 small head savoy cabbage, shredded
½ cup chopped fresh cilantro
   (about 1 bunch), for garnish

1. Prepare the Basic Cooked Chickpeas, Tunisian Harissa Sauce, and Rich Chicken Stock. Reserve.

2. Preheat the oven to 350°F. Arrange the chicken thighs on a baking sheet and sprinkle with salt and pepper. Roast for 45 minutes, or until thoroughly cooked and tender. The juices should run clear when the thighs are pierced in their thickest parts. Reserve in a warm oven.

3. While the chicken is roasting, pour 3 cups of the Rich Chicken Stock into a medium pot. Arrange a sieve or colander over the pot. Pour the couscous into the sieve. Cover tightly with a lid or a double layer of heavy-duty aluminum foil, so the steam doesn't escape. Bring to a boil, reduce the heat and steam for about 20 minutes, or until small white dots appear on the couscous. Transfer the steamed couscous into a large bowl. Add 2 tablespoons of the oil and season to taste with salt. Using your clean hands, work the oil and salt into the couscous until all the lumps disappear and the grain is fluffy. Return the fluffed couscous to the sieve set over simmering stock. Cover and steam for 20 minutes longer.

Cook's Note ❧ ❧ ❧

If you're short of time, you can prepare the couscous without steaming it. Simply heat the Rich Chicken Stock with the olive oil and about 2 teaspoons salt to boiling. Stir in 2 cups of couscous, stir gently to combine and remove from the heat. Cover and set aside for a few minutes to allow the grain to absorb the liquid. Fluff up and serve.

4. Meanwhile, in a large pan, heat the remaining 4 tablespoons olive oil. Add the onion, squash, rutabaga, artichokes, and limas, and cook until crisp-tender, about 10 minutes. Add the remaining 2 cups Rich Chicken Stock, chickpeas, and cabbage. Bring to a boil and cook for 5 to 10 minutes at high heat to reduce the liquid.

5. To serve, place a pyramid-shaped mound of the couscous in the center of each plate. Place 1 roasted chicken thigh on each plate and cover with some of the vegetable mixture and a generous ladleful of their cooking juices. Sprinkle with the chopped cilantro and serve accompanied by a bowl of harissa sauce.

COOKING WITH A COUSCOUSIER

A couscousier is an ancient two-part steaming pot of Berber origin that is used to make the myriad versions of couscous—the national dish of north Africa. The couscous is steamed in the upper section of the couscousier over a flavorful broth or stew in the bottom section. The couscousier I use is made of hammered copper with a tinned interior and brass fittings. It is not necessary to use an authentic couscousier to make good couscous. However, it does make it easier and the eye appeal is wonderful. (See Sources, page 323.)

INDIVIDUAL CHICKEN POT PIES
WITH ASSORTED LEGUMES

It seems that in every restaurant I've cooked or consulted for, I've had to develop a special pot pie recipe. This version is a bit time consuming to make because of the preparation of the chicken, vegetables, broth, and pastry. However, it's always received with pleasure by grown-ups and children alike, and can be varied endlessly to suit your taste and the vegetable you have on hand. This version is for bean lovers because it calls for green beans, black-eyed peas, and sugar snap peas.

Makes 8 to 12 individual pies •

4 cups Rich Chicken Stock
  (see page 303)

3 pounds boneless, skinless
  chicken thighs

¼ pound (1 stick) unsalted butter

¼ cup unbleached all-purpose flour

½ cup dry white vermouth

Salt, freshly ground black pepper,
  and cayenne

½ cup diced onion

½ cup diced carrots

½ cup diced celery (or celery root)

1 cup diced sweet or golden potato

1 cup fresh green beans, cut into
  1-inch lengths

1 (12-ounce) package frozen black-eyed
  peas, rinsed and drained

1 cup trimmed sugar snap peas

¼ cup chopped fresh tarragon leaves
  (about 1 bunch)

½ cup chopped fresh dill
  (about ½ bunch)

¼ cup unbleached all-purpose flour

1. Prepare the Rich Chicken Stock.

2. Heat the stock in a large pot. Add the chicken thighs and bring to a boil. Skim off and discard the white foam impurities that appear. Reduce the heat to a simmer and cook for 20 minutes or until tender. Remove the chicken from the stock and cover with damp paper towels. Strain the stock through a sieve or cheesecloth and then wipe out the pot. Transfer the stock back to the pot.

3. In a small pan, make a roux by melting 4 tablespoons of the butter over low heat, then stirring in the flour and cooking for 5 to 10 minutes, stirring occasionally. Whisk the roux into the strained chicken stock. Bring to a boil, stirring occasionally, until the stock thickens. Add the vermouth and continue to cook until thick enough to coat a spoon. Season the sauce generously with salt, black pepper, and cayenne.

4. Shred the cooked chicken meat into large pieces, removing and discarding any gristle, fat, or bone. Add to the sauce and proceed with the recipe. Otherwise, if making this dish ahead, place the large pot in an ice bath to cool it quickly. Reserve in the refrigerator.

1 pound Buttermilk Dough (see page 305), or 1 (17-ounce) package puff pastry sheets (preferably all-butter), defrosted in the refrigerator

2 egg yolks

$1/4$ cup heavy cream

Cook's Note ❧ ❧ ❧

To make the pot pies ahead of time, make the Rich Chicken Stock and the Buttermilk Dough ahead of time and refrigerate or freeze until you're ready to proceed. You can also make the filling up to the point of adding the chicken (but without the vegetables) and refrigerate and freeze it. Add the vegetables fresh, finish with the pastry, and you'll have a perfectly tasty dish to serve. Before stirring in the vegetables, be sure to defrost the filling if frozen.

5. In a pan, sauté the onion, carrots, celery, potato, and green beans in the remaining 4 tablespoons butter until crisp-tender. Remove from the heat and stir in the black-eyed peas and snap peas. Cool the vegetables to room temperature and then stir into the chicken mixture with the tarragon and dill. Or, if making ahead, cool and reserve, covered, in the refrigerator up to 1 day.

6. On a lightly floured surface, roll out the Buttermilk Dough to an $1/8$-inch thickness. Wrap in plastic wrap and refrigerate for at least 30 minutes. Assemble 8 to 12 large ovenproof bowls or individual casserole dishes. Cut the chilled dough into shapes to match the dishes, making them 1 inch larger all around than the size of the dishes. Chill the pastry cutouts if they become too soft to handle.

7. In a small bowl, lightly beat together the egg yolk and heavy cream to make an egg wash. Spoon the chicken filling into the ungreased individual serving dishes. Brush the outside edges of the dishes with the egg wash. Carefully lay a pastry cutout over each bowl or casserole. Press down on the outside of the dish to seal. Brush the tops of the pastry with the remaining egg wash to make a shining glaze. Cut a 2-inch cross into the pastry top of each potpie with a sharp knife. (If desired cut out leaves or other decorative shapes from any dough scraps, place on top and brush with the egg wash.)

8. When ready to bake, preheat the oven to 350°F. Place the potpies on a baking sheet and bake for 30 minutes or until tops are brown and the filling is bubbling. Remove from the oven and cool for 5 to 10 minutes before serving.

SKILLET-ROASTED CHICKEN WITH BLACK-EYED PEAS, COUNTRY HAM, AND SAVORY

If you think chicken is boring, try an excellent-quality grain-fed or organic chicken to remind yourself of just how special chicken can be. A strong, cured country ham, like a Smithfield ham, is perfect here. I love the little black-eyed peas and ham with the chicken. Try to find fresh savory for this dish, a wonderful herb with poultry and beans. For this recipe, you'll need to have two cast iron skillets to weigh down the chicken so it browns thoroughly.

Serves 4 to 6 •

2 grain-fed or organic chickens
  (4 to 5 pounds total), split and flattened
Salt and freshly ground black pepper
Olive oil, for seasoning pan
2 tablespoons vegetable oil
$1/4$ pound country ham, cut into
  small dice
$1/2$ pound fresh or frozen black-eyed peas
1 bunch scallions, cut diagonally into
  1-inch lengths
1 cup Light Chicken Stock
  (see page 301)
$1/2$ cup dry white vermouth
1 tablespoon chopped fresh savory leaves,
  or 1 teaspoon dried
2 tablespoons unsalted butter

1. Assemble 2 well-seasoned cast-iron skillets, each about 10 inches in diameter. Remove the backbones from the chickens. Cut 2 to 3 slashes in each chicken thigh. Season the chicken halves with salt and pepper.

2. Preheat 1 skillet and coat the inside with a little olive oil. Cooking in two batches, place the chicken halves skin side down in the skillet and cover with the second skillet to weigh down. Cook over medium heat for about 10 minutes, then turn them over. When chicken halves are cooked through, remove them from the skillet and keep warm in a 200°F oven. Pour off and discard any excess fat from the skillet. Repeat.

3. Heat the vegetable oil over high heat and quickly cook the diced ham until crispy. Add the black-eyed peas and scallions and cook for a few minutes. Remove ham-pea mixture from the pan and scatter over the chicken.

4. In the same skillet, bring the Light Chicken Stock and vermouth to a boil. Cook until reduced to a syrupy consistency. Stir in the savory and butter. Ladle the sauce over the chicken and serve immediately.

SMOKED TURKEY CHILI
WITH BLACK-EYED PEAS

This chili is tasty, relatively low in fat, and great to feed a hungry crowd. How good can it get? It's also inexpensive. I like to play around with my outdoor smoker, so I brine and then smoke inexpensive turkey thighs on the bone. I then pull the meat from the bone and use the bones to make a fabulous soup stock for black bean or split pea soup.

Serves 8 •••

1/4 cup olive oil

1 large Spanish onion, diced

2 large carrots, diced

4 bell peppers (preferably a mix of red, yellow, and orange), seeded and diced

1 tablespoon chopped garlic

2 pounds poblano peppers, roasted, peeled, seeded (see Roasted Red Bell Peppers, page 314) and cut into 1-inch squares

1 teaspoon ground allspice

1 tablespoon ground cinnamon

1 tablespoon dry oregano

2 tablespoons chile ancho powder

2 tablespoons salt

1 teaspoon freshly ground black pepper

2 tablespoons all-purpose unbleached flour

1 cup Light Chicken Stock (see page 301)

4 pounds smoked turkey parts on the bone, or 2 pounds boneless turkey meat

2 (12-ounce) packages frozen black-eyed peas

3 cups tomato sauce, purchased or homemade

1/2 bunch fresh cilantro sprigs, for serving

1 cup sour cream, for serving

1/4 pound shredded sharp Cheddar or pepper Jack cheese, for serving

1 red onion, thinly sliced, for serving

1. In a large, heavy-bottomed Dutch oven, heat the olive oil over medium heat. Add the onion, carrots, bell peppers, garlic, and poblano peppers and cook until softened but not browned, about 7 minutes. Stir in the allspice, cinnamon, oregano, chile ancho powder, salt, and black pepper. Cook for about 5 minutes, or until the aromas are released, stirring to combine.

2. Stir in the flour and cook for 2 to 3 minutes, stirring until well mixed. Add the Light Chicken Stock and bring to a boil, stirring occasionally, to make a smooth thick sauce. Stir in the smoked turkey, black-eyed peas, and tomato sauce. Reduce the heat and simmer for 30 minutes or until the turkey is tender and the chili has thickened.

3. When the chili is done, serve immediately, garnishing each portion with cilantro, sour cream, cheese, and red onion. If you want to serve the chili within the next few days, chill it in an ice water bath, especially if you make this recipe during hot, humid weather. Cover and refrigerate until ready to use.

MAKING HOMEMADE SMOKED TURKEY THIGHS

FOR 10 POUNDS OF TURKEY THIGHS, COMBINE 2 CUPS MOLASSES, 6 TABLESPOONS KOSHER SALT, 2 TABLESPOONS EACH OF GROUND CORIANDER, GROUND JUNIPER BERRY, GROUND FENNEL SEED, AND GROUND ALLSPICE IN A LARGE BOWL. COMBINE WITH 3 QUARTS WATER AND SOAK THE TURKEY THIGHS IN THE BRINE MIXTURE OVERNIGHT OR UP TO 2 DAYS IN THE REFRIGERATOR. DRAIN AND SMOKE THE TURKEY THIGHS ACCORDING TO THE SMOKER MANUFACTURER'S DIRECTIONS USING FRUITWOOD CHIPS, SUCH AS CHERRY OR APPLE, FOR 5 HOURS OR UNTIL THE THIGHS ARE TENDER.

RAGOUT OF FLAGEOLETS, CHICKEN-BASIL SAUSAGE, AND SPINACH

Chef Alfonso Contrisciani, captain of the 2000 U. S. Olympic Team, is one of only fifty-three Certified Master Chefs in the country, a title earned in a grueling ten-day examination. He is also a skilled charcutier and believes in making everything in his kitchen from scratch, including his own chicken-basil sausage. This ragout—which is just a fancy French word for stew—features delicate flageolets beans in a rich broth topped with grilled portabella mushrooms and homemade chicken-basil sausage. Like many a chef's creation, this one depends on advance preparation of all ingredients. Once you've assembled all the components, it's relatively easy to complete the dish.

Serves 6 •

3 cups Basic Cooked Flageolets
   (see page 232)
1 cup Rich Chicken Stock (see page 303),
   or diluted demi-glace or veal stock
   (see Sources, page 323)
6 Crostini (see page 53), for serving
1 tablespoon olive oil
1 teaspoon chopped garlic
1 tablespoon chopped shallot
¼ cup diced onion
1 cup quartered white mushrooms
1 cup sliced shiitake mushroom caps
1 teaspoon chopped fresh thyme leaves
1 tablespoon chopped fresh basil leaves
¼ teaspoon hot red pepper flakes
½ teaspoon dried oregano
2 tablespoons brandy
¼ cup dry white wine
3 tablespoons olive oil
2 tablespoons balsamic vinegar
6 large portabella mushrooms caps

1. Prepare the Basic Cooked Flageolets, the Rich Chicken Stock, and the Crostini. Reserve.

2. In a medium pan, heat the 1 tablespoon olive oil over medium-high heat. Add the garlic and shallots. Stir-fry until the garlic turns golden, then add the onion and the white and shiitake mushrooms, stirring to combine. Add the thyme, 1 tablespoon basil, red pepper flakes, and oregano. Continue to stir-fry until the onion is translucent, about 3 to 4 minutes.

3. Add the brandy and, keeping your face away from the flame, carefully light the mixture with a match to flambé. When the flames die down, add the cooked flageolets and the chicken stock. Add the white wine. Simmer over a high heat to reduce and thicken the liquid slightly, about 5 to 10 minutes. Reserve the sauce until ready to finish the dish. (It can be made up to 1 day ahead of time, covered and refrigerated.)

4. To cook the portabella mushrooms and sausage, prepare a hot grill. If using natural hardwood charcoal, wait until the flames die down.

1¹/₂ pounds commerical chicken-basil
   sausage (see Sources, page 323)
1 (12-ounce) bag fresh spinach leaves,
   stems removed
¹/₄ cup shredded fresh basil leaves,
¡ for garnish (about ¹/₂ bunch)
4 tablespoons unsalted butter
1 cup sliced bottled imported roasted red
   peppers, for garnish

Cook's Note ≈ ≈ ≈

*For the home cook, I recommend
purchasing one of the fine commercially made chicken-basil sausages,
now available in specialty meat
departments (see Sources, page 323).
If you can't find basil-flavored
chicken sausage, substitute with
plain chicken sausage or one flavored with sun-dried tomatoes.*

5. In a small bowl, whisk together 2 tablespoons of the olive oil and the balsamic vinegar. Brush the portabella mushroom caps with the mixture and grill, starting with the top sides down, for about 5 minutes or until grill marks are visible. Remove the mushrooms from the grill, reserving on a plate to collect the juices. Grill the sausage until cooked through, about 10 minutes. Cool slightly and then cut into ¹/₄-inch diagonal slices. Reserve.

6. In a medium pan, heat the remaining 1 tablespoon olive oil over medium heat. Add the spinach and cook until wilted but still intensely green in color. Drain and reserve.

7. To finish the ragout, reheat the reserved sauce and gradually stir in the ¹/₄ cup basil and butter. Divide the ragout among 6 large, shallow soup plates, heated if possible. Place 1 grilled portabella mushroom cap on each, drizzling with any accumulated juices. Top with the sausage slices, roasted pepper strips, and wilted spinach. Serve immediately with 1 Crostino on the side of each plate.

SPICED DUCK IN PORT WINE SAUCE WITH GREEN LENTILS AND SAVOY CABBAGE

Here's a lovely, fancy dish to serve for a special wintertime dinner. It's what I adore about French cuisine: the contradictory combination of the earthy cabbage and lentils with the elegant medium-rare duck breast in its deep ruby-colored sauce. I fell in love with the cabbage confit after tasting Chef Georges Perrier's version. The large Moullard-type duck breasts are available at specialty meat markets. The sauce, cabbage, and green lentils can all be made up to two days ahead of time. On the day of your dinner, the only thing you'll need to do is reheat them, and sear and carve the duck.

Advance preparation required. Serves 6 •

3 cups Basic Cooked French Green
   Lentils (see page 233)
4 cups Rich Chicken Stock
   (see page 303), or duck stock

SPICED DUCK
1 tablespoon ground cinnamon
1 tablespoon ground coriander
1 tablespoon ground anise seed
1 tablespoon kosher salt
2 teaspoons freshly ground black pepper
6 large boneless Moullard duck breast
   halves, fat pricked all over (without
   piercing the flesh)

SAVOY CABBAGE CONFIT
1 head savoy cabbage
1/4 cup duck fat (see Sources, page 323)
   or bacon fat
1 teaspoon kosher salt
1/4 teaspoon freshly ground black pepper

1. Prepare the Basic Cooked French Green Lentils and Rich Chicken Stock. Reserve.

2. Prepare the Spiced Duck: Combine the cinnamon, coriander, anise, salt, and black pepper. Rub lightly into the duck breasts on both the skin and flesh sides. Cover and refrigerate overnight.

3. Prepare the Savoy Cabbage Confit: Bring a large pot of salted water to a boil. Cut the cabbage into quarters. Trim off and discard a triangle-shaped piece of the core and the larger ribs from each quarter. Add the cabbage leaves to the boiling water and blanch for 5 minutes, then drain in a colander. Cook the duck fat, cabbage, salt, and pepper in a medium pot over low heat for 20 minutes. Strain the cabbage in a colander or sieve to drain off the fat. Pat dry on paper towels and reserve.

4. Prepare the Port Wine Sauce: In a small pan over medium heat, sauté the shallots in 1 tablespoon of the butter until they are browned. Stir in the sugar and cook until the sugar melts and caramelizes (it will be brown in color and smell like caramel). Add the vinegar and cook for 2 minutes. Add the port wine, reserved chicken stock, and thyme. Bring to a boil and cook until the liquid is reduced to 1 1/2 cups. Whisk in the remaining 1 tablespoon butter and season with salt and pepper to taste. Strain through a fine sieve and reserve in a warm place.

PORT WINE SAUCE

$1/2$ cup chopped shallots

2 tablespoons unsalted butter

$1/4$ cup sugar

$1/4$ cup cider vinegar

2 cups port wine

2 tablespoons chopped fresh thyme leaves
   (about $1/2$ bunch)

Salt and freshly ground black pepper

5. Place the spiced duck breasts in a cast-iron skillet, skin sides down and sear on low heat to render the excess fat. Drain fat once or twice (saving for another use). When skin is evenly and lightly browned, removed from skillet and cool slightly.

6. Have ready 6 large heated dinner plates. Place a mound of lentils in the center of each plate. Surround by the cabbage. Carve the duck into thin slices, using an electric knife if available. Arrange the duck slices over the lentils and ladle over about $1/2$ cup of Port Wine Sauce for each portion.

Cook's Note ✌ ✌ ✌

Moullard ducks are sterile hybrids of Barbary and Nantes ducks that are raised especially for their enlarged livers (or fois gras). The large breasts of these ducks are suitable for cooking rare and serving thinly sliced, like a steak.

COUNTRY-STYLE MACARONI
(Maccherone alla Contadina)

About five years ago, I was asked by Gabriel Marabella to develop a new fast Italian food concept with him. Gabe's parents had started the Philadelphia area's famous Marabella's restaurants many years before and later the three brothers ran the rapidly expanding business with the help of their mother. After most of the original restaurants were sold, Gabe decided it was time to venture out on his own. His successful concept was Parma, where he serves prepared from scratch "old world food" quickly and at moderate prices. I developed this dish for the original Parma as a hearty, satisfying vegetarian pasta dish. Though not a vegetarian myself, I adore all kinds of vegetables, including the delicious bitter-edged broccoli rabe called for here.

Serves 6 •

4 cups Oven-Cooked Vegetarian Beans (see page 230), or Oven-Cooked Italian-Style Beans (see page 228), prepared with cannellini beans

12 to 16 Oven-Roasted Plum Tomatoes, cut into strips (see page 289)

1 pound maccherone pasta or rigatoni, or ridged penne

1 bunch broccoli rabe, bottom 2 inches of stem discarded

1/4 cup extra-virgin olive oil

1 tablespoon fresh chopped garlic

1/2 teaspoon hot red pepper flakes

1/2 cup grated aged Provolone cheese

1. Prepare the Oven-Cooked Italian-Style Beans. In a blender or food processor, purée half of the beans, leaving the remaining beans whole. Reserve.

2. Prepare the Oven-Roasted Plum Tomatoes. Reserve.

3. Bring a large pot of salted water to a boil. Add the pasta and cook for about 9 minutes or until al dente or firm to the tooth. Drain and reserve.

4. Bring a small pot of water to a boil. Cut the rabe into 1/2-inch-thick slices. Add the rabe to the boiling water and cook for 1 minute, until the strips turn bright green. Drain and rinse under cold water. Reserve.

5. In a large, heavy-bottomed pan heat the olive oil over medium. Add the garlic and red pepper flakes. Cook until the garlic sizzles and gives off its aroma. Stir in the broccoli rabe and cook 5 minutes more. Add the puréed and whole cannellini beans and the tomato strips. Bring the sauce to a boil. Add the pasta, toss to combine, and sprinkle with the Provolone. Serve immediately.

GREEN AND YELLOW BEAN CURRY WITH CAULIFLOWER

This colorful, aromatic vegetable curry calls for many wonderful Indian spices. Indian groceries are the best places to buy fresh and inexpensive spices, but many of these spices or substitutes are available in supermarkets, too. The black mustard seeds listed put a sharp edge on the flavor of the curry, but yellow mustard seeds can be substituted. The acrid aroma of fenugreek says "curry," but is optional. The *garam masala* or traditional Indian spice mix, which typically includes black pepper, fragrant sweet spices, such as cinnamon, clove, and allspice, is also available in specialty stores and Indian groceries, but I have included a recipe. Recipes for garam masala vary according to regional styles and personal tastes.

Serves 6 •

SEASONING PASTE

1 (2-inch) piece fresh ginger,
  peeled and cut up
3 cloves garlic, peeled
1 jalapeño pepper, seeded
1 teaspoon turmeric
1/2 teaspoon ground fenugreek
1/2 teaspoon Garam Masala
  (see page 294), or purchased
1 teaspoon ground cumin
1/4 cup fresh lime juice (about 2 limes)

VEGETABLES

2 tablespoons peanut oil
2 teaspoons black mustard seeds
1 white onion sliced into strips
1 head cauliflower or broccoflower,
  cut into florets
1/2 pound fresh green beans,
  cut into 2-inch lengths
1/2 pound fresh wax beans,
  cut into 2-inch lengths
2 red or yellow peppers,
  cut into 1-inch squares
1/2 pound sugar snap peas, trimmed
1 cup diced plum tomatoes
  (fresh or canned)

1. Prepare the Seasoning Paste: In a blender or food processor, process the ginger, garlic, jalepeño, turmeric, fenugreek, garam masala, cumin, and lime juice until smooth. Reserve.

2. Prepare the Vegetables: Heat the peanut oil in a large skillet over medium heat. Add the mustard seeds and cover the pan to prevent seeds from popping out. As the seeds start to pop, add the onion and cook for 3 minutes more. Add the cauliflower, and green and wax beans. Cook for 3 minutes more. Add the peppers and sugar snaps.

3. Stir the seasoning paste into the vegetables and cook for 5 minutes. Stir in the tomatoes and serve immediately.

VEGETARIAN CHILI WITH RED BEANS AND WHITE HOMINY

This vegetarian chili, which I developed for the take-out department of a specialty foods store, features a knockout presentation when served in steamed acorn squash halves. This chili is even better when you reheat it a day or two later.

Advance preparation required. Serves 8 to 10 •

1 pound dried giant white corn (hominy)

1½ cups dried black turtle beans, cooked and drained (see Basic Cooking Chart, page 43), or 4 cups canned black beans, rinsed and drained

1½ cups dried red kidney beans, cooked and drained (see Basic Cooking Chart, page 43), or 4 cups canned kidney beans, rinsed and drained

8 cups (2 quarts) cold water

4 bay leaves

½ cup olive oil

1 pound onions, chopped

1 pound carrots, diced

¼ cup chopped garlic

2 (28-ounce) cans chopped Italian plum tomatoes

1 celery root, diced

1 rutabaga, diced

1 small butternut squash, peeled, seeded, and cubed

Salt and freshly ground black pepper

¼ cup chopped chipotle chiles in adobo sauce (including sauce)

2 teaspoons ground allspice

2 tablespoons dried oregano

2 tablespoons ground toasted cumin seeds (see Toasting Seeds, page 217)

1 cup cilantro sprigs (about 1 bunch), for garnish

1. In a large bowl, soak the giant white corn in enough cold water to cover for 12 hours or overnight.

2. Prepare the black turtle and red kidney beans. Reserve.

3. Drain the corn, rinse, and place in a large pot. Cover with the 8 cups cold water and add the bay leaves. Bring to a boil, cover, and reduce the heat to a bare simmer. Cook for 2 hours or until firm but cooked through. Drain, discarding the bay leaves, and reserve.

4. Heat the olive oil in a large Dutch oven. Add the onions and carrots and cook over medium heat for 3 to 5 minutes, until crisp-tender. Add the garlic and cook 3 minutes longer. Add the chopped tomatoes, celery root, and rutabaga and return to a boil. Reduce the heat, cover, and simmer for 15 minutes, then stir in the squash and bring back to a boil. Cover and simmer 15 minutes, stirring occasionally. Season to taste with salt and pepper.

5. Add the chipotle chiles, allspice, oregano, and cumin and stir to mix well. Add the black and red beans, and the white corn. Bring to a boil. Reduce the heat and cook for 20 minutes, stirring often, until the chili is well thickened. Taste for seasonings, adding more salt if necessary. Serve garnished with chopped cilantro.

Cook's Note ❧ ❧ ❧

This makes a large batch of chili, but it freezes so beautifully, it doesn't make sense to prepare less. After cooling the chili, divide it into quart-sized plastic freezer bags, label, and freeze.

CHINESE STEAMED CLAMS WITH FERMENTED BLACK BEAN SAUCE

Here is a dish of steamed clams in a sauce made from pungent fermented black beans accented with chopped ginger and garlic. Steamed clams seem to cry out for wine, garlic, and hot pepper. The Italian classic steamed clams in white wine sauce is made with white wine, garlic, and hot red pepper flakes. Here the wine becomes rice wine, and the garlic and hot red pepper remain but the ginger and the two derivatives of the soybean family (soy sauce and fermented black beans) give it a Chinese flavor. Although it's not traditional, serve with a crusty French baguette to mop up the delicious sauce, and there won't be any left.

Serves 6 •

1/2 cup bottled clam juice or Light
　Chicken Stock (see page 301)

2 tablespoons soy sauce

2 teaspoons sugar

1/4 cup rice wine

2 teaspoons cornstarch

2 tablespoons soybean oil

2 tablespoons fermented black beans,
　coarsely chopped

1 bunch scallions, white and green parts
　sliced separately

1 1/2 tablespoons chopped garlic

1 1/2 tablespoons chopped fresh ginger

1 teaspoon Korean red pepper flakes, or
　hot red pepper flakes

48 littleneck clams, scrubbed
　(see Cleaning Clams below)

1. In a small bowl, combine the clam juice, soy sauce, and sugar. In a separate bowl, combine the rice wine and cornstarch. Reserve both.

2. Heat a wok (or a large skillet) over high heat, then add the oil and swirl around until coated. Add the black beans, white parts of the scallions, garlic, ginger, and pepper flakes. Stir-fry for about 30 seconds, or until the mixture releases its fragrance. Add the clam juice mixture, and heat until boiling, stirring constantly.

3. Add the clams, cover and cook, shaking the wok occasionally, until most of the clams have opened. (So as not to overcook the clams, pry open the last few partially opened clams using the edge of a pair of tongs, a clam knife, or the edge of an icing spatula.) Discard any clams that have sand inside or that do not open.

4. Scoop the clams out of the pot, placing them in a deep bowl to keep warm. Slowly, while stirring constantly, add the rice wine mixture to the pot and bring to a boil. Spoon the sauce over the clams and sprinkle with the sliced green scallions. Serve immediately.

CLEANING CLAMS

To clean the fresh clams, first place them in a sinkful or large pot of cold water. Scrub the clams well, using a scrub brush or a clean scrubby pad and lots of cold water. Discard the water and place the clams in fresh water and allow them to soak for 20 to 30 minutes to purge them of any sand inside. Remove and keep cold until ready to cook.

MISO-MARINATED GLAZED HALIBUT

This delicately flavored dish of glazed fish was popularized by Japanese chef, Nobu Matsuhisa, at the restaurants Matsuhisa in Los Angeles and Nobu in New York. Originally made with Pacific Black Cod (also known as Alaska cod, black sablefish, and butterfish), it is also good with firm, white halibut or the more oily, but still white-fleshed Chilean sea bass. Miso is a Japanese fermented soybean paste that is made in many varieties, each with its own characteristic color and flavor. Shiro miso is light yellow and mild in flavor. Mirin is a sweet, syrupy Japanese cooking wine available in Asian markets. This is an excellent dish to make when you buy fish but don't want to eat it the same day. The fish must marinate for two days to absorb the flavors and yield a deep-brown, shiny caramelized glaze.

Advance preparation recommended. Serves 4 •

½ cup shiro miso

6 tablespoons sugar

3 tablespoons saké

¼ cup mirin

1½ pounds boneless halibut or cod,
    cut into 8 pieces

1. To prepare the marinade, thoroughly combine the miso, sugar, saké, and mirin in a small heatproof mixing bowl with a wooden spoon until smooth. Place over a pot of simmering water and cook for about 30 minutes, until hot and fragrant. Remove from the heat and cool. Pour half the marinade into a shallow glass or ceramic dish. Arrange the halibut over the marinade in the dish, then cover with the remaining marinade. Cover and refrigerate for 2 days.

2. When ready to serve, preheat the broiler. Remove the fish from the marinade, allowing the excess to drip off. Arrange the fish pieces, skin sides up on a broiler or shallow baking pan and place under the broiler, 6 to 8 inches from the heat source. Broil for 10 minutes, then turn over and broil about 3 minutes longer, or until the fish flakes easily.

BLACK SEA BASS
WITH FRENCH GREEN LENTILS

This recipe was given to me by the wonderful Lyonnais chef Pierre Orsi who made it traditionally with gilt-head bream (*dorade*). Because the French-prized *dorade*, a royal member of the bream or porgy fish family, is almost unattainable in the United States (unless you are a restaurant chef with access to the finest imported fish), you'll probably need to substitute another fish such as black sea bass, striped bass, grouper, tilefish or even Chilean sea bass for this dish.

Serves 4 •

1/2 pound (1 cup) French green lentils

1/2 onion

1/2 carrot

1 sprig fresh thyme

Fine sea salt and freshly ground
  black pepper

1/4 cup olive oil

1 shallot, peeled and sliced

1/4 cup red wine vinegar

1/4 cup heavy cream

4 black sea bass fillets
  (about 10 ounces each)

2 tablespoons olive oil

1 tomato, peeled, seeded, and diced

1 sprig fresh tarragon, chopped

2 tablespoons snipped fresh chives
  (about 1/2 bunch)

1. Place the lentils in a large pot, cover with cold water and bring to a boil. Reduce the heat and simmer for 5 minutes, then drain and rinse under cold running water. Place the lentils back into the pot, add the onion, carrot, thyme sprig, and enough water to cover by about 1 inch. Bring to a boil, then reduce the heat, and simmer for about 30 minutes, or until cooked through but still firm. Drain, then season to taste with salt and pepper.

2. Heat the 1/4 cup olive oil in a medium pot over medium heat. Add the shallots and cook until softened but not colored. Add the lentils and the red wine vinegar. Bring to a boil. Reduce the heat and simmer for about 10 minutes to evaporate the excess liquid. Add the cream and return to a boil. Season to taste with salt and pepper. Reserve in a warm place.

3. If the dorade fillets are thicker then 1/2 inch, cut 2 to 31/2-inch-deep slashes in them using a kitchen scissors so they will cook faster. Grouper and Chilean sea bass are firmer and could benefit by this treatment; black sea bass, however, are delicate-fleshed fish that won't need slashing.

4. Heat the 2 tablespoons olive oil in a large nonstick skillet over high heat. Place the fish fillets, skin sides down into the skillet and cook on both sides for 3 minutes, until flaky but still moist. Season to taste with salt and pepper.

5. When ready to serve, add the tomato, tarragon, and chives to the reserved lentils and mix well. Place the fish fillets, skin sides down, onto 4 large heated dinner plates. Surround the fish with the lentils and their sauce. Serve immediately.

SALMON SCALLOPPINE
WITH CHINESE BLACK BEAN SAUCE

Here is a crowd-pleasing, quick-cooking dish of salmon scallops in an orange-scented fermented black bean sauce. Inspired by a dish served at Susanna Foo's, a nationally celebrated restaurant located along Philadelphia's prestigious Restaurant Row, this is a perfect melange of Chinese ingredients and French technique that Chef Foo has made her trademark. By cutting the salmon fillet on the bias into thin scalloppine that resemble veal scallops, one pound of salmon will easily feed four people. Serve with Sesame Sugar Snaps (see page 258), if desired.

Serves 4 •

¹/₄ cup chopped shallots

2 tablespoons chopped garlic

¹/₄ cup chopped peeled fresh ginger

2 tablespoons peanut oil

2 cups dry white vermouth

¹/₂ cup frozen orange juice concentrate, thawed

2 tablespoons molasses

2 teaspoons coriander seeds, crushed

1 cup fermented black beans (available in Asian markets)

2 tablespoons grated orange zest

¹/₂ pound (2 sticks) unsalted butter, softened

1 pound salmon fillet, pinbones removed

¹/₄ cup thinly sliced fresh chives, or Chinese chives (about 1 bunch)

Cook's Note ❧ ❧ ❧

To make the sauce ahead, prepare up to Step 2, but don't add in the butter. Allow the sauce to cool and refrigerate for up to 4 days. Reheat over low heat until bubbling, then stir in the butter. Continue as directed.

1. Place the shallots, garlic, ginger, and peanut oil in a medium stainless steel or enameled pan and cook until the shallots are transparent. Add the vermouth, juice concentrate, molasses, and coriander, and bring to a boil. Reduce the heat and simmer until the liquid has reduced by half. Transfer to a food processor or blender and purée until smooth. Strain through a food mill or sieve. Reserve.

2. When ready to serve, bring the sauce to a boil, cooking until thick bubbles appear all over the surface. Stir in the black beans and orange zest, then beat in the butter a little at a time. Reserve the sauce in a warm place.

3. Cut the salmon into eight (2-ounce) diagonally-sliced scalloppines. Heat a large nonstick pan over medium-high heat until hot. Working in batches, arrange the salmon scalloppines in a single layer (without crowding) in the hot pan and cook until browned. Flip each scalloppine over and cook until browned but still juicy and not quite cooked in the middle. Using a flat spatula, remove the salmon from the pan and drain briefly on paper towels.

4. Arrange 2 scalloppines on each plate and ladle about ¹/₄ cup of the sauce over top. Sprinkle with the chives and serve immediately.

RICE STICK NOODLES WITH SHRIMP, BEAN SPROUTS, AND PEANUTS *(Pad Thai)*

This classic recipe was given to me by the owners of one of Philadelphia's finest Thai restaurants, Thai Garden. Thai cooks and prep people formed the backbone of Philadelphia's first restaurant renaissance that flourished in the early seventies. Many of the early restaurants couldn't have run without their large contingent of Thai staff, many of whom went on to open their own resturants.

Serves 2 (or 4 as an appetizer)

½ pound dried rice stick noodles

2 tablespoons nam pla (Asian fish sauce)

1 teaspoon Thai Sriracha sauce,
   or 1 tablespoon of chili sauce

4 teaspoons sugar

¼ cup soybean oil

2 tablespoons coarsely chopped garlic

¾ pound large shrimp, peeled and
   deveined, tail shell left on

2 eggs, lightly beaten

¼ cup coarsely chopped roasted peanuts

2 cups fresh bean sprouts

1 bunch scallions, diagonally sliced into
   1-inch lengths

2 limes, quartered

2 tablespoons shredded Thai purple basil,
   or 1 tablespoon shredded sweet basil
   and 1 tablespoon shredded mint

ABOUT PAD THAI VARIATIONS

PAD THAI CONSISTS OF RICE STICK NOODLES SAUTÉED WITH BEAN SPROUTS, GARLIC, PEANUTS, AND SHRIMP. IT'S MADE IN MANY VERSIONS AND CAN INCLUDE MORE EXOTIC INGREDIENTS LIKE DRIED SHRIMP, SALTED RADISH, TAMARIND, AND BROWN BEAN SAUCE. IN THAILAND, PAD THAI IS SERVED ACCOMPANIED BY SMALL BOWLS OF CHOPPED PEANUTS, GROUND DRIED CHILE PEPPERS, SUGAR, LIME WEDGES, AND FRESH CHINESE CHIVES.

1. Soak the noodles in warm water to cover for 15 minutes, or until soft and limp. Drain well.

2. Combine the nam pla, Thai Sriracha sauce, and sugar in a small bowl, stirring until sugar is dissolved. Reserve.

3. Heat a wok or large skillet, such as a cast-iron skillet, over medium-high heat. Add 2 tablespoons of the oil and heat until very hot. Add the garlic and stir-fry until golden, about 30 seconds. Add the shrimp and stir-fry until pink and opaque, about 1 minute. Remove from the wok and reserve.

4. Add the beaten egg to the wok and spread it out into a thin sheet. As soon as the eggs set, stir to break them up into small chunks. Remove from the pan and reserve with the shrimp.

5. Add the remaining 2 tablespoons of oil to the wok, heat until very hot. Add the softened noodles. Using a spatula, spread the noodles into a thin layer. Allow them to cook for 1 minute, then scrape up the noodles and spread them out again into a thin layer. Cook for 1 minute. Repeat once again, and then add the reserved nam pla mixture and most of the peanuts. Toss together until the noodles are evenly coated.

6. Reserving a few for garnish, add the bean sprouts, scallions, and the reserved shrimp and eggs to the noodle mixture. Cook for 1 minute, turning often. Transfer the noodles to the serving platter and squeeze the juice of half the limes over the top. Garnish with the remaining bean sprouts, 1 tablespoon peanuts, lime wedges, and basil. Serve at once.

GRILLED CURED SALMON
ON A BED OF BELUGA LENTILS

Perhaps because almost all salmon in the markets these days is farm-raised, I find it rather bland and flabby. To bring back some of the firmer texture and more assertive flavor of the true wild salmon, I cure the salmon for a day before grilling it. This step also removes the need for a sauce to enhance the flavor of the fish. If you prefer, serve the lentils topped with simply grilled salmon and sprinkled with fresh herbs. The beluga lentils called for here are, naturally, a tiny black caviar-shaped lentil that makes a strikingly beautiful bed for the salmon. Beluga lentils absorb flavors very easily. If you can't find them, the best substitute is the French green or Spanish pardina lentils.

Advance preparation required. Serves 6 to 8 •

¼ cup kosher salt (not table salt)

¼ cup packed dark brown sugar

½ cup chopped mixed fresh herbs
  (such as dill, thyme, marjoram,
  tarragon, or chervil)

3 shallots, chopped

2 teaspoons crushed black peppercorns

2 teaspoons crushed coriander seeds

1 tablespoon crushed fennel seeds

¼ cup brandy

1 (2- to 3-pound) salmon fillet,
  pinbones removed

3 cups (1 recipe) Basic Cooked French
  Green Lentils (see page 233), prepared
  with black beluga lentils

2 tablespoons unsalted butter

2 tablespoons chopped shallots

Freshly ground black pepper

Olive oil, for brushing

Lemon wedges, for garnish

1. Combine the ¼ cup kosher salt, brown sugar, herbs, shallots, crushed black pepper, coriander, fennel, and brandy in a small bowl. Spread the resulting wet paste onto both sides of the salmon. Place on a wire rack (such as a cooling rack) over a pan to catch the drippings. Cover with plastic wrap, place another pan on top, and add several cans to the top pan to weigh down the fish. Leave salmon to cure for 24 hours in the refrigerator. When ready to proceed, remove the salmon from pan, draining off and discarding any excess liquid that accumulated.

2. Prepare the black beluga lentils. Reserve.

3. In a small pot, heat the butter and shallots until the shallots are softened but not browned. Stir in the reserved lentils and continue to cook until heated through. Season to taste with salt and black pepper. Keep warm while the salmon is cooking.

4. Thoroughly heat a grill. Remove the salmon fillet from the pan. Quickly rinse with water and pat dry, wiping off most of the spices on the surface. Cut into portions of about 6 ounces each.

5. Lightly brush both sides of the salmon with olive oil, then lay them, flesh sides down, on the grill at an angle on the racks. Grill for 5 to 6 minutes or until the salmon releases easily from the grill when prodded with a spatula. Rotate to crisscross the grill marks and cook for 2 to 3 minutes longer. Turn over and grill until cooked to your taste (medium-rare is pink in the middle; medium-well flakes apart.)

6. To serve, spoon a mound of beluga lentils onto each plate, cover with a salmon fillet, and garnish with the lemon wedges.

SHRIMP AND GREEN BEANS IN ORANGE-RED CURRY SAUCE

This quick-to-prepare and impressive meal blends brightly colored crunchy fresh green beans with succulent shrimp and a sweet-spicy curry sauce. The intense flavor of the red curry paste is tempered with orange juice and butter to make a rosy pink, spicy, but not too fiery, sauce.

Serves 6 ••

ORANGE-RED CURRY SAUCE

2 shallots, chopped

1 (2-inch) length fresh ginger, peeled and chopped

1 (1-inch) length fresh galanga, peeled and chopped, or 1 tablespoon dried galanga (optional)

2 tablespoons curry powder

2 tablespoons unsalted butter

2 tablespoons Thai red curry paste

$^1/_2$ (6-ounce) can frozen orange juice concentrate, thawed

Grated zest of 1 orange

$^3/_4$ cup heavy cream

1 tablespoon salt

SHRIMP AND GREEN BEANS

$1^1/_2$ pounds fresh green beans, trimmed

1 tablespoon vegetable oil

$1^1/_2$ pounds large shrimp, peeled and deveined, with tails intact

2 tablespoons chopped fresh cilantro leaves

2 tablespoons shredded fresh basil (preferably Thai purple basil)

3 cups cooked rice, for serving (optional)

1. Prepare the Orange-Red Curry Sauce: In a large pan or wok over low heat, cook the shallots, ginger, galanga, and curry powder in butter for 10 minutes or until softened. Whisk in curry paste and cook for 3 minutes longer. Add the orange concentrate and zest. Bring to a boil, reduce the heat and simmer until the liquid is somewhat reduced and thickened. Stir in the cream and salt. Reserve.

2. Prepare the Shrimp and Green Beans: Bring a pot of water to a boil. Add the beans and cook for 2 minutes, or until they turn bright green. Rinse under cold water and reserve.

3. Heat the oil in a wok or large skillet over high heat until it shimmers. Add the shrimp and reserved green beans and stir-fry until the shrimp are opaque, about 4 minutes. Add the curry sauce and bring to a boil. Stir in the cilantro and basil and serve immediately over cooked rice, if desired.

Cook's Note ❧ ❧ ❧

I like the flavor of shrimp mixed with other ingredients better than eating it alone. Also, mixed like this you can afford to buy better shrimp, such as South American pinks, rather than the less expensive warm-water tiger shrimp from Asia. The pinks have a more intense shrimp flavor and a firmer texture.

CLASSIC CHILI CON CARNE

Chili con carne seems to have originated in the early 1800s in towns near the Mexican border, like San Antonio, Texas. By the turn of the century, a German immigrant from New Braunfels, Texas invented pre-blended chile powder. Chile powder is a blend mostly of ground red chile peppers, seasoned with oregano, cumin, and garlic. Each manufacturer has their own secret blend, so taste and compare to find one you like. After the invention of chile powder, chili con carne started to become popular throughout the rest of the country. The classic version of this dish (according to many chili authorites) is made with meat only, with the beans served on the side. Here I've taken the outrageous liberty of cooking the meat and beans together—with delicious if not traditional results.

Serves 8 •

1½ cups dried pinto, red kidney, or pink,
    or red chile beans, cooked and drained
    (see Basic Cooking Chart, page 43),
    or 4 cups canned, rinsed and drained
¼ cup vegetable oil
2 pounds coarsely ground beef chuck
3 cups thinly sliced onions
1 tablespoon chopped garlic
3 cups tomato sauce (purchased or
    homemade)
2 tablespoons yellow cornmeal
2 teaspoons dried oregano
¼ cup prepared chile powder
    (hot or mild as preferred)
2 teaspoons salt
½ teaspoon freshly ground black pepper
Steamed white rice, for serving
    (optional)
Chopped white onion, shredded cheddar
    cheese, diced tomato, for garnish
    (optional)

1. Prepare the pinto beans. Reserve.

2. In a large skillet, heat the oil and brown the beef over high heat in batches and reserve. Pour off most of the fat from the pan and add the sliced onions. Cook the onions until brown, stirring often. Add the garlic and cook for 2 minutes longer.

3. Transfer the onion mixture to a large heavy pot with a lid. Stir in the beans, tomato sauce, cornmeal, oregano, chile powder, and beef. Bring to a boil. Reduce the heat, cover and simmer for 1½ hours, stirring occasionally. Remove from the heat. Stir in the salt and black pepper. Serve with steamed white rice and small bowls of the optional garnishes.

FIVE-WAY CINCINNATI-STYLE CHILI

Fantastically funny food maven Calvin Trillin writes about Cincinnati chili in his book *American Fried*. According to Trillin, a Greek immigrant named Kiradjieff introduced Cincinnati-style chili in his Empress Diner in 1922. The Skyline Diner was also famous for its version of this unique chili. This slightly sweet, cinnamon-accented chili is served 3-way (chili and cheese over spaghetti), 4-way (chili and cheese over spaghetti topped with chopped onions), or 5-way, which includes all of the above, plus beans.

Serves 6 to 8 •

¾ cup dried red kidney beans
   (see Basic Cooking Chart, page 43),
   or 2 cups canned kidney beans,
   rinsed and drained
4 medium onions, chopped
2 tablespoons vegetable oil
1 clove garlic, minced
2 pounds ground beef
Spice Sachet (4 whole dried chiles,
   35 whole allspice berries, 5 bay
   leaves tied in a cheesecloth bag
   with kitchen string)
4 cups (1 quart) water
2 tablespoons white vinegar
1 (12-ounce) can tomato paste
2 tablespoons mild chile powder
1 tablespoon ground cinnamon
1 teaspoon Tabasco brand hot sauce
2 dashes Worcestershire sauce
Salt and freshly ground black pepper
1 pound spaghetti
½ pound sharp Cheddar cheese,
   shredded, for serving
1 onion, chopped, for serving

1. Prepare the red kidney beans. Reserve.

2. In a large, heavy-bottomed pot or Dutch oven, cook the onions in oil over medium heat until lightly browned. Stir in the garlic and cook for 1 minute. Add the beef and cook until the meat is browned. Add the spice sachet, water, vinegar, tomato paste, chile powder, cinnamon, hot sauce, and Worcestershire sauce, season to taste with salt and pepper, and bring to a boil. Reduce the heat and simmer for 1 hour, stirring occasionally. Taste for seasoning and keep hot. Remove and discard the spice sachet.

3. Bring a large pot of salted water to a boil. Cook the spaghetti for 7 minutes, or until firm but cooked through. Drain and place on the bottom of a large serving bowl. Spoon the reserved beans over top and then ladle the chili over the spaghetti. Cover with cheese and the chopped onions and serve immediately.

SEARED SALMON WITH SUGAR SNAPS AND RHUBARB SAUCE

Here, three springtime treats are in one dish—salmon, sugar snap peas, and rhubarb. Because the salmon is rich and slightly oily, the crunchy, fresh sugar snaps and the tart rhubarb with its hint of honey-sweetness both serve to cut the richness and make this a perfectly balanced dish. It makes an eye-catching main dish for a dinner party that's easy to make and quickly cooked. You can prepare the rhubarb sauce up to two days ahead of time, reheating gently just before serving.

Serves 4 (makes 1½ cups sauce) •

RHUBARB SAUCE

1 bunch rhubarb (about 1 pound), trimmed and stems cut into 1-inch lengths, or 1 (12-ounce) package frozen rhubarb

2 bay leaves

¼ cup honey

6 star anise

½ cup heavy cream

Salt and freshly ground black pepper

SALMON AND SUGAR SNAPS

1 tablespoons olive oil

2 pounds salmon fillet, de-boned, cut into 4 portions

Salt and freshly ground pepper

1 cup trimmed sugar snap peas

Cook's Note ❧ ❧ ❧

Rhubarb leaves are poisonous because they contain so much oxalic acid. Normally they are removed before being sold. If you grow your own, be sure to remove the leaves.

1. Prepare the Rhubarb Sauce: Combine the rhubarb, bay leaves, honey, and two of the star anise in a medium pot. Simmer over medium heat until the rhubarb is soft. Add the cream, increase the heat, and bring to a boil. Remove from the heat. Season to taste with salt and pepper. Remove and discard bay leaves and anise. Reserve.

2. Prepare the Salmon and Sugar Snaps: Lightly oil the salmon fillets and season with salt and pepper. Preheat a large nonstick pan over medium-high heat. Arrange the salmon fillets in the pan, skin sides down, and cook until the skins are well browned and crispy, about 3 minutes on each side. Flip over and continue cooking until the salmon is medium to medium-rare. Remove from the pan and drain on paper towels.

3. In a separate small pan, bring a small amount of water to a boil. Add the sugar snap peas and cook until they are bright green, about 2 minutes. Remove from the water, drain, and reserve. Ladle the rhubarb sauce onto 4 large, heated dinner plates. Place one portion of salmon, skin side up, on each plate. Surround the salmon with the reserved sugar snaps and garnish with remaining 4 star anise.

CHAPTER NINE

ONE-POT DISHES

BIRD-STYLE BEANS
(Fagioli all'Ucceletto)

The people of Tuscany are known as *mangiafagioli* or "bean-eaters." This dish is a poor man's version of the traditionally prepared wild game birds that are so plentiful in the Tuscan hills that surround the city of Florence. Cranberry or pink beans are closest to the favorite Tuscan, borlotti, but baby lima beans make a delicious substitute.

Serves 6 •

1 pound (2 cups) dried borlotti,
   cranberry or pink, soaked
   (see Soaking Chart, page 41)
3 cups Light Chicken Stock
   (see page 301)
3 cups water
1/2 cup olive oil
8 cloves garlic, peeled
1/4 cup snipped fresh sage leaves,
   or 1 tablespoon dried rubbed sage
   (about 1/2 cup)
1 pound ripe plum tomatoes, peeled,
   seeded, and diced
2 teaspoons salt
Freshly ground black pepper

1. In a large pot, place the dried beans, Light Chicken Stock, and water. Bring to a boil and skim off any white foam impurities that rise to the surface. Reduce the heat and simmer until the beans are half-cooked, about 30 minutes. Remove from heat. Reserve.

2. Preheat the oven to 325°F. Place the olive oil, garlic, and sage in the bottom of a large, heavy Dutch oven. Cook over low heat for about 5 minutes, or until the garlic becomes golden. Add the beans with their liquid, tomatoes, and salt. Bring to a boil. Cover the Dutch oven and place in the oven. Bake about 30 minutes, then stir gently. Cover and bake for 30 minutes longer, or until the beans are quite soft, but still juicy. Remove from the oven and season to taste with a little more salt and pepper. Serve piping hot as an accompaniment to grilled meats or poultry.

Cook's Note ❧ ❧ ❧

For a real treat, prepare this dish when fresh cranberry beans (in their pink and white pods) are in season in October and November. After shelling the beans, cover them with Light Chicken Stock only (no water) and cook for 15 minutes. Proceed with the recipe as directed.

DINER-STYLE BAKED BEANS WITH BACON

What good is a diner without baked beans? I developed this simple but delicious recipe while consulting for the Country Club Diner in Philadelphia. The second-largest diner ever built, this large well-established eatery has been a local institution for forty years for everyone from families with young children to older customers who've been loyal from the beginning. This recipe makes a large quantity and it reheats and freezes well.

Serves 12

2 pounds (4 cups) dried great Northern beans

1 pound bacon, sliced into thin strips

3 onions, cut into small dice

1 cup dark corn syrup

1 cup prepared German-style mustard (such as Gulden's brand)

1 cup Worcestershire sauce (such as Lea & Perrin brand)

1 cup ketchup

1 cup tomato purée

1 tablespoon salt

½ teaspoon freshly ground black pepper

1. Place the beans in a large pot and add enough cold water to cover them. Bring to a boil. Cook for 5 minutes, then drain, discarding the liquid. Reserve.

2. Cook the bacon in a large pan over medium heat until crisp, stirring to prevent burning. Transfer the bacon to paper towels to drain, reserving the fat. In the same pan, cook the onions in the bacon fat until transparent.

3. In a large bowl, whisk together the corn syrup, mustard, Worcestershire, ketchup, tomato purée, bacon, and onions. Add to the reserved beans.

4. Preheat the oven to 325°F. Place the bean mixture in a large Dutch oven. Bake for 2 hours. Season the beans with salt and pepper (do not season before 2 hours). Cover and continue baking for 2 hours longer or until the beans are tender and have absorbed the liquid.

❧ ❧ ❧ ABOUT HEINZ BAKED BEANS ❧ ❧ ❧

An older version of baked beans was introduced by the H.J. Heinz Company of Pittsburgh, Pennsylvania and became one of the very first popular brand-name canned foods. While other brands of pork and beans had appeared in tins as far back as 1880, they really started to take off under the Heinz name. The company tried to introduce these profitable beans into England in 1905 without much success. In the 1920s the head of the British branch of Heinz is said to have vowed, "I'm going to manufacture baked beans in England, and they're going to like it!"

"LIZ TAYLOR" BEEF CHILI
TOPPED WITH CORN BREAD

When I first moved to Philadelphia from Washington, D.C. in the late sixties, good restaurants were few and far between. It was quite a change from the full array of ethnic restaurants that Washington had to offer. Then came the "restaurant renaissance," when quite a few brave entrepreneurs opened their own storefront restaurants. The recipe for this dish was passed around the restaurant community at that time with many claimants to the title of original. It is based on the chili recipe at the late, great Chasen's Restaurant in Los Angeles. Liz Taylor supposedly had this chili sent to the set of *Cleopatra* when she was filming. I'm not sure where the corn bread topping came from; maybe it was a local addition.

Serves 8 •

3 cups (¹/₂ recipe) Basic Black Turtle
    Beans (see page 231)

¹/₄ pound dried New Mexico chiles,
    or 1 whole ancho chile, or ¹/₄ cup chile
    ancho powder

2 pounds stewing beef (chuck or
    top rib), cut into ¹/₂-inch cubes

1 cup peanut oil

2 onions, cut into ¹/₄-inch dice

2 tablespoons chopped garlic

2 jalapeño peppers, seeded and chopped

¹/₄ cup ground toasted cumin seeds
    (see Toasting Seeds, page 217)

¹/₄ cup dried oregano

1 tablespoon ground toasted allspice
    seeds (see Toasting Seeds, page 217)

1 (16-ounce) can plum tomatoes,
    seeded, drained and chopped

1¹/₂ tablespoons salt

4 cups (¹/₂ recipe) Buttermilk Corn Bread
    batter (see page 307)

1. Prepare the Basic Black Turtle Beans. Reserve in the refrigerator.

2. Soak the New Mexico chiles or ancho chile in warm water to soften.

3. In a large, heavy skillet over medium-high heat, brown the beef in small batches using the peanut oil. Transfer to a plate and reserve. Drain off the excess fat from the pan. In the same pan, using ¹/₄ cup of fresh peanut oil, brown the onions, garlic, and jalapeños. Stir in the cumin, oregano, allspice, and cook for 3 minutes. Remove from the heat and reserve.

4. Preheat oven to 325°F. Drain the soaked chiles, reserving the water. Seed and discard the stems. In a blender, purée the softened, cleaned chiles with the reserved soaking liquid. Transfer the chile purée to the pan containing the onion mixture. Add the tomatoes. Bring to a boil. Add the reserved browned meat, the salt, and bring back to a boil.

5. Bake the chili for 2 hours or until the meat is quite tender. Check several times to see if more water is needed; add more if the chili begins to stick to the bottom of the pan. The chili can be prepared to this point and reserved for later. Cool the pot of chili quickly in an ice bath and then place, tightly covered, in the refrigerator. It will keep up to 5 days.

6. When ready to serve, heat the oven to 375°F. Prepare the Buttermilk Corn Bread batter. Reserve.

7. Spread a layer of the reserved black beans on the bottom of 1 large (8-quart) glass or ceramic 2-inch-deep baking dish or 8 individual deep casseroles. Top with the chili, leaving 1 inch of room at the top. Pour the reserved corn bread batter over the chili. Place the dish on a baking sheet and bake 30 to 40 minutes, or until the corn bread is golden brown and the chili is bubbling hot.

BOSTON BAKED BEANS
WITH STEAMED BROWN BREAD

What could be more frugal than a pot of baked beans and steamed brown bread? Thrifty colonial New England cooks knew how to make the most out of the few ingredients in their pantry. Yankee traders in the West Indies brought home barrels of the inexpensive molasses left over from the sugar refining process and New Englanders developed an enduring taste for its mellow dark sweetness. What's surprising is how good baked beans and brown bread tastes: simple but satisfying. Perhaps that's another reason why this combination has held its place in our modern repertoire. It is for these baked beans that Boston is known as "bean town." Interestingly, the Puritans were very strict about not working on their Sabbath. Like the Jews during Sabbath cholent, they sent the family's bean pot to the baker's oven, usually in the cellar of a nearby tavern. The baker then returned the baked beans complete with a bit of brown bread on Sunday morning. Note that the bread tastes best made with whole-grain flours.

Serves 8 (makes 1 loaf of bread) •

BOSTON BAKED BEANS

1 pound (2 cups) dried great Northern
   beans
22 cups (5 ½ quarts) cold water
1 large onion stuck with 5 whole cloves
1 cup molasses
1½ cups packed dark brown sugar
1 tablespoon dry mustard
1 tablespoon ground ginger
1 teaspoon salt
1½ teaspoons freshly ground
   black pepper
½ pound salt pork, scored

STEAMED BOSTON BROWN BREAD

2 tablespoons unsalted butter, softened
1 cup rye flour
1 cup cornmeal
1 cup oat flour
2 teaspoons baking soda
1 teaspoon salt
2 cups buttermilk
¾ cup molasses

1. Prepare the Boston Baked Beans: Place the beans in a large pot and add 8 cups of the cold water. Bring to a boil and cook for 2 minutes. Remove from the heat and allow the beans to soak for 1 hour. Drain the beans; cover with another 8 cups of the cold water. Bring to a boil, reduce the heat, and simmer for about 1 hour, until half done (a bean cut in half still has a hard center). Drain the beans, discarding any liquid.

2. Preheat the oven to 250°F. Place the onion in the bottom of a large bean pot or Dutch oven and cover with the partially cooked beans. In a large bowl, combine the molasses, 1 cup of the brown sugar, the mustard, ginger, salt, pepper, and the remaining 6 cups of cold water. Whisk together to combine, then pour this mixture over the beans. Add the salt pork, pushing it slightly beneath the surface. Cover tightly and bake in the center of the oven for 4 hours.

3. Prepare the Steamed Boston Brown Bread: Butter a clean, empty 1-pound coffee can and two 24 x 12-inch pieces of heavy-duty foil, doubled over. Whisk together the rye flour, cornmeal, oat flour, baking soda, and salt in a large bowl. In

I adapted the Boston baked bean and brown bread recipes from my copy of Fanny Farmer's 1923 edition of *The Boston Cooking-School Cook Book*. According to Farmer, "The fine reputation which Boston Baked Beans have gained has been attributed to the earthen bean-pot with small top and bulging sides in which they are supposed to be cooked." If you don't have one of these half-brown glazed bean pots—a good item to look for at flea markets—don't despair. Farmer adds, "Equally good beans have often been eaten where a five-pound lard pail was substituted for the broken bean pot." These beans will taste great no matter what pot you use, though an old-fashioned, half-glazed ceramic bean pot is ideal. If you have an old-fashioned steamed pudding mold with a cover, use it to make the brown bread in an appealing shape.

another medium bowl, combine the buttermilk and molasses. Stir into the dry ingredients until well combined and the mixture resembles a thick, smooth pancake-like batter. Scrape the batter into the buttered can. (The batter should fill the can two-thirds.) Cover tightly with the buttered doubled foil and, without puncturing the foil, secure the foil to the can by tying with a string.

4. Place a round wire rack, trivet, or 2 empty tuna cans (with both ends removed) in the bottom of a tall, large pot with a lid. (This is to keep the bread mold off the bottom of the pot.) Place the mold upright on the rack in the bottom of the pot. Add enough hot water to reach halfway up the side of the can. Cover the pot, bring the water to a boil, and reduce the heat to a simmer. Steam for 2½ to 3 hours or until a skewer inserted into the center of the bread comes out clean. (Check the water level occasionally, since it may need to be replenished.) When done, remove the cover, and allow the steam to escape. Carefully remove the can from the pot. Allow the bread to cool for 10 minutes in the can, then turn upside down. The bread should slide right out. Cool to room temperature on a cooling rack.

5. When the beans have cooked for 4 hours, remove the cover and sprinkle with the remaining ½ cup brown sugar. Bake for another 30 minutes and serve directly from the Dutch oven. Using a serrated knife, cut the cooled brown bread into thin slices. Serve with butter and the baked beans.

Boston is known as "Beantown" in honor of the significance of beans in the Bostonian diet, mainly in the form of Boston baked beans.

CASSOULET WITH DUCK CONFIT, LAMB, AND HARICOTS LINGOTS

Cassoulet is an ancient rich baked stew of white haricot beans and meats that originated in Southwestern France. The French word *cassoulet* shares its origin with a word that has become as American as apple pie: casserole. It's probably the original potluck casserole. Three towns in the area of the Languedoc claim to produce the most authentic version of this endlessly varied dish. In Castelnaudary, they make it with fresh pork, ham, and pork sausages. In Toulouse, they make it with Toulouse sausage and confit of duck or goose, and in Carcassonne, they add pieces of mutton or lamb. These days, the regional differences have been blurred. I make my cassoulet with what I think are the tastiest in this panoply of meats: duck confit, lamb, bacon, and smoked pork sausage. Be aware that if you plan to make the Confit of Duck Legs, you will need to prepare them one week in advance.

Advance preparation required. Serves 12 •

12 Confit of Duck Legs (see page 310)
  or purchased (see Sources, page 323)

BEANS

2 pounds (4 cups) dried haricots lingots
  or cannellini beans, soaked (see
  Soaking Chart, page 41)

8 cups (2 quarts) Light Chicken Stock
  (see page 301)

8 cups (2 quarts) cold water

4 pounds smoked ham hocks

3 large yellow onions, peeled

1 bunch fresh thyme, tied with
  kitchen string

6 bay leaves

1 head garlic, ½ inch sliced off the top to
  expose the cloves

½ pound pork rind, bacon rind,
  or prosciutto skin (optional)

1. Prepare the Confit of Duck Legs. Reserve.

2. Prepare the Beans: Place the beans in a large stockpot and add enough cold water to cover them. Bring to a boil, and cook for 2 minutes. Drain and discard the liquid. Reserve.

3. In the same stockpot, bring to a boil the Light Chicken Stock, 8 cups water, ham hocks, onions, thyme, bay leaves, garlic, and pork rind. Reduce the heat and simmer for 2 hours. Strain through a sieve, reserving the liquid and the ham hocks, discarding the other solids. Cool the ham hocks, then remove the meat from the bones. Save the meat and discard the bones. Clean out the pot if you with to reuse it.

4. Combine the strained stock, reserved beans, and ham hock meat in the cleaned pot. Bring to a boil, reduce the heat to a simmer and cook until the beans are firm-tender, about 2 hours. (They should have a hard center kernel when cut in half, but otherwise they should be soft.)

MEATS

½ pound thick-cut smoked bacon,
    cut into ½-inch strips
1 pound boneless lamb shoulder,
    cut into 2-inch chunks
1 pound garlic pork sausages
    (kielbasa, cotechino, or saucisson),
    cut in ½-inch-thick slices
1 pound yellow onions, diced
1 tablespoon chopped garlic
¼ cup chopped fresh thyme leaves
    (about ½ bunch)
1 (28-ounce) can plum tomatoes,
    seeded and diced, liquid strained
    and reserved
2 cups dry white vermouth
Kosher salt and freshly ground
    black pepper
2 cups fresh bread crumbs
    (country-style bread)
½ cup melted duck, or bacon fat, or lard
½ cup chopped Italian parsley leaves
    (about 1 bunch)

5. Prepare the Meats: In a large pan, render the fat from the bacon over medium heat, reserving both the fat and the crisp bacon bits. In the same pan with the fat, brown the lamb on all sides. Remove and reserve. Brown the sausages, pricking in several places. Remove and reserve. Brown the reserved duck legs. Remove and reserve.

6. In the same pan, brown the onions over medium heat in the remaining fat. Add the garlic and thyme and cook for 2 to 3 minutes. Add the tomatoes, vermouth, and season to taste with salt and pepper. Bring the liquid to a boil and cook for 10 minutes or until slightly thickened.

7. Preheat the oven to 300°F. In a small bowl, combine the bread crumbs, duck fat, and parsley. Reserve.

8. In a large Dutch oven (using 2 if you have only small pots), arrange a layer of half the meats, followed by half the beans. Repeat the layers. Pour the tomato-vermouth sauce over top. (There should be enough liquid to just cover the beans. If not, add a little water.) Cover and bake for 1 hour.

9. Sprinkle the top of the cassoulet with the reserved bread crumb mixture. Bake, uncovered, for 2 hours longer, or until the crust is crunchy and most of the liquid has been absorbed. Remove from the oven and cool slightly before serving directly from the Dutch oven.

THE HOLY WAR OF CASSOULET

EVER SINCE THE PERSECUTION OF PROTESTANTS, A HOLY WAR HAS BEEN WAGED IN THE AREA OF SOUTHERN FRANCE KNOWN AS THE LANGUEDOC. THE VARIOUS WAYS OF MAKING CASSOULET ARE AT STAKE, FOR THERE IS NOT JUST ONE CASSOULET. EACH VERSION HAS ITS FANATICAL SUPPORTERS. EVERY TOWN PROCLAIMS THAT IT ALONE PRACTICES THE TRUE RITE, AND, AFTER ALL, RITES RATHER THAN RECIPES ARE INVOLVED HERE. THE DISH'S NAME COMES FROM CASSOLE, A SPECIAL EARTHENWARE POT THAT IS MADE IN A TOWN NEAR CASTLENAUDARY. BEFORE THE DISCOVERY OF NEW WORLD HARICOT BEANS, CASSOULET WAS MADE WITH FAVA BEANS, KNOWN AS FAVOLLES. THE PREFERRED HARICOT BEAN TO USE IS THE MONK-BEAN OR MOUNJETE, A PLUMP BEAN SUPPOSEDLY RESEMBLING A CAPUCHIN FRIAR. THE DISH MUST BE FIRST COOKED ON TOP OF THE STOVE AND THEN FINISHED IN THE OVEN. ITS CRUST OF BREADCRUMBS SHOULD BE BROKEN SIX TIMES. THE SEVENTH CRUST-A MAGICAL NUMBER IS THE APOTHEOSIS OF THE DISH. IN TOULOUSE, BREAST OF MUTTON AND THE FAMOUS LOCALLY MADE SAUSAGE ARE ESSENTIAL. IN CARCASSONNE, THEY ADD PORK CHOPS. IN CASTLENAUDARY, PRESERVED DUCK OR GOOSE IS INCLUDED ALONG WITH PERHAPS GARLIC SAUSAGE. IN CORBIÈRES, IT WOULD BE SACRILEGE TO MAKE CASSOULET WITHOUT INCLUDING LIGHTLY SALTED PIG'S TAIL AND EAR.

CHICKPEA AND EGGPLANT MOUSSAKA WITH GOAT CHEESE TOPPING

Years ago, I worked as a chef at the well-known White Dog Cafe, an eatery and gathering place near the University of Pennsylvania. I developed this hearty casserole dish for the many vegetarian customers we served. It combines a few of my favorite foods: eggplant, chickpeas, and goat cheese. Many people are afraid of cooking eggplant because it's so oil-hungry. I've found this method of hot-roasting eggplant cubes prevents oil absorption—and it's easy and tasty, too.

Serves 6 •

CHICKPEA MIXTURE

3/4 cup dried chickpeas, cooked and
  drained (see Basic Cooking Chart,
  page 43), or 2 cups canned
  chickpeas, rinsed and drained
1 large onion, diced
1 tablespoon chopped garlic
1/2 cup extra-virgin olive oil
1 (28-ounce) can plum tomatoes,
  chopped
1/2 cup dry white vermouth
1 tablespoon ground toasted cumin seeds
  (see Toasting Seeds, page 217)
1 tablespoon ground toasted coriander
  seeds (see Toasting Seeds, page 217)
3 bay leaves
Salt and freshly ground black pepper
1/4 pound mild goat cheese, crumbled

1. Prepare the Chickpea Mixture: Prepare the chickpeas. Reserve.

2. Preheat the oven to 400°F. In a medium pan, cook the onion and garlic in the olive oil over medium heat, until softened but not browned. Add the tomatoes, vermouth, cumin, coriander, and bay leaves. Bring to a boil. Reduce the heat and simmer until thickened, stirring occasionally, about 20 minutes. Discard the bay leaves and season to taste with salt and pepper. Reserve.

3. Prepare the Eggplant: Toss the eggplant cubes with oil, marjoram, garlic, salt and black pepper, and red pepper flakes in a large bowl. Spread out in a single layer on a large shallow baking pan. Roast for 20 minutes, then shake the pan to release the eggplant and turn the pieces over so they cook evenly. Return to the oven and bake for 20 minutes longer or until the eggplant is brown and crusty on the outside and creamy on the inside. Spread on the bottom of either 1 large shallow baking dish about 2 quarts or 6 individual ovenproof casserole dishes. Reserve.

EGGPLANT

1 (1-pound) firm, shiny eggplant,
  cut into 1-inch cubes

¼ cup extra-virgin olive oil

2 tablespoons chopped fresh marjoram
  leaves, or 1 tablespoon dried oregano

1 tablespoon chopped garlic

Kosher salt and freshly ground
  black pepper

1 teaspoon hot red pepper flakes, or
  Korean red pepper flakes

4. Stir the chickpeas into the onion mixture and cook about 10 minutes, or until somewhat thickened. Spread the chickpea mixture over the eggplant in the dish, then top with the crumbled goat cheese. (The dish may be prepared to this point up to 2 days before finishing. Cover and refrigerate.)

5. When ready to serve, preheat the oven to 400°F. Bake for 30 minutes or until bubbling and the cheese is browned. Allow the dish to cool for 5 or 10 minutes before serving.

⋄ ⋄ ⋄ TOASTING SEEDS ⋄ ⋄ ⋄

I toast whole seed spices such as cumin, coriander, allspice, fennel, anise, and nigella to intensify their flavors. To toast, heat a small skillet (preferably uncoated, such as steel or cast-iron) without any oil until quite hot. Add about ¼ cup of the whole seeds and toast, shaking occasionally just until the seeds are lightly browned and fragrant, about 4 minutes. (Watch the spices carefully at this point; you don't want blackened bitter seeds.) Remove from the heat, and cool to room temperature. Grind in a small coffee grinder, preferably reserved for spices. Alternatively, crush the seeds using a mortar and pestle. Using a funnel, pour into a reserved clean small glass jar, such as an empty spice, mustard, or jelly jar and cover tightly. The toasted spices will keep quite well for 2 to 3 months.

HOPPIN' JOHN

This southern dish, made of black-eyed peas, pigeon peas, or cowpeas mixed with rice, is served traditionally on New Year's Day to ensure good luck for the year. It was a staple of the African slaves who populated southern plantations, especially those of the Gulla country in the Sea Islands of South Carolina. According to the ever-reliable *Time-Life Food of the World Series Book of Southern Cooking*, Hoppin' John must be eaten before noon on New Year's Day to ensure good luck in the coming year.

Serves 8 •

1 pound (2 cups) dried black-eyed peas, soaked (see Soaking Chart, page 41)

½ pound salt pork, or thick-cut bacon, cut into small dice

1 onion, chopped

1 clove garlic, chopped

1 sprig fresh thyme

8 cups (2 quarts) water

Salt and freshly ground black pepper

1½ cups raw long-grain rice

1. Drain the soaked black-eyed peas. Reserve.

2. In a large, heavy-bottomed pot, cook the salt pork, onion, garlic, and thyme over medium-high heat until the vegetables are soft. Add the soaked peas and water and bring to a boil. Cover, reduce the heat to low, and simmer for 1 hour. Season generously with salt and pepper.

3. Stir in the rice. Continue to cook for 30 minutes, or until the beans and rice are cooked through and the liquid has been absorbed. (Add more water if the liquid is absorbed before the beans and rice are cooked through.)

❧ ❧ ❧ ABOUT HOPPIN' JOHN ❧ ❧ ❧

The origin of the name Hoppin' John is obscure and there seem to be lots of theories. According to John Thorne, author of *Simple Cooking*, it may have come from a corruption of *pois à pigeon* (meaning pigeon peas), a French-Caribbean term for a similar dish. Another source, *The American Heritage Cookbook* says the name may have been derived from an old custom that children had to hop once around the table before the dish was served, or that it may have been the name of a lively waiter. According to Southern cooking doyenne, Edna Lewis, in her book *The Pursuit of Flavor*, the dish originated in Charleston, South Carolina and was named after a crippled man, who peddled beans in the streets of Charleston.

HOPPIN' DON
(A Lighter Version)

Don Mauer, ebullient author of *Lean Cuisine* and *A Guy's Guide to Great Eating*, shared his low-fat version of Hoppin' John with me. He says, "I was born in the Chicago area, where I almost never saw or ate black-eyed peas. Then I moved to North Carolina where I couldn't turn around twice without seeing black-eyed peas. I learned that a very special black-eyed pea dish—Hoppin' John—is always prepared as a New Year's Day part of the meal, to bring good fortune for the remainder of the year." His version has less fat per serving than the traditional favorite. I've adapted it just slightly here.

Serves 8 •

¹/₂ pound (1 cup) dried black-eyed

1 tablespoon extra-virgin olive oil

1 cup diced onions

2 garlic cloves, minced

¹/₂ teaspoon hot red pepper flakes

¹/₂ pound (about 1¹/₄ cups) long-grain rice

4 cups Light Chicken Stock
   (see page 301), skimmed of all fat

1 pound low-fat smoked sausage,
   sliced crosswise into ¹/₂-inch slices

1 bay leaf

1 tablespoon chopped fresh thyme leaves,
   or 1 teaspoon dried thyme leaves,
   crumbled

¹/₈ teaspoon ground cloves

Salt and freshly ground black pepper

1. Place the black-eyed peas in a large pot and add enough water to cover them by 2 inches. Bring to a boil. Reduce the heat and simmer for 25 to 30 minutes, or until just tender. Drain and reserve.

2. Remove the top oven rack and place the remaining rack at its lowest position. Preheat the oven to 325°F.

3. Add the olive oil to a 5-quart ovenproof saucepan and place over medium heat. When the oil is hot, add the onions, garlic, and red pepper flakes. Cook, stirring, for about 6 minutes, until the onions are translucent. Add the rice and stir until coated with the oil. Stir in the Light Chicken Stock, sausage, and black-eyed peas and bring to a boil. Stir in the bay leaf, thyme, and cloves. Cover the saucepan and place in the oven. Bake for 20 minutes, or until the rice is tender. Season to taste with salt and pepper. Remove and discard the bay leaf and serve immediately.

BEEF, BEAN, AND BARLEY CASSEROLE
(Jewish Sabbath Cholent)

Observant Jews don't light a fire on the Sabbath, relying instead on an oven or burner left on low heat for the entire twenty-four hours the Sabbath is observed. In times past when gas and electric stoves didn't exist and fires had to be kept stoked, Jewish cooks turned to their neighborhood bakers for help. After the bread baking was finished for the day, the baker would allow people to bring their dishes (usually hermetically sealed with a flour-and-water paste) and place them in the still-hot hearth oven. The dishes would cook slowly overnight in the retained heat of the baker's oven. It's easy to see how the cholent, though made with beef and perhaps goose, could evolve into the southwest French masterpiece: cassoulet. Just like the word chowder, even the name "cholent" is probably derived from *chaud* in French, meaning hot, and *lent*, meaning slow.

Serves 8 •

1½ pounds beef chuck, trimmed off excess fat and cut in 2-inch cubes

3 tablespoons paprika (preferably Hungarian)

2 tablespoons kosher salt

1½ teaspoons freshly ground black pepper

4 large carrots, sliced into coins

2 large onions, diced

3 ribs celery, sliced

1 cup dried baby limas

1 cup dried red kidney beans

1 cup medium pearl barley

2 pounds all-purpose potatoes, peeled and cut into 1-inch-thick half slices

1. Preheat the oven to 250°F. In a large bowl, toss the beef with 1 tablespoon of the paprika, 1 tablespoon of the salt, and 1 teaspoon of the pepper.

2. In a large deep ovenproof Dutch oven, arrange the following ingredients in 4 layers, sprinkling each layer with some of the remaining 2 tablespoons paprika, 1 tablespoon salt, and ½ teaspoon pepper: layer 1 is the carrots, onions, and celery; layer 2 is the beef; and layer 3 is the limas, kidney beans, and barley; layer 4 is the potatoes.

3. Fill the Dutch oven with enough cold water to cover the potatoes by about 2 inches. Cover and bring to a boil on top of the stove, then bake for at least 8 hours or overnight. Check the water level once or twice, adding more if all of the liquid has been absorbed. When the dish is done, the water should be almost completely absorbed and the potatoes should be browned and soft. Serve piping hot.

❧ ❧ ❧ A 1918 RECIPE ❧ ❧ ❧

Here is the recipe for *schalet* or *tscholnt* as it appeared in the highly influential 1918 edition *International Jewish CookBook* by Florence Greenbaum: "Wash one pint of white haricot beans and one pint of coarse barley and put them into a covered pot or pan with some pieces of fat meat and some pieces of marrow bone, or the back of two fat geese, which have been skinned and well spiced with ginger and garlic. Season with pepper and salt and add sufficient water to cover. Cover the pot up tightly. If one has a coal range it can be placed in the oven on Friday afternoon and let remain there until Saturday noon. The heat of the oven will be sufficient to make the schalet if there was a nice clear fire when the porridge was put in the oven. If this dish cannot be baked at home it may be sent to a neighboring baker to be placed in the oven there to remain until Saturday noon when it is called for. This takes the place of soup for the Sabbath dinner."

During World War II, a person who waited on tables was known as a "bean jockey," no doubt a reference to this common staple in a soldier's diet.

BLACK TURTLE BEANS WITH EPAZOTE

I t's hard to believe now, but it wasn't that long ago when fresh herbs (other than curly parsley and maybe dill) were tough to come by in the supermarket. We owe their current availability to folks like Paul Tsakos, an herb and exotic vegetable grower who long ago came into a kitchen where I was chef with an assortment of fresh herbs to sell. I snapped them up and started buying from him every week. He's still the only grower I know in my area that sells fresh epazote (a strong-tasting resinous herb in the oregano family), the natural partner to black beans in Mexican cookery.

Serves 6 •

1 pound (2 cups) dried black turtle beans, soaked (see Soaking Chart, page 41)

4 cups Light Chicken Stock (see page 301) or Vegetable Stock (see page 304)

2 large sprigs fresh epazote, or 2 tablespoons dried

4 cups cold water

1/2 pound thick-sliced bacon, diced

1 large onion, diced

2 carrots, diced

2 ribs celery, diced

4 cloves garlic, chopped

1 tablespoon pure red chile powder, such as chile ancho or New Mexican chile

1 tablespoon ground toasted cumin seeds (see Toasting Seeds, page 217)

2 tablespoons salt

12 (6-inch) corn tortillas, for serving

1/4 pound crumbled Queso Añejo, or mild French feta, or ricotta salata, for garnish

1/4 cup chopped pickled jalapeño peppers, for garnish

1/2 pound bacon, cooked and crumbled, for garnish

1. Preheat the oven to 300°F. Drain and rinse the black beans. Place the beans, Light Chicken Stock, the epazote, and water in a large ovenproof Dutch oven. Bring to a boil on top of the stove, then transfer to the oven. Cover and bake for 2 hours.

2. Meanwhile, in a large skillet, cook the bacon over medium heat until crispy and the fat is rendered. Remove and reserve the bacon, leaving the fat in the pan. Add the onion, carrots, celery, and garlic to the fat. Cook over medium heat until the vegetables are softened, but not browned.

3. Remove the pot of beans from the oven and uncover. Taking care not to touch the hot pot or lid, stir the cooked vegetable mixture into the beans with the chile powder, cumin, and salt. Cover and bake beans for 1 hour longer, or until the liquid has been absorbed and the beans are thoroughly cooked.

4. Preheat a grill pan over medium-high heat. Add the tortillas and grill on each side until lightly charred, about 3 minutes. Serve the beans accompanied by the grilled tortillas. Garnish each portion with the cheese, pickled jalapeños, and the crumbled bacon.

ABOUT EPAZOTE

THE STRONG, ALMOST TURPENTINELIKE, SMELL OF EPAZOTE COULD PUT YOU OFF AT FIRST, BUT I SWEAR IT GROWS ON YOU. IT'S ALSO A NATURAL CARMINATIVE, MEANING THAT IT PREVENTS GAS, ALWAYS A CONSIDERATION WHEN EATING BLACK BEANS. YOU CAN BUY DRIED EPAZOTE FROM MANY HERB COMPANIES. ON MY LAST TRIP TO TEXAS, I EASILY FOUND BAGS OF FRESH EPAZOTE IN THE PRODUCE DEPARTMENT OF THE LOCAL SUPERMARKET.

VENETIAN RICE AND PEAS
(Risi e Bisi)

If you make this dish on April 25, you will be carrying on an ancient tradition from the days of the Republic of Venice. This springtime dish of creamy rice and peas was, and still is, made in Venice and its surroundings areas to celebrate the feast day of its patron Saint Mark. More of a soup, *risi e bisi* should be served as a course of its own, befitting its stature. In days past, it was presented on Saint Mark's Day with much ceremony to the doge, the leader of Venice. You can streamline this dish by using frozen small peas but you won't get the delicate flavor of the pea-pod scented stock.

Serves 6 •

8 cups (2 quarts) Light Chicken Stock
  (see page 301)
2 pounds fresh young English green peas,
  shelled, pods reserved
$^1/_2$ pound imported prosciutto including
  the fat, cut into small dice
1 large yellow onion, finely diced
6 tablespoons unsalted butter
2 cups raw arborio or other short-grain
  Italian rice, such as canaroli
$^1/_2$ cup dry white vermouth
1 tablespoon salt
$^1/_2$ teaspoon freshly ground black pepper
$^1/_4$ pound grated Parmigiano-Reggiano
  (about 1 cup)
2 tablespoons chopped Italian
  parsley leaves

1. In a 3-quart pot with a lid, combine the Light Chicken Stock and pea pods. Bring to a boil, reduce the heat, and simmer, partially covered, for 30 minutes to flavor the broth with the pea pods. Strain and reserve the broth, discarding the pods.

2. In a large, heavy saucepan over medium heat, cook the prosciutto and onion in 4 tablespoons of the butter, stirring constantly until the onion is translucent, about 5 minutes. Add the rice and stir to coat with the butter. Add the vermouth and about 2 cups of the reserved broth. Bring to a boil, then reduce the heat and simmer until the liquid is absorbed, stirring occasionally. Continue to add the broth in 2-cup increments, stirring occasionally, and waiting until the previous addition is absorbed before adding more.

3. When about half the broth (4 cups) has been added, stir in the peas, salt, and pepper. Continue to cook until all the liquid has been added and the dish is quite creamy and almost soupy. Remove from the heat, stir in the cheese, parsley, and the remaining 2 tablespoons butter. Serve immediately.

SOUTHWEST BEANS WITH CHILE ANCHO

The Anasazi® beans called for here are a medium-sized oblong bean with vivid streaks of deep red over cream. The beans were given their romantic name after the lost tribe of Anasazi Indians who lived in cliff dwellings in Arizona. (Read more about the Anasazi in Tony Hillerman's mysteries that take place in their region.) I've bought organic Anasazi® beans packed by Colorado's Arrowhead Mills in natural food stores. You can certainly substitute pinto, cranberry, or pink beans because this delicious dish—fragrant with orange zest, chile ancho, and roasted cumin and mellowed with molasses—is a real winner.

Serves 6 •

1 pound (2 cups) dried Anasazi®, pinto, pink, or cranberry beans, soaked (see Soaking Chart, page 41)

¹⁄₂ pound bacon, diced

1 large onion, diced

3 carrots, diced

2 tablespoons chopped garlic

2 tablespoons chile ancho powder, or pimentón (see About Pimentón, below)

1 whole chile ancho, seeded, soaked in cold water until soft (about 30 minutes), and minced

2 tablespoons ground toasted cumin seeds (see Toasting Seeds, page 217)

¹⁄₂ cup molasses

Grated zest of 1 orange

Juice of 1 orange

1 (28-ounce) can plum tomatoes, chopped

1¹⁄₂ teaspoons freshly ground black pepper

1 tablespoon salt

1. Drain the Anasazi® beans. Reserve.

2. Cook the bacon in stainless steel pan over low heat until crispy. Transfer the bacon onto paper towels and reserve. In the same pan, cook the onion, carrots, and garlic in the bacon fat until softened. Add the minced chile ancho, cumin, molasses, orange zest, and juice. Cook for 3 minutes. Transfer the mixture to a large ovenproof Dutch oven with a lid.

3. Preheat the oven to 300°F. Add the reserved beans, tomatoes, and bacon to the Dutch oven. Bring to a boil on top of the stove. Cover and bake in the oven for 2 hours or until the beans are almost soft. Season the beans to taste with the pepper and salt. Stir well, cover, and place back in oven 30 minutes longer or until the beans are soft and the liquid has been absorbed. (If the water has been absorbed before the beans are done, add 1 to 2 cups to beans while baking.)

❧ ❧ ❧ ABOUT PIMENTÓN ❧ ❧ ❧

If you can find it, vary the basic recipe by substituting 1 tablespoon *pimentón* (smoked paprika grown exclusively in Spain's Extremadura region) for 1 tablespoon of the chile ancho powder. Lately, I've been able to find this extraordinary wood-smoked paprika—in mild, medium, and hot versions—in specialty food shops.

SPANISH ONE-POT SOUP
(Cocido)

There are numerous versions of this dish in Spain, all invariably containing chickpeas. This meal-cooked-in-a-big-pot is closely related to the French *pot-au-feu*, the Italian *bollito misto* and even the New England boiled dinner, which all contain a variety of meats and hearty root vegetables cooked in a rich broth. Traditionally this soup is served in three separate courses: first the broth alone in a soup tureen with fresh crusty bread for dunking, then the vegetables and chickpeas, and finally, the assorted meats. Strongly flavored condiment sauces, such as a green sauce made from crushed herbs and vinegar, may accompany the meats. In America, we might serve the meats with prepared horseradish or mustard.

Serves 8 to 10 •

1 pound (2 cups) dried chickpeas, soaked
   (see Soaking Chart, page 41)
4 pounds whole chicken legs
   (thighs attached)
2 smoked ham hocks
2 pounds veal shank,
   cut into 1- to 2-inch rounds
8 cups Light Chicken Stock
   (see page 301)
2 cups dry white wine
4 cups (1 quart) cold water
2 pounds smoked chorizo
1 large onion, chopped
1 tablespoon chopped garlic
$1/2$ pound yellow potatoes, peeled, diced,
   and placed in a bowl of cold water
$1/2$ pound parsnips, peeled, diced, and
   placed in a bowl of cold water
$1/2$ pound carrots, peeled and diced
2 bay leaves
2 tablespoons hot paprika or pimentón
   (Spanish smoked paprika)
Salt and freshly ground black pepper

1. Drain and rinse the chickpeas. Place in a large soup pot. Add the chicken, ham hocks, veal shanks, Light Chicken Stock, white wine, and water. Bring to a boil, skim off the white foam impurities, and reduce the heat. Simmer for 2 hours. Add the chorizo, onion, garlic, potatoes, parsnips, carrots, bay leaves, and paprika. Return to a boil, reduce the heat, cover, and simmer for 1 hour longer.

2. Remove the ham hocks and veal shanks from the soup. Remove and discard the bay leaves. When cool enough to handle, remove the meat from the bones. Add the meat back to the pot and season to taste with salt and pepper. Serve immediately, making sure that each guest gets 1 piece each of the chorizo and chicken.

CHAPTER TEN

SIDE DISHES AND RELISHES

OVEN-COOKED ITALIAN-STYLE BEANS

If you live near an Italian neighborhood, you can probably find prosciutto trimmings and tail ends for a low price. This is a valuable ingredient in cooking beans because it gives not only a good deep flavor but also a smooth, unctuous texture. Be sure the prosciutto bone is whole and not cut; the fat inside is likely to be rancid from the aging process. The rind of the prosciutto (or the cotenna) is also wonderful for the velvety, creamy quality it imparts to slow-cooked beans.

Serves 6 to 8 (makes 6 cups) •

1 pound (2 cups) dried red kidney beans, or cannellini beans, soaked (see Soaking Chart, page 41)

$1/2$ pound prosciutto (or cotenna) trimmings and bones

1 small whole onion, peeled

1 head garlic, $1/2$ inch sliced off the top to expose the cloves

1 bunch fresh marjoram, tied with kitchen string

8 cups (2 quarts) cold water

1. Preheat the oven to 300°F. Drain and rinse the beans. In a large pot, cover the kidney beans with cold water and bring to a boil. Cook for 5 minutes, then drain, discarding the water.

2. Combine the beans, prosciutto trimmings, onion, garlic, and marjoram in a heavy-bottomed Dutch oven with a tight-fitting lid and add the water. Bring to a boil over medium heat. Cover and bake for 2 to $2^{1/2}$ hours, or until the beans are tender when pierced with a fork. Remove from the oven, cool slightly then discard the cooking liquid, prosciutto trimmings, onion, garlic, and marjoram.

OVEN-COOKED COUNTRY-STYLE BEANS

Ham hocks are just about the least-expensive way of flavoring and enriching beans. Buy ham hocks in most grocery stores or ethnic markets. They freeze quite well, so buy five pounds and keep the extra frozen. Aside from the smokiness, the hocks add a velvety, creamy quality to slow-cooked beans. Because this is a basic recipe to be used in many dishes, why not double it and cook two pounds of beans at a time, freezing the extra.

Serves 6 to 8 (makes 6 cups) •

1 pound (2 cups) dried cannellini,
   cranberry, or pinto beans, soaked
   (see Soaking Chart, page 41)
1 ham hock
1 small onion, peeled
1 head garlic, $1/2$ inch sliced off the top
   to expose the cloves
1 bunch fresh thyme,
   tied with kitchen string
8 cups (2 quarts) cold water
Salt and freshly ground black pepper

1. Preheat the oven to 300°F. Drain and rinse the beans. In a large pot, cover the beans with cold water and bring to a boil. Cook for 5 minutes, then drain, discarding the water.

2. Combine the beans, ham hock, onion, garlic, and thyme in a Dutch oven with a tight-fitting lid and add water. Bring to a boil over medium heat. Cover and place in the oven. Bake $1 1/2$ hours. Season to taste with salt and pepper. Continue baking for about 1 hour, until the beans are tender when pierced with a fork. Remove from the oven, cool somewhat then discard the cooking liquid, onion, garlic, and thyme. If you wish, remove the gelatin-rich meat from the ham hocks and add to the beans.

OVEN-COOKED VEGETARIAN BEANS

Here is a full-flavored method of cooking larger dried legumes, such as red kidney beans or cannellini beans, without any meat products. If you can find the natural wood-smoked Spanish paprika (*pimentón*), you'll find it adds a natural smoky flavor to the beans without using meat. Serve these beans hot or at room temperature (not cold) as a side dish or dressed while still warm with Cumin-Lime Citronette Dressing (see page 296), Roasted Red Pepper Vinaigrette (see page 286), Lemon-Garlic Vinaigrette (see page 287), or French Tarragon-Shallot Vinaigrette (see page 288).

Serves 6 to 8 (makes 6 cups) •

1 pound (2 cups) dried dark red kidney beans, or cannellini beans, soaked (see Soaking Chart, page 41)

6 cups (1½ quarts) cold water

¼ cup extra-virgin olive oil

1 whole onion, peeled and stuck with 4 whole cloves

1 head garlic, ½ inch sliced off the top to expose the cloves

3 bay leaves

½ bunch fresh thyme, tied with kitchen string

1 (3- to 4-inch) strip lemon zest (yellow part only)

1 whole dried red chile pepper, or 1 tablespoon pimentón (Spanish smoked paprika)

1 teaspoon ground allspice

Salt and freshly ground black pepper

1. Preheat the oven to 300°F. Drain and rinse the soaked kidney beans. In a large pot, cover the beans with cold water and bring to a boil. Cook for 5 minutes, then drain, discarding the water.

2. In a large, heavy ovenproof Dutch oven with a lid, combine the beans, water, oil, onion, garlic, bay leaves, thyme, lemon zest, chile, allspice, and salt and pepper. Bring to a boil on top of the stove.

3. Cover and bake for 3 hours for large beans or about 2 hours for smaller beans. Remove from the oven, uncover, and cool slightly. Remove and discard the onion, garlic, bay leaves, thyme, lemon zest, and chile pepper. Cool without stirring, to avoid breaking up the beans.

BASIC BLACK TURTLE BEANS
(Frijoles Negros)

Most American-grown dried beans don't need much sorting. However, some imported beans are not cleaned as well and should be picked over carefully. For some reason, dried black turtle beans are especially prone to foreign matter being mixed in, perhaps because the dirt clumps or little stones are easily disguised. Before proceeding with the recipes, pick the beans over carefully, removing and discarding any small stones or clumps of dirt.

Serves 8 (makes 6 cups) •

1 pound (2 cups) black turtle beans,
 soaked (see Soaking Chart, page 41)
1 ham hock, or 1 teaspoon liquid smoke
1 whole onion stuck with 6 whole cloves
2 bay leaves
2 to 3 sprigs of fresh epazote tied with
 kitchen string, or 2 tablespoons dried
 oregano, or marjoram
2 teaspoons salt

1. Rinse the soaked black beans under cold water. Place in a large pot and cover generously with cold water. Bring to a boil, then drain, discarding the water.

2. Add the ham hock, onion, bay leaves, and epazote sprigs. Cover with water and bring to a boil again. Reduce the heat and simmer for about 2 hours, and then stir in the salt. Continue to cook 1 hour longer or until tender to the bite.

3. Remove from the heat and allow the beans to cool. Remove the ham hock and remove the meat from the bone and add it back to the beans. Discard the ham hock, onion, bay leaves, and epazote.

BASIC COOKED FLAGEOLETS

A dish of these simple lemon- and thyme-flavored elegant flageolets makes a perfect side dish to accompany roasted chicken or meat.

Serves 6 (makes 4 cups) •

1 (12-ounce) package (1½ cups) dried flageolets

1 whole peeled onion stuck with 4 whole cloves

1 (3 to 4-inch) strip lemon zest, made using a potato peeler

2 bay leaves

½ bunch fresh thyme, tied with kitchen string

6 cups (1½ quarts) cold water

Place the flageolets, onion, lemon zest, bay leaves, and thyme in a medium-sized heavy-bottomed pot. Cover with the water and bring to a boil. Skim off and discard the white foam impurities that rises to the top. Reduce the heat to a bare simmer and cook slowly for about 1 hour or until the beans are close to tender. Remove from the heat, pour off any remaining water and discard the onion, lemon zest, bay leaves, and thyme.

BASIC COOKED FRENCH GREEN LENTILS

The special French green lentils, called *lentilles du Puy*, are raised in Puy, a southwest region of France. They are small, speckled deep green, and firm when cooked. They also take only a short time to cook. Because of their attractive appearance and ease of cooking, they are the darlings of French and American chefs. Use these basic cooked lentils in recipes like the French Green Lentil Salad with Bacon and Tomato (see page 85), French Green Lentils with Black Truffles and Caramelized Shallots (see page 138), and in the Spiced Duck in Port Wine Sauce with Green Lentils and Savoy Cabbage (see page 190).

Serves 6 (makes 3 cups) •

1 (12-ounces) package (1½ cups)
   imported lentilles du Puy
   (French green lentils)

3 bay leaves

½ bunch fresh thyme,
   tied with kitchen string

½ peeled onion stuck with
   4 whole cloves

1 head garlic, top ½ inch cut off
   and discarded

4 cups (1 quart) cold water

1. Place the lentils, bay leaves, thyme, onion, and garlic in a medium pot. Add the cold water and bring to a boil. Skim off any white foam and discard. Cover, reduce heat, and simmer for about 1 hour, or until the lentils are quite soft.

2. Remove from the heat, and discard the bay leaves, thyme, onion, and garlic. Cool slightly, then drain off and discard any excess liquid.

BASIC COOKED CHICKPEAS

Dry chickpeas are the most challenging bean to cook. Check that your chickpeas come from a source that sells through its stock quickly. Shriveled, dried-out chickpeas will never get soft, no matter how long you cook them. I buy mine from a Mexican or Latino, Indian, or Middle Eastern grocery because all those cuisines have many dishes made from chickpeas. More than any other type of legume, chickpeas need to cook in softened water (water that doesn't have a lot of minerals). Most tap water is too hard (acidic and mineral laden) to cook them properly. To ensure that your cooking water is soft enough to cook chickpeas, always add a little baking soda. If the beans are still hard after cooking two hours, add more. Too much baking soda makes the beans mushy and their skins slip off.

Serves 8 (makes 6 cups) •

1 pound (2 cups) dried chickpeas, soaked
   (see Soaking Chart, page 41)
$^1/_2$ to 1 teaspoon baking soda,
   depending on hardness of water
2 bay leaves
1 whole red chile pepper

Cook's Note ❧ ❧ ❧

Because they give off so much foam, it's not a great idea to cook chickpeas in a pressure cooker. It's possible, though unlikely, that the valve could get clogged. If you're short on time, and wish to use your pressure cooker, make sure that you don't fill it more than half-full to give the beans plenty of room to expand.

1. Drain and rinse the soaked chickpeas. Chickpeas gives off a great deal of white foam impurities when cooked. To ensure that this foam doesn't end up in your final product, cook them briefly before the final cooking step. To do this, cover the chickpeas with fresh cold water and bring to a boil. Boil for 3 to 5 minutes, skimming off and discarding the foam that rises to the top.

2. In a large pot, cover the par-cooked chickpeas with about 8 cups cold water. Bring to a boil, along with the smaller quantity of baking soda, bay leaves, and chile pepper. Skim off and discard the white foam that rises to the top. Cover, reduce the heat and simmer for 2 to 3 hours, or until the chickpeas are tender to the core but not mushy. Cool and drain the chickpeas. Remove and discard the bay leaves and chile pepper.

❧ ❧ ❧ YOU SAY GARBANZO ❧ ❧ ❧

The word "garbanzo," which supposedly derives from Greek and prehistoric German, is the Spanish name for chickpeas. In seventeenth-century England, the word evolved into "calavance," a term first used for chickpeas and eventually for all types of legumes. The old-English word for chickpeas was "chichis," similar to the contemporary Italian word, *ceci*.

EARTHENWARE-COOKED BEANS
(Frijoles de Olla)

These soupy cooked beans are served at Mexican meals after the main course, or alongside it in a small separate bowl. Diners soak up the yummy liquid by mopping it with a fresh corn tortilla. These beans taste even better reheated the next day, after the flavors have had a chance to mellow. In the old style, these beans were cooked in an earthenware pot, or *olla*, nestled in the coals of a live fire. According to Rick Bayless, author of *Authentic Mexican*, "Those who've tasted the beans that come from it know that the olla and its contents share an earthy exchange of flavors."

Serves 8 (makes 6 cups) •

1 pound (2 cups) pinto, dark red kidney, or black turtle beans

¼ pound bacon, chopped fine

1 onion, chopped fine

1 tablespoon seeded and chopped red chiles

1 tablespoon chopped garlic

1 tablespoon salt

1. Rinse and drain the beans if they appear at all sandy. In a large pot, cover the beans with cold water and bring to a boil. Cook for 5 minutes, then drain, discarding the water.

2. Return the beans to the pot. Add the bacon, onions, chile, and garlic and enough cold water to cover them by about 4 inches. Bring to a boil. Reduce the heat and, stirring occasionally, simmer, partially covered, for 2 hours.

3. Stir in the salt and simmer for about 1 hour, or until the beans are very tender and the cooking liquid has thickened. Taste for seasoning and serve as is, or cool to use for refried beans.

❧ ❧ ❧ PAINTED BEANS ❧ ❧ ❧

The pinto bean is a variety of kidney bean speckled with brownish-red blotches, its name means "painted" in Spanish. Another colloquial name is the crabeye bean because it supposedly resembles the beady bean-shaped eye of the crab.

REFRIED BEANS
(Frijoles Refritos)

These mashed and fried beans are called "refritos" because they are recooked after the first preliminary cooking stage. Although lard, which is called for here, has a bad reputation, it has wonderful flavor. Though completely nontraditional, I've used duck fat with excellent results. I always make a large batch of refried beans because they freeze so well. Use them in Chile Ancho Empanadas with Frijoles Filling (see page 58) and Ranch-Style Eggs with Refried Beans (see page 146).

Serves 8 •

6 cups (1 recipe) Earthenware-Cooked
 Beans (see page 235)
1/4 cup lard, or melted duck fat
 (see About Duck Fat, page 310),
 or olive oil
1 cup finely chopped onion

1. Prepare the Earthenware-Cooked Beans. Reserve.

2. Heat the lard in a large cast-iron or nonstick skillet. Add the onion and cook for 2 to 3 minutes or until transparent but not browned. Stir in one-fourth of the beans. As the beans begin to bubble, crush them with a potato masher. Cook the beans until thickened, stirring often with a wooden spoon and mashing. Add another one-fourth of the beans and repeat, cooking until thickened. Add the remaining beans in the same fashion. Cook the beans until they resemble mashed potatoes. These beans reheat quite well in the microwave and freeze perfectly.

TRICOLOR SUCCOTASH

Succotash is a dish made in many versions with a long history. Originally, it was an Algonquin Indian dish consisting of butter beans (large limas) and corn kernels cooked together in bear fat. The Narragansett Indians called it *misckquatash* and made it with kidney beans instead of limas. It may have been one of the first recipes taught to the settlers at Plymouth Rock. The recipe in my 1923 *Boston Cooking-School Cook Book* couldn't be simpler: "Cut hot boiled corn from cob, an equal quantity of hot boiled shelled beans; season with butter and salt; reheat before serving." As they do at Georgia Brown's Restaurant in Washington, D.C., serve this dish as a bed for Maryland-style crab cakes.

Serves 8 •

¾ cup dried dark red kidney beans,
    cooked and drained (see Basic Cooking
    Chart, page 43), or 2 cups kidney beans
    canned, rinsed and drained
2 cups cooked shelled fresh lima beans
    (see Basic Cooking Chart, page 45),
    or 2 cups frozen baby limas, rinsed
¼ cup unsalted butter
4 cups fresh yellow corn kernels
    (about 8 ears)
Salt and freshly ground black pepper
Freshly grated nutmeg

1. Prepare the kidney and lima beans. Reserve.

2. In a large, heavy pan, melt the butter, add the kidney beans, limas, and corn. Stir or toss to coat evenly with the butter and cook over medium heat for 5 to 10 minutes, until bubbling hot. Season to taste with salt, pepper, and nutmeg. Serve immediately.

INDIAN-SPICED CHICKPEAS

The exotic flavors of Indian cooking are finally starting to gain the attention of American chefs and diners. I haven't been in England since I was about twenty, but I can still taste the wonderfully complex dishes served in a few fine Indian restaurants I visited. The fresh chutneys, raitas, and breads were outstanding. Although I served Indian-inspired dishes as a chef all during my career, not enough customers understood or appreciated the food. Finally, it has become the "hot" cuisine of the day. It's about time! If desired, serve these spicy vegetarian chickpeas over rice sprinkled with black sesame seeds for a simple garnish.

Serves 8 (makes 6 cups) •

1¹/₂ cups dried chickpeas, cooked and
   drained (see Basic Cooking Chart,
   page 43)
¹/₄ cup vegetable oil
1 large onion, chopped
2 tablespoons chopped garlic
1 fresh green chile, such as jalapeño,
   chopped
1 tablespoon chopped fresh ginger
1 tablespoon ground coriander
1 tablespoon ground cumin
2 teaspoons ground turmeric
1 tablespoon sweet paprika
1 (15-ounce) can chopped plum
   tomatoes
2 teaspoons Garam Masala
   (see page 294) or purchased
1 tablespoon amchur, or juice of 2 limes
Salt
Black sesame seeds, for garnish

1. Prepare the chickpeas. Reserve.

2. Heat the oil in a large pan with a lid. Add the onion, garlic, chile, and ginger. Cook gently until lightly browned. Add the coriander, cumin, turmeric, paprika, and tomatoes. Bring to a boil, then add the drained chickpeas, Garam Masala, amchur, and season to taste with salt. Reduce the heat and simmer for 5 to 10 minutes, or until the sauce has thickened. Sprinkle with black sesame seeds before serving.

FLAGEOLETS WITH FENNEL, TOMATO, AND GREEN OLIVES

A recipe for flageolets that once appeared in a Williams-Sonoma catalog immediately caught my eye. It was on the same page as the pressure cooker in which to cook them. (I'm a big fan of pressure-cooked beans.) I adapted the original recipe to suit my taste for the Mediterranean flavors I crave, including the wonderful preserved lemons from north Africa. Substitute small navy beans if you must, but there is nothing like the elegant pale green flageolets grown only in France. I've added tomatoes to the dish for color and to balance the saltiness of the lemons and olives.

Serves 6 •

1 (12-ounce) package (1½ cups) French flageolets, soaked (see Soaking Chart, page 41)

2 bay leaves

2 sprigs fresh thyme

1 head garlic, ½ inch sliced off the top to expose the cloves

4 cups Light Chicken Stock (see page 301)

1 large fennel bulb, trimmed

2 tablespoons fresh lemon juice (about 1 lemon)

¼ cup extra-virgin olive oil

½ cup dry white vermouth

1 cup chopped plum tomatoes (fresh or canned)

2 tablespoons chopped fresh thyme leaves (about ½ bunch)

¼ cup diced purchased preserved lemon rind (see Sources, page 323)

½ cup coarsely chopped pitted green olives

2 tablespoons chopped Italian parsley leaves

Freshly ground black pepper

1. Drain and rinse the soaked flageolets. In a large pot, combine the flageolets, bay leaves, thyme, garlic, and Light Chicken Stock. Bring to a boil. Reduce the heat and simmer for 1½ to 2 hours, or until tender to the tooth. Cool slightly, then discard the bay leaves, thyme, and garlic. Reserve.

2. Meanwhile, cut the fennel bulb into small dice and toss with the lemon juice to prevent discoloration. In a large stainless steel or enameled pan, heat the olive oil, then add the fennel and stir-fry for 3 to 4 minutes, or until lightly browned. Add the vermouth, tomatoes, chopped thyme, preserved lemon rind, and olives. Simmer for 5 minutes, then add the flageolets and any cooking liquid. Return to a boil, reduce the heat, and simmer for 10 minutes, or until the liquid has almost completely evaporated.

3. Sprinkle with the parsley before serving either hot or at room temperature. Season to taste with pepper. (You might need salt but taste first, as both the olives and preserved lemon are salty.)

MEXICAN DRUNKEN BEANS

(Frijoles Borrachos)

There is a whole family of "drunken" dishes, called *borracho* in Mexico or *ubriaco* in Italy, that are cooked in copious amounts of alcoholic beverages, usually beer or wine. Here it refers to cowboy-style pinto beans cooked in dark beer with roasted poblanos and tomatoes. Serve them over rice or as an accompaniment to charcoal-grilled skirt steak or flank steak.

Serves 6 to 8 •

1 pound (2 cups) dried pinto beans,
   soaked (see Soaking Chart, page 41)
2 (12-ounce) bottles dark beer
4 cups cold water
1 large onion, quartered
2 poblano peppers
2 ripe beefsteak tomatoes
½ pound chorizo sausage,
   casing removed
Salt
½ cup chopped fresh cilantro leaves
   (about 1 bunch)

1. Drain and rinse the soaked pinto beans. Place in a large heavy pot with a lid. Add the beer and water and bring to a boil. Cover, reduce the heat, and simmer for about 1 hour, or until the beans are cooked through but still firm. Reserve.

2. Over a gas flame or directly on an electric coil, char the onion, poblano peppers, and tomatoes until their skins are blackened but the flesh is still firm. Place in a bowl to cool. When cool enough to handle, rub off and discard the blackened skins. Seed the peppers and tomatoes. Chop the vegetables reserve together in a bowl.

3. Place the chorizo in a hot skillet and cook over medium heat until well browned, breaking up the meat as it cooks.

4. Add the browned sausage, along with its fat, and the charred vegetables to the cooked beans. Season to taste with salt and continue to cook for another 30 minutes, or until the sauce thickens and beans are tender, stirring occasionally. Remove from the heat and taste for seasoning. Stir in the cilantro and serve.

BABY LIMA BEANS
WITH TOMATO AND ROSEMARY

Here is a delicious and easy-to-prepare side dish. If you use larger, starchier limas, you will need to pre-cook them first in boiling water until tender *before* combining with the tomato sauce. Otherwise the acid in the tomatoes will prevent the limas from softening. If fresh baby limas are in season, by all means use them. Don't skimp on the olive oil, rosemary, or garlic; the beans absorb these flavors resulting in a mellow, rich-tasting dish with only a few ingredients. This dish both reheats and freezes well.

Serves 6

¼ cup extra-virgin olive oil

12 cloves garlic, thinly sliced

2 large sprigs fresh rosemary

2 (10-ounce) packages frozen Fordhook
  lima beans

1½ cups tomato sauce
  (homemade or prepared)

Salt and freshly ground black pepper

1. Place the olive oil, garlic, and rosemary sprigs in the bottom of a medium, heavy saucepan. Cook over low heat for about 5 minutes, stirring constantly, until the garlic is golden.

2. Add the beans and tomato sauce and bring to a boil. Reduce the heat and simmer for 20 minutes or until the beans have absorbed most of the liquid. Season to taste with salt and pepper. If desired, discard the rosemary sprigs before serving.

The original term "beanfeast" came from the practice of English employers (up until the nineteenth century) giving their workers an annual blowout party in which beans with bacon were a major part of the menu. Beanfeast gradually came to be used for any celebration, especially a free party. In printers' jargon, the word was shortened to "beano" (which is now the commercial name of an effective anti-flatulence remedy).

TUSCAN BEANS COOKED IN A FLASK
(Fagioli Cotti al Fiasco Toscana)

In Tuscany, it was an old custom to cook fresh shelled white beans in a heavy glass wine flask buried in the cinders of a hardwood fire. The beans would cook slowly, absorbing all the flavor inside the bottle. Here is an example of Italian cooking at its best: the simplest of ingredients cooked slowly in a bean pot to make an exquisite dish. Instead of potatoes, Tuscan bean lovers serve this dish as an accompaniment to a rare grilled T-bone steak seasoned *alla Fiorentina*, or rubbed with chopped fresh rosemary, garlic, sea salt, and black pepper.

Serves 6 •

4 cups fresh shelled white beans, or fresh
   cranberry beans
$1/2$ cup extra-virgin olive oil
   (preferably Tuscan)
1 bunch fresh sage
4 cloves fresh plump garlic
3 cups cold water
Sea salt and freshly ground black pepper

1. Preheat the oven to 325°F. Combine the beans, oil, sage, garlic, and water in an earthenware bean pot or Dutch oven. Cover and place in oven. Reduce the heat to 275°F and cook for 3 hours or until beans are plump and tender.

2. Remove the beans from the oven, transfer them to a bowl and season generously with salt and freshly ground black pepper. Serve piping hot or at room temperature.

SARDINIAN-STYLE CRANBERRY BEANS WITH FENNEL AND SAVOY CABBAGE

This rustic, earthy dish comes from the island of Sardinia. Now home to several ultra-exclusive resorts, in the past Sardinia was extremely isolated with little choice in foods. I've never been to Sardinia, but I did spend several weeks living on the neighboring island of Corsica. The countryside is dramatic, the rocky landscape interspersed with struggling herbs that develop extraordinary flavor. In this dish, dried beans are combined with powerful wild fennel and the tender curly green *verza* or savoy cabbage.

Serves 4 •

3/4 pound (1 1/2 cups) dried cranberry
  beans, soaked (see Soaking Chart,
  page 41)
2 wild fennel bulbs, or 2 small domestic
  fennel bulbs plus 2 tablespoons ground
  fennel seeds
1 small head savoy cabbage, shredded
1 large onion, sliced
3 to 4 cloves garlic, peeled
1/4 pound fresh pork fat, or olive oil
1/2 cup imported Italian tomato paste
Salt

1. Drain and rinse the soaked cranberry beans. In a large pot, add enough fresh cold water to cover them by 2 to 3 inches. Bring to a boil. Reduce the heat and simmer until almost tender, about 1 1/2 hours.

2. Trim and finely slice the fennel bulb. Add the fennel, cabbage, and onion to the bean pot. Simmer for 10 to 15 minutes, or until the vegetables are tender.

3. Chop the garlic and pork fat together (or mix the garlic with the olive oil) until it forms a paste. Stir into the beans with the tomato paste, and salt to taste. Cook for 15 minutes longer until the beans and vegetables are tender and the flavors have blended.

PUERTO RICAN-STYLE PINK BEANS
(Habichuelas Rojas)

This recipe was given to me by Chef Guillermo Pernot, owner of the acclaimed Latino hot-spot in Philadelphia, ¡Pasion! A native of Buenos Aires, Pernot has gained a lot of national attention for his Nuevo Latino cooking. In his travels he learned to make this Puerto Rican dish using the firm, orange calabaza squash found in Latino markets. You can easily substitute butternut squash, especially the squash sold in supermarket produce departments. Pernot recommends serving this dish with a tangy, green herb condiment called *recaito criollo*. Vitarroz makes a good all-natural version. Both the calabaza and the recaito criollo are sold in Latino markets.

Serves 12 •

2 pounds (4 cups) dried pink or kidney
   beans, soaked (see Soaking Chart,
   page 41)

¹/₄ cup olive oil

¹/₂ pound ham, diced

16 cups (4 quarts) cold water

6 medium onions, chopped

2 green bell peppers, seeded and chopped

1 pound calabaza, or butternut squash,
   peeled and cut into ¹/₂-inch dice

1 pound all-purpose potatoes, peeled and
   cut into ¹/₂-inch dice

1 cup chopped Italian parsley leaves
   (about 1 large bunch)

2 chicken bouillon cubes
   (such as Knorr brand)

¹/₄ cup tomato paste

¹/₂ teaspoon ground cumin

¹/₂ teaspoon Mexican oregano

1 teaspoon salt

Freshly ground black pepper

1¹/₂ cups purchased recaito criollo,
   for serving

1. Drain the soaked pink beans. Reserve.

2. In a large pot, heat the oil. Add the ham and cook for 5 minutes over medium heat. Add the pink beans and water. Bring to a boil. Reduce the heat, cover, and simmer for about 2 hours or until the beans are tender.

3. Stir in the onions, green peppers, calabaza, potatoes, parsley, bouillon cubes, tomato paste, cumin, and oregano. Simmer for about 10 minutes longer, or until the calabaza and potatoes are tender. Season to taste with salt and black pepper. Serve with the recaito criollo.

TRIO OF SAVORY BEANS

Savory is *the* herb for beans. It is another member of the large mint family along with basil and sage. Use either the winter variety with fibrous leaves and a pungent flavor or the summer variety with tender leaves and a milder flavor. I've read that every little garden in Switzerland has a savory plant, called *bohnenkraut* or string bean herb. Both my winter and summer savory seem to grow very easily in my front yard herb garden with little to no attention. The blossoms of both kinds are lovely and long lasting, though lavender winter savory blossoms are especially beautiful.

Serves 6 •

³/₄ cup dried cranberry beans, cooked and
    drained (see Basic Cooking Chart,
    page 43)

¹/₂ pound fresh green beans,
    cut diagonally into 1-inch pieces

¹/₂ pound shelled fresh fava beans,
    or fresh baby lima beans

¹/₄ cup extra-virgin olive oil

3 large shallots, chopped

1¹/₂ tablespoons chopped fresh savory
    leaves, or 1¹/₂ teaspoons dried

Salt and freshly ground black pepper

Fresh savory sprigs (with blossoms if
    available), for garnish

1. Prepare the cranberry beans. Reserve.

2. Bring a large pot of salted water to a boil. Add the green beans and cook for 2 minutes. Remove with a slotted spoon and rinse under cold water to set the color and stop the cooking. Return the water to a boil. Add the fava beans and cook for 2 minutes. Drain and rinse under cold water. Slip off each of the fava skins and discard, reserving the favas.

3. Heat the olive oil in a large pan over medium-low heat. Add the shallots and savory. Cook for 5 minutes or until the shallots are softened and lightly browned. Add the reserved cranberry beans, green beans, and favas and toss to coat evenly. Cook for 2 to 3 minutes or until thoroughly heated, then season to taste with salt and pepper. Serve immediately garnished with savory sprigs.

CHINESE YARD-LONG BEANS WITH BLACK BEAN AND GARLIC SAUCE

Not a dish for the faint of heart, these delightful beans are stir-fried in a pungent fermented black bean sauce with plenty of garlic. The tangerine zest called for here has a wonderful perfume, sweeter and spicier than orange.

Serves 6 •

¼ cup soy sauce

¼ cup rice wine, or dry sherry,
   or Marsala

1 tablespoon sugar

2 teaspoons cornstarch

½ cup cold water

1 pound Chinese Yard-Long beans,
   washed, trimmed and cut into 6-inch
   lengths

2 tablespoons vegetable oil

2 tablespoons, coarsely chopped
   fermented black beans

Grated zest of 1 tangerine,
   or 1 tablespoon orange zest

1-inch length fresh ginger,
   peeled and grated

2 teaspoons chopped garlic

1 teaspoon hot chile paste, or hot red
   pepper flakes

1. In a small bowl combine the soy sauce, rice wine, sugar, cornstarch, and cold water. Reserve.

2. Bring a pot of water to a boil. Add the long beans, return to a boil, and boil for 3 to 4 minutes. Drain and rinse under cold water to set the color and stop the cooking. (The beans may be prepared to this point up to 1 day ahead.)

3. In a large skillet or a wok, heat the oil over medium-high heat until it just begins to smoke. Add the cooked, drained beans and stir-fry for 3 to 4 minutes or until slightly green in color. Add the black beans, zest, ginger, garlic, and chili paste. Stir-fry for 2 minutes longer. Pour in the soy sauce mixture and stir to coat the beans. Bring to a boil, toss to combine well, and serve immediately.

Cook's Note ❧ ❧ ❧

Long beans grow up to one and a half feet long and are closely related to the black-eyed pea. They have stronger bean flavor than our more watery green beans. Long beans are best suited to stir-frying or braising. Choose thin, blemish-free beans without noticeably developed seeds. Prepare by cutting off both ends.

LADY PEAS WITH CAROLINA RICE AND GREEN TOMATO RELISH

During a fabulous weekend of shopping, cooking, and eating with the Carolina low country culinary authority, John Martin Taylor or "Hoppin' John," I was introduced to this unpretentious dish. John decided to make it after passing a farmer's stand where they sold the delicate lady peas called for here. This smaller, more delicate version of black-eyed peas is found mostly at farmer' markets and is not commercially grown. You can certainly substitute fresh or frozen rather then dried black-eyed peas. The famous long-grain Carolina rice is hardly grown in South Carolina low country any longer, where rice plantations have a long and venerable history. Most of our rice now comes from Texas.

Serves 6

11 cups cold water

2 ham hocks (about 1 pound)

4 cups fresh lady peas, or fresh or frozen black-eyed peas

1 teaspoon salt

1 tablespoon unsalted butter

1½ cups long-grain rice (preferably Carolina)

Green tomato relish, or piccalilli (see Sources, page 323), or Pennsylvania-Dutch Chow-Chow (see page 63), for garnish

1. Place 8 cups of the water and the ham hocks in a large soup pot. Bring to a boil. Reduce the heat and simmer for 30 minutes, skimming off any white foam impurities that rise to the surface. Add the lady peas and return to a boil. Reduce the heat and simmer for 30 minutes or until the peas are plump and tender. (There should be several cups of liquid in the pot.) Reserve, discarding the ham hock.

2. In a heavy-bottomed 2-quart pot with a lid, bring the remaining 3 cups water, salt, and butter to a boil. Add the rice. Return to a boil, cover, and reduce the heat as low as possible. Cook for 15 minutes or until the water is absorbed. Turn off the heat and allow the rice to steam for another 10 minutes. Uncover and fluff lightly with a fork or a rubber spatula. Reserve.

3. Place a generous mound of steaming hot rice in the center of a salad-sized plate. Make a hole in the middle, spreading the rice out to make a ring. Ladle the peas and their cooking liquid into the center. Serve with a bowl of green tomato relish to garnish each serving.

GARDEN PEAS À LA FRANCAISE

This most delicate springtime dish is worth making when you find sweet young garden peas in the pod. The Boston lettuce and scallions enhance the subtle taste of the sweet peas. The lettuce shreds also form a web that captures the flavors of the mild scallions, sweet butter, and grated fresh nutmeg.

Serve 4 to 6 •

2 tablespoons unsalted butter

2 pounds fresh garden peas, shelled

1 small head Boston lettuce,
  sliced into thin shreds

1 bunch scallions, sliced

Salt and freshly ground black pepper

Freshly grated nutmeg

In a medium pan over low heat, heat the butter until foaming. Add the peas, lettuce, and scallions. Cook until the peas are bright green. Season to taste with salt, pepper, and nutmeg and serve immediately.

❧ ❧ ❧ CHOOSING GARDEN PEAS ❧ ❧ ❧

Choose garden peas with rounded pearl-shaped peas that perfectly fill their pods, but aren't bulging. Stay away from overgrown, starchy peas that are flattened against each other, resembling a set of teeth. Peas will maintain almost all of their sweetness for three to four days if they're placed in a closed plastic bag and refrigerated.

GEORGIAN GREEN BEANS
IN WALNUT SAUCE

Georgia, in Eurasia, reaches from the Black Sea to the Caspian Sea. This country was often featured in the mythology of ancient times and to this day maintains a strong national identity and cuisine traced back to the origins of the Georgian peoples 2,500 years ago. It is a fabled land of bounty, tucked away in mountain valleys and fertile lowlands. Georgia's most famous of many sauces is this walnut sauce, *satsivi*. It may be served with poultry, fish or, as in this recipe, with vegetables. According to Darra Goldstein, author of *The Georgian Feast*, their sauces are so delicious that people say "with a Georgian sauce, you can swallow nails."

Serves 6 •

2 pounds fresh green beans,
   cut into 2-inch pieces

¼ pound light-skinned walnuts

2 cloves garlic, peeled

1 small onion, finely chopped

½ bunch fresh cilantro leaves, chopped
   (about ¼ cup), reserving a few whole
   leaves for garnish

1 teaspoon ground coriander

2 tablespoons olive oil

2 tablespoons red wine vinegar

2 tablespoons fresh lemon juice
   (about 1 lemon)

2 teaspoons sweet paprika

½ cup Light Chicken Stock
   see page 301)

Salt

1. Bring a medium pot of lightly salted water to a boil. Add the green beans, return to a boil, and cook for 2 minutes. Drain and rinse under cold water to set the color and stop the cooking. Reserve.

2. Place the walnuts and garlic into the bowl of a food processor and purée to a paste. Transfer to a medium-size bowl. Add the onion, cilantro, coriander, olive oil, vinegar, lemon juice, paprika, and Light Chicken Stock and process until smooth. Season to taste with salt. Reserve.

3. Arrange the green beans on a serving platter. Drizzle decoratively with the walnut sauce and sprinkle with the reserved whole cilantro leaves. Garnish with additional paprika for color.

GREEN BEAN AMANDINE

Is there anyone out there who doesn't love this tried-and-true combination of green beans with butter-toasted almond slices? It may be simple but it certainly is delicious. If you happen across haricots verts (velvety-coated pencil-thin green beans) in season, don't miss the opportunity to enjoy this classic. I prefer unblanched sliced almonds to matchstick-cut slivered almonds that are skinless and blander tasting and looking. You can substitute pine nuts for a terrific variation.

Serves 6 •

1 pound young green beans,
   stem ends trimmed
¼ cup unsalted butter
½ cup sliced unblanched almonds
¼ cup chopped shallots
¼ cup water
1 wedge lemon
Salt and freshly ground black pepper

1. Steam the green beans until they turn emerald green. Drain. (If you're preparing the beans ahead of time, run them under cold running water to set the color. If you're serving them immediately, this step is not necessary.)

2. In a medium skillet, melt the butter, continuing to cook until the butter solids lightly caramelize and the butter starts to give off an aroma of hazelnuts. Add the sliced almonds and shallots. Sauté 1 to 2 minutes or until the shallots are softened and the almonds lightly browned. Add the green beans and water and cook over high heat until the green beans are hot and the sauce coats the beans.

3. Squeeze the lemon wedge into the beans. Season to taste with salt and pepper and serve immediately.

GREEN BEANS IN LEMON-MARJORAM CREAM

Except for roadside farm stands, old-fashioned hand-picked green beans are hard to come by. Unfortunately, these days, most beans are machine picked. The combination of the lemony-cream and the pungent marjoram makes this dish something special.

Serves 6

1 pound tender green beans or haricots verts, trimmed

³/₄ cup heavy cream

2 tablespoons chopped fresh marjoram leaves (about ¼ bunch)

Grated zest of 1 lemon

¼ cup fresh lemon juice (about 2 lemons)

Salt and freshly ground black pepper

1. Cook the green beans in plenty of boiling salted water for 2 minutes, or until they turn bright green. Drain and rinse under cold running water to stop the cooking and set the color. Reserve.

2. In a small pot, heat the cream over medium heat, about 10 minutes, until it's thickened and bubbles appear over the entire surface of the sauce. Transfer to a pan and add the green beans, marjoram, lemon zest, and juice. Season to taste with salt and pepper. Quickly toss together and cook 1 to 2 minutes to reheat the beans. (Don't cook any longer or the green beans will lose their emerald color.)

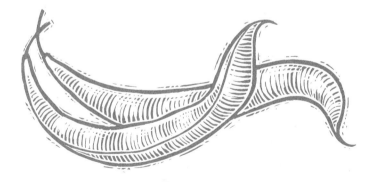

WAX BEANS WITH DILL

Here's a simple, attractive way to prepare wax beans, a pale buttery-looking variety of green beans. I like the contrast of the grassy-green dill-butter flecks over the light yellow wax beans. Wax beans can be on the tough side, so look for slender pods with small unobtrusive seeds inside. They should be crisp enough to make a "snap" sound when broken in half. Wrap and refrigerate any remaining dill butter tightly in plastic wrap or place in a small freezer bag and freeze for another time. This butter is an excellent way to have fresh herb flavor on hand in a convenient form.

Serves 6

¼ pound (1 stick) unsalted butter, softened

1 bunch fresh dill, stems discarded, leaves washed and dried

2 shallots, peeled

2 teaspoons salt

½ teaspoon freshly ground black pepper

2 pounds fresh yellow wax beans, stem ends trimmed

1. Combine the butter, dill, shallots, salt, and pepper in the bowl of a food processor. Process until well combined but not puréed. (There should still be visible dill pieces.) Remove from the bowl and reserve.

2. Bring a large pot of salted water to a boil. Add the beans and cook for about 5 minutes, or until they are bright yellow with no white spots. Drain and toss with about half the dill butter. Serve immediately. Refrigerate or freeze remaining dill butter.

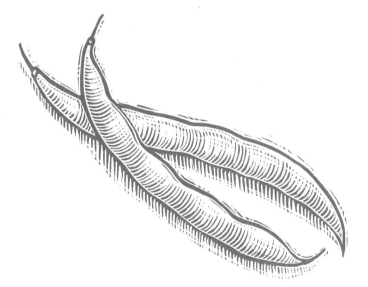

GREEN SOYBEANS
WITH CANTONESE BACON

I first tasted this unexpected treat at Chef Philippe Chin's tiny original restaurant, Chanterelles. While I've never been much of a dried soybean fan, I've always loved fresh green favas. These green soybeans reminded me most of fresh favas. The best part is, you can buy green soybeans in the frozen food section of many Asian markets even if they're not in season. The Cantonese bacon is not smoked but it is cured (much like pancetta, which makes a good substitute). If you can only find smoked bacon, then par-cook it first in boiling water for one minute to reduce the smoked flavor, which would interfere with the oyster sauce in this recipe.

Serves 6

4 cups fresh shelled green soybeans
   (about 2 pounds whole beans),
   or frozen soybeans
½ onion, chopped
1 shallot, chopped
1 tablespoon unsalted butter
3 (¼-inch-thick) slices Cantonese,
   or regular bacon, cut into small dice
1 teaspoon sugar
1 tablespoon balsamic vinegar
1 teaspoon soy sauce
2 tablespoons oyster sauce (see below)
2 tablespoons chopped parsley leaves

1. Bring a pot of salted water to a boil. Add the soybeans and cook for 2 minutes. Drain and rinse under cold water to set the color and stop the cooking. Drain and reserve. (The soybeans can be prepared to this point up to 1 day ahead.)

2. In a pan over medium heat, cook the onion and shallot in the butter for 5 minutes. Add the bacon and sugar and cook until the mixture is golden brown.

3. Add the soybeans. Deglaze the pan with the vinegar and soy sauce, scraping up any brown bits with a spoon. Add the oyster sauce and parsley and serve immediately.

❧ ❧ ❧ ABOUT OYSTER SAUCE ❧ ❧ ❧

Oyster sauce is a dark-brown, thick and concentrated liquid made from oyster, brine, and soy sauce. It's popular as a seasoning for stir-fries and as a table condiment. It imparts a rich but not overpowering flavor. When choosing a brand, always look at the ingredients to make sure oyster is one of the first listed. It is not necessary to refrigerate it.

PROVENÇAL-STYLE HARICOTS VERTS
(Haricots Verts à la Provençale)

I happen to adore green beans prepared in almost any fashion, as long as they're tender, green, and without any developed bean within. Here the elegant haricots verts, a special kinds of green bean picked when literally no thicker than thin cord, are served in a lovely, light sauce made in the Provençal style with fresh tomatoes, garlic, and basil. You can, of course, approximate this dish with full-sized green beans and canned tomatoes for a tasty but less extraordinary dish. Many of the haricots verts available for sale these days are raised in Guatemala. These can be good, but if you get the chance to buy them from a local specialty grower, you'll understand why the French are so crazy about these beauties.

Serves 6 •

1¹/₂ **pounds haricots verts, stem ends trimmed**

1 **red onion, cut into slivers**

2 **tablespoons extra-virgin olive oil**

3 to 4 **large cloves garlic, thinly sliced**

3 **ripe beefsteak tomatoes (about 1 pound), cored, seeded, and diced**

¹/₄ **cup shredded fresh basil leaves**

Salt and freshly ground black pepper

Cook's Note ❧ ❧ ❧

Because of the acid in the tomatoes, the beans will lose their bright green color quickly and turn a less attractive olive green color. That's why it's important not to add the tomatoes to the beans until ready to serve.

1. Bring a pot of salted water to a boil. Add the haricots verts and bring back to a boil, stirring so they cook evenly. As soon as the haricots verts are evenly bright green in color but still crispy, about 2 minutes, drain and rinse under cold running water to set their color and stop the cooking.

2. In a medium pan, cook the red onion in the olive oil over medium heat until softened but not browned. Add the garlic and cook for 1 minute longer, or until the garlic releases its fragrance. Add the tomatoes and cook over high heat for about 5 minutes or until the tomatoes have softened but still have their shape. (The dish can be prepared up to 1 day at this point.) Just before you're ready to serve the dish, add the haricots verts and basil to the onion mixture. Toss together and cook for about 1 minute, or until the beans are thoroughly heated. Season with salt and pepper to taste and serve immediately.

MINTED FRESH FAVAS BEANS

As a young (and driven) chef in my first major job, I did some crazy things in my search for authenticity, such as personally clean fifty-pound boxes of squid in order to obtain their tiny ink sacs to make my own black squid ink pasta. Perhaps my most notorious act was choosing to serve fresh, green fava beans for the opening of the restaurant, an event to which several hundred guests had been invited. I joined the staff in cleaning about six bushels of favas, which involved opening the large, tough outer pods, removing the inner beans, blanching them, and then individually removing the covering skin from each fava. The task seemed endless but the results were extraordinary because no one (for good reason) had ever been served fresh favas in a restaurant. Favas are best in season in early June.

Serves 6 •

2 to 3 pounds fresh fava beans in their
  pods
¼ cup extra-virgin olive oil
¼ cup chopped fresh mint
  (about ½ bunch)
¼ cup water
Salt and freshly ground black pepper

1. Remove the fava beans from their spongy outer pods and discard the pods.

2. Bring a pot of salted water to a boil. Add the favas and cook for about 2 minutes or long enough to loosen the outer skin. Drain and rinse under cold water. Slip the individual favas from their skins and reserve. (If the favas are overly mature and have turned yellow rather than bright green, blanch them again in boiling water until they're tender.)

3. In a medium pan, heat the olive oil and mint just until the mint gives off its aroma. Add the favas and water and cook until the favas are tender and coated with mint oil. Season to taste with salt and pepper. Serve immediately.

WHOLE FAVAS WITH SALT

ACCORDING TO THE RENOWNED PROVENÇAL CULINARY AUTHORITY, JEAN-NOËL ESCUDIER, IT IS AN ANCIENT CUSTOM IN THE REGION TO ENJOY THE FIRST, MOST TENDER GREEN BROAD BEANS—CALLED *fevettes*—RIGHT FROM THEIR PODS, AS AN HORS D'OEUVRE PERHAPS WITH A GLASS OF THE RIVIERA'S BELOVED *pastis* (THE ANISEED-FLAVORED LIQUOR, SIMILAR TO PERNOD AND RICARD). YOU WILL ONLY BE ABLE TO SERVE THIS DELICACY IF YOU GROW YOUR OWN FAVAS OR KNOW A FRIENDLY FARMER WHO DOES. ONCE THE BEANS START TO MATURE, THEY LOSE THEIR FLEETING SWEETNESS AND BECOME TOO STARCHY. TO SERVE EIGHT AS AN HORS D'OEUVRE YOU'LL NEED ABOUT ONE POUND VERY YOUNG FAVA BEANS IN THEIR PODS AND A DISH OF FRENCH SEA SALT. EACH PERSON SPLITS OPEN THE PODS AND SLIPS THE FAVAS OUT OF THE INNER SKIN, REVEALING THE BRIGHT GRASS GREEN FAVA BEAN HALVES. DIP THE FAVAS LIGHTLY INTO THE SALT AND EAT THEM AS IS.

PIEDMONTESE RED BEANS IN RED WINE

One of my first and still favorite Italian cookbooks written in English is *Northern Italian Cooking* by Francesco Ghedini, an Italian nobleman who came to the United States as a journalist specializing in food. Published in 1973, this little book is a treasure of simple, authentic recipes from Northern Italy. Unfortunately, Ghedini had only just completed this one book before his death. I adapted this recipe for red kidney beans cooked with red wine from my much stained copy of his book. I found a similar recipe in Escudier's Provençal cookbook. There must be an old connection between these two dishes dating from the days of the Kingdom of Savoy, which included Savoy, Piedmont, Monaco, and Nice.

Serves 6 to 8 •

1 pound (2 cups) dried dark red
   kidney beans
4 cups cold water
2 cups dry red wine (preferably
   Piedmontese, such as Barbera,
   Barbaresco, or Gattinara)
$1/2$ pound piece prosciutto rind, or salt
   pork, rinsed and drained
1 large onion stuck with 2 whole cloves
2 bay leaves
1 tablespoon salt
$1/2$ pound pancetta, or diced bacon
2 tablespoons unbleached
   all-purpose flour
2 tablespoons unsalted butter
Freshly ground black pepper

1. In a large pot, combine the kidney beans with enough cold water to cover. Bring the water to a boil, reduce the heat and simmer for 5 minutes. Drain, discarding the water.

2. Combine the beans with the 4 cups cold water, wine, prosciutto rind, onion, and bay leaves. Bring to a boil, skim off any white foam impurities that rise to the surface, and reduce the heat. Simmer for 1 hour, covered. Add the salt, cover and cook for about 30 minutes, or until the beans are soft but not mushy. Remove and discard the prosciutto rind, onion, and bay leaves.

3. In a small pan over medium heat, cook the pancetta to render the fat and brown the meat. Stir in the flour. Add this mixture to the cooked beans along with the butter. Season to taste with pepper. Bring back to a boil and serve.

SCARLET RUNNER BEANS IN BROWN BUTTER AND SHALLOTS

My friends Mark and Judy Dornstreich have been growing extraordinary organic greens, herbs, edible flowers, and vegetables for more than twenty years. As their first restaurant customer, I take pride in having introduced other chefs to their produce. It's hard to describe the experience of handling, cooking, and eating what they grow. Scarlet runner beans fit in beautifully at their farm because they are as decorative as they are delicious. They are commonly planted as an ornamental, rather than an edible plant, because of their beautiful, large scarlet-red blossoms.

Serves 4 to 6 •

1 pound fresh scarlet runner beans, shelled, or 2 cups fresh green lima beans

$1/4$ cup unsalted butter

$1/2$ cup thinly sliced shallots

1 tablespoon chopped fresh lemon thyme, or regular fresh thyme plus 1 teaspoon grated lemon zest

Salt and freshly ground black pepper

1. Bring a pot of salted water to a boil. Add the scarlet runner beans and return to a boil. Cook for 5 to 10 minutes, or until the beans are tender but not mealy. Drain and reserve.

2. Heat the butter in a medium pan and cook over medium heat until it begins to brown, shaking constantly. Add the shallots and sauté until caramelized on the edges. Stir in the scarlet runner beans and the thyme and cook just until the beans are heated thoroughly. Season to taste with salt and pepper, and serve.

❧ ❧ ❧ ABOUT SCARLET RUNNERS ❧ ❧ ❧

The scarlet runner bean gets its name from the tendrils or runners it produces for support when climbing up the nearest convenient beanpole or lattice. It was first introduced into Britain in the seventeenth century as a decorative plant because of its attractive bright red flowers. Around that time it occurred to the British to eat the young pods, a habit that didn't catch on much in other parts of the world where it was cultivated. At one time it was used as a mildly insulting slang name for an English soldier because of their red coats. It is also called "stick bean."

SESAME SUGAR SNAPS

Sugar snap peas are versatile and make a good addition to any quickly cooked mixed vegetable dish, such as a sauté or stir-fry. Here, served in a simple Asian-style sauce, they are flavored with sesame in two forms—the roasted oil and the seeds. Sugar snap peas wilt quickly, so plan on cooking them just before you're ready to serve them.

Serves 4 to 6 •

1 pound fresh sugar snap peas

1 tablespoon sesame seeds

1 tablespoon roasted Japanese sesame oil

2 tablespoons unsalted butter

2 tablespoons soy sauce

1. Preheat the oven to 300°F. Trim the peas by removing the stem ends and side strings with your thumb and forefinger. Reserve.

2. Lightly toast the sesame seeds in a small baking pan for 5 minutes, checking often. Reserve.

3. In a wok or a large pan, heat the sesame oil and butter. Add the sugar snaps, and toss together, cooking for 1 to 2 minutes or until the peas turn a bright, light green. Sprinkle in the soy sauce and toss. Serve immediately sprinkled with the toasted sesame seeds.

❧ ❧ ❧ ABOUT SUGAR SNAPS ❧ ❧ ❧

Sugar snap peas have been around at least one hundred years. They didn't become famous until twenty-five years ago when a grower in Idaho perfected the variety and won a gold medal for his accomplishment. Sugar snaps have been a favorite of home gardeners ever since. Look for unblemished sugar snaps that are crispy with no visible peas bulging out.

STIR-FRIED SNOW PEAS AND BOK CHOY WITH GINGER

Here is a simple fresh-tasting stir-fry that combines slightly chewy, sweet snow peas with the juicy, mild-tasting bok choy (it's hard to believe it's in the cabbage family). Make this dish when you can find fresh snow peas that have no round spots, which indicate spoilage. These can be hard to find because snow peas are a relatively expensive specialty item, so supermarkets tend to move their inventories slowly. Even as little as a quarter pound of snow peas is noticeable in this dish but a half pound is even better.

Serves 4

1 large head bok choy, or 1 pound
   light green-white or dark green-white
   baby bok choy

¹⁄₄ cup rice wine

2 tablespoons soy sauce

2 teaspoons cornstarch

1 teaspoon Chinese five-spice powder, or
   a pinch each of ground cinnamon and
   ground cloves

2 tablespoons soybean oil

1 bunch scallions, sliced diagonally
   into 1-inch pieces

2 tablespoons finely chopped
   fresh ginger

¹⁄₄ to ¹⁄₂ pound snow peas, trimmed

1. Trim off and discard any wilted leaf ends of the bok choy. Cut crosswise into 1-inch-wide strips, discarding the core near the bottom of the stalk. Wash in a large bowl of water, then scoop out and drain in a colander. Reserve.

2. In a small bowl, stir together the rice wine, soy sauce, cornstarch, and five-spice powder. Reserve.

3. In a wok or a large pan, heat the oil over medium-high heat, then add the scallions and ginger. Stir-fry for 1 minute to release the flavors. Add the bok choy and snow peas and stir-fry for about 2 minutes or until the bok choy begins to wilt and the snow peas are shiny green.

4. Stir the rice wine mixture and add to the pan. Bring to a boil, stirring to coat the vegetables. Serve immediately.

TENNESSEE PICKLED YELLOW WAX BEANS IN SOUR CREAM DRESSING

Prepare this country-style dish from Tennessee one or two days before you want to serve it to allow the green beans to pick up the flavors of the pickling liquid. A great addition to a summer buffet table or a barbecue, try bringing these to your next pot luck dinner. The Sour Cream Dressing is also delicious mixed with steamed golden potatoes.

Advance preparation required. Serves 6 to 8 •

PICKLED WAX BEANS

2 cups water

3 cloves garlic, slightly crushed

1/4 cup sugar

1 cup cider vinegar

1/4 cup vegetable oil

2 tablespoons salt

1 tablespoon mixed pickling spices (wrapped in cheesecloth or enclosed in a tea ball)

2 pounds yellow wax beans, trimmed, blanched and refreshed in ice water

1 large sweet onion (such as Vidalia or Texas Sweet 100s), thinly sliced

SOUR CREAM DRESSING

1/2 cup sour cream

1/4 cup mayonnaise

2 tablespoons fresh lemon juice (about 1 lemon)

2 teaspoons dry mustard

1 tablespoons prepared horseradish

1/4 cup snipped chives (about 1 bunch)

1. Prepare the Pickled Wax Beans: Place the water, garlic, sugar, vinegar, oil, salt, and pickling spices in a 2- to 3-quart stainless-steel or enameled pot. Bring to a boil. Boil for 5 minutes then turn off the heat and allow the mixture to cool to room temperature.

2. Layer the wax beans, onion, and cooked garlic cloves in a large, deep stainless steel, glass, or ceramic bowl or jar. Strain the pickling liquid over the beans and onion in the bowl. Cover and refrigerate for at least 12 hours or preferably overnight. (The beans can be stored in the liquid for up to 3 days before finishing the dish.)

3. Prepare the Sour Cream Dressing: In a medium bowl, whisk the sour cream, mayonnaise, lemon juice, dry mustard, horseradish, and all but some of the chives.

4. Drain the pickled beans well. Toss with enough of the dressing to coat thoroughly. Serve as a side dish or relish with the reserved chives sprinkled on top.

MARINATED BEAN SPROUTS AND JÍCAMAS

This simple relish makes a good snack on its own, or as a garnish to your next green salad. According to the marvelous Chinese restaurateur, cookbook author, and chef, Susanna Foo, these full-trimmed sprouts are called "silver sprouts." The smaller sprouts with a tiny head end, about 2 inches long, come from green mung beans. In China, the root end is removed. For extra-special occasions, the yellowish head end is also removed. You may also see larger, 3- to 4-inch-long sprouts with a larger yellow head. These are soybean sprouts, which are not as tender. You must remove the head end of the soybean sprout before using. In both kinds, look for fresh-smelling, firm, and silvery white sprouts.

Serves 6 •

1 (8-ounce) package fresh mung bean sprouts (about 2 cups)

1 jícama (about 8 ounces), pared and cut into matchsticks

¼ cup rice wine vinegar

2 tablespoons roasted Japanese sesame oil

2 tablespoons soybean oil

2 tablespoons light soy sauce

1 clove garlic, crushed

½ teaspoon hot red chile paste, or cayenne, or hot pepper sauce

1. Bring a medium pot of water to a boil. Add the bean sprouts and boil for 2 to 3 minutes. Drain and lightly squeeze out the water.

2. In a medium bowl, combine the sprouts, jícama, vinegar, sesame and soybean oils, soy sauce, garlic, and chili paste. Marinate in the refrigerator for at least 1 hour and up to 3 days before serving.

HAITIAN RED BEANS AND RICE

Growing up in Washington, D.C., I developed friendships with kids from around the world, including one close friend from Senegal and another from Haiti. The son of the military attaché to the Haitian Embassy, he introduced me to Haitian-style music and planter's punch, which I loved. I also loved to eat dinner at his house, where their cook would make this dish. I don't know what there was about it, but I could never get my fill; the textural combination of the nutty, almost dry red beans and the creamy rice was delicious. From Caribbean friends like my neighbor from Belize, I picked up the habit of always serving a bottle of hot sauce to sprinkle on all rice and bean dishes.

Serves 6 to 8 •

1 pound (2 cups) dried small red beans
  (pequeños)
1 ham hock
2 bay leaves
8 cups (2 quarts) cold water
1/4 pound sliced bacon, diced
1 large onion, diced
2 large shallots, chopped
1 green bell pepper, seeded and diced
1 hot green chile pepper, such as jalapeño
  or serrano, seeded and minced
2 cups long-grain white rice
2 tablespoons salt
2 tablespoons butter
Hot sauce, for serving (optional)

1. Place the beans, ham hock, bay leaves, and water in a large, heavy pot. Bring to a boil. Cover, reduce the heat, and simmer for 1½ to 2 hours, or until the beans are tender. Cool slightly, then drain the beans, reserving both the cooking liquid and the beans. Measure out 4 cups of the bean liquid, discarding any extra. Reserve. Discard the ham hock and bay leaves.

2. Preheat the oven to 300°F. In an ovenproof Dutch oven, cook the bacon over medium heat until most of the fat has been rendered. Add the onion, shallots, bell pepper, and green chile and cook for 5 minutes or until softened but not browned. Stir in the rice and cook for 2 minutes or until the rice is translucent but not browned. Add the reserved beans, cooking liquid, and salt. Bring to a boil, then reduce the heat, cover and place in the oven.

3. Bake for 20 minutes or until the liquid has evaporated. Cool for about 10 minutes, then lightly fluff and stir in the butter. Serve with the hot sauce.

The great Louis Armstrong loved the creole favorite red beans and rice so much, he signed his letters "Red Beans and Ricely Yours."

CUBAN BLACK TURTLE BEANS AND RICE

(Moros e Christianos)

This popular dish of beans and rice is whimsically referred to as "Moors and Christians" due to the black and white colors of the dish. The culantro called for here is a more flavorful flat-leafed relative of cilantro, which can be substituted for a less pungent flavor. To make this into a Cuban one-dish meal, top each portion with a fried egg and a garnish of fried sweet plantains.

Serves 6

1 cup dried black turtle beans, cooked and drained (see Basic Cooking Chart, page 43)

1/2 cup diced Roasted Red Bell Peppers (see page 314), or purchased

1/2 cup olive oil

1 medium onion, chopped

1 green bell pepper, diced

1 bunch scallions, thinly sliced

2 tablespoons chopped garlic

4 cups Light Chicken Stock (see page 301)

2 teaspoons dried oregano

2 teaspoons ground cumin

Salt and freshly ground black pepper

2 cups raw long-grain rice

1/4 cup chopped fresh culantro or cilantro leaves (about 1/2 bunch)

1. Prepare the black turtle beans and Roasted Red Bell Peppers. Reserve.

2. Preheat the oven to 350°F. Heat the olive oil in a large ovenproof Dutch oven with a lid. Stir the onion, green pepper, roasted red peppers, scallions, and garlic. Cook for about 5 minutes, or until softened but not brown. Add the Light Chicken Stock, oregano, cumin, and season to taste with salt and black pepper. Bring to a boil. Stir in the rice and beans, cover, and place in the oven.

3. Bake for about 25 minutes, or until the liquid has been absorbed. Remove from the oven and let stand for 5 to 10 minutes to steam, then stir in the culantro and season to taste with salt and black pepper.

GOLDEN RISOTTO WITH BABY LIMAS AND RED PEPPER

The saffron called for here is the world's most expensive spice, costing about forty-five dollars an ounce. In this case more is not better because a little goes a long way. The powerful, slightly acrid flavor of the saffron permeates this risotto and tints it an unmistakable rich, warm golden color. Overdo it on the saffron and it could taste medicinal. This is a variation on the classic Milanese risotto, which is simmered with saffron and traditionally served with braised veal shanks called osso buco. The favas add a bright bit of color and their own sweet pealike flavor and mouth-pleasing texture to the risotto, while the red pepper lends sweetness and additional bright color.

Serves 4

4 cups Vegetable Stock (see page 304) or Rich Chicken Stock (see page 303), simmering

1 large pinch saffron threads

2 tablespoons unsalted butter

1/2 cup chopped onion (about 1 medium)

2 tablespoons chopped shallot (about 1 large)

1 red bell pepper, seeded and diced

1 teaspoon chopped garlic

1 cup raw arborio, or other short-grain rice

1 (10-ounce) package frozen baby lima beans, or green favas

1/4 cup freshly grated Parmesan-Reggiano

2 tablespoons chopped Italian parsley leaves

Salt and freshly ground black pepper

1. Prepare the Vegetable Stock. Add the saffron and reserve.

2. In a large saucepan over medium heat, melt the butter. Add the onion, shallot, and red pepper and cook for about 5 minutes, stirring frequently, or until the onion is tender. Stir in garlic and rice. Cook 2 minutes, stirring constantly. Stir in about 1 1/2 cups of the hot stock. Heat to boiling, then reduce the heat. Simmer, uncovered, stirring occasionally, until most of the liquid is absorbed. Stir in 1 1/4 cups of the remaining stock and the lima beans. Simmer, uncovered, stirring occasionally, until most of the liquid is absorbed. Add the remaining 1 1/4 cups stock and continue cooking until the liquid has been absorbed and the rice is tender, about 15 minutes. Stir in the cheese, parsley, and season to taste with salt and black pepper. Sprinkle each portion with additional black pepper as desired.

CHICKPEA SPAETZLE

Spaetzle is a dish of soft dumplings known throughout the former Austro-Hungarian Empire. They are made from a batter that is halfway between a pancake batter and a pasta dough and can be flavored with everything from chestnuts and chestnut flour, to spinach, pumpkin, and chickpea flour. Spaetzle are an especially good side dish to serve at a party because they can be made ahead and then cooked until toasty-brown in butter. I first tasted these chickpea spaetzle at a meal I enjoyed at the exotic and adventurous Indian-inspired restaurant, Tabla, at New York's Madison Square Park. I thought it was such a good idea that I had to try making them myself.

Serves 6

2 cups unbleached all-purpose flour

2 cups chickpea flour

2 teaspoons salt

1 teaspoon freshly grated nutmeg

4 eggs

4 cups whole milk

¼ cup unsalted butter

1 cup soft bread crumbs

½ cup chopped Italian parsley leaves (about 1 bunch)

1. Combine the all-purpose flour, chickpea flour, salt, and nutmeg in bowl. Whisk together the eggs and milk in a large bowl. Beat the egg mixture slowly into the flour mixture until the dough is smooth and the consistency is halfway between a pancake batter and a dough.

2. Bring water to a boil in a large wide pot. Working in batches, press the dough through the holes of a colander or a spaetzle maker directly into the boiling water. Stir gently to prevent sticking. The spaetzle are ready when they float to the surface, about 5 minutes. Remove with a slotted spoon and reserve.

3. Melt the butter in a pan, over medium heat. Add the bread crumbs and cook until evenly toasted, stirring frequently. Toss the spaetzle with the toasted crumbs and parsley. Serve as a side dish with spicy meats.

WHITE BEAN PURÉE

urées are a classic side dish in the elegant cuisine of France. Serve this smooth, flavorful purée hot as a side dish with roast chicken or roast beef.

Serves 6 •

1 pound (2 cups) dried white emergo
   beans, or haricots lingots, or haricots
   soisson, or other large creamy white
   beans, soaked and drained (see Basic
   Soaking Chart, page 41)
1 bunch fresh savory, or thyme
4 cups Vegetable Stock (see page 304) or
   Light Chicken Stock (see page 301)
$1/4$ cup unsalted butter
1 large onion, diced
2 tablespoons chopped garlic
1 teaspoon ground allspice
Grated zest of 1 lemon
2 russet potatoes, peeled and diced
1 cup heavy cream
Salt and freshly ground black pepper

1. Prepare the white emergo beans. Combine the beans with the savory and Vegetable Stock in a large pot. Cover with a lid. Bring to a boil. Reduce heat and simmer for $1\frac{1}{2}$ hours.

2. In a small pan, melt the butter. Add the onion, garlic, allspice, and lemon zest, and cook over medium heat until the onion is transparent. Add the beans along with the potatoes. Continue cooking for 30 minutes longer, or until the beans are very soft. Remove from the heat and discard the savory. (Some of the leaves will remain in the pot.) Drain and reserve any excess liquid.

3. Purée the contents of the pot in a food processor. Pour in the cream and process again. If the mixture is still stiff, pour in up to $1/2$ cup of the reserved cooking liquid to form a smooth, soft consistency. Season to taste with salt and pepper.

CHAPTER ELEVEN

DESSERTS

MOLASSES CARAMEL CORN WITH PEANUTS

In 1871 a German immigrant, F. W. Rueckheim, brought the recipe for the ever-delicious delight that became known as Cracker Jack® to Chicago. With his entire fortune of $200, Rueckheim started a small shop selling his specialty. The treat's popularity increased enormously in 1893 after being introduced at the first World's Fair held in the same city. Essential to this recipe are the small, rounded, red-skinned Spanish peanuts called for here.

Makes about 16 cups (4 quarts) •

¼ **pound (1 stick) unsalted butter**

1 tablespoon peanut oil

1 cup raw popcorn kernels

1 cup sugar

½ **cup light corn syrup**

¼ **cup molasses**

1 tablespoon vanilla extract

2 cups small red-skinned Spanish peanuts, roasted and salted

A funny name for the peanut is "monkey nut," so called because of its popularity for feeding to the monkeys at zoos in the early twentieth century.

1. Preheat the oven to 275°F. Rub a large roasting pan with 1 tablespoon of the butter and reserve. In a large (2-gallon), heavy-bottomed pot with a lid, heat the oil with 3 popcorn kernels, covered, over medium heat. When the kernels pop, add the remaining popcorn. Cover, shaking the pot occasionally, until the popping slows to several seconds between each pop. Remove from the heat, uncover, and cool to room temperature. Reserve in a large, heatproof bowl.

2. In a small, heavy saucepan over medium heat, bring to a boil the sugar, remaining 7 tablespoons butter, corn syrup, and molasses. Cook over medium heat until the mixture reaches the "soft crack" stage (275°F on a candy thermometer). If not using a thermometer, the syrup should form hard but pliable threads when dropped into a bowl of cold water. Remove from the heat and slowly stir in the vanilla, taking care as the syrup will bubble up.

3. Working quickly, add the peanuts to the hot syrup and stir to coat. Immediately pour the peanuts and syrup over the reserved popcorn and stir to combine, using a wooden spoon (or a high-heat silicon spatula).

4. Spread the mixture out onto the prepared roasting pan. Bake for 30 minutes, stirring every 10 minutes. The mixture should be the color of dark caramel and the nuts should be toasted. Remove from the oven, cool completely, and then break into chunks. Store in an airtight cookie tin.

CARAMEL APPLES
WITH SALTED PEANUT CRUNCH COATING

This is a great snack for kids either on the stick or cut into wedges with the seeds removed. If you serve it on a stick, you will need eight short wooden dowels available in most cookware stores or where candy making supplies are sold. You can substitute inexpensive wooden chopsticks cut into halves. When choosing apples, look for the smaller ones that come packed in a 2- to 3- pound plastic bag. They're less expensive than the larger ones and will have a good apple-to-coating ratio.

Makes 8 apples •

8 small firm red apples (such as Winesap, Jonathan, McIntosh)

1 (1/2-pound) can roasted salted peanuts (not dry roasted)

1 pound good-quality soft, chewy caramel candies, unwrapped

1 tablespoon vanilla extract

1. Have ready a baking sheet covered with waxed or parchment paper. Twist the stems off the apples then stick a dowel or skewer 2 to 3 inches into the stem end of each apple. Reserve.

2. Coarsely chop the peanuts, then shake them through a wire sieve set over a bowl to remove any dusty bits. You should have only chunky nuts left in the sieve. Place the chunky peanuts in a bowl and reserve.

3. Place the caramels and vanilla in a deep microwaveable bowl. Microwave on medium power (50%) for 2 to 3 minutes, then stir. Microwave again for 2 minutes, or until almost liquid. (Alternatively, place the caramels in a heatproof bowl and set over a pot of simmering water. Stir until melted and smooth. The mixture should be hot to the touch but not burning.)

4. Holding an apple by its wooden dowel, dip into the melted caramel, tilting the bowl of caramel and twirling the apple to coat completely. Allow any excess caramel to drip off, then dip the bottom of the apple into the bowl of reserved chopped peanuts. Place on the prepared baking sheet. Repeat with the remaining apples.

5. Chill in the refrigerator for 30 minutes or until the caramel is set. Serve the apples as is or cut each into 6 wedges and remove the core and seeds.

FRIED DESSERT WON TONS
WITH RED BEAN PASTE FILLING

How can beans be a dessert? In China, red adzuki beans are reserved for sweet rather than savory dishes. The color red is said to bring good luck. This is probably why dishes made with these beans are associated with festivals. Here, in a somewhat Westernized variation, the tiny mild red mung beans are combined with chopped dates, vanilla, and brandy and cooked until they form a thick paste reminiscent of chocolate. Rather than the more traditional filled Chinese steamed buns, here I use the red bean filling to stuff won ton skins, and then deep-fry them. To make the stuffed won tons ahead, spread them out on a single layer on a waxed- or parchment paper-lined baking sheet, then freeze until firm. Transfer to a freezer bag, pressing out the excess air before sealing. Freeze until ready to cook.

Serves 8 (48 won tons) •

RED BEAN PASTE

1 pound (2 cups dried) red adzuki beans, soaked (see Soaking Chart, page 41)

6 cups cold water

½ pound pitted dates

¼ pound (1 stick) unsalted butter

1 cup sugar

1 teaspoon salt

2 tablespoons vanilla extract

¼ cup brandy

1 (4-ounce) package won ton skins (thawed if frozen)

4 cups soybean oil, for frying

Confectioners' sugar, for serving

1. Prepare the Red Bean Paste: Drain the soaked adzuki beans. Place in a large pot and cover with the cold water. Bring to a boil, then reduce the heat and simmer for 1½ to 2 hours, or until the beans are soft but not mushy. (The water should have evaporated by the time the beans are cooked.) Drain and discard any water left in the pot.

2. Soak the dates for 15 minutes in 1 cup boiling water to soften. Reserve.

3. Purée the cooked beans in a food processor until they form a smooth paste, scraping down the side of the bowl several times. (If desired, strain the puréed beans through a sieve or food mill to remove the skin pieces for a more refined texture.) Transfer the beans to another bowl and reserve. Without washing the processor bowl, purée the dates and their soaking liquid until smooth.

ABOUT ADZUKI BEANS

❧ ❧ ❧

Called simply red beans in Chinese and adzuki or azuki beans in Japanese, these are small red mung beans related to black-eyed peas, cow peas, and pigeon peas. In Japan and China, these beans are associated with sweets. They are prepared in a sweet bean paste filling for steamed buns or are cooked and sugar coated as a confection. When these same adzuki beans are skinned and split, they become the Indian staple porridge, dal.

4. In a large heavy-bottomed saucepan, melt the butter and sugar together. Add the salt, reserved red bean purée, and the date purée. Stir to combine and cook over low heat, stirring frequently until a thick paste forms (similar to the paste for refried beans). Remove from the heat and immediately stir in the vanilla and the brandy. Cool, covered, and then refrigerate until chilled, about 1 hour. The paste can be made 3 to 4 days ahead.

5. Prepare the won tons: Place 1½ teaspoons of the bean paste just below the diagonal center of each won ton skin. Do not get any filling on the edges of the skin. With a finger dipped into a bowl of water, moisten the edges of the wrapper. Bring the wrapper up over the filling, forming a triangle, and press the edges to seal. Take the 2 points of the triangle along the bottom folded edge and bring them together, pinching tightly to form a stuffed ring shape with a pointy cap so that it looks like a tortellini. As the won tons are finished, arrange them on a waxed or parchment paper-lined pan, without touching. Chill until ready to serve.

6. Heat the oil in a deep pan or wok until a light haze forms above it, about 365°F on a deep-frying thermometer. Carefully place 6 to 8 won tons, one at a time, into the oil. Fry for 2 to 3 minutes, turning them to cook evenly, until golden brown and crispy. Remove with a slotted spoon and drain on paper towels. Sprinkle generously while still warm with confectioners' sugar and serve immediately.

PEANUT BUTTER AND
JELLY SANDWICH COOKIES

I first made these cookies for a television presentation and I've been thinking about them ever since. The funny thing is, I always hated PB and J sandwiches. Somehow, in cookie form I find it an irresistible combination. To shape the cookie dough, you will need a fairly large (4-inch) round cutter, fluted if possible, and a small (1-inch) round cutter or the bottom of a metal pastry tip.

Makes 2 dozen sandwich cookies •

5 cups unbleached all-purpose flour
  (1¼ pounds)
1 tablespoon baking powder
1 teaspoon baking soda
1 teaspoon salt
1 teaspoon ground allspice
2 cups chunky peanut butter
¾ pound (3 sticks) unsalted butter
2 cups confectioners' sugar
1 pound dark brown sugar (use light
  brown sugar for less of a molasses flavor)
3 eggs
2 tablespoons vanilla extract
1 (15-ounce) jar good-quality raspberry
  or strawberry jam

ABOUT GOOBERS
PEANUTS ARE A MEMBER OF THE LEGUME FAMILY AND HAVE MANY ALIASES. THEY HAVE BEEN CALLED "GOOBERS," A WORD OF AFRICAN ORIGIN FROM THE CONGO THAT HAS BEEN USED SINCE THE NINETEENTH CENTURY; GROUNDNUT, A NAME USED BY BOTANISTS BECAUSE THE SEED CASE OF THE PLANT BURROWS DOWN INTO THE EARTH TO RIPEN; EARTHNUT; AND GROUND PEA.

1. In a bowl, stir together flour, baking powder, baking soda, salt, and allspice. Reserve.

2. In the bowl of an electric mixer, beat together the peanut butter, butter, confectioners' sugar, and brown sugar until light and fluffy. Beat in the eggs, one at a time. Add the vanilla. Stir in the dry ingredients. Wrap the dough tightly in plastic wrap and chill for about 1 hour or until firm.

3. Preheat the oven to 325°F. On a floured board, roll out the dough (a portion at a time) into a ¼-inch-thick sheet. Cut out circles with a 4-inch round cutter. Place the circles, spaced 2 inches apart, on parchment paper-lined baking sheets. Chill the cutout dough rounds, then count them. You should have about 48 cookie rounds. Cut out the centers of half the chilled dough rounds with a 1-inch round cutter. (Reroll these small dough rounds or bake as is, for mini cookies, if you like.)

4. Bake the cookies for 15 minutes or until lightly browned on the edges, turning the baking sheets halfway through baking time for even browning. Remove from the oven and allow the cookies to cool to room temperature on a rack.

5. Warm the jam for 2 minutes in the microwave oven on low (20%) power (or over low heat in a small pot for 2 minutes) until runny but not hot to the touch. To form each sandwich cookie, spoon 1 tablespoon of the jam into the center of each baked solid cookie round. Cool slightly to set, then lay a cutout top over the jam and press to join together. Chill before serving to set the filling.

CHINESE FIRECRACKER-JACKS

As a food consultant, I am sometimes hired to develop recipes for specialty foods companies. This generally means that I'm overwhelmingly immersed in a particular food for a time while I try and retry recipes. Once it was lobster bisque and Guinness Irish stew; another time it was endless batches of bolognese sauce. For a time I worked on popcorn recipes for my friend Ronna Schultz, who owns the Society Hill Nut Company, where they make praline-coated nuts in giant old copper kettles. She had the idea that flavored and coated popcorn was a natural extension of her existing line. This recipe is one of my favorites from that time, when I seemed to be always popping corn and making caramel.

Makes 8 cups •

1 tablespoon peanut oil

1 cup raw popcorn kernels

2 cups roasted, salted peanuts, with skins on (if possible)

2 tablespoons sesame seeds

2 tablespoons grated fresh ginger

1 tablespoon dry mustard

Grated zest of 1 orange

2 tablespoons soy sauce

2 tablespoons roasted Japanese sesame oil

$1/2$ cup sugar

$1/4$ cup orange marmalade

$1/4$ cup light corn syrup

$1 1/2$ tablespoons Korean red pepper flakes, or hot red pepper flakes

1. In a large heavy-bottomed pot with a lid, heat the oil and 3 popcorn kernels, covered, over medium heat. When the kernels pop, add the remaining popcorn. Cover, shaking the pot occasionally, until the popping slows to several seconds between each pop. Remove from the heat, uncover, and cool to room temperature. Place the cooled popcorn and peanuts in a large, heatproof bowl. Reserve.

2. Preheat the oven to 300°F. In an ovenproof pan, lightly toast the sesame seeds, about 10 minutes. Reserve.

3. In a bowl, whisk together the ginger, dry mustard, orange zest, soy sauce, and sesame oil.

4. In a small, heavy-bottomed pot, bring to a boil the sugar marmalade, and corn syrup. Continue cooking over medium heat until the mixture reaches 275°F on a candy thermometer. Slowly stir the spice mixture into the hot syrup, being careful not to get burned, as the mixture may bubble up.

5. Pour the hot syrup over the cooled popcorn and peanuts and toss to mix. Sprinkle with the red pepper flakes and sesame seeds and toss again. Cool, then store in an airtight cookie tin.

ROASTED PEANUT-MACADAMIA BRITTLE WITH BOURBON

Last time I made this homemade brittle, I had to give the second half of the batch away because I couldn't stop eating it. Although I've outgrown my ridiculously demanding sweet tooth, there are still a few candies that tempt me. This brittle is one of them. The combination of the bourbon with the indulgently rich macadamia nuts is perfectly balanced by the salted, toasted peanuts.

Makes 3 pounds •

1 (1-pound) can roasted and salted
   peanuts (not dry roasted)

4 cups sugar

½ cup light corn syrup

¼ pound (1 stick) unsalted butter

1 teaspoon baking soda

2 teaspoons vanilla extract

¼ cup bourbon

¼ pound roasted, salted macadamia
   nuts, split in halves

Cook's Note ❧ ❧ ❧

To test without using a candy thermometer, have ready a small bowl filled with cold water. Drop a small spoonful of hot sugar syrup into the bowl. Remove and squeeze the ball. The syrup should form a rigid ball when pressed between your fingers.

1. Preheat the oven to 200°F. Spread the peanuts, with excess salt shaken off, onto a baking pan. Warm the nuts in the oven while making the brittle.

2. Using nonstick vegetable spray, generously spray two (15 × 10-inch) jelly-roll pans. In a heavy (not nonstick) medium saucepan with a lid, combine both the sugar and the corn syrup. Cook over medium heat, covered, stirring occasionally with a wooden spoon. Heat until the sugar has melted and is no longer grainy. Increase the heat to medium-high and cook, without stirring, to the hard-crack stage (300°F on a candy thermometer; see Cook's Note), about 10 minutes.

3. Stir in the butter, which will reduce the temperature. Continue cooking until the mixture returns to the soft-crack stage (280°F on a candy thermometer) and then remove from the heat.

4. In a small bowl, combine the baking soda, vanilla, and bourbon. Stir the soda mixture into the candy pot, continuing to stir as the candy foams. Remove the peanuts from the oven and quickly stir in the warm peanuts and macadamias, using a wooden spoon. Carefully pour the mixture onto the 2 prepared jelly-roll pans. Use spring tongs to spread out the brittle to fill the pan, then flip the brittle over. Allow the brittle to cool enough to handle (gingerly) and stretch thinner, like taffy. Allow the brittle to cool completely then break into large shards. Store in an airtight cookie tin.

PEANUT CREAM-FILLED CHOCOLATE CUPS

I don't know anyone who doesn't love chocolate peanut butter cups. To make them, you will need two dozen paper-lined foil petit four cups (1-inch muffin papers), available at kitchenware stores.

Makes about 2 dozen miniature chocolate cups •

CHOCOLATE SHELLS

8 ounces high-quality semisweet chocolate, broken into small chunks

1 tablespoon vegetable oil

CREAMY PEANUT FILLING

1 cup creamy peanut butter

4 tablespoons unsalted butter

$1/2$ cup confectioners' sugar

2 teaspoons vanilla extract

BECAUSE OF THEIR CLOSE ASSOCIATION WITH SLAVES, PEANUTS WERE LONG CONSIDERED LOWLY COUSINS OF TREE NUTS AND WERE OFTEN SHUNNED BY WHITE CONSUMERS. ABOUT 100 YEARS AGO, THE KELLOGG BROTHERS (OF CORN FLAKES FAME) BEGAN TURNING PEANUTS INTO PASTE. PEANUT BUTTER SOON BECAME A STAPLE IN THE AMERICAN PANTRY. MORE THAN HALF OUR ANNUAL CROP OF PEANUTS GETS TURNED INTO PEANUT BUTTER. IN THIS COUNTRY WE CONSUME ABOUT 700,000,000 POUNDS OF PEANUT BUTTER A YEAR.

---

1. Prepare the Chocolate Shells: Arrange 24 paper-lined petit four foils on a baking sheet.

2. Place 6 ounces of the chocolate and the oil in a microwaveable bowl or measuring cup. Heat on low power (20%) for 1 minute. Stir and microwave at 1-minute intervals or until the chocolate has melted completely, stirring between each interval. Remove from the microwave and stir in the remaining 2 ounces of chocolate. Continue stirring until the chocolate is completely smooth. Reserve. (Or, place the chocolate in a clean, dry heatproof bowl over a pot of simmering water until melted. Remove from the heat.)

3. Pour about 1 tablespoon of the melted chocolate into each paper-lined foil cup. Using a spoon, spread some of the chocolate up the side of each paper. Place the sheet of chocolate-lined cups in the refrigerator for 10 minutes or until the chocolate has set. Keep the remaining chocolate warm.

4. Prepare the Creamy Peanut Filling: Process the peanut butter, butter, confectioners' sugar, and vanilla in a food processor until smooth. Transfer the filling to a pastry bag fitted with a round piping tip or heavy-duty plastic freezer bag with one corner snipped off. Pipe the filling into the prepared chocolate shells, snipping off $1/8$ to $1/4$ inch more of the bag if necessary to make it easier to pipe.

5. Reheat the remaining chocolate in the microwave or over a pot of boiling water just until warm enough to pour. Transfer the melted chocolate to a separate pastry bag fitted with a small round piping tip or a clean, dry heavy-duty plastic freezer bag with a very small corner snipped off (just large enough for the chocolate to drizzle out with using slight pressure). Drizzle the chocolate over the tops of the peanut filled cups to cover and refrigerate again until set. Store in the refrigerator until ready to serve.

ALL-AMERICAN PEANUTTY DEVIL'S FOOD CAKE

I've combined several American favorites here: deep-dark devil's food cake flavored with strong coffee, a rich peanut cream filling, and the simplest chocolate icing of sour cream melted with chocolate chips. It's rich, it's delicious, and it's relatively easy to make. Why not make two cakes while you're at it? As long as it's well-wrapped, the cake freezes beautifully. This devil's food cake is at its best at room temperature so that the chocolate icing melts in your mouth and the peanut filling tastes rich and creamy.

Serves 12 (makes one 9-inch layer cake) •

CAKE

½ cup Dutch-processed cocoa

1 cup hot freshly brewed strong coffee

2 tablespoons instant coffee granules (optional)

1½ cups unbleached all-purpose flour

1 teaspoon baking soda

1 teaspoon salt

½ teaspoon baking powder

¼ pound (1 stick) unsalted butter, softened

1 cup dark brown sugar

½ cup granulated sugar

1 teaspoon vanilla extract

2 eggs

1. Prepare the Cake: Preheat the oven to 350°F. Spray a 9-inch springform pan generously with nonstick vegetable spray.

2. In a small bowl, whisk together the cocoa, coffee, and coffee granules—use these if you like a strong coffee flavor. Set the mixture aside to cool to room temperature.

3. In a separate bowl, combine the flour, baking soda, salt, and baking powder. Reserve.

4. In the bowl of an electric mixer, cream together the butter, brown sugar, granulated sugar, and vanilla until creamy and light. Beat in the eggs, 1 at a time. Alternately, add the dry ingredients and the coffee liquid, beginning and ending with the dry ingredients and beating well after each addition.

5. Pour the batter into the prepared pan. Bake for 40 minutes, or until the cake comes away from the side of the pan and forms a slightly rounded top and a toothpick inserted into the center comes out clean. Cool in the pan on a wire rack for 10 minutes. Remove the sides of the springform pan and refrigerate until chilled before filling.

CHUNKY PEANUT FILLING

1½ cups chunky peanut butter

8 ounces cream cheese, softened

1 cup confectioners' sugar

2 teaspoons vanilla extract

CREAMY CHOCOLATE ICING

1 (12-ounce) package semisweet
chocolate chips

1 cup sour cream

1 cup coarsely chopped roasted,
salted peanuts, for garnish

6. Prepare the Chunky Peanut Filling: In the bowl of an electric mixer, beat the peanut butter, cream cheese, and confectioners' sugar until light and creamy, scraping the side of the bowl halfway through to prevent lumps. Add the vanilla and beat until well mixed. Reserve.

7. Prepare the Creamy Chocolate Icing: Combine the chocolate chips and sour cream in a microwaveable bowl. Microwave on low power (20%) for 1 to 2 minutes. Stir and microwave again for 1 to 2 minutes or until the chocolate is almost completely melted. Or place the chocolate in a clean, dry heatproof bowl and set over simmering water until completely melted. Chill in the refrigerator until it reaches a spreadable consistency, about 1 hour.

8. Using a long, serrated knife, cut the cake horizontally into 2 layers. Spread the peanut filling on 1 layer. Top with the second layer, cut side up. Smooth the side and chill the cake for 20 minutes in the freezer. Remove from the freezer and spread the top and side with the Creamy Chocolate Icing. Sprinkle the top with the chopped peanuts and refrigerate again until ready to serve. Cut the cake using a sharp knife. Dip the knife in hot water before each cut and wipe the blade clean after each cut.

Amedeo Obici, an Italian immigrant, founded the Planters Peanut Company. In 1918 he turned a sketch by a Virginia schoolboy into Mr. Peanut, the monocled, top-hatted mascot of his company who became famous around the world.

TUNISIAN CHICKPEA COOKIES *(Ghraiba)*

These unusual cookies are made from toasted chickpea flour and rolled in white sesame seeds. Chickpeas are particularly high in soluble fiber and are quite high in protein. So, not only do these cookies taste good, they're also very healthful and nourishing. In Tunisia, they are typically served accompanied by a glass of hot, sweet mint tea. The name *ghraiba* means "foreign," indicating that the original recipe was brought to Tunisia from somewhere else, perhaps the Middle East. The chickpea flour called for here (available at Middle Eastern and Indian groceries and health food stores) is inexpensive.

Makes 2 dozen cookies •

1½ cups toasted chickpea flour

½ cup unbleached all-purpose flour

¼ teaspoon baking powder

½ cup sugar

2 tablespoons olive oil

4 tablespoons melted unsalted butter

1 to 2 tablespoons water

½ cup hulled white sesame seeds

1. Preheat the oven to 325°F. In a blender or food processor, place the toasted chickpea flour, all-purpose flour, baking powder, and sugar. Add the olive oil and butter and process to combine. Add the water, using only enough to moisten the dough. As soon as the dough comes together into a ball, it is ready.

2. Remove the dough from the blender and knead slightly on a lightly floured surface until smooth. Divide the dough into 6 equal portions. Roll each portion into a log about ¾ inch in diameter. Spread the sesame seeds out evenly on a baking sheet.

3. Lightly roll the dough logs in the sesame seeds until coated. Cut the rolls diagonally into 2-inch-thick slices. Arrange on a separate baking sheet lined with parchment paper. Bake for 15 minutes or until lightly browned. The cookies should be crunchy on the outsides and soft on the insides. Transfer the cookies to a cooling rack and let cool. To store, place in a cookie tin and keep up to 4 days.

"Dog's body," a most unsavory-sounding dish, was nineteenth-century British naval slang for pease pudding boiled in a cloth.

VIENNESE WHITE BEAN AND HAZELNUT TORTE

This unusual Viennese-style torte uses not only the usual ground nuts to replace the flour, but also contains white bean purée, which makes it moist. It's easy to make and not too sweet because it is filled with apricot jam rather than covered with an icing. I recommend using a high-quality imported jam, such as Hero brand, for the best fruit flavor here. To prevent nuts from becoming oily when ground, freeze them first. As long as the nuts are cold, the oil can't escape. For the neatest results when cutting the layers, bake the cake a day ahead of time so it has time to become firm.

Serves 10 (makes one 10-inch round cake) •

²/₃ cups dried navy or great Northern
   beans, cooked and drained
   (see Basic Cooking Chart, page 43),
   or 2 cups canned navy beans,
   rinsed and drained
4 eggs, separated
1 cup sugar
1 tablespoon vanilla extract
3 tablespoons dark rum, or brandy, or
   whiskey, or bourbon
1½ cups finely ground skinless, toasted
   hazelnuts, or almonds
½ cup apricot jam
½ cup confectioners' sugar

1. Prepare the navy beans. Allow to cool. Put through a food mill to make a smooth thick purée. Reserve.

2. Preheat the oven to 350°F. Spray a 10-inch springform pan with nonstick vegetable spray.

3. Beat the egg yolks with ½ cup sugar, vanilla, and rum until light and fluffy. Fold in bean purée and ground hazelnuts. Reserve.

4. In a separate clean medium bowl, beat the egg whites until soft peaks form. Gradually add the remaining ½ cup sugar, beating between each addition, until the whites are firm and glossy and the meringue sticks to the side of the bowl.

5. Fold one-third of the meringue into the egg yolk mixture to lighten, then fold in the remaining meringue in two parts. Pour the mixture into the prepared pan. Bake for about 1 hour, or until the torte is set and has begun to shrink away from the side of the pan. Cool thoroughly in the pan at room temperature (preferably overnight).

6. To finish the torte, cut it horizontally into 2 even layers using a large serrated knife. Melt the apricot jam in a small saucepan over low heat until warm and runny, but not hot. Spread the jam onto the cut side of the bottom layer. Cover with the top layer, cut side down. Dust generously with the confectioners' sugar and cut the cake into 10 pieces with a serrated knife.

CHAPTER TWELVE

PANTRY
SALAD DRESSINGS · SAUCES · STOCKS · DOUGHS

ADOBO COLORADO MARINADE

This versatile and delicious marinade not only imparts a great flavor and beautiful red-gold color to grilled foods like chicken and tuna, it also tenderizes dark meat chicken, making it as moist and succulent as can be. Serve adobo-marinated chicken or tuna to accompany Black Turtle Beans with Epazote (see page 222) or make it a full meal with a side of Refried Beans (see page 236) and a basket of warm fresh tortillas.

Makes about 3 cups

1 (14-ounce) package anchiote paste

1 cup vegetable oil

1 cup cider vinegar

2 tablespoons ground toasted cumin (see Toasting Seeds, page 217)

1/4 cup finely chopped garlic

2 tablespoons dried oregano

1 1/2 teaspoons ground allspice

2 teaspoons salt

1. Blend the anchiote paste, oil, vinegar, cumin, garlic, oregano, allspice, and salt in a small bowl. Cover tightly and refrigerate for up to 2 to 3 months.

2. Use to marinate boneless, skinless chicken thighs, or firm fish, such as tuna, swordfish, and mahi-mahi. Marinate the chicken for between 6 and 48 hours, and the fish for 2 to 6 hours before grilling.

LEMON-PEPPER MOJO

Mojo or *môlho* is a Brazilian term for a fresh salsa. Serve this mojo with Black Turtle Beans with Epazote (see page 222), Chile Ancho Empanadas with Frijoles Filling (see page 58), or with lime- and chile-marinated grilled fish or shrimp.

Makes 1 1/2 cups

1/4 cup pickled jalapeño peppers, drained and chopped

1/2 cup finely diced white onion

1 teaspoon chopped garlic

1/4 cup fresh lemon juice (about 2 lemons)

1/2 cup drained, diced imported roasted red peppers

1/4 cup diced green bell pepper

1/4 cup chopped fresh cilantro leaves

In a small bowl, combine the jalapeños, onion, garlic, lemon juice, roasted red bell peppers, and green bell peppers. Cover and refrigerate until chilled. Stir in the cilantro just before serving so it keeps its color.

BARLEY MALT VINAIGRETTE

This is kind of a "macho" dressing, strong and bold in flavor and not meant for the fainthearted. It is especially suited to bean salads because the flavor of milder dressings tends to get lost when absorbed into the starchy beans.

Makes about 2 cups •

1/2 cup malt vinegar
1 tablespoon Dijon mustard
1 tablespoon Pickapeppa Sauce
2 tablespoons barley malt syrup
1 teaspoon hot pepper sauce
2 large shallots, coarsely sliced
1 teaspoon salt
1/2 teaspoon freshly ground
   black pepper
1/4 cup chopped marjoram
1 1/2 cups peanut oil, or sunflower oil

Place the vinegar, mustard, Pickapeppa Sauce, malt syrup, hot sauce, shallots, salt, black pepper, and marjoram into a mixing bowl. Whisk until creamy looking. Slowly pour in the oil, whisking constantly, until well combined. Keep refrigerated for up to 2 weeks.

PEPITA-TOMATILLO SAUCE

This is a light green creamy and rich sauce made with ground pumpkin seeds (*pepitas*) and the Mexican green-husked tomatoes (*tomatillos*). The lemony tasting, crisp-tender tomatillos are counterbalanced by the rich creaminess of the pumpkin seeds. The method of using ground nuts to thicken sauces can be traced back to the Spanish colonists who brought the technique with them from the Mediterranean where they were more likely to use almonds or pine nuts. Pepitas are a new world food that became adapted to Old World methods.

Makes 4 cups •

1/2 cup diced onion
2 teaspoons chopped garlic
1/2 pound tomatillos, husked
2 tablespoons olive oil
1 cup shelled green pumpkin seeds
   (pepitas), lightly toasted
2 sprigs epazote (optional)
1/2 bunch fresh cilantro leaves
1 jalapeño pepper, chopped
2 cups Light Chicken Stock (see page
   301) or Vegetable Stock (see page 304)

In a medium pan, heat the onion, garlic, and tomatillos in olive oil until transparent. In a blender, purée the pumpkin seeds, epazote, cilantro, jalapeño, and Light Chicken Stock. Combine with the onion mixture and refrigerate for up to 3 weeks.

ROASTED RED BELL PEPPER VINAIGRETTE

For this dressing I use roasted red bell peppers, either fresh or from a jar. I prefer bottled bell peppers that are imported from Europe. Greece, Spain, and Italy all produce firm, slightly smoky, bottled roasted peppers. The peppers have several functions: they impart a beautiful orangy-red color and sweet pepper taste and they also thicken the dressing, thereby keeping the other ingredients from separating. Use this dressing to drizzle over a plateful of Oven-Cooked Italian-Style Beans (see page 228) or Oven-Cooked Vegetarian Beans (see page 230), or simply drizzled in a zigzag pattern over steamed green beans.

Makes about 2 cups •

1 teaspoon chopped garlic

¼ cup grated Pecorino Romano

1 cup Roasted Red Bell Peppers
   (see page 314), or 1 (15-ounce) jar
   roasted red peppers, well drained

1 tablespoon chopped fresh
   marjoram leaves

1 teaspoon salt

½ teaspoon freshly ground black pepper

½ cup balsamic vinegar

1 cup vegetable oil

½ cup extra-virgin olive oil

1. In a small bowl with a hand-held blender or in a standard blender, combine the garlic, cheese, roasted peppers, marjoram, salt, black pepper, and vinegar. Then, with the blender running, slowly drizzle in the oils, until completely absorbed and the dressing is creamy.

2. Pour into a glass jar with a lid and refrigerate until needed. The dressing will keep well for up to 2 weeks if tightly covered and refrigerated.

LEMON-GARLIC VINAIGRETTE

For this dressing I include the grated zest of the lemon. The pure lemon oil contained in the tiny pockets in the skin give the lemon its marvelous sunny aroma. Sometimes I make the dressing closer to an Eastern Mediterranean style with garlic and lemon juice, but no shallots and sherry vinegar, which give more of a western European cast. If you use straight lemon juice, increase the quantity to 1 cup. Be sure the garlic is plump, juicy, and white without any bitter-tasting green sprout in the center. Bottled lemon juice has a metallic aftertaste that is especially noticeable in a dressing like this. Use this versatile dressing on Niçoise Pasta Shell Salad with Green Beans, Chickpeas, and Tuna (see page 86) and in the Provençal Chickpea Salad with Tuna Caviar (see page 80).

Makes 2 cups •

2 cloves garlic, peeled

1 large shallot, coarsely chopped

1/2 teaspoon freshly ground black pepper

1 teaspoon salt

1/4 cup sherry vinegar

Grated zest of 1 lemon

1/4 cup fresh lemon juice (about 4 lemons)

1 cup olive oil

1. In a medium bowl with a hand-held blender, or in a standard blender, combine the garlic, shallot, pepper, salt, vinegar, and lemon zest and juice. With the blender running, slowly drizzle in the olive oil, until completely absorbed and the dressing is creamy.

2. Pour into a glass jar with a lid and refrigerate until needed. The dressing will keep well for up to 2 weeks if tightly covered and refrigerated.

CHINESE SHANXI VINEGAR DRESSING

An easy dressing to make with a well-balanced mix of pungent Chinese flavors. The Shanxi vinegar is a mild vinegar fermented from barley, sorghum, and peas with a mellow, sweet taste reminiscent of balsamic vinegar, which makes the best substitute. The mushroom soy sauce has an extra depth of flavor from the dried mushrooms used to flavor it. Plain soy sauce could easily be substituted if you don't have mushroom soy sauce on hand. I've found, though, that I use mushroom soy sauce more and more, especially for cold dishes where flavors tend to fade.

Makes 2 cups •

2 shallots, peeled and chopped

1 (2-inch) piece fresh ginger, peeled
  and chopped

1/2 cup peanut oil

2 tablespoons roasted Japanese sesame oil

1/2 cup Shanxi vinegar, or balsamic vinegar

1/4 cup mushroom soy sauce or soy sauce

Grated zest of 1 tangerine or orange

1. In a medium bowl with a hand-held blender, or in a standard blender, purée the shallots, ginger, oils, vinegar, soy sauce, and tangerine zest until smooth and creamy.

2. Pour into a glass jar with a lid and refrigerate until needed. The dressing will keep for up to 2 weeks if kept refrigerated.

FRENCH TARRAGON-SHALLOT VINAIGRETTE

This is a classic French vinaigrette dressing flavored with the characteristic trio of culinary musketeers: shallots, tarragon, and Dijon mustard. Use it when making the French Navy Bean and Shrimp Salad (see page 83) and the French Green Lentil Salad with Bacon and Tomato (see page 85). This dressing is also wonderful as a light coating on strong-flavored salad greens, such as Belgian endive, arugula, frisée, and spinach.

Makes 3 cups •

¼ pound shallots, peeled and coarsely chopped

½ cup tarragon vinegar

¼ cup Dijon mustard

1 cup extra-virgin olive oil

1 cup chopped Italian parsley leaves (about 2 bunches)

¼ cup chopped fresh tarragon leaves (about 1 bunch)

Salt and freshly ground black pepper

1. In a blender or food processor, purée the shallots, vinegar, mustard, and olive oil. Add the parsley and tarragon. Blend again until the herb leaves are in small pieces but not puréed. Season to taste with salt and pepper.

2. Pour into a glass jar with a lid and refrigerate until needed. Will keep for up to 2 weeks if kept refrigerated.

CUCUMBER-YOGURT RAITA

A raita is a refreshing salad based on yogurt that is a standard condiment at the table in India. Because yogurt is high in protein, it is especially important in vegetarian meals. Indian yogurt is thick, creamy, and a bit sweet. Traditionally, it is made from buffalo milk, which has a high fat content, and is drained through a cloth before using to make it thick. This raita is particularly cool and delightful because it is made from firmer seedless cukes and refreshing mint.

Makes 3 cups •

2 cups natural, unsweetened whole milk yogurt

1 large seedless English cucumber, peeled

1 fresh green chile pepper (such as jalapeño, or pasilla) seeded and minced

1 teaspoon toasted ground cumin seeds (see Toasting Seeds, page 217)

2 tablespoons chopped fresh mint leaves

1 teaspoon salt

1. Place a sieve lined with a cheese cone (yogurt cheese funnel), or clean dampened cotton, linen, cheesecloth, or muslin napkin over a large bowl. Place the yogurt into the lined sieve and allow it to drain for about 1 hour. (This step is optional but makes for a thicker raita with more body.)

2. Grate the cucumber into a medium bowl, and add the chile pepper, drained yogurt, cumin, mint, and salt. Cover and refrigerate for at least 30 minutes before serving. The sauce will keep refrigerated for only 2 days; after that the cucumbers will become soggy.

OVEN-ROASTED PLUM TOMATOES

Make these wonderful tomatoes when large, ripe plum tomatoes are plentiful. It's really not worth making in quantities of less than five pounds of tomatoes, because they shrink so much when baked. When the tomatoes are all used, strain the olive oil and reserve in the refrigerator. It is fabulous in pasta sauces, but must be kept refrigerated or it will spoil.

Makes about 80 tomato halves (6 cups) •

5 pounds ripe plum tomatoes
  (about 40), tops sliced off
¼ cup kosher salt (do not substitute
  table salt)
½ bunch fresh thyme sprigs
½ bunch fresh rosemary sprigs
½ bunch fresh sage sprigs
1 head garlic, cloves peeled and
  coarsely chopped
3 cups extra-virgin olive oil

1. Wash the tomatoes well to remove any waxy coating. Cut into halves lengthwise. Arrange the tomato halves, cut sides up, in a single layer on large baking sheets. Sprinkle evenly with the salt and let stand at room temperature for 1 hour.

2. Preheat the oven to 225°F. Drain and discard any juices that collect on the tray. Place the tomato halves in the oven and slowly roast for 4 to 5 hours. (The tomatoes should be dried and wrinkly-looking, but still plump.) Remove the tomatoes from the oven, and cool to room temperature.

3. In a large (½-gallon) container with a lid, arrange the tomatoes, herbs, and garlic in layers, covering each layer with olive oil. Press the tomatoes down so the olive oil covers them. Cover and refrigerate overnight. For best flavor, marinate for at least 2 days before using. The tomatoes will keep for up to 1 month in the refrigerator if you make sure to completely cover them with more olive oil each time you remove some.

MEXICAN TOMATO SAUCE WITH ALLSPICE

This Mexican-style sauce is perfect for Ranch-Style Eggs with Refried Beans (see page 146), or as an alternative choice when making Black Bean Quesadillas with Pepita-Tomatillo sauce (see page 67). Although the recipe calls for lard, which gives it an authentic flavor, you can use bacon fat or olive oil. If you have fresh, ripe plum tomatoes, use them for the sauce, but strain through a food mill or sieve after cooking to remove the rather tough skin pieces.

Makes 6 cups •

1 large onion, peeled and cut into quarters

4 cloves garlic, peeled

2 jalapeño peppers

2 (28-ounce) cans plum tomatoes

1 teaspoon allspice

1/2 teaspoon cinnamon

2 teaspoons salt

1/4 teaspoon freshly ground black pepper

1/4 cup lard, bacon fat, or olive oil

1. In a food processor or blender, process the onion, garlic, and jalapeños until chunky. Add the tomatoes with their liquid, allspice, cinnamon, salt and black pepper and process again, quickly, to maintain a chunky texture.

2. Melt the lard over medium-high heat in a skillet. Pour the tomato liquid into the lard, stirring carefully so it doesn't spatter. Cook for about 20 minutes, or until the oil rises to the top. To store, let cool and transfer to a glass container with a lid. Store in the refrigerator for up to 1 week.

DATE-TAMARIND CHUTNEY

Unlike the well-known commercially made mango chutney, which is chunky with pieces of chewy mango, this recipe from Bombay is a smooth, thick, dark condiment. This simple, fat-free chutney is made from a combination of dates and tamarind, two ingredients that have an ancient history in the East. Serve with Yellow Split Pea and Rice Pancakes (see page 60) or with Crispy Lentil Wafers (see page 52). Tamarind is usually sold in small 12-ounce blocks. The fruit pulp and large seeds are dried and pressed into a block that will keep indefinitely. You must soak the block to soften it and then strain out the solids to obtain the usable fruit pulp.

Makes 1½ cups •

1 cup pitted dates, soaked overnight in cold water

½ cup dried tamarind (see Preparing Tamarind below), soaked overnight in 1 cup cold water, seeds removed

1 teaspoon salt

1 teaspoon ground coriander seeds

1 teaspoon dark brown sugar

1. In a blender or food processor, purée the softened, seeded tamarind, including the soaking liquid. Strain through a sieve to remove any fibers. Stir in the salt, ground coriander seed, and brown sugar.

2. Pour into a glass jar with a lid and refrigerate until needed. The chutney will keep for up to 2 weeks if kept refrigerated.

❧ ❧ ❧ PREPARING TAMARIND ❧ ❧ ❧

To quick-soak the dried tamarind, place the dried tamarind block in hot water to cover for about 30 minutes, or until softened. While it is soaking, break the pulp up with your hands to speed the process. Rub the tamarind with the soaking liquid through a sieve or food mill, discarding the fibers and seeds. The strained tamarind liquid is ready to use and will keep for at least 1 month in the refrigerator. If you prefer, substitute tamarind with ½ cup dried tamarind with 6 tablespoons soaked prunes puréed with 2 tablespoons lemon juice. Indian groceries also sell pre-made tamarind concentrate. If you use this, cut down on the amount of salt in this recipe.

COCONUT-CILANTRO CHUTNEY

This dip is great with Chickpea Fries (see page 59) or Crispy Lentil Wafers (see page 52). I was so happy when I discovered Goya's brand of frozen grated coconut in my local Latino market. I had been making this extraordinary fresh chutney with coconut meat that I removed from the shell, peeled, and then grated. Now fresh coconut is a wonderful thing, miles from packaged, dried coconut, but it is a lot of work to hammer open that coconut and pry out the meat. Now I've got the best of both worlds: fresh coconut taste and quick preparation.

Makes 4 cups •

2 tablespoons peanut oil

1 tablespoon black mustard seeds

1 bunch fresh cilantro, leaves and roots, if available

2 jalapeño peppers, seeded and sliced

1 (2-inch) piece fresh ginger, peeled and sliced

4 cloves garlic, peeled

2 cups frozen or fresh grated coconut meat

1 cup plain yogurt

2 teaspoons salt

2 tablespoons fresh lemon juice (about 1 lemon)

1. Heat the oil in a small pan and add the mustard seeds. Cover and cook until the seeds pop. Cool.

2. Process the cilantro, jalapeños, ginger, and garlic in a food processor to a paste. Stir in the coconut, yogurt, salt, lemon juice, and mustard seeds with their oil. Cover and refrigerate until ready to serve.

YEMENITE FENUGREEK *(Hilbeh)* SAUCE

In the 1950s almost all of the members of the ancient Jewish community of Yemen were airlifted into Israel where they have since made their home. They brought with them special foods, like this sauce, which have become a part of the multifaceted cooking of Israel. Hot and spicy foods are particularly loved by the Yemenites who flavor their exotic foods with fenugreek, cardamom, black cumin, caraway, turmeric, and even saffron. Serve this sauce with Crunchy Falafel (see page 66) or with Pan-Grilled Falafel with Salad in Garlic Dressing (see page 68). It's also good spread on fresh pita or other flatbreads.

Makes 1 cup

2 tablespoons whole fenugreek seeds, soaked in cold water overnight

4 cloves garlic, peeled

$^1/_2$ cup chopped fresh cilantro (about 1 bunch)

2 teaspoons salt

$^1/_4$ cup fresh lemon juice (about 2 lemons)

1 small dried hot chile pepper, seeded

Drain the fenugreek seeds, which should be softened and have a jellied coating. Process in a blender or food processor with the garlic, cilantro, salt, lemon juice, and hot pepper until the mixture becomes a coarse purée. Store in the refrigerator for up to 1 week.

ABOUT FENUGREEK

FENUGREEK IS A SPICE THAT IS ACTUALLY A MEMBER OF THE PEA FAMILY. THESE SMALL AROMATIC YELLOW-BROWN SEEDS ARE MOST COMMONLY USED IN INDIAN COOKERY, THOUGH THEY ARE ALSO POPULAR IN NORTH AFRICA AND YEMEN. THE ANCIENT EGYPTIANS PROBABLY USED FENUGREEK IN THEIR COOKING BUT THE NAME IS DERIVED FROM ANOTHER USE, AS ANIMAL FODDER. THE ROMANS CALLED THIS PLANT *fenum graecum*, WHICH MEANS GREEK HAY. THE TINY, PEBBLELIKE SEEDS ARE ROASTED TO ENHANCE THEIR PUNGENT AROMA. THEY HAVE A UNIQUE BITTERSWEET, SOMEWHAT ACRID TASTE AND ARE QUITE POWERFUL, SO USE IN MODERATION. GROUND FENUGREEK SEEMS TO LOSE ITS FRAGRANCE RATHER QUICKLY, SO CHECK THE QUALITY BEFORE YOU USE IT. FENUGREEK SEEDS ARE QUITE HARD, SO CRUSH THEM IN A MORTAR AND PESTLE OR WITH A HAMMER.

GARAM MASALA

This versatile mix of roasted spices is used in many Indian dishes. It is made in various styles in different regions of India. Many spice companies make an excellent prepared version of garam masala, convenient if you're only planning to use a little bit. However, it is easy and fun to make and the warm, sweet fragrance will perfume your house better than any aromatherapy candle or oil. Store in a tightly sealed glass jar out of the light for up to four months. After that it will start to lose the subtleties of its aroma. Among the many additions to the basic formula are mace, nutmeg, fennel seeds, mustard seeds, and ajwain (carom or lovage) seeds.

Makes 1¹/₂ cups •

3 (2- to 3-inch) cinnamon sticks

¹/₂ cup white (or green) cardamom pods, or 2 tablespoons ground cardamom

4 bay leaves

³/₄ cup coriander seeds

¹/₂ cup cumin seeds

¹/₄ cup black peppercorns

1 tablespoon whole cloves

1. Using a hammer, break up the cinnamon sticks into small shards. Break open the cardamom pods, remove the hard black seeds, and discard the pods. Crumble the bay leaves.

2. Heat a small skillet, preferably uncoated (such as steel or cast-iron), without any oil over high heat. Add the cinnamon, cardamom seeds, coriander, cumin, peppercorns, and bay leaves and cloves. Toast, shaking the pan occasionally, until the spices are lightly browned and fragrant. (Watch the spices carefully at this point so they don't turn black and become bitter.)

3. Remove from the heat and cool to room temperature. Grind to a powder in a small coffee grinder, preferably reserved for spices. Alternatively, crush the seeds using a mortar and pestle. Using a funnel, pour into a clean, dry small glass jar, such as an empty spice, mustard, or jelly jar, and cover tightly. Store for up to 4 months.

SPICY GUACAMOLE

Homemade guacamole with plenty of fresh-squeezed lime juice is a real weakness of mine, even though I know it's full of fat from the oil-rich avocados (the only fruit that I know of that contains oils). It's definitely a challenge to buy and ripen avocados just right. If you buy green avocados (preferably Haas; see Cook's Note below), ripen them at room temperature for one to two days. When ready, they should be firm, with a dull, not shiny skin, and the tip of the stem end should be easy to pull off. Also, when cutting an avocado, if the skin peels back from the flesh without sticking, it's at its peak.

Serves 6 to 8 (makes 1½ cups)

2 firm, but ripe, Haas avocados
  (see Cook's Note below)

¼ cup fresh lime juice

1 teaspoon salt

½ cup finely diced white onion,
  or thinly sliced scallions

1 jalapeño pepper, seeded and finely
  diced, or 1 tablespoon drained chopped
  pickled jalapeños

½ cup seeded and diced ripe plum
  tomatoes

¼ cup chopped fresh cilantro leaves
  (about ½ bunch)

1. Peel, pit, and quarter the avocados. In a medium bowl, mash together the avocados, lime juice, and salt using a heavy whisk or potato masher. The finished mixture should contain small lumps. Stir in the onion, jalapeño pepper, tomatoes, and cilantro.

2. Cover tightly, pressing plastic wrap directly on the surface of the guacamole and reserve in the refrigerator for up to 2 days. (After a few hours, the guacamole may discolor on top, due to oxidation. Simply scrape off the darkened layer, which will have an off taste, and use the remainder.)

Cook's Note

Haas avocados, the pebbly black-skinned type, tend to be more buttery tasting than other types. Fuerte avocados make a good substitute.

AVOCADO MOUSSE

Here I combine avocados with other ingredients to preserve their color. The cream cheese coats the avocado with fat and the limes and pickled jalapeños are acidic, preventing oxidation. Lay the plastic wrap or waxed paper directly onto the surface of the mousse to maintain the green color.

Makes 2 cups •

4 ounces cream cheese, softened

4 firm, but ripe, Haas avocados,
    peeled and pitted

1 bunch scallions, chopped

2 pickled jalapeño peppers, chopped

2 tablespoons fresh lime juice
    (about 1 lime)

1/2 bunch fresh cilantro leaves

Salt

Process the cream cheese in a food processor until smooth. Add the avocados and process until chunky. Add the scallions, jalapeños, lime juice, and cilantro and process briefly to maintain the chunky texture. Season to taste with salt. Transfer to a bowl and place a piece of plastic wrap directly on the surface of the mousse. The mousse will keep 1 week if tightly covered and refrigerated.

CUMIN-LIME CITRONETTE DRESSING

Here's a dressing that combines three of my favorite flavors: lime, toasted cumin, and cilantro. Fresh lime juice is less acidic than vinegar, so I've combined it with nutty-sweet but strong sherry vinegar for a deeper level of acidity. You could also make the same dressing with lime juice only, increasing the amount to 1 cup. When using lime zest, it's especially important not to include any of the bitter white pith that lies under the green skin. Look for firm, rough-skinned limes for easier grating. If your limes are too soft to grate, omit the zest.

Makes 2 cups •

2 teaspoons toasted ground cumin seeds
    (see Toasting Seeds, page 217)

2 teaspoons cayenne hot pepper sauce

1 teaspoon salt

1/4 cup chopped fresh cilantro leaves
    (about 1/4 bunch)

1/2 teaspoon grated lime zest

1 teaspoon dried oregano

1 cup peanut oil

6 tablespoons fresh lime juice
    (about 2 limes)

1/4 cup sherry vinegar

Blend together the cumin, pepper sauce, salt, cilantro, lime zest, oregano, oil, lime juice, and vinegar using a hand-held blender or a standard blender. Pour into a covered jar and refrigerate for up to 3 weeks.

TUNISIAN HARISSA SAUCE

I first learned how to make this spicy Tunisian red pepper paste from the two Tunisian Jewish brothers who owned a Mediterranean bistro in Philadelphia during the eighties where I was the chef. They showed me how to combine three different types of red peppers, hot and sweet, and oven roast them to concentrate their flavors. I learned that caraway, rather than the cumin listed in many recipes, was the seasoning of choice in harissa. Later, I discovered this somewhat simpler way to make this sauce from Taieb Dridi, the Tunisian owner of a bakery in Philadelphia that specializes in Mediterranean-style flatbreads.

Makes about 1 1/2 cups •

3 large (about 3/4 pound) red bell peppers, roasted (see page 314), or 2 cups prepared imported roasted red peppers, drained

2 ounces (about 4) fresh hot red chile peppers (such as red jalapeños, red Korean peppers, red Holland hot peppers, or pasillas)

1/2 cup sweet Hungarian paprika

1/4 cup extra-virgin olive oil

6 garlic cloves, peeled

1 tablespoon ground caraway seeds, or 3 tablespoons whole seeds, freshly ground

1. Purée the roasted red bell peppers, hot peppers, paprika, oil, garlic, and caraway in a food processor. Use sparingly as a condiment.

2. Pour into a glass jar with a lid and refrigerate until needed. The harissa will keep well for 2 months if tightly covered and refrigerated.

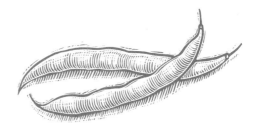

SPICY PEANUT DIPPING SAUCE

Americans take quite easily to Asian-style peanut sauces, which can range in textures from smooth, like this one, to chunky, to a Southeast-Asian creamy style, which combines peanuts with rich coconut milk. The nam pla called for here is a thin, liquid sauce made from salted, fermented fish that is vital to Thai and Vietnamese cooking. It provides the characteristic undertone of flavor. Fish sauce takes a little getting used to because of its strong smell, but here it helps emphasize the savory qualities of the sauce.

Makes about 2 cups •

1 cup smooth peanut butter

1 tablespoon coarsely chopped fresh ginger

2 teaspoons coarsely chopped garlic

2 shallots, coarsely chopped

¼ cup dry sherry

¼ cup soy sauce

¼ cup roasted Japanese sesame oil

¼ cup packed dark brown sugar

2 teaspoons nam pla (Asian fish sauce)

2 teaspoons hot chile oil, or hot red pepper flakes

¼ cup cilantro leaves

½ cup thinly sliced scallions (about ½ bunch)

Process the peanut butter, ginger, garlic, shallots, sherry, soy sauce, sesame oil, brown sugar, fish sauce, and chile oil in a food processor to a smooth paste, scraping down the side of the bowl once or twice. Add the cilantro and scallions. Use immediately or transfer the mixture to a storage container. Cover and refrigerate for up to 2 weeks. (If the sauce seems too thick, thin by whisking in a little cold water before serving.)

❧ ❧ ❧ MORE ABOUT PEANUTS ❧ ❧ ❧

It is the salted, roasted variety of peanuts that has become such a universally popular snack, second only to potato chips. Peanut butter was first concocted in the early 1900s and quickly became an American staple. Other cultures, particularly Indonesian and Thai, have long used ground peanuts as a key ingredient to enrich and thicken their sauces.

MIXED GREENS
WITH GARLIC AND OLIVE OIL

I like to combine greens for more interesting texture and a rounder flavor. The three I use here are all quite different: the broccoli rabe is slightly bitter; the chard echoes the sweetness of its close relative, the beet; and the kale has a mild, broccolilike taste. Other good greens to substitute would be Chinese broccoli for the broccoli rabe, beet greens for the chard, and if you like strong tastes, sharp mustard greens for the milder kale. Unlike most vegetable dishes, these greens reheat quite well. I also enjoy them at room temperature or cold drizzled with a little Shanxi or balsamic vinegar.

Serves 6

1 pound fresh broccoli rabe, bottom 2 inches of stalks trimmed and discarded

1 pound fresh Swiss chard, ribs removed and saved for another use, leaves trimmed

1 pound fresh kale, bottom 2 inches of stalks trimmed and discarded

1/4 cup olive oil

1/4 cup chopped garlic (about 6 cloves)

1/2 teaspoon hot red pepper flakes

2 teaspoons salt

1. Cut the broccoli rabe into 1-inch-wide strips. Wash well and drain. Cut the Swiss chard into 1-inch-wide strips. Wash and drain. Remove and discard the center ribs of the kale and cut the leaves into 1-inch-wide strips. Wash and drain the kale. Steam or boil all the greens together until bright green and fully wilted, about 5 minutes. Drain the greens, rinsing them under cold running water to set color. Reserve. (The greens can be cooked up to 2 days ahead and refrigerated.)

2. Heat the olive oil in a large pan over medium heat. Stir in the garlic, red pepper and salt. Cook for 3 minutes. Add the greens and heat until piping hot and the liquid has evaporated, about 8 minutes. Serve immediately.

PICO DE GALLO SALSA

This uncooked salsa's name translates to "rooster's beak " and is so called in the Southwest and the West in America because of its bright colors. In Mexico, it's known simply as "salsa Mexicana." Whatever the name, I could eat this salsa every day and not get tired of it, especially when local tomatoes are in season. If using larger beefsteak tomatoes, it's a good idea to sprinkle them with the salt and allow them to drain for 15 to 20 minutes to draw off the excess water. It's not necessary to do this step with meatier plum tomatoes.

Makes 2 cups •

1 pound ripe plum or beefsteak
  tomatoes, seeded and cut into small dice
1 sweet white onion, cut into small dice
2 fresh or pickled jalapeño peppers,
  seeded and finely chopped
¼ cup fresh lime juice (about 2 limes)
1 tablespoon salt
½ cup chopped fresh cilantro leaves
  (about 1 bunch)

In a large bowl, combine the tomatoes, onion, jalapeños, lime juice, salt, and cilantro. Season to taste then cover tightly, pressing plastic wrap directly on the surface of the salsa. Refrigerate until ready to serve. The salsa will keep for 2 to 3 days, but will become more watery each day as the liquid is released from the tomatoes and onions. If necessary, drain off this excess liquid before serving.

LIGHT CHICKEN STOCK

Do you really have to bother making your own stock? The answer is no, canned will do. However, I get a particular enjoyment out of making "stone soup," or something out of nothing. I save all the trimmings from onions (though not red because they give an off color to the stock), carrots, celery, tomatoes, and mushrooms as I prepare different dishes, along with stems of thyme, tarragon, and chives. I place the trimmings into a freezer bag and keep adding to my stash until I have enough to make a large pot of stock. I also save roasted chicken carcasses, chicken wing tips, backbones, and other trimmings and supplement as needed with inexpensive purchased chicken legs and thighs. After cooling the stock, I ladle it into three plastic one-quart containers (or even freezer bags, sealed carefully) and freeze. The stock just needs a minute or two in the microwave to melt enough so that it slides right out of the bag and is ready.

Makes 12 cups (3 quarts) •

5 pounds mixed chicken parts
  (necks, backs, wings, and legs),
  preferably from grain-fed chickens
16 cups (4 quarts) water
4 bay leaves
1 teaspoon coriander seeds
1 teaspoon fennel seeds
1 teaspoon black peppercorns
1 onion, peeled
2 carrots
2 ribs celery
A small handful of tender herb trimmings
  (parsley, chervil, tarragon)

1. In a large stockpot, combine the chicken parts, water, bay leaves, coriander, fennel, peppercorns, onion, carrots, celery, and herbs. Bring to a boil, skimming off and discarding the white foam impurities that rise to the surface. Reduce the heat to a bare simmer and cook , partially covered, for 8 hours, or until the chicken meat falls easily off the bones. Strain through a sieve into another pot, discarding the solids.

2. Place the pot of strained stock into a larger pot or deep pan containing ice water, allowing the stock to cool for about 1 hour. Refrigerate overnight to solidify the fat. Remove and discard any fat from the surface. If desired, freeze the stock at this point.

SMOKED TURKEY STOCK

I got the idea of making a smoked turkey stock because I learned that some people substituted smoked turkey legs for ham hocks when they were looking for a lighter or pork-free diet. Flavorwise, it's not that different. You can find inexpensive smoked turkey legs, wings, and even necks in most supermarkets or ethnic markets. I buy extra and keep them in the freezer to use as needed.

Makes 12 cups (3 quarts) •

5 pounds smoked turkey drumsticks,
    necks, and/or thighs
16 cups (4 quarts) water
4 bay leaves
1 teaspoon coriander seeds
1 teaspoon fennel seeds
1 teaspoon black peppercorns
1 onion, peeled
2 carrots
2 ribs celery
A small handful of tender herb trimmings
    (parsley, chervil, tarragon)

1. In a large stockpot, combine the turkey, water, bay leaves, coriander, fennel, peppercorns, onion, carrots, celery, and herbs. Bring to a boil, skimming off and discarding the white foam impurities that rise to the surface. Reduce the heat to a bare simmer and cook, partially covered, for 8 hours, or until the turkey meat falls easily off the bones. Strain through a sieve into another pot, discarding the solids.

2. Place the pot of strained stock into a larger pot or deep pan containing ice water. Allow the stock to cool for 1 hour. Refrigerate overnight to solidify the fat. Remove and discard any fat from the surface. If desired, freeze the stock at this point.

RICH CHICKEN STOCK

When you're looking for a more substantial foundation for a sauce or a soup, use this roasted chicken and vegetable stock. The caramelized roasted vegetables add a note of underlying sweetness. Use this stock for Hot and Sour Soup with Duck, Pea Shoots, and Fresh Tofu (see page 110), Moroccan Golden Split Pea and Pumpkin Soup (see page 120) and to make the French Green Lentils with Black Truffles and Caramelized Shallots (see page 138).

Makes about 8 cups (2 quarts) •

5 pounds mixed chicken parts (necks, backs, wings, and legs), preferably from grain-fed chickens

1 whole onion, unpeeled, cut up

2 carrots, cut up

2 ribs celery, cut up

16 cups (4 quarts) cold water

6 bay leaves

1 teaspoon coriander seeds

1 teaspoon fennel seeds

1 teaspoon black peppercorns

¼ bunch fresh thyme

¼ pound mushrooms or mushroom trimmings (optional)

A small handful tender herb trimmings (parsley, chervil, tarragon)

1. Preheat the oven to 400°F. Arrange the chicken parts in a large roasting pan. Roast for 30 minutes. Add the onion, carrots, and celery to the pan. Continue roasting for 30 minutes. Remove the pan from the oven and place the roasted chicken parts and vegetables in a large stockpot.

2. Place the roasting pan over a burner and add 3 cups of the water to the pan. Bring the liquid to a boil. Reduce the heat and simmer for 5 to 10 minutes, scraping up the browned bits with a wooden spoon. Pour the contents of the pan into the stockpot with the remaining 13 cups water. Bring to a boil, skimming off and discarding the white foam impurities that rise to the surface. Add the bay leaves, coriander, fennel, peppercorns, thyme, mushrooms, and herbs. Reduce the heat to a bare simmer and cook, partially covered, for 8 hours or until the chicken meat falls easily off the bones. Strain through a sieve into another pot, discarding the solids.

3. Place the pot of stock into another larger pot filled with ice water to cool for 1 hour. Refrigerate immediately. Remove and discard any fat that has solidified. If desired, freeze the stock at this point.

VEGETABLE STOCK

Here's a mild-flavored stock for vegetarians or those who enjoy the fresh flavor of vegetables. If you save the liquid from steamed vegetables, add it to this stock. Although it won't have the body that comes from gelatinous-rich meats, this stock will provide a flavorful foundation.

Makes 8 cups (2 quarts) •

1 tablespoon black peppercorns

1 tablespoon coriander seeds

4 bay leaves

1 bunch fresh thyme, or 2 teaspoons dried

2 cups dry white vermouth or water

8 cups (2 quarts) water

2 cups chopped tomatoes, fresh
   or canned

2 cups coarsely chopped celery

4 cups coarsely chopped mushrooms,
   including the stems (shiitake, white
   mushrooms, and/or cremini)

1 cup coarsely chopped yellow onion,
   including the skin

In a large stockpot, combine the peppercorns, coriander, bay leaves, thyme, vermouth, water, tomatoes, celery, mushrooms, and onion. Bring to a boil, skimming off and discarding any white foam that rises to the surface. Reduce the heat and simmer, partially covered, for 1 hour. Strain through a sieve into another pot, pressing down well to extract the vegetable juices. Discard the solids. Cool and refrigerate for up to 4 days, or freeze for up to 1 month. Use as directed in soups or other dishes as a substitute for chicken stocks.

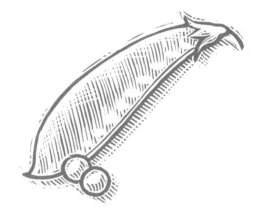

BUTTERMILK DOUGH

I've discovered that dry buttermilk powder made by the Saco company and sold in many well-stocked super-markets and specialty food stores is a wonderful product to have on hand for baking. Not that different from the idea of powdered milk, this buttermilk powder makes a particularly flaky short crust dough. If you can't find the buttermilk powder, substitute ½ cup liquid buttermilk mixed with 1 egg for the ½ cup beaten eggs.

Makes about 1 pound dough (enough for 16 pot pies) •

3 cups (12 ounces) unbleached
   all-purpose flour
2 teaspoons salt
¼ cup dry buttermilk powder
¼ pound (1 stick) unsalted butter,
   cut into bits
½ cup eggs (about 3 large eggs),
   lightly beaten

1. In the bowl of an electric mixer, combine the flour, salt, and buttermilk powder and mix together lightly. Top with the butter bits but don't mix. Place the bowl in the freezer for 30 minutes to chill (or for 1 hour if you're working on a really hot day).

2. Beat the chilled flour mixture until it resembles cold and crumbly oatmeal. Pour in the eggs and beat until the mixture just comes together into a ball. Place in a large resealable plastic food storage bag and then flatten the dough to fill the bag. Chill for at least 30 minutes before rolling out. The dough can be refrigerated for up to 2 days before using. Roll out the dough on a floured board to a thickness of about ⅛ to ¼ inch. Cut as needed. This dough freezes quite well if double-bagged in heavy-duty freezer bags. Defrost overnight in the refrigerator when ready to use.

DURUM PASTA DOUGH

Durum wheat flour, the golden-yellow flour used to make Italian semolina bread, is the flour of choice for pasta. Its appealing color enhances the color of the egg yolks that enrich the pasta. Durum flour is sometimes sold as pasta flour. It is not the same thing as semolina, which is the hard germ of the same wheat kernel. I especially like using durum flour because it produces a firm pasta with a bit of resistance to the bite and non-stickiness. Use this dough to make homemade ravioli as in the Ravioli with Spring Greens and Creamy White Bean Sauce (see page 152) or to make *maltagliati* for Pasta and Beans (see page 169).

Makes 1 pound •

4 cups durum wheat flour
  (about 1 pound)
5 eggs, at room temperature

SHAPING MALTAGLIATI
❧ ❧ ❧

To make the *maltagliati*, which means badly-cut in Italian, lay a sheet of the pasta dough, rolled slightly thicker than for ravioli, onto a board. Cut parallel lines about 2 inches apart along the length of the dough. Cut crosswise strips on the diagonal to create rough diamond shapes from the dough, measuring about 1½ inches on a side. Spread out the cut pieces on a lightly floured surface to dry, making sure the pieces do not touch each other. When you're ready to cook the pasta, be sure to shake off the excess flour before adding the pasta to the cooking water.

1. Place the flour in the bowl of a food processor. Add 4 eggs, 1 at a time, processing until the dough is crumbly. Add the last egg, processing just until the dough forms a ball. (The dough will be quite stiff, so keep a close watch over it and stop processing immediately after it forms the ball.)

2. Remove the dough to a floured board and knead by hand until smooth and elastic. Place the dough in a plastic food storage bag, seal, and let rest at room temperature for at least 1 hour.

3. Using a manual or electric pasta machine, roll about ½ cup of the dough at a time into thin (but not paper thin) sheets. Feed the dough through the rollers, starting with a wide setting at number 1 and finishing with a narrow setting at number 6. Keep sheets covered with plastic wrap until ready to use.

BUTTERMILK CORN BREAD

Maybe I'm overly particular about ingredients, but if you make this corn bread with standard granulated cornmeal, you just won't get the same corn-rich taste and mouth-pleasing texture of the whole-grain cornmeal. Whole-grain cornmeal is to granulated cornmeal as whole wheat flour is to white flour. It is particularly important to keep whole-grain cornmeal in the freezer or refrigerator to keep bugs out of its rich nutrients. Rumford's brand is the only aluminum-free baking powder on the market these days. I prefer it because it doesn't leave that faintly metallic aftertaste that other baking powders can.

Serves 12 (makes one 13 × 9-inch pan)

3 cups sifted unbleached all-purpose flour

1½ cups whole-grain yellow cornmeal

1 tablespoon baking powder

1 teaspoon baking soda

¼ cup sugar

2 teaspoons salt

2 cups buttermilk

6 tablespoons unsalted butter, melted

4 eggs

1. Preheat the oven to 350°F. Spray a 13 × 9-inch baking pan with nonstick vegetable spray. Combine the flour, cornmeal, baking powder, baking soda, sugar, and salt in a large bowl and make a well in the center of the ingredients.

2. Lightly beat together the buttermilk, melted butter, and eggs. Pour the liquid mix into the well in the dry bowl and whisk together until mostly combined. Using a rubber spatula, fold the batter together until no dry spots remain. Don't overbeat or you will toughen the cornbread.

3. Spread the batter into the prepared pan. Bake for 40 minutes or until a toothpick inserted in the center comes out clean and the cornbread comes away from the sides of the pan. Cool slightly, then cut with a serrated knife and serve with butter.

HOME-GROWN BEAN SPROUTS

Freshly picked sprouts taste the best since they start to deteriorate as soon as they've been harvested. If you don't have access to good-quality commercial bean sprouts (such as those sold fresh in Asian markets and health food stores), sprouting your own is a good way to go. You can buy a commercial sprouter with separate racks that will allow you to sprout several different types of beans at once. Bean sprouts are extremely nutritious and add a delightful crunchiness to stir-fries, salads, and sandwiches. Stir delicate mung bean sprouts and stronger tasting soybean sprouts into clear soups several minutes before serving.

. . . .

1 cup organically grown beans, peas, or lentils (do not use limas or favas because they are toxic when raw)

4 cups tepid water

FDA SPROUT RECOMMENDATIONS

ACCORDING TO THE U. S. FOOD AND DRUG ADMINISTRATION (FDA), ALL RAW SPROUTS, WHETHER HOME OR COMMERCIALLY GROWN, MAY POSE A HEALTH RISK, ALTHOUGH ALFALFA AND CLOVER SPROUTS TEND TO BE THE MOST PROBLEMATIC. MANY ILLNESSES HAVE BEEN ATTRIBUTED TO CONTAMINATED SEEDS. IF PATHOGENIC BACTERIA ARE PRESENT IN OR ON THE SEED, THEY CAN GROW TO HIGH LEVELS DURING SPROUT-ING EVEN UNDER CLEAN CONDITIONS. TO SIGNIFICANTLY REDUCE THE RISK OF ILLNESS, THE FDA RECOMMENDS COOKING SPROUTS FIRST.

---

1. Have ready a large glass jar, some cheesecloth, and a rubber band.

2. Pick through the legumes, discarding any damaged or moldy ones. Rinse about 2 cups of the beans, then place them in a bowl covered by tepid water and allow them to soak overnight.

3. After soaking overnight, drain and rinse the beans. Place them into the glass jar. Cover the top of the jar with a piece of cheese-cloth and secure it to the jar with a rubber band. Add water to the jar and rinse the beans again. Invert the jar to let them drain. Position the jar in a dark place, such as a closet, that is about 70°F. Store the jar on its side to spread the beans over a larger area. Note: Bright light or sunlight will make the seeds dry out, too high a temperature will promote mold and too low of a temper-ature will prevent the seeds from sprouting. The place you choose should be convenient because you will have to rinse the sprouts 2 to 3 times a day. This rinsing is critical because it prevents fun-gus from growing on the sprouting seeds. Never eat any sprouts that have even a trace of mold on them as it could be toxic.

Bean sprouts require anywhere from 3 to 5 days to grow, depending on the size of the bean and the room temperature. The sprouts are ready when they are about 1 inch long. The larger the bean, the smaller the sprout should be. If sprouts grow too large, they will lose their tenderness.

～ ～ ～

Lentil sprouts have a chewy texture and are small, only about ½ inch long.

～ ～ ～

Mung beans are easy to sprout and are delicious added to almost any Asian-style stir-fry. These sprouts deteriorate quickly once they reach their full size of 1 to 2 inches long. For the best taste and texture, use mung bean sprouts within 1 day of picking. Cook mung bean sprouts if they are more than 1 day old. Mung beans and soybeans can take up to 1 week to sprout.

～ ～ ～

Pea sprouts taste like fresh peas and make a lovely garnish for salads and a tasty addition to sandwiches. Soybean sprouts can be purchased in Asian markets. These larger sprouts with a yellowish head and 2- to 3-inch-long stem are difficult to sprout at home because they ferment so easily. If you do sprout soybeans, you must rinse them frequently and thoroughly.

～ ～ ～

Larger sprouted beans will need to boil for thirty minutes to one hour until they are tender enough to eat. Once harvested, refrigerate sprouts in a loosely covered container to give air a chance to circulate, until ready to use.

CONFIT OF DUCK LEG

Confit is a wonderful way that frugal cooks from the southwest of France have long used to preserve duck parts like legs and even gizzards (delicious, believe it or not). These same ducks have sacrificed their engorged livers for foie gras. Their breasts are served pan-seared rare and carved like a steak. What's left is the plentiful duck fat and the leg-thigh portions, destined for confit. The duck is first cured by salting and spicing, then cooked ever so slowly in a large pot of duck fat. The duck is then aged in the same duck fat, which seals and helps to preserve it. After two weeks, the spices have mellowed and the duck is tender enough for the meat to fall off the bone when it is crisped in a pan. Duck confit will keep refrigerated for at least two months, if fully covered in duck fat. You can also purchase duck confit (see Sources, page 323).

Makes 4 pounds •

¼ cup kosher salt

2 tablespoons ground coriander seeds

2 tablespoons ground ginger

2 tablespoons ground anise seeds

2 tablespoons ground allspice

2 tablespoons crushed bay leaves

2 tablespoons crushed black peppercorns

5 pounds duck leg-thigh pieces
    (the best duck to use is from the
    large Moullard ducks)

24 garlic cloves (about ½ pound),
    separated but not peeled

2 pounds duck fat, goose fat, or lard

1. Combine the salt, coriander, ginger, anise, allspice, bay leaves, and peppercorns in a small bowl. Rub generously onto each duck leg, coating completely. Arrange the duck legs on a wire rack set over a pan. Cure in the refrigerator for 48 hours, turning after 24 hours. Drain off and discard any excess liquid from the pan.

2. Preheat the oven to 300°F. Rinse the spice mixture off the legs, pat dry, and arrange in a large roasting pan. Add the garlic cloves and duck fat to the pan and cover with foil. Bake for 2 to 3 hours or until very tender. (Test for tenderness by jiggling a thigh bone; it should move easily in the joint.) Remove the pan from the oven, uncover, and let the duck legs cool.

3. Using a large fork or tongs, remove the duck legs from the pan and arrange in a heatproof container large enough to hold them. Strain the fat and juices from the pan through a sieve into the container. (You should have enough fat to cover the legs completely. Push the legs down to cover, if necessary.) Cover and refrigerate for at least two weeks to allow the flavors to mature and the duck to become even more tender. As needed, remove legs from container, wiping off excess fat.

ABOUT DUCK FAT

DUCK FAT IS A DELICIOUS COOKING FAT SUITABLE FOR MANY LEGUME DISHES. IF YOU ROAST YOUR OWN DUCK, SAVE THE DRIPPINGS AND POUR INTO A SMALL, NARROW CONTAINER. CHILL OVERNIGHT. THE FAT WILL HAVE CONGEALED TO A HARD WHITE SUBSTANCE. REMOVE AND RESERVE THE LAYER OF FAT, DISCARDING THE JELLIED COOKING JUICES. SIMMER THE RESERVED DUCK FAT IN A SAUCEPAN OVER VERY LOW HEAT, SKIMMING OFTEN TO REMOVE ANY FOAM IMPURITIES, UNTIL THE FAT IS CLEAR. REFRIGERATE FOR 3 MONTHS; FREEZE FOR UP TO 6.

NOTES ON INGREDIENTS

ROASTED RED BELL PEPPERS

There's nothing like a freshly roasted bell pepper. The object in roasting peppers is to char (blacken) the skin of the pepper while keeping the flesh firm and uncooked. Charring gives the peppers an extra dimension of smoky intensity. Beyond flavor, there are two reasons for removing the skin: ripened red bell pepper skin is especially thick and it is also indigestible. Char red bell peppers over direct heat for best results. Ideally, grill the peppers on an outdoor barbecue over hardwood charcoal burned down to coals. If you're lucky enough to own an indoor electric grill, this also works well. For those who struggle with an electric range, try placing the peppers directly on preheated electric coils. On a gas range, turn the flame up high. Alternately, roast the peppers under a preheated broiler, though this is not ideal. Since the peppers are not placed directly on the heat source, they tend to collapse from overcooking. If your heat source is less than intense, try rubbing the peppers lightly with oil. The oil helps the pepper skins char more easily.

Place the peppers, next to each other, on a preheated grill. Char for about 5 minutes (the time depends on the quantity and initial heat). As the skins blacken, turn using a pair of tongs. If the peppers are thin-walled or overcooked, there won't be much meat left after roasting. After evenly roasting the peppers on all sides, turn them so the stalk end chars a few minutes (trimming off the stem first, if necessary). Then turn upside-down so the blossom ends also chars.

Place the peppers in a large stainless steel bowl and cover with plastic wrap. Or put them in a plastic bag and seal. The peppers will steam as they cool, making it easier to remove the skins. Working near a source of cool running water, rub the skins off the charred peppers. Rinse off the blackened skin pieces from your hands under water. Avoid rinsing the peppers themselves as water strips flavor too. Store covered in a refrigerator for up to 2 weeks.

SALT

I prefer to use kosher salt in the kitchen for a number of reasons: its large flakes make it easy to pick up in a pinch of the fingers and sprinkle on evenly. It's also relatively mild so you won't be likely to oversalt. Because it's unmistakable as salt, you won't ever get it mixed up with the sugar, which happens more often than you might think in restaurant kitchens. Kosher salt is, however, only half as strong as the heavier, fine-crystal table salt. I've tested all these recipes using kosher salt (available in most supermarkets). If you prefer sea salt, go ahead and substitute it. Just remember that sea salt is the strongest and most concentrated of all the salts and you must use it judiciously.

HERBS

I'm rather a fanatic about using fresh herbs, though these dishes will certainly taste good if you substitute half the amount of dried for the fresh. I can't cook happily without lots of fresh chopped herbs and toasted home-ground spices. I wash herbs only if they feel sandy as many of them come from greenhouses these days. Local field-grown herbs, such as basil, dill, and cilantro can be loaded with dirt but their pungent aroma and strong healthy leaves make the washing worth the extra effort.

FLOUR

In recipes using flour, I prefer—and have tested these recipes using—a good unbleached all-purpose flour, such as Ceresota, Hecker's, or King Arthur's brands. For these recipes, sift *before* measuring.

CORNMEAL

I love the taste of natural cornmeal and recommend a ground whole kernel corn variety from Arrowhead Mills in Texas. Compared to commercial cornmeal, it's like using whole wheat flour versus white.

BUTTER

I always specify unsalted butter because it must be fresher than salted butter (the salt in butter acts as a preservative). You can certainly substitute salted butter or margarine, but be sure to taste before adding any additional salt to the recipe. I recommend Land O' Lakes brand for its quality and availability.

OILS

I fry with a combination of oils depending on the flavor I'm trying to achieve. I prefer soybean oil for general frying because it's light and mild and has a relatively high smoking point. For vegetable tempura, I blend roasted Japanese sesame oil into the soybean oil for its nutty flavor and aroma. I like peanut oil for frying stronger flavored foods like fish and calamari. I use a strong extra-virgin olive oil that comes from north Africa for all of my Mediterranean-flavored dishes. I find most French and Ligurian olive oils too bland for my tastes. When I refer to Japanese sesame oil in these recipes, I mean roasted sesame oil used as a seasoning. Almost all of this roasted sesame oil is imported from Japan. I recommend Kadoya brand. Do not substitute the clear cold-pressed sesame oil sold in natural foods stores.

ONIONS

I call for three basic types of onions in this book: yellow-skinned or Spanish, white-skinned or sweet, like Vidalia or Texas 100s, and red-skinned or Bermuda onions. A standard medium onion will work for most recipes. I specify "sweet" onions when I want their special flavor and crisp texture. I use red onions in many salads for their color—and I like the rich flavor they add to Mediterranean dishes. You can substitute when necessary, as long as your onions are firm and without odor—an indication of spoilage.

GLOSSARY AND SOURCES

GLOSSARY

ACHIOTE PASTE

An orangy-red seasoning paste from the Yucatan, achiote is made from a combination of crushed red annatto seeds and an assortment of seasonings, such as oregano, garlic, black pepper, cumin, and cloves. I combine the prepared achiote paste with more fresh seasonings to make a marinade that I rub over chicken thighs, swordfish, and tuna before roasting or grilling. The achiote not only flavors the meats, it also makes them juicy and tender. Achiote paste is available from Mexican and Latino groceries. I use DelMayaB.

ALEPPO PEPPER (OR NEAR EAST PEPPER)

This mildly hot, very aromatic, deep-red ground pepper comes from Aleppo in Syria. Its warm, rich flavor is highly sought after among Middle Eastern cooks. Because it contains only the dried pepper flesh and no seeds, Aleppo pepper has a more vegetablelike flavor. Its attractive color is another plus. Buy Aleppo pepper from Middle Eastern and Indian groceries. Keep refrigerated.

AMCHUR (OR AMCHOOR)

Amchur is a dried and powdered form of unripe mango. This pale, beige-colored powder has a mangolike flavor and a tangy, sour taste. It is used much like lemon juice in Indian cookery, and because of India's hot climate and lack of refrigeration, it is preferred over fresh perishable citrus juice.

ANNATTO SEEDS

Very hard, deep-red triangular seeds commonly used in Caribbean cookery for color and a mild flavor. The Mexican name for them, achiote, is also the name for a seasoning paste made from crushed annatto seeds, garlic, oregano, and other spices. In Puerto Rico, the seeds are lightly cooked in oil and then strained out. This red oil is then used for cooking.

ASAFETIDA

A super-powerful, even evil-smelling spice extracted from the sap of the asafoetida, a member of the parsley family. The spice is sold in lump and powdered form. It is used in minute quantities in Indian cookery as a flavor enhancer and as a substitute for onions. It used especially in legume dishes because it is reputed to be an antiflatulent.

ASIAN SHRIMP WAFERS (OR *Krupuk*)

These Indonesian "crackers" are sold in thin, flat oblongs that resemble an uncooked potato chip. They will keep a long time if uncooked and kept in a cool, dry spot. To prepare krupuk, heat about two inches of oil in a wok, then drop in the crackers one at a time. After about 15 seconds they will puff up to two or three times their original size. Remove from the oil and drain. Serve them as a snack chip or as a garnish for salads.

BACALA (OR BACALAO, BACALHAU)

The Italian, Spanish, and Portuguese terms for dried salt cod are very similar. Bacala was originally used by Portuguese and Scandinavian fisherman as a way of preserving cod during the long sea voyage home from the Grand Banks fishing grounds east of Canada. Because of its strong aroma and stringy consistency, bacala is somewhat of an acquired taste. Bacala must be soaked in cold water, changing the water several times if it is extremely salty. If you buy bacala fillet, you only need to soak the fish, not clean it.

BEAN THREAD (OR CELLOPHANE NOODLES)

These very fine, translucent threads are made from the starch of green mung beans. Sold dried in Asian markets, they must be soaked in water to soften before using. They generally don't need to be precooked.

BLACK MUSTARD SEEDS

The two main types of mustard seeds are white and brown. Whole brown mustard seeds (commonly called black mustard seeds) are ubiquitous in Indian cookery. They are popped in oil before using (like popcorn), which transforms the seeds from hot to sweet and nutty.

BLACK SESAME SEEDS

A variety of sesame seed that is sold with black hulls intact. Black sesame seeds are popular in Japanese and Chinese cookery and have become more common here because many chefs like their dramatic look and mild flavor.

CAPER BERRIES

Caper berries are the fruit of a caper bush and have a similar flavor to the tiny pickled flower buds from the same bush called nonpareil capers. They are a large oval shape and are pickled complete with their stems.

CHILE PASTE (OR *Sambal oelek*)

Sambal oelek is a hot, vermilion-red paste from Indonesia made from cooked red chile peppers and their seeds. The chiles are crushed to a chunky paste with salt and a little vinegar. There are also Chinese versions of chile paste, some flavored with garlic and other spices. Purchase chile paste in Asian groceries and specialty food markets. Once opened, keep the chili paste refrigerated. Use judiciously as chile pastes can be extremely hot.

CHICKPEA FLOUR

There are two kinds of chickpea flour, raw and toasted. The raw kind, called gram flour, is sold in Indian groceries. The toasted kind is tan colored with a nutty aroma, and is sold in Middle Eastern groceries. Save this flour in the freezer.

CHIPOTLE CHILIES (OR CHILE PEPPERS)

Chipotle peppers are smoke-dried jalapeño chiles. When purchased whole, they smell quite smoky, even through the package. Chipotles are light brown in color, brittle and wrinkled with the shape of a fresh jalapeño. Philly Chili Company makes an excellent chipotle hot sauce with a pourable consistency. (See Sources, page 323.)

CHIPOTLE CHILES IN ADOBO SAUCE

These are dried, smoked, red jalapeño peppers that are rehydrated in a spicy tomato-based sauce and packed in small cans. Both the chipotles (with or without their seeds) and the packing liquid is used. Many specialty and Hispanic groceries carry this product. La Preferida, Embasa, and San Marcos are among the many good brands available.

CHILE ANCHOS, CHILE ANCHO POWDER

Ancho, also called mulato and pasilla (a misnomer), is the name for the red, ripe dried form of the dark green fresh poblano peppers. A relatively mild, smoky and sweet tasting powder is made from the crushed peppers. Use along with toasted cumin, garlic, and oregano for a homemade chile powder. Seed and stem the dried form before soaking in hot water to soften or grinding to a powder.

CHORIZO (OR *Chouriço*)

This highly seasoned, coarsely ground pork sausage is flavored with garlic and paprika. It is widely used in different versions in Mexico, Spain, and Portugal. Chorizo is available fresh, smoked, and dried.

COTENNA

The skin of a prosciutto or other cured pork product, cotenna is used for the large amounts of natural gelatin it contains. Cooking beans with cotenna gives them a rich, creamy, smooth texture. Pork or bacon rind imparts an equivalent texture, though not the same prosciuttolike flavor.

CULANTRO

Culantro is a wide-leaved relative of the herb we call cilantro. It has an even more pronounced pungent flavor than cilantro and is sold fresh in Hispanic markets. Like cilantro, culantro must be used fresh because it doesn't dry or freeze well. Cilantro leaves may be substituted.

DEMI-GLACE

This rich classic French base for meat sauces, which means "half-glaze," is a concentration of veal stock and veal bones that requires two levels and many hours of slow roasting and cooking to achieve a rich, brown, thick, flavorful sauce. To obtain the desired richness in this sauce, one gallon of the veal stock must be reduced to one quart of demi-glace. Few home cooks make this sauce from scratch. There are a number of excellent commercial demi-glace sauces available (see Sources, page 323).

EPAZOTE

A wild herb and common weed, epazote is also known as wormseed, goosefoot, and Jerusalem oak. It has spiky, 2- to 3-inch long leaves with a strong, almost turpentinelike flavor that can get quite addictive. It is reputed to be an antiflatulent and is a requisite ingredient in Mexican bean cookery, especially black turtle beans.

FENUGREEK SEEDS

A legume plant common in Indian cookery, fenugreek is used for both its greens and seeds. You might recognize its aroma as being familiar to curry.

FERMENTED BLACK BEANS

These salted black beans are a Chinese specialty of small black soybeans (not black turtle beans) that have been preserved in salt. They have a strong pungent, salty flavor. Available in most Asian markets.

FOIE GRAS

Literally translated, foie gras means "fat liver." Foie gras is a very delicate and unctuous tasting specialty of France, especially Alsace and the southwest region. It has been well-loved in France for centuries where Alsatian farm women, many of them Jews, specialize in raising these geese. Even the Romans knew and prized foie gras. For a long time, the only form of foie gras available in this country was canned as "pâté de foie gras." In the last 20 years, foie gras has been produced in the United States, originally only on one farm in New York started by Michael Ginor, author of a book called *Foie Gras*. Now it is also produced in California and much of what is consumed in France comes from Israel.

GHEE

Usli ghee (or clarified butter) is the preferred cooking and seasoning fat in northern India, though these days vegetable shortenings are often substituted. To make ghee, butter is heated and skimmed of its white foam, then cooked very, very slowly until all the water evaporates and any remaining solids stick to the bottom of the pot. The clear cooked butterfat is then poured off and used for cooking. Ghee is especially important in India where refrigeration is scarce to nonexistent because, once clarified, the butter will keep quite well even at room temperature.

GENOA SALAMI

A type of uncooked, cured, and air-dried pork sausage, originally from Genoa, Italy. The Genoa-style is made with a mixture of beef and pork, boldly seasoned with garlic and studded with white peppercorns.

GIANT WHITE CORN (WHITE HOMINY)

White hominy is made from dried white corn kernels from which the hull and the germ have been removed, making it easier to digest. In a process developed ages ago by Native Americans, the corn is soaked in some form of alkaline slaked lime such as fireplace ashes. At one time crushed oyster shells were used. The giant white corn hominy is a specialty of Peru and is sold by the Goya Company, Vitarroz, and Indian Harvest (see Sources, page 323).

HAZELNUT OIL

A fragrant, sweet, and nutty oil pressed from hazelnuts and used mostly for salads. Most hazelnut oil comes from France and is rather expensive. Keep it in the refrigerator to prevent rancidity. You will still get the flavor of the oil if you blend it with a bland oil such as soybean or canola.

HOISIN SAUCE

A prepared sauce made from soybeans, spices, chile pepper, and garlic, hoisin is thick, reddish-brown and sweet. It is widely used in Chinese cooking. Once opened, it will keep indefinitely if tightly covered and refrigerated.

JÍCAMA (MEXICAN YAM BEAN)

The jícama is a turnip-shaped underground tuber of a plant in the legume family and can be eaten raw or cooked. Originally from Mexico, the plant was imported by the Spanish in Mexico to their colonies in the Philippines during the seventeenth century. From there it was quickly adapted by Chinese cooks. It has a crunchy, juicy ivory-colored flesh with a texture very similar to fresh water chestnuts. Jícama must first be peeled of its tough, beige outer skin before it is ready to eat. Look for jícama at the supermarket and in Asian groceries. It deteriorates quickly, so choose unblemished, plump jícama without any pockmarks.

KIELBASA

This Polish smoked sausage is made from pork flavored with garlic and sometimes beef added. It is about 2 inches in diameter and is usually sold precooked.

FRENCH GREEN LENTILS (LENTILLES DU PUY)

The tiny French lentilles du Puy are raised in a special region of France called Puy. They are small, dark-green to brownish-black in color and firm when cooked. They also take a short time to cook.

MACCHERONI

These medium-large cut pasta tubes are often ridged and look similar to rigatoni. The artisanal Italian pasta manufacturer, Martelli, that forms its pasta using brass rather than Teflon-coated dies, makes a firm, chewy, golden maccheroni (see Sources, page 323).

MERGUEZ SAUSAGE

This thin lamb sausage is popular in north Africa and highly flavored with garlic and hot red pepper. It is available from specialty food stores (see Sources, page 323).

MIRIN

Mirin is a very special Japanese rice wine used only in cooking. It adds a mild sweetness and glazes grilled foods when used in a basting sauce. Mirin has the consistency of a thin, golden syrup. Find it in Japanese and other Asian food stores. English labels read something like "sweet cooking rice wine." Only a few tablespoonfuls are needed to prepare most dishes, so it will last a long time. If you can't find mirin, Shizuo Tsuji, author of *Japanese Cooking: A Simple Art*, recommends substituting 1 teaspoon of sugar for every tablespoon of mirin.

MUSHROOM SOY SAUCE

Mushroom soy sauce is a seasoned black soy sauce flavored with dried Chinese black mushrooms. It has a rounded, almost meaty, flavor.

MOLASSES, UNSULPHURED

A by-product of sugar refining. Molasses is produced by squeezing the liquid from sugar cane or sugar beets and cooking it down to extract the sugar crystals. The remaining warm brown liquid is the molasses. Use light (from the first boiling) or dark (from the second boiling) for cooking here. The type of molasses known as blackstrap is thick, very dark, and somewhat bitter. It's too strong for the recipes included here. I use Grandma's brand.

Nam Pla (Asian Fish Sauce)
A thin, liquid sauce made from salted, fermented fish that is vital to Thai and Vietnamese cooking provides their undertone of flavor. It has a strong aroma that dissipates after cooking. The closest comparison would be to anchovy paste. Squid Brand is common and excellent.

Nigella Seeds
These angular black seeds called variously *negilla*, *kalonji*, and *charnushka* have a distinctive aroma and a mild flavor, acrid and nutty at the same time, a bit like a pungent poppy seed. Nigella is the seed of choice on Russian-style black bread and New York rye bread, where it is called charnushka, the Russian name. The same seed is mixed with bread dough to make Indian nan bread and used to flavor lentil pappadum wafers. Purchase nigella seeds from Indian and Middle Eastern groceries like Kalustyan in New York and Bitar's in Philadelphia or from specialty spice companies like Penzey's.

Oil-cured Black Olives (Sicilian-style)
These wrinkly-looking ripe black olives come from Sicily. They are cured first in salt and then in olive oil and resemble a dried raisin in consistency. Once the jar has been opened they can be refrigerated indefinitely. Press down with your thumb to flatten the olive and loosen the pit, then open into two halves to remove and discard the pit.

Oregano (Mexican and Greek)
Oregano is one of the few herbs that does well when dried. It seems to concentrate its unmistakable aroma. Most commercial oregano is the Mediterranean type. If you can find Greek or Mediterranean oregano on the branch, it is wonderfully aromatic (see Sources, page 323). Mexican oregano is milder and more mintlike and is, in fact, a different variety than the European type. In some Yucatan recipes it is toasted before using, which intensifies its flavor. Buy Mexican oregano from a Mexican grocer or from an herb and spice specialty company.

Pancetta
An Italian specialty product of pork belly, pancetta is the same cut as bacon, cured with salt and black pepper as for prosciutto, and then air-dried rather than smoked. Unlike bacon, pancetta is made without sugar.

Pickapeppa Sauce®
This bottled savory sauce belongs to the family of British-inspired sauces like Worcestershire and A1 Steak Sauce. It comes from Shooters Hill in Jamaica in the West Indies and is used to add a sweetly pungent flavor that's jazzy but not hot to soups, meats, and seafood. Like Worcestershire and other bottled sauces, Pickapeppa Sauce contains tamarind along with tomatoes, onions, raisins, vinegar and other spices. Look for the bottle with the parrot on the label in the condiment aisle at the supermarket.

Pimentón (Spanish Paprika)
An extraordinary wood-smoked paprika produced from special peppers grown exclusively in Spain's Extramadura region, buy pimentón from specialty food stores such as Caviar Assouline and The Spanish Table (see Sources, page 323). It comes in mild, medium, and hot versions and is packed in beautifully decorated small home-size cans and large food service cans. Adding pimentón to vegetarian dishes is an excellent way to create natural smoked flavor without using any meat.

Popcorn Salt
This super-fine almost powdery salt comes in a small container and is usually sold in the supermarket with the popcorn. It is ideal for salting any snack food because you can sprinkle on an even, fine coat without producing any overly salty spots. Substitute fine sea salt.

Poutarge
This preparation of strong-flavored pressed and dried mullet or tuna roe is used in the south of France and along the Italian Mediterranean coast where it's known as bottarga.

Preserved Lemon
A north African way of curing and preserving lemons is to either soak them in a salt water brine or salt and then layer them in olive oil to cure. Either way, the edible part is the yellow zest, not the lemon pulp, which is to be discarded. Available from specialty foods stores (see Source, page 323).

Queso Añejo (or Queso de Cotija)
A very dry, crumbly aged cheese that is a bit of acidic and quite salty. It was originally made in the farming town of Cotija. It is usually grated very finely and sprinkled on top of enchiladas and other dishes, like beans.

Raw peanuts

You can buy creamy white colored raw, shelled peanuts that are unroasted at most natural foods or specialty nut stores. Store raw peanuts in the freezer.

Recaito Criollo

This tangy green herb condiment is sold in Latino markets.

Rice Stick Noodles (or Pad Thai Noodles)

Rice noodles come in various shapes and widths. The flat, fettuccine-size noodles are sometimes labeled "chantaboon" and are perfect for pad Thai.

Saucisson

This large French pork sausage is flavored with garlic and used in cassoulet or to wrap with brioche for an hors d'oeuvre. The closest easily available substitute is Polish kielbasa, though specialty sausage companies now produce French-style saucisson in many cities.

Saké

A clear Japanese rice wine (sometimes referred to as a beer) that is made from fermented rice.

Shanxi Vinegar

This mild vinegar is fermented from barley, sorghum, and peas with a mellow, sweet taste reminiscent of balsamic vinegar. Made in a remote northern province of China, this vinegar has been brewed in the traditional way for thousands of years.

Sesame Seeds

These tiny flat seeds are sold hulled (white) and unhulled (tan) in most grocery stores and Asian markets. Instead of toasting your own sesame seeds, you can buy unhulled, natural light tan sesame seeds that have already been roasted.

Sumac

These purplish red, ground dried berries of a special edible variety of sumac are used in Eastern Mediterranean cookery for their special acidity. Buy only from a Middle Eastern grocery or a spice company; do not attempt to pick your own wild sumac, as it can be poisonous.

Tarama

Salted orange carp roe from Greece, tarama is usually sold in small jars. Used like strong caviar, it is often combined with lemon and olive oil to moderate its powerful and concentrated fish flavor. It is also good as a flavorful garnish.

Tamarind

Also known as an Indian date, tamarind is the large fruit pod of a tamarind tree. The sour, pruny-flavored pulp surrounding the seeds is widely used as a flavoring in Middle Eastern, Indian, and Indonesian cuisines. Tamarind is available dried and in liquid form.

Tomatillos

Tomatillos resemble a green or acid tomato encased in a dry parchmentlike inedible husk. These Mexican green tomatoes aren't tomatoes at all but rather a variety of Cape Gooseberry or ground cherry, all in the *Physalis* family. Peel off and remove the husk and lightly steam and purée or chop to make a salsa. Tomatillos keep for several weeks in the refrigerator, but they will eventually become sticky, indicating that they are beginning to break down.

Urud dal

These white split gram beans look like tiny white seeds. They are closely related to green and red mung beans, and are used roasted as a spice in Indian cookery.

Zaatar

One of several varieties of thyme from Lebanon, zaatar has a longer, thinner leaf than traditional thyme and a fragrance somewhere between savory, oregano, and thyme. A blend of dried zaatar leaves, sumac, and sesame seeds, also called zaatar, is used to sprinkle on pita bread, salads, and kabobs.

SOURCES

ADOBE MILLING
P.O. Box 596
Dove Creek, CO 81324
Phone: 1-800-542-3623
Anasazi® beans, pinto beans, black beans, bean soup mixes

AIDELL'S SAUSAGE COMPANY
1625 Alvarado Street
San Leandro, CA 94577
Phone: 1-800-AIDELLS
Fax: 510-614-2287
www.aidells.com
Huge variety of fresh all-natural sausages such as chicken
and turkey sausage with sun-dried tomatoes and basil.
Available in two 3-pound packs of uncooked sausage
(Sausage freezes well if carefully wrapped)

BITAR'S SPECIALTY FOOD STORE & GRILL
947 Federal Street
Philadelphia, PA 19147
Phone: 215-755-1121
Fax: 215-755-8445
E-Mail: pitahut@aol.com
Catalog available
Aleppo pepper, dried mint, dried yellow split favas, dried
chickpeas, frozen green favas, nigella seeds (also called
kalonji, onion seed, and charnushka), sumac, tamarind,
turnip pickle (torshi), zaatar leaves and mix, pita bread,
zaatar pita, toasted chickpea flour

CAVIAR ASSOULINE
505 Vine Street
Philadelphia, PA 19123
Phone: 1-800-521-4491
Fax: 215-627-3517
www.caviarassouline.com
Catalog available
Chickpea flour, French white coco beans, French green
lentils (lentilles de Puy), flageolets de Chevrier, haricots
lingots, Shanxi vinegar, saffron (available by the ounce)
hazelnut and walnut oils, pimentón (Spanish smoked
paprika), preserved lemons, Mortelli maccheroni pasta,
Merguez sausage

D'ARTAGNAN
399-419 St. Paul Avenue
Jersey City, NJ 07306
Phone: 1-800-DARTAGNan
Fax: 201-792-0588
Catalog available
Duck fat, fresh foie gras, moullard duck breast and legs,
chorizo sausage, merguez lamb sausage

DEAN & DELUCA
560 Broadway
New York, NY
Phone: 1-800-221-7714
www.dean-deluca.com
Spices, high-quality dried beans, sun-dried tomatoes, olives

HOPPIN' JOHN (THE "KING OF LOWCOUNTRY COOKING")
Phone: 1-800-828-4412
www.hoppinjohns.com
Specialty foods, such as 15-ounce pop-tab cans of Tony the
Peanut Man brand peanuts, and cookbooks

INDIAN HARVEST SPECIALTIFOODS, INC.
P.O. Box 428
Bemidji, MN 56619-0428
Phone: 1-800-294-2433
www.indianharvest.com
Catalog available
Giant white corn (white hominy). Excellent variety of
dried beans, peas, lentils, and chickpeas, including golden
chickpeas, also heirloom and specialty beans

INDIAN ROCK PRODUCE
539 California Road
Quakertown, PA
Phone: 1-800-882-0512
Fresh cranberry beans, fresh green fava beans (shelled or in
the pod), fresh green soybeans, haricots verts, pea shoots,
pea sprouts, romano beans (flat green beans), sugar snap
peas, wax beans, wing beans, yard-long beans

KALUSTYAN'S
123 Lexington Avenue
(between 28th and 29th Streets)
New York, NY 10016
Phone: 212-685-3451
Fax: 212-683-8458
www.kalustyans.com
Herbs, spices, and legumes—especially Indian and Middle Eastern items—such as nigella seeds, green chickpeas, black sesame seeds, yellow lentils, red lentils, tamarind, Aleppo pepper, amchur, white emergo beans, beluga lentils, and golden chickpeas

MERIEME IMPORTS
c/o Farmer's Bakery
4905 North 5th Street
Philadelphia, PA 19120
Phone: 215-329-2196
Fax: 215-329-9202
Copper couscousiers, Tunisian products

MORE THAN GOURMET
115 W. Bartges Street
Akron, OH 44311
Phone: 330-762-6652
Fax: 330-762-4832
Veal demi-glace, chicken broth concentrate, beef broth concentrate, vegetarian glace concentrate

PENZEY'S SPICES
W19362 Apollo Drive
Muskego, WI 53150
Phone: 414-679-7207
Fax: 414-679-7878
www.penzeys.com
Catalog available
Selection of exotic spices, including exotics like black cumin (kala jeera), sumac, nigella, whole and ground chile ancho, chipotle and ajwain seed

SADAF MIDDLE EASTERN FOODS
Soofer Company
2828 S. Alameda Street
Los Angeles, CA 90058
Phone: 1-800-852-4050
Fax: 323-234-2447
www.sadaf.com
Wide range of Middle Eastern and Persian products, including large split yellow favas, dark red kidney beans, yellow split peas

THE SPANISH TABLE
1427 Western Avenue
Seattle, WA 98101
Phone: 206-682-2827
Fax: 206-682-2814
E-mail: tablespan@aol.com
Spanish products including dry and canned premium beans and dry specialty varieties, wines, olives, pequillo peppers, tuna packed in olive oil

VANN'S SPICES LTD.
1238 E. Joppa Road
Baltimore, MD 21286
Phone: 800-583-1693
Fax: 800-583-1617
E-mail: vanns@balt.mindspring.com
Large variety of heirloom and specialty beans, grains, and high-quality non-irradiated spices, and spice blends

HEIRLOOM BEAN SOURCES

LANDIS VALLEY MUSEUM-HEIRLOOM SEED PROJECT
2451 Kissel Hill Road
Lancaster, PA 17601
Phone: 717-569-0401
Catalog available of rare and endangered varieties of historic plants, including many heirloom bean seeds

THE SEED SAVERS EXCHANGE
3076 North Wiunn Road
Decorah, IA 52101
Phone: 319-382-5990
Yearly membership provides access to an international network of seed savers and offerings from the seed library of Heritage Farm, maintained by the organization

SELECTED BIBLIOGRAPHY

Algar, Ayla Esen. *Complete Book of Turkish Cookery*. London: Kegan Paul International, 1985.

Anderson, Jean. *The Foods of Portugal*. New York: William Morrow and Company, 1986.

Anthony, Dawn, Elaine and Selwa. *The Lebanese Cookbook*. Sydney: Lansdowne Publishing Pty Ltd., 1978.

Ayto, John. *The Diner's Dictionary: Food and Drink from A to Z*. New York: Oxford University Press, 1993.

Berry, Elizabeth and Fabricant, Florence. *Elizabeth Berry's Great Bean Book*. Berkeley, California: Ten Speed Press, 1999

Boxer, Arabella et al. *The Encyclopedia of Herbs, Spices and Flavorings*. London: Octopus Books Ltd., 1984.

David, Elizabeth. *A Book of Mediterranean Food*. London: John Lehman, 1950.

Davidson, Alan. *The Oxford Companion to Food*. Oxford: Oxford University Press, 1999

der Haroutunian, Arto. *Middle Eastern Cookery*. London: Pan Books, 1984.

Escudier, Jean-Noël. *The Wonderful Food of Provence*. Translated by Peta J. Fuller. Boston: Houghton Mifflin Company, 1968.

Farmer, Fanny Merritt. *The Boston Cooking School Cookbook*. Boston: Little, Brown and Company, 1923.

Foo, Susanna. *Susanna Foo Chinese Cuisine*. Shelbourne: Chapters Publishing Ltd., 1995.

Ghedini, Francesco. *Northern Italian Food*. New York: Hawthorn Books, Inc., 1973.

Gosetti della Salda, Anna. *Le Ricette Regionale Italiane*. Milan: Casa Editrice Solares, 1977.

Gray, Patience. *Honey from a Weed*. San Francisco: North Point Press, 1990.

Greenbaum, Florence Kreisler. *Jewish CookBook*. New York: Bloch Publishing Co. Inc., 1933.

Grigson, Jane. *Jane Grigson's Vegetable Book*. Middlesex: Penguin Books Ltd., 1980.

Hearn, Lafcadio. *La Cuisine Creole*. 1885. Reprint, New Orleans: Pelican Publishing House, 1967.

Herbst, Sharon Tyler. *Food Lover's Companion*. Hauppauge: Barron's Eductional Series, Inc., 1990.

Johnson, Mireille. *The Cuisine of the Sun*. New York: Random House, 1976.

Kasper, Lynn Rossetto. *The Italian Country Table*. New York: Scribner, 1999

Kennedy, Diana. *The Art of Mexican Cooking*. New York: Bantam Books, 1989.

Kouki, Mahomed. *Cuisine et Patisserie Tunisiennes*. Tunis: Le Patrimoine Tunisien, 1997.

LaFray, Joy. *Cuba Cocina*. New York: William Morrow and Company, 1994.

Lang, Jennifer Harvey, ed. *Larousse Gastronomique*. New York: Crown Publishers Inc., 1988.

Mallos, Tess. *Complete Middle East Cookbook*. Willoughby: Weldon Publishing, 1979.

McGee, Harold. *On Food and Cooking: The Science and Lore of the Kitchen*. New York: Charles Scribner's Sons, 1984.

Miller, Ashley. *The Bean Harvest Cookbook*. Newtown: The Taunton Press, 1997.

Milorandovich, Milo. *The Art of Cooking with Herbs & Spices*. Garden City: Doubleday & Company, 1954.

Ortiz, Elisabeth Lambert. *Complete Book of Caribbean Cooking*. New York: M. Evans and Company, Inc., 1973.

Owen, Sri. *Indonesian Food and Cookery*. London: Prospect Books, 1986.

Perrier, Georges with Aliza Green. *Georges Perrier: Le Bec-Fin Recipes*. Philadelphia: Running Press, 1997.

Roden, Claudia. *The Book of Jewish Food*. New York: Alfred A. Knopf, Inc., 1996.

Rosengarten, David with Joel Dean and Giogia DeLuca. *The Dean & DeLuca Cookbook*. New York: Random House, 1996.

Sahni, Julie. *Classic Indian Cooking*. New York: William Morrow and Company, 1980.

Senderens, Alain. *The Table Beckons: Thoughts and Recipes from the Kitchens of Alain Senderens*. Translated and adapted by Michael Krondl. New York: Farrar, Straus and Giroux, 1993.

Simon, André L. *Concise Encyclopedia of Gastronomy*. New York: Harcourt, Brace and Company, 1952.

Tsuji, Shizuo. *Japanese Cooking: A Simple Art*. Toyko: Kodansha International, 1980.

Weaver, William Woys. *Heirloom Vegetable Gardening*. New York: Henry Holt and Company, 1997.

Withee, John E. *Growing and Cooking Beans*. Dublin: Yankee, Inc., 1980.

Wolfert, Paula. *The Cooking of Eastern Mediterranean*. New York: HarperCollins Publishers, 1994.

FOR OUR INTERNATIONAL AUDIENCE

Conversion Tables

Generic Formulas for Metric Conversion

Ounces to grams....................multiply ounces by 28.35
Pounds to grams ....multiply pounds by 453.5
Cups to liters ....multiply cups by .24
Fahrenheit to Centigrade .....subtract 32 from Fahrenheit,
                    multiply by five and divide by 9

Metric Equivalents for Volume

U.S.	Imperial	Metric	
$\frac{1}{8}$ tsp.	—	. 6 mL	
$\frac{1}{2}$ tsp.	—	2. 5 mL	
$\frac{3}{4}$ tsp.	—	4. 0 mL	
1 tsp.	—	5. 0 mL	
$1\frac{1}{2}$ tsp.	—	7. 0 mL	
2 tsp.	—	10. 0 mL	
3 tsp.	—	15. 0 mL	
4 tsp.	—	20. 0 mL	
1 Tbsp.	—	15. 0 mL	
$1\frac{1}{2}$ Tbsp.	—	22. 0 mL	
2 Tbsp. ($\frac{1}{8}$ cup)	1 fl. oz	30. 0 mL	
$2\frac{1}{2}$ Tbsp.	—	37. 0 mL	
3 Tbsp.	—	44. 0 mL	
$\frac{1}{3}$ cup	—	57. 0 mL	
4 Tbsp. ($\frac{1}{4}$ cup)	2 fl. oz	59. 0 mL	
5 Tbsp.	—	74. 0 mL	
6 Tbsp.	—	89. 0 mL	
8 Tbsp. ($\frac{1}{2}$ cup)	4 fl. oz	120. 0 mL	
$\frac{3}{4}$ cup	6 fl. oz	178. 0 mL	
1 cup	8 fl. oz	237. 0 mL	(.24 liters)
$1\frac{1}{2}$ cups	—	354. 0 mL	
$1\frac{3}{4}$ cups	—	414. 0 mL	
2 cups (1 pint)	16 fl. oz	473. 0 mL	
4 cups (1 quart)	32 fl. oz	—	(.95 liters)
5 cups	—	1185. 0 mL	(1.183 liters)
16 cups (1 gallon)	128 fl. oz	—	(3.8 liters)

Oven Temperatures

Degrees Fahrenheit	Degrees Centigrade	British Gas Marks
200°	93.0°	—
250°	120.0°	—
275°	140.0°	1
300°	150.0°	2
325°	165.0°	3
350°	175.0°	4
375°	190.0°	5
400°	200.0°	6
450°	230.0°	8

Metric Equivalents for Weight

U.S.	Metric
1 oz	28 g
2 oz	58 g
3 oz	85 g
4 oz ($\frac{1}{4}$ lb.)	113 g
5 oz	142 g
6 oz	170 g
7 oz	199 g
8 oz ($\frac{1}{2}$ lb.)	227 g
10 oz	284 g
12 oz ($\frac{3}{4}$ lb.)	340 g
14 oz	397 g
16 oz (1 lb.)	454 g

Metric Equivalents for Butter

U.S.	Metric
2 tsp.	10.0 g
1 Tbsp.	15.0 g
$1\frac{1}{2}$ Tbsp.	22.5 g
2 Tbsp. (1 oz)	55.0 g
3 Tbsp.	70.0 g
$\frac{1}{4}$ lb. (1 stick)	110.0 g
$\frac{1}{2}$ lb. (2 sticks)	220.0 g

Metric Equivalents for Length
(use also for pan sizes)

U.S.	Metric
$\frac{1}{4}$ inch	. 65 cm
$\frac{1}{2}$ inch	1. 25 cm
1 inch	2. 50 cm
2 inches	5. 00 cm
3 inches	6. 00 cm
4 inches	8. 00 cm
5 inches	11. 00 cm
6 inches	15. 00 cm
7 inches	18. 00 cm
8 inches	20. 00 cm
9 inches	23. 00 cm
12 inches	30. 50 cm
15 inches	38. 00 cm

INDEX